KAZ COOKE

GIRL STUFF

Your full-on guide to the teen years

ROUGH GUIDES

CONTENTS

Introduction 1

PART 1 BODY → 5

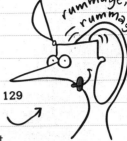

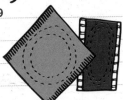

Credits and Publishing Information

Copyright © Kaz Cooke 2007, 2009
Illustrations copyright © Kaz Cooke 2007, 2009
The moral right of the author has been asserted.

Designed by Adam Laszczuk © Penguin Group (Australia)
Kazza font created by Kaz Cooke, digitalised by DiZign Pty Ltd
Typeset in 9/14 pt Stone Serif by Post Pre-press Group/Dan May, Rough Guides
Printed in Singapore by Toppan Security Printing Pte. Ltd.
Edited by: Tracy Hopkins and Peter Buckley
Proofreading: Sam Cook
Production: Rebecca Short and Vicky Baldwin

Rough Guides Reference
Editors: Peter Buckley, Tracy Hopkins, Matt Milton, Joe Staines, Ruth Tidball
Director: Andrew Lockett

First published as Girl Stuff by Penguin Group (Australia) 2007
This edition first published May 2009 by Rough Guides Ltd:
80 Strand, London WC2R 0RL
www.roughguides.com
mail@roughguides.com
Distributed by the Penguin Group:
Penguin Books Ltd, 80 Strand, London WC2R 0RL

528 pages; includes index

ISBN 978-1-84836-018-1

A catalogue record for this book is available from the British Library

3 5 7 9 8 6 4

Intro

This book is designed to be your friend through the teenage years – it will tell you the whole truth and let you make up your own mind about things. It doesn't care if you're in the cool group, or whether you need new jeans, or about something that happened three months ago that still makes you blush.

GIRL STUFF is on your side.

You start your teens as a kid, and you leave them as an adult. In between, there's heaps of change, and it's not just that your favourite colour isn't Barbie pink any more.

I'm an adult now, so how do I know what girls want to read about? I set up a Girl Stuff website with a survey, and there were more than 4000 responses. Girls said they wanted to know about body changes, food, exercise, hair, their brain, their feelings, drinking, drugs, family, love, sex, confidence, what to believe in, helping other people, school, work, money, shopping, clothes, make-up, and their rights.

Then I asked a whole bunch of health and other experts what they thought girls should know. More than seventy generous and adorable ones lent this book their time and knowledge, often answering many follow-up questions. All of them wanted to help get girls the most up-to-date and useful info possible.

Being a teenager can be the most exciting, fun time in your life, when you sometimes can't stop laughing, you make great friends, and you get to work out who you are and some of the things you want to do with your life. But it also has its challenges. GIRL STUFF is about how to make the most of being a teenager, and how to handle some of the problems that can turn up and make you want to scream into a pillow. The book covers a lot of "problems". But don't worry – that doesn't mean you'll necessarily have any or all of the problems, or that they'll happen all at once. It just means there's lots of info on everything in case you do need help.

Some advice in books for teenage girls starts at periods and end with "moods", on the way referring vaguely to hormones without explaining them. Others say, "Be confident!" – but nobody seems to explain how. Or they suggest that you find out what your body shape is, then use the info to work out how to relate to people, become incredibly popular and marry a prince.

Some books and magazines for teenage girls are full of pictures of rich models who look as if their whole life is one long beach holiday (because everyone can relate to that, right?). And some seem to say that your eyebrow shape is more important than whether or not you're happy.

Then there are the adults who suggest teenage girls are evil, selfish fiends. Some people don't respect girls. Sadly this is a problem you'll strike all through your life – you just graduate to meeting people who don't respect women either. The best revenge is to try to make them irrelevant to your life. This book talks about how to grow up to be a strong, independent young woman, and how to find out what you're good at and make the most of your life, not just your eyebrows.

A lot of adults see teenagers as a "problem": they think girls are a bunch of bubble-headed idiots who don't care about anything but themselves. I don't agree – although I'm sure we've all met a couple of airheads in our time. I think girls are smart and funny, and that they care about the world and what they can do to make a difference to others and build a great future for themselves. They're creative, emotional, thoughtful, loving and, yes, sometimes self-centred. But who wouldn't be, faced with a new body, new feelings and a media culture that urges us to hero-worship some of the most self-centred women on the planet?

It's up to you to decide whether you're old enough to hear about, or ready for, certain things. If you're not interested in drinking, or drugs, or sex, for example, that's absolutely fine. You can either leave those chapters until some time in the future, or read the stuff now so that you can make good decisions later. Knowing about something doesn't mean you should do it. Sometimes knowing about stuff means you understand it's a good idea not to do it, or not to do it yet. As the saying goes, "Knowledge is power", and you need that power to make smart and informed decisions about your life.

The quotes used throughout the book are from the thousands of girls who filled in the survey on the Girl Stuff website. They're all real. But if you think you know somebody who's quoted – you don't, unless it was you. Lots of names have been changed to protect girls from possible embarrassment, or from getting into trouble with parents or teachers. We're keeping everybody's secrets.

The four Parts of GIRL STUFF each have a theme: Body; Head; Heart; and Info to Go. You don't have to read the book all in one go, from start to finish, like a story. You can use the Contents list (at the front) or the Index (at the back) to just pick the bit you're interested in at the moment. I've included some websites, books and other information at the end of sections or chapters so that if you want to find out more about a specific subject you've got a head start. Books, even if they are published overseas, can be ordered through your neighbourhood bookshop. Local libraries and school librarians can help you chase things up or give you other useful recommendations.

Where possible I've suggested UK websites, or the best ones from overseas. Please be savvy when going online: beware of people being creepy, or trying to sell you stuff or get you onto a list so they can send you hundreds of advertising emails. I've attempted to choose non-commercial websites (those that aren't trying to sell stuff). If one is a commercial site, I'm *not* recommending whatever it's selling; I'm trying to help you find some good info on it.

Some of the stuff explored in this book is covered by magazines as well as websites. Many of their stories are really helpful and well researched, but you can't rely on magazines with advertisers to give you totally independent advice. There *are* no beauty or fashion "essentials", whatever the magazines and ads say. That's just a way to get you to buy things. What you'll find in GIRL STUFF is the lowdown, without the hard sell (or the hidden sell).

And this book, unlike a magazine, doesn't give you 173 tips on nail polish. Because frankly it would bore us half to death. So dive in, anywhere you like, and start finding out about GIRL STUFF.

Kaz x

I used to smoke and not eat just to lose weight. Let everyone know it's a myth. All it does is

make you get sick. And don't try eating just Pot Noodles. It will make you sick.   Tara, 18

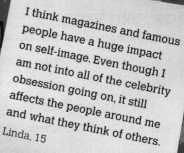

I think magazines and famous people have a huge impact on self-image. Even though I am not into all of the celebrity obsession going on, it still affects the people around me and what they think of others.

Linda, 15

Get into team sports – it can be so great coz u have regular exercise and a wider group of

friends with different thoughts and attributes to ur skool mates.   Millie, 18

PART 1

BODY →

CHANGE

1

GIRL CLUB

I'm sorry to break it to you like this, but Mother Nature is a bit of a mad old nutbag. Some natural things can be a pain in the butt – such as going through the changes of "puberty". These include growing hair in places where there wasn't any, getting periods, changing body shape and feeling new emotions.

Some girls start puberty at age 8 or 9, others at 15 or 16, but most begin around 11 or 12. Luckily the various changes happen over a few years until you've reached your full height, as early as 14 or 15, or as late as 18 or so.

Mother Nature doesn't care what problems you have on the way through puberty – she couldn't give a flying fig if you get pimples, miserable or pregnant. In fact, her job is pretty much confined to trying to **GET** you pregnant. It's okay, though, because you also have a brain you can use while you're growing from a girl into a woman. And the changes are gradual. Getting your first period doesn't mean you're ready to have sex, or a baby, or run your own airport maintenance business. **You're still a girl**.

This chapter should smooth out any worries and questions you might have. Let's get down to it.

Reasons you may not want to change

Puberty can sound freaky and scary before you go through it. The natural changes can be confusing or annoying if you don't understand them or don't feel ready. Here are some of the common worries.

It seems gross

The changes can freak you out when they're new, but after a while you get used to your new body, and to having a period every month, and don't really think about it any more.

Someone gets weird about you changing

Sometimes parents or other relatives find the idea that you're growing up very confronting and might say to you, "It's too early. You're too young." Remind them that it's obviously the right time for you, it doesn't mean you're a woman yet, and you need their support. (Or show them this paragraph.) Some adults have forgotten what it's like to go through the changes, so they say thoughtless things.

You don't have somebody to talk to about it

If you can't talk to your mum, try your big sister, dad, auntie, cousin, older friend, teacher, school nurse or counsellor, local doctor or friend's mum. This book should also answer most of your questions.

You're the first or the last of your class or friends to begin the changes

You won't always be the first or the last to go through a stage: things even out in the end. Don't feel you have to talk to anyone of your own age about any of it if you don't want to.

You don't want people to look at you or comment on the changes

Well, they shouldn't. Most people who say rude things are either ignorant and determined to annoy you, or trying desperately to draw attention away from their own changes or lack of changes.

Grow UP?
I'm not going to!

When I was first developing breasts, hair, etc I was VERY self-conscious about it and DIDN'T want it to happen, but then I got used to it and now it's not a problem. But I remember it was hard getting used to it.   Megan, 15

So what are you in for?

During your teen years there are major changes you can see, and others happening inside your body that you can't.

You get bigger

You might get taller steadily through the teen years, or have a few growth jumps or one big growth spurt. Some girls grow several centimetres in a year; usually the time of quickest growth is around 12 or 13.

Your hands and feet are the first to grow bigger, followed by your arms and legs, and then your spine lengthens. Your muscles get bigger and stronger. For some girls these changes are gradual; for others they seem overnight. Changing quickly can affect your sense of balance, and make you feel awkward or clumsy while you get used to your new self, but you'll adjust quickly.

Your breasts, hips and thighs will probably get bigger and rounder. Some girls will be curvier than others, but getting larger is a natural process.

Teenage girls often worry about their tummy "sticking out". This bump is natural for many girls. It's normal to have a flat or a rounded tummy. Some girls will stay lean and not very curvy, even when they're fully grown, and that's fine too.

Inside, your girly bits, including your ovaries and uterus, are also growing (there's more coming up on those in a moment).

You get fluffier

By the end of your teen years you'll have:

- ❻ underarm hair
- ❻ pubic hair, which grows between your legs and on the pubic mound – the bump at the front
- ❻ leg hair that's more noticeable
- ❻ hair on your forearms (below the elbows) that also may be more noticeable
- ❻ perhaps some extra hair here and there.

Body hair is usually about the same colour as your eyebrows or a bit darker (there's more info in the Hair chapter).

You get leakier

I know this seems appalling at first, but you just get used to it because it's normal. Your skin and hair may become oilier, and you sweat more (see the Skin and Hair chapters). And you'll see that your vagina (the middle opening between your legs) leaks some

What to say to rude comments about your changes

"Ooh, look, you've got boobies!"

"Oh, is that what they are. I thought I was getting antlers."

"Show us ya tits!"

"Show us ya brain!"

"Oh, aren't you getting taller!"

"Yes, I believe it's compulsory."

"You're getting a big butt."

"What's the matter with you? Why are you looking at my bum?", or "So what? *You're* getting ruder and more stupid."

"You're becoming a woman."

"Actually I'm just becoming a teenager/ I'm not even a teenager yet. But if you really think I'm grown up, how about a car?"

"Ooh, you have put on weight."

"Yes, the alternative is to wither away and die – so, tough decision", or

"Yes, lucky isn't it? Otherwise I'd look like a 9-year-old all my life."

clear or whitish fluid now and then, and also some blood, known as a period, for several days every month. (More on all this later on.)

You get moodier

During the teen years various organs in your body make some new hormones; these chemicals then roam around your body, causing the physical changes but also messing with your brain and helping to cause different moods. You can feel sad, angry, weepy or wildly happy without exactly knowing why (see the Feelings chapter). Some girls get crabby or emotional and teary before their periods.

The order of the changes

Here's the order that the changes usually go in, taking about four to six years to get from little-girl body to full-on young-woman's body.

The secret stage   This can happen any time between the ages of 8 and 11. Glands and organs inside (such as your ovaries) start getting bigger and sending hormone messages.

Your hands and feet may get bigger and you may grow taller.

The bosom stage   Breasts usually start to form any time between 9 and 14. First you get breast buds, a hard little lump under each nipple (often one comes before the other). Months, or even years, later the nipples push out, and your breasts start to grow.

You can also have a growth spurt, getting taller and bigger all over.

The pubic hair stage   This usually happens a little while after the budding bosoms stage. About one in five girls gets some pubic hair before she sees any bosom action, which is also normal. The first hairs start out fine and straight.

The period stage   Usually about a year or two after the first sign of bosom business, you'll get your first period (doctors call this first one the menarche – pronounced men-ark – but we won't bother). Most girls get it at 12 or 13, but thousands of girls get it earlier or later (any time between 9 and 15) and the difference is no big deal. (See your doctor just for a check-up if it hasn't come before your sixteenth birthday.)

Your breasts keep growing, and your pubic hair usually gets a little thicker, darker and curlier. Your body is still growing taller and, although you can't tell, your vagina is enlarging (which helps if you want to use tampons during your period). You're probably also noticing a small amount of clear or whitish fluid on your knickers, which comes from your vagina.

The underarm hair stage   This can happen any time between 10 and 16, with the average age being 13 or 14.

Hair also starts to fill in the sort of triangle-shaped pubic area.

The nipple area will also develop at this time, and inside you your ovaries are releasing an egg now and then, but probably not yet regularly once a month (see "Insidey bits" later in this chapter).

> At first you think you're weird because your breasts grow oddly and you begin to get wild hair and your period becomes out of control, but really you're just like everyone else.
> Sarah, 14

The it's-all-going-on stage   Usually by about the age of 16, your breasts and body hair are "finished", and you're at or near your adult height. Your period comes about once a month, and you regularly release an egg inside about halfway between each period.

> I didn't really notice any changes straight away. It all happened really slowly, which I guess is good, 'cause I didn't have a real awkward stage.   Kate, 18

> It can be embarrassing if you're the first one of your friends to go through it.
> Alex, 13

More info on body changes

Your local doctor (GP), the practice nurse at your GP's surgery or the school nurse can answer any questions about your physical changes and whether you're on schedule (the Body Maintenance chapter has info on seeing a doctor).

NHS Direct health line: 0845 46 47 (or NHS 24 in Scotland: 08454 24 24 24) 24-hour confidential medical helpline; questions answered; gives details of local health services for a check-up.

www.likeitis.org
Website with info about puberty and periods; interactive girly-bits diagram; heaps of FAQs.

www.youngwomenshealth.org
US hospital-based site that has fact pages about the body.

Puberty Girl by Shushann Movsessian, Allen and Unwin
Friendly book about puberty changes.

Breasts

Bosoms, boobs, bust: call 'em whatever you like (but maybe not melons, jugs or hooters). Once they start growing, breasts usually take three to five years to get to their final size. If you have a baby one day, your breasts will make milk. (There's no milk in your breasts now.)

Nipples

Nipples, the pointy bit of your breasts, have tiny hidden holes like a sprinkler system so the milk can come out.

During the teen years the nipples and the coloured area surrounding them can get darker, and they become darker still during pregnancy and stay darker (probably so they are easier for a hungry baby to see and latch onto).

Nipples can get erect – harder and pointier – when it's cold, when you're having sexy thoughts, or when you touch them. This is perfectly normal. Some girls worry about their nipples being seen through their clothes. You can try wearing a crop top or vest top or a thick bra under your clothes, and a patterned top (rather than a solid block of colour) or a loose shirt.

Innies and outies   Some girls have nipples that always stick out. Some have turned-in ones, called inverted nipples (which are also normal). Inverted nipples

> I started hating my body for being different. It might have helped if someone had told me that sooner or later the other girls would catch up.
> Annie, 16

> If girls are worried that they're late bloomers – don't worry, it'll happen!
> Manda, 17

usually pop out and say hello if they're cold or if you're having sexy thoughts.

Colour   The coloured area around each nipple is called the areola (pronounced arry-ole-ah); the plural is areolae (pronounced arry-ole-eye). When they're growing, each areola forms a slightly mounded shape that will either stay that way or go back to looking flat. Some areolae (often on fair skin) are a very light pink or apricoty colour; others are dark plum or deep brown. The shape of the areolae can be round, oval or almost oblong.

> I woke up one morning and I swear my boobs just grew over night.
>
> Amy, 18
>
> It's stupid how people want bigger breasts when most guys don't really care.
>
> Zoe, 13

Ouchy ones   Sometimes your tender new nipples get rubbed sore from bouncing around and rubbing against your clothes. You can wear a firm-fitting crop top or a bra under your clothes to stop them bouncing so much. You're most aware of your breasts when they're "new". They may feel fuller and even a bit sore before your period.

Lumps and bumps   Many girls and women have naturally lumpy breasts. Most lumps and bumps have absolutely nothing to do with breast cancer, which is very rare in young women, although it does happen. If you have a sudden or unusual lump you must see a doctor straight away – within a day or so (there's more on this in the Body Maintenance chapter).

Your breast size

Your breasts will probably start and finish growing at different times from your friends'. Most people have one breast slightly larger than the other. Frustratingly the two may grow at different rates (it's the same for your feet). Nobody ever notices this about someone else.

The size and shape that your breasts are meant to be is programmed, before you're born, by the genes you inherit from both sides of your family. There's nothing you can do to make them bigger or smaller or firmer, and this includes exercises, diet, pills and "firming" creams and lotions. People make claims in advertising that you can, but liar, liar, their pants are on fire.

After your breasts are fully grown, their size will only change when you gain or lose weight; before a period and when you're on the contraceptive pill (they get slightly bigger); and during pregnancy and breastfeeding (bigger again).

Littlies   Some girls worry that their bosoms aren't growing fast enough or big enough, but there's no such thing as "too small". Your breasts are just right for you. If you get teased, remind yourself that girls with big breasts also get teased about theirs, and girls with middle-sized breasts get teased about something else or are told their breasts are too big or too small.

Companies make bras that hoist breasts up, push them together to create "cleavage" or pad them, not because there's anything wrong with small breasts, but because if they can make you think you need those bras, they make more money.

idiots wiLL TaLK to YouR BReaStS

Big 'uns   Bosoms are right there, out the front, and difficult to hide. Teenage boys and the odd man tend to stare at bigger breasts. It's just plain rude if someone can't see past your boobs to talk to your face and discover the person behind them. Some people also assume a girl with large breasts is older and more sexually experienced than she is (of course they are utter morons, but it's still annoying).

Some girls with very big breasts can develop a protective shyness and physical problems. Big breasts can be uncomfortable when it's hot, change a girl's balance while she gets used to them, and get in the way of activities such as sport. For some girls with very large breasts, carrying their weight can create headaches and back, neck and shoulder pain.

Girls with big breasts who feel they need extra physical support should get bras with wide shoulder straps and be professionally fitted by an assistant in a lingerie shop or in the underwear section of a department store (see the "Getting a bra" section below). (Lingerie is French for underwear and is pronounced lon-jer-ray.)

A few women make the big decision to have breast reduction surgery: girls need to wait until their breasts have stopped growing (see the "Cosmetic surgery" section in the Shape chapter).

Love the ones you're with   So any combination of size, shape and colour is normal, and you may as well learn to love or at least be friendly to your breasts no matter what they look like, and whether they point east, west, north or south-south-west. Don't waste time wondering why they don't look like your friends'. Your knees aren't the same either. (And whether or not you care what guys think, they love breasts no matter what size, shape or colour they are.)

> One breast is always bigger than the other!!!! Aaagghhhh!!
> Lucy, 14

> I hate guys liking me for my breasts, rather than myself.
> Kelly, 16

Do you need a bra?

Hundreds of millions of pounds are spent each year on ads telling you to buy bras. The lacier and prettier they are, the more bras usually cost.

Companies get supermodels, singers or actresses to put their names to their bras (and matching undies) in the hope that you'll buy them thinking some of the glamour might rub off on you.

But the basic reason for a bra is simple: to stop jiggling and bouncing, especially during strenuous activity. Bouncing breasts can cause pain, be annoying or attract unwanted staring. Only a bra made of metal could stop *all* jiggling, which would be uncomfortable and weird, so bras are really jiggle minimizers, not jiggle killers. (If you start a band called the Jiggle Killers please invite me to your first gig.)

Many girls only need a bra when they're doing bouncy things such as exercising, dancing or playing sport. If you don't mind a bit of bouncing, then you don't need one.

Bras don't stop your breasts from sagging when they get older, or from changing shape after pregnancy. The body ligaments that support your breasts should be allowed to do their work sometimes, instead of never being used because a bra is doing all the work for them.

Bra alternatives Instead of a bra you can wear a camisole (a top with little straps) made of stretchy fabric, or a crop top or vest top. Some tops now have a double layer of fabric in the breast area, sometimes with a little elastic "shelf" underneath, to cut down concern about visible nipples and the jiggle factor.

Getting a bra

A bra should be comfortable and not dig in or leave red marks when you take it off.

Bra sizes There are two parts to a bra size: the chest size and the cup size. It's important not only that the cups are the right size for your breasts, but also that the bra is not too tight or too loose around the back. Most bras have adjustable shoulder straps, as the distance

> If you are flat-chested you will get picked on and if you have got big boobs you'll get picked on. Tracy, 17

between shoulder and breast varies. Your size will keep changing until your breasts stop growing.

Some starter bras and crop tops are sold in sizes according to age, 9–10, 11–12, 13–14 and so on, but most bras are sold using a number related to chest size in inches (28, 30, 32, 34, 36, 38 and so on), plus a cup size related to breast size (AA being the smallest, then A, B, C, D, DD – "double D" – and so on through the alphabet). This means your size might be something like 28AA or 32D or 36B.

> It just seems unfair that it happens to some girls so young. I was 7 when I first started developing breasts. I wasn't ready for it.
> Sophie, 15

You can measure yourself with a tape measure, but translating your measurements into the right bra size can be tricky. Always take two measurements: one underneath the breasts and all the way around your body to get the chest size in inches; and the other across the fullest part of your breasts and all the way around your body for the cup size.

Many bra-selling websites will calculate your size once you've put in your two measurements (search "bra size calculator"), but bra sizes are worked out differently all over the world. Cup sizes are often about the same everywhere, but chest sizes are measured in different ways. If you're a 34 in the UK, you'll probably be a 75 in Europe and a 12 in Australia, so you should always try on a new bra to check the fit before you buy it.

It's really upsetting when guys go "She's hot, she's got a huge rack", when you just want them to look at your face and comment about your personality for once …

I also hate going shopping. Nothing fits me right and I end up leaving the shop with zero confidence.   Veronica, 15

I love the changes that took place now. I would never have said that though while they were happening!   Ruby, 16

Older people constantly say they envy us for our youth, but what is the point of youth when you are so freaked out at your own body?   Sian, 15

I was comfortable with the changeover process from girl to womanhood as I felt it was relatively quick and barely noticeable.   Rachel, 17

Having a bra fitting The best way to get the right bra is to ask an assistant in a lingerie department or shop to help you work out your size. Sales assistants do this all day long, fitting thousands of women a year, so there's no reason to be shy. Just say, "Hi, I need some help to work out my bra size."

An experienced bra fitter will measure you accurately, make sure the size you get is right, and suggest styles or brands that suit you. Don't be afraid to ask for something cheaper or simpler.

Let nature do what it has to do!
Jennifer, 16

People pay so much money for larger breasts but, I'm telling you now, being a DD is not that fun!
Michelle, 17

More info on bras

www.figleaves.com/uk/fitting_room.asp
You don't have to buy from this online lingerie shop to get all sorts of info about bras. Choose "Bra fitting" (size calculator, fitting advice) and "Your bra and your lifestyle" (changes in bra size, first bras and maternity bras).

www.marksandspencer.com
The department store's "Lingerie advice" section has size charts, FAQs, bra fitting tips and washing and style guides.

Your girly bits

Otherwise known as the female reproductive system, your girly bits include inside organs and outsidey parts, which are called genitals (pronounced jen-it-tals) by very serious medical staff who need to loosen up and wear a party hat occasionally.

Even though you don't need all the female equipment inside you yet, your body is making sure it's ready in case one day you want to have a baby. Already it has been producing hormones with particular jobs to do. The main hormones for girls and women are:

6 oestrogen (pronounced ees-tro-jen)

6 progesterone (pronounced pro-jes-ter-own).

When your body starts to produce a lot more oestrogen it triggers the puberty changes. In a way the hormone tells your physical bits what to do.

The main hormone for guys and men is testosterone (tes-tos-ter-own), but we girls have a little bit of it too (and guys and men have some oestrogen).

Insidey bits

The following are the girly bits hidden away inside you:

- ❻ **Ovaries**   These are two little glands that start off the size of a raisin (or an almond, depending on the snack habits of the doctor you ask) and grow to about the size of a walnut in your teens. During pregnancy they will be the size of a fruit-and-nut chocolate bar. (No, I made that up.) Ovaries make the oestrogen and, on instructions from your brain, send it out around your body. Each ovary contains thousands of eggs smaller than this full stop. Each egg is called an ovum (the plural is ova). The ovaries' job is to ovulate: one of them releases an egg each month into a fallopian tube (they usually take it in turns).

- ❻ **Fallopian tubes**   These two tiny, narrow tubes lead down from the ovaries to the uterus. They are usually seven to twelve centimetres long, and as thick as a strand of wool on their outside but as narrow as a piece of cotton inside. If, on its way along one of the tubes, an egg is fertilized by a sperm, you'll become pregnant. This can happen if you have sex with a guy without using contraception (more on this in the Sex chapter).

- ❻ **Uterus** (pronounced you-ter-us)   Also known as the womb, the uterus grows during your teens from the size of a thumb to about the size of a (hollow) upside-down pear. If you ever have a baby in there, the uterus will grow along with the baby so that it always fits, and then shrink back to pear size afterwards.

- ❻ **Cervix** (pronounced ser-vicks)   This spongy disk at the bottom of your uterus has a small opening leading into your vagina. The opening will stretch to about ten centimetres wide during childbirth, to allow the baby to pass from the uterus to the vagina and out into the world. (This stretching doesn't happen at any other time.)

- ❻ **Vagina** (pronounced vaj-eye-nar)   This is a passage made of stretchy skin leading into your body from the middle opening between your legs (the one between the openings for wee and poo). This is where your period blood comes out, it's where a penis will go if you have sex with a guy, and it's where a baby will come out if you have one (unless it's delivered by a caesarean operation).

Outsidey bits

You can see your pubic mound – that plump, roundish area of skin where your pubic hair is going to be or is already – if you stand in front of a mirror, especially if you look at yourself sideways.

You can look at your girly bits between your legs with a small hand-mirror. You may want to lock the bedroom or bathroom door before making your inspection: this isn't a good time to be surprised by a visitor. "I'm just plucking my eyebrows" isn't really going to be all that believable when the hand-mirror is between your thighs. Okay, now let's take a guided tour.

☾ **Vulva**   This is the name for the whole area between your legs. Look at that, all pink and sort of glistening and possibly hairy here and there. Now, I know what you're thinking: that can't possibly be what's between every woman's legs – but it is. It's absolutely right and natural for it to look like that – and the reason why you might be feeling appalled is because people who want to sell us razors and stuff have made us horrified by the idea of hair, or skin that's not perfectly smooth. But don't worry, your vulva is bound to be completely normal.

> As the years go on, you get more and more used to talking about things like that.
>
> Bianca, 15

☾ **Labia majora** (pronounced lay-bee-ah ma-jor-rah), **or outer labia**   These are the large "lips" that surround and protect the vagina's entrance (and the front opening, where wee comes out). Pubic hair grows here too. A lot of girls think their "lips" are too big, or too small, or too uneven – but all variations are absolutely normal. When you have sexy feelings there is a rush of blood to this area and it can feel tingly, tender and hot.

☾ **Labia minora** (pronounced lay-bee-ah my-nor-rah), **or inner labia**   If you pull your outer labia lips open you will see that inside there are two smaller lips, which don't have hair on them. They look a bit like two teeny tongues. They may be barely visible or long and thick, they can range from light pink to purplish or dark brown, and one lip can be bigger than the other. The labia are like curtains that can be parted, and make a nice spongy covering over your vagina opening. (Lots of artists have portrayed the entrance to the vagina as a beautiful, delicate flower.)

☾ **Vagina opening and hymen**   The hymen is a stretchy piece of skin, with a few blood vessels, which surrounds and perhaps covers some of the vagina opening, found between your labia. Your hymen has one hole or a few holes in

---

I honestly did not care about going through puberty. No stress for me, I just took it all in my stride. I had bigger things to worry about than the body.   Nic, 18

Is there any way that I can hurry the process up?   Shell, 15

I hate pubic hair! It just gets in the bloody way! My boobs could be a B cup! I hate periods! Guys don't have to get or worry about getting pregnant! Why girls?!   Chloe, 13

Can it be called metamorphosis rather than puberty? It just sounds so much cooler!

Anonymous, 17

it so that period blood can come out, and over the years it stretches or "tears" painlessly. After that's happened – usually when you're dancing or playing sport of some kind – it looks sort of like a little scrunchie, or a doughnut with a hole in the middle. Most girls don't even feel it when their hymen stretches or breaks. (Some girls don't have a hymen at all, which is not a problem, so don't worry if you can't see yours.)

ⓖ **Clitoris** (pronounced kli-tor-iss)   This is a small round bump that all girls have. At the front where the inner labia meet there's a skin fold called the clitoral hood, which connects to your clitoris. If you pull the hood up with your fingers you can get a better look at the little bump. Its only purpose is to make you feel good when it's touched in the right way (you don't have to make use of it yet, but it will be there when you need it). This is the most sensitive part of your body – made from the same sort of skin as the tip of a penis. If you touch your clitoris with your finger you'll probably feel a slight tingle. If you gently rub it you'll probably feel a harder bit underneath, which is its shaft.

While you're down there with your hand-mirror you may also see your urethra (or, if you prefer the classier title, wee-hole): between the clitoris and the vagina opening is another hood-like shape housing the teeny urinary opening (so teeny that you may not be able to see it easily), where your wee comes out.

Furthest towards your back you'll be able to see your anus, or bottom hole, where your poo comes out. It's separated from the vulva by a little area of flat skin called the perineum (pronounced perry-nee-um).

More info **on your girly bits**

Most diagrams and photos of girly bits are a bit over the top – they're either medical-textbooky or show very unusual, diseased or strange girly bits. If you're worried, you can get your girly bits checked out by your local GP or practice nurse.

www.childrenfirst.nhs.uk/teens
Choose "Puberty body tour" for interactive diagrams of your girly bits and info about all the phsical changes you'll go through during puberty.

en.wikipedia.org/wiki/Vulva and
en.wikipedia.org/wiki/Clitoris
Diagrams and facts about girly bits and real photos (unless somebody's hacked in and left a picture of the prime minister).

www.nhsdirect.nhs.uk and
www.nhsdirect.wales.nhs.uk
Search for your local GP or youth advisory clinic; or get info by calling the NHS Direct health line: 0845 46 47. In Scotland, use www.nhs24.com or call the NHS 24 health line: 08454 24 24 24. In Northern Ireland, use www.healthandcareni.co.uk.

www.ourbodiesourselves.org/book
Choose "Sexual anatomy, reproduction and the menstrual cycle" for a guided tour of your girly bits.

Clear or white stuff

You'll start to notice on your undies the clear or white secretions (pronounced se-cree-shuns) that come out of your vagina. All girls and women have these secretions. Around the time of ovulation, when there's an egg ready to be fertilized, the stuff is usually clearer and thinner (easier for sperm to swim through). When it dries on your knickers it can look yellowy and dusty.

These secretions are always a small amount, like a dab of clear jam – nothing that anyone else would ever notice – but they're why companies try to sell you "everyday pads" or "panty liners" so you can feel "fresh". The pads just soak up the little bit of stuff. These pads have only been around for the last few years: they're expensive and you don't have to use them. As long as you wear new undies and wash every day you will be fresh and clean.

If you have a very thick, lumpy secretion (sometimes called a discharge) or one that smells kind of "off", and your vulva feels itchy or as if it's burning when you wee, these could be signs of an infection that needs treatment to make it go away. (You don't have to have had sex for this discharge to happen.) Any secretion that's unusual for you should be checked by your local doctor. There's more info about infections in the Body Maintenance chapter.

Girls find it hard to talk about things like this. Even though we are all going through the same thing you still feel a little uncomfortable. Now that I'm 15 my girlfriends and I, we joke about it. We are so over it!   Punita, 15

I think that it sucks that you go through all of these physical changes in the first twenty years of your life, then the rest of it is just boring.   Kelly, 16

A lot of girls will actually be so upset when they have to mature!   Alisha, 17

At first I found the changes in my body scary and alien – almost disgusting. Now I've grown used to it I am sort of happy to look like a woman rather than a girl.   Amy, 15

Your period

Here's a reminder of why you get a period. About once a month after the oestrogen call has gone out – "Release the egg!" – and one of your ovaries has popped out a teeny egg, the egg tootles off, heading for the uterus.

The call goes out to the ovary...

Although it only has ten or so centimetres to travel down the nearest fallopian tube, the egg can take about two or three days to get there – your eggs may be potentially miraculous but they are not speedy. The egg hangs around in the fallopian tube in case a sperm turns up to fertilize it. If this doesn't happen, the egg finally gives up, dawdles down into the uterus and dissolves away to nothing.

While it has been waiting for the egg, your uterus has grown a lovely soft lining of endometrium (pronounced endo-me-tree-um). A fertilized egg can implant itself and grow in the special blood cells of the endometrium. If the egg isn't fertilized, or if it is but your body decides it isn't a good one, the uterus packs it all in and sends the lining down the chute, as a period. The endometrium slowly breaks down into blood and begins to slide away, down the walls of the uterus, through the cervix into the vagina, and then out between your legs.

A menstrual (pronounced men-strewl) period, which is the technical term, usually lasts four to six days. Five to nine days after your period finishes, another egg is released from an ovary and the whole palaver starts all over again.

When to get ready

Because most girls get their first period anywhere between the ages of 9 and 15, as you've seen earlier, it's a good idea to be ready by having some pads in your bedroom or bathroom and school bag.

FACT

Other names for periods   Menses (doctor-speak); the monthly (very old-fashioned granny word); Fred; a little visitor; time of the month; having the painters in; women's troubles; and the curse (calm down, everybody!). I've even heard of rebooting the ovarian operating system, but I think we can stop right there.

What to expect

The first time it happens you'll see the red period blood on your undies. Sometimes you'll feel the blood come out of your vagina or sense some wetness between your legs, but often you won't.

How much blood comes out during a period? Although it may seem as if a lot of blood is coming out, the actual amount is very small. Your whole period is about two tablespoons of liquid.

Some girls will bleed only a little, others more; others will have some clots (which look a bit like dark red jam) – this is just because some of the endometrium cells are clumped together rather than being liquid.

Generally the amount of blood is heaviest at the start, then gets less and less and finally fades to nothing. More than two-thirds of a period's total blood usually slides out in the first two or three days.

If it seems to you like the bleeding is too much or is going on for too long, or there's a lot more than usual, see your doctor.

What colour should the blood be? Often on the first day of your period the blood is bright red, then it can become rust-coloured or browner towards the end as it gets "older". As blood dries on a pad it also goes browner.

Does period blood smell? Period blood does have the very faintest of odours – but nothing that another person would be able to smell as long as you change pads and tampons every two to four hours during the day and wash regularly. It's only "old" blood that tends to smell noticeably as the air gets to it.

Your menstrual cycle

The pattern of hormonal changes, egg release and periods is called your menstrual cycle, and each cycle lasts about 28 days – but some people have cycles that are a bit longer or shorter than this, or vary a bit from month to month. Day One of your menstrual cycle is Day One of your period.

Even though you will usually have a period each month, it may not be like that when you start. You may get the first one, then go for a couple of months before the next one, and so on. That's fine – eventually you'll settle down.

See the "Reasons to see the doctor" box further on if there's something about your cycle that you think you should maybe check out.

When you first get your period you need someone to talk about it with. I needed that but didn't really have anyone.
Rachel, 15

Periods shouldn't be so secret.
Jessica, 14

A period calendar   Using your diary, a calendar or a personal organizer, you can keep a record so you know when to expect your next period. Count 28 days from the first day of your last period, then write "period due" (or mark the due date with a half moon or other secret symbol). Obviously if you find your period tends to come on day 29, or follows some other pattern, count and mark accordingly.

You can use a photocopy or scan of the period calendar opposite , and maybe keep it in your diary. You can also record different symptoms on it, using a code (which is helpful for a doctor if you have period pain or other worries).

Pre-period hassles

After a while you may start to recognize when your period is on the way. Known as premenstrual syndrome (PMS), or sometimes premenstrual tension (PMT), the symptoms in the few days before a period can include:

- feeling tearful
- being clumsy
- getting grumpy
- having fuller breasts and/or a bloated tum (don't worry, that's not because there's heaps of blood to come out but because your body is retaining other fluid).

Symptoms can vary wildly between people. If PMS is getting in the way of you enjoying your life you need help.

How to fight PMS

- To help reduce bloating and fluid retention, wee a lot. Drink plenty of water and cut down on dehydrating salty foods (check the ingredients on a packet and if salt, or sodium, is high on the list give the food a miss), caffeine (it's in coffee, tea, chocolate, cola, and energy and guarana drinks) and alcohol.

- To stop fuller, tender breasts feeling sore, try wearing a firm crop top or bra.

- To keep your energy levels up, eat healthy snacks between meals (that doesn't mean a Snickers bar – it means a small handful of almonds and some veggies or fruit).

Do NOT DISTURB 🔔 Person with period!

↑
door knob
hanger

Medical herbalists may prescribe a range of herbal, vitamin and mineral supplements to deal with the general symptoms, often with an emphasis on vitamin B6, magnesium, vitamin E and evening primrose oil. (Make sure your herbalist belongs to the National Institute of Medical Herbalists.) It's important to always let your GP and herbalist know what the other has prescribed for you. There are some problems a herbalist won't be able to help you with, and you may need medical treatment from your GP.

I was the first at my school to get my period and it was so embarrassing.   Marie, 14

Period calendar (for photocopying)

Circle each day you have your period and you'll soon see if it's "regular" and how long it usually goes on for. You can also add little notes in code to record other symptoms.* Add whatever else you want to factor in.

Jan 1	29	26	25	22	20	17	15	12	9	7	4	2	30
2	30	27	26	23	21	18	16	13	10	8	5	3	31
3	31	28	27	24	22	19	17	14	11	9	6	4	Jan 1
4	Feb 1	[29]	28	25	23	20	18	15	12	10	7	5	2
5	2	Mar 1	29	26	24	21	19	16	13	11	8	6	3
6	3	2	30	27	25	22	20	17	14	12	9	7	4
7	4	3	31	28	26	23	21	18	15	13	10	8	5
8	5	4	Apr 1	29	27	24	22	19	16	14	11	9	6
9	6	5	2	30	28	25	23	20	17	15	12	10	7
10	7	6	3	May 1	29	26	24	21	18	16	13	11	8
11	8	7	4	2	30	27	25	22	19	17	14	12	9
12	9	8	5	3	31	28	26	23	20	18	15	13	10
13	10	9	6	4	Jun 1	29	27	24	21	19	16	14	11
14	11	10	7	5	2	30	28	25	22	20	17	15	12
15	12	11	8	6	3	Jul 1	29	26	23	21	18	16	13
16	13	12	9	7	4	2	30	27	24	22	19	17	14
17	14	13	10	8	5	3	31	28	25	23	20	18	15
18	15	14	11	9	6	4	Aug 1	29	26	24	21	19	16
19	16	15	12	10	7	5	2	30	27	25	22	20	17
20	17	16	13	11	8	6	3	31	28	26	23	21	18
21	18	17	14	12	9	7	4	Sep 1	29	27	24	22	19
22	19	18	15	13	10	8	5	2	30	28	25	23	20
23	20	19	16	14	11	9	6	3	Oct 1	29	26	24	21
24	21	20	17	15	12	10	7	4	2	30	27	25	22
25	22	21	18	16	13	11	8	5	3	31	28	26	23
26	23	22	19	17	14	12	9	6	4	Nov 1	29	27	24
27	24	23	20	18	15	13	10	7	5	2	30	28	25
28	25	24	21	19	16	14	11	8	6	3	Dec 1	29	26

*Code: S: spotting   B: bleeding   HB: heavy bleeding   DP: dull pain   C: cramps   BC: bad cramps
T: tearful   G: grumpy   SB: sore bosoms   _____

Doctors sometimes suggest going on the contraceptive pill ("the Pill"), which adjusts hormone levels, but this usually has more effect on the length and heaviness of the period than on PMS symptoms.

Period pain

Most girls don't have any pain for the first few years of their periods. Later some girls get pains called cramps, which are often a squeezy feeling, usually in the first day or so of their period. That's because the uterus actually *is* squeezing a bit, trying to help the blood slide out. Sometimes you can feel the individual cramps; sometimes there's a dull achy or draggy feeling in your lower tummy area (but it's nothing to do with your stomach where you digest your food).

Ways to deal with the pain

- Put up with it – this only works if the pain is slightly annoying rather than seriously hurty.

- Do some exercise – walking and swimming are good because they won't stress the body or bounce sore breasts too much. Exercising before your period's due is best, and can stop some of the pain.

- Find some relaxing activities (cramps can be worse if you're stressed) – these can include taking a nice warm bath, meditation or gentle yoga over the month, but ask your yoga teacher which are the exercises not to do when you have a period because some make the pain worse.

- Put a warm (not boiling) hot-water bottle or wheat bag on your tum.

- Take drugs that have an effect on the prostaglandin hormones causing the cramps. Ask your GP or chemist which one could be good for you. If the pain is bad enough for you to feel you need painkillers each month, see a doctor.

- Take herbal remedies prescribed by a qualified herbalist – some herbs make the uterus cramp less, some are "warming" and some regulate hormones. Complementary therapists may suggest supplements with omega 3 fatty acids, calcium and magnesium.

To help with period pain either curl up with a book and a cup of something warm and a hot-water bottle, or do some stretches. That helps. That and sleep.   Sharon, 15

⑥ Take the Pill if your doctor recommends it – many doctors prescribe it because it usually makes a period less painful and less heavy.

> I am 16 and still don't have my periods. For the time being my friends are all jealous that I don't have to worry about these problems, and I don't care that I haven't got them.
>
> Emily, 16

Stuff you need for periods

Otherwise known as "feminine hygiene products", for gawd's sake, pads and tampons are the small, disposable items we use to soak up (absorb) period blood. You can buy them at all supermarkets and chemists and most corner shops and convenience stores.

When they're just starting periods, most girls try pads first because they don't feel ready to use tampons, which are pushed up inside the vagina. (If you're a virgin a tampon doesn't change that – there's more on this in the Sex chapter.)

Sometimes a pad or tampon will take in all the blood it can absorb within a couple of hours, especially during those first days when most of the blood comes out (often called "heavy" days), so you should change it every few hours.

There are pads and tampons made of cotton, with no chemical additives to help absorption, which are sold as "natural" alternatives. These are way less absorbent than synthetic ones with chemical additives and may need to be changed a lot more often.

Pads

A pad (or sanitary towel) is rectangular, with curved ends. It has a sticky strip on the back: you stick the back to the inside of your undies' gusset (the bit between your legs). Some pads also now have sticky "wings" or flaps on the sides that wrap around your underwear to help hold the pad in place. Before ways to make them more absorbent were invented, pads of yesteryear were up to four centimetres thick: wearing one felt like having a single mattress in your undies. (And before they were invented, girls had to wear folded-up rags in their pants, which they then had to wash out by hand and re-use.)

PADS of yesteryear were much more obvious...

1978

When to change a pad   On the heavier days of your period you'll need to change the pad up to every two hours, then later every four hours (whether there's much blood or not), to be fresh and clean. This can be hard when you're stuck on a school bus trip. Bigger, "overnight" pads are good for these times, but it's best not to wear any kind of pad for longer than four hours during the day.

Types of pads

- Ⓖ Panty pads/liners: these are just to keep your pants fresh and protected from non-period vaginal shenanigans (see the "Clear or white stuff" section earlier) and are definitely not absorbent enough to deal with the period flow.
- Ⓖ Ultra-thin pads: they are very thin but have a lot of absorbency.
- Ⓖ Regular, super and overnight pads: the terms indicate their different degrees of absorbency, but all are more absorbent than the ultra-thins. During your first few periods you probably won't need anything more than regular, but see how you go.

Be careful where you put your adhesive strip...

Tampons

A tampon is a super-compressed roll of absorbent material. It has a rounded tip to make it slide more easily into the vagina, and a securely attached string at the other end, which you pull gently on to drag it out.

A tampon is less messy than a pad because it soaks up the blood before it comes out of your body. You can swim with a tampon in – you can't swim with a pad.

Only one tampon should be used at a time.

When to change a tampon Like pads, tampons need to be changed every couple of hours on heavy days, and no kind of tampon should be worn all night or for more than four hours max because of the rare chance of the dangerous infection toxic shock syndrome (see the "Reasons to see the doctor" box further on).

You need to wash your hands before you touch a tampon that you're about to use.

Types of tampons

- Ⓖ Mini tampons – these thinner-than-ordinary tampons are for young girls having their first few periods.

I got my period a little before I turned 10 and I was practically the only girl in my school who had it. It was difficult to go through physical and emotional changes when you had no one to share your thoughts and feelings with. Chantelle, 14

Disposal

Most public and school toilets have a sanitary bin next to each loo to put your used pad or tampon in. (Signs often call pads and tampons "sanitary items".) If there's no special sanitary bin, you can put anything with blood on it in a plastic bag, then dispose of it in the nearest bin (or carry it in your period kit or bag until you can get to a bin at home). When you haven't got a bag with you, wrap the pad or tampon in toilet paper.

Don't try to flush a pad down the loo – this could cause an overflow, and a spectacular waterfall is not what you need right now. Tampons and baby wipes shouldn't be put down the loo either.

⊙ "Silky" ones – these are designed to slip in and come out more easily, and are also good for girls new to tampons.

⊙ Light, regular, super and super plus – the super and super plus ones (the most absorbent) can be used during the first couple of days or for heavy periods.

⊙ Tampons with applicators – each tampon has a small, disposable cardboard "syringe" to push it up inside you.

⊙ Twinpacks – these usually combine packs of super and regular tampons so that you can use the supers in the first couple of days, then move on to the regulars.

> I used to hate having periods, but now I don't really mind. It's just a part of growing up.
> Mia, 13

> Periods are annoying at first but get easy to deal with after a while.
> Sonia, 15

Getting a tampon in First lock the door of the bedroom, bathroom or toilet for privacy. It's easiest if you lie on a bed with your legs open, or squat, or stand with one foot on the toilet lid or the edge of the bath. Follow the instructions on the pamphlet inside the box of tampons, and unravel the tampon string before you start.

You may need to practise lots of times. Start with mini tampons, and don't worry if you fluff up the ends of a couple trying to get them in. Just chuck them away, and try again with a new one.

Try to relax when you're putting in a tampon, and always point and push it slightly towards the small of your back, rather than straight up towards your head.

A tampon also needs to be pushed a little way up from the entrance of your vagina, otherwise it'll be uncomfortable all the time. When it's correctly in place you can't feel it.

(Sometimes when you're wearing a tampon the string will end up in a position that annoys your vulva – you just need to get to a loo and move the string.)

You can't push the tampon in too far – you'll always be able to reach the string, even if it gets a bit bunched up just inside your vagina. You can't lose a tampon inside you because it's too big to get pushed up out of the vagina, through the tiny cervix opening and into the uterus.

If tampons still hurt when you're practising, try again with different ones another time – you can always use pads in the meantime.

When you want to change a tampon, pull gently on the string. If your vagina is dry and there is hardly any blood a tampon might feel a little resistant, but don't worry – the string won't break.

I was terrified about getting my period. I really didn't want it. It's not so bad now. I don't mind it. At least it shows my body is working OK!
Bec, 17

Your period kit

You'll soon work out what you need yourself, but here are some suggestions:

- ✪ tampons and/or pads
- ✪ baby wipes for washing yourself (although toilet paper is fine)
- ✪ spare undies in case you get blood on the pair you're wearing
- ✪ two or three folded-up small plastic or brown-paper bags for putting used pads or tampons in before you throw them in a bin. (Some pads come in their own wrappers, which you can roll used pads up in before putting them in the bin.)

Replace supplies the day you use them.

emergency period kits

"Emergencies"

If you're caught short without pads or tampons because you've run out of them, or your period has come unexpectedly, you can ask someone if they have a spare. (Women who don't know each other often do this in public toilets.) Most adult women will carry tampons, but not pads.

A more reliable alternative is to make up a few little emergency period kits: a small make-up bag with a zip is perfect. You can keep one in your school bag, sports bag, backpack, school locker, work locker or desk, the glove box of the car, or a house at which you often stay – wherever you think would be handy. If all your friends also keep emergency kits you'll be able to help each other out.

Reasons to see the doctor

✳ You haven't had your first period before you're 16 (lots of girls don't so there's probably nothing wrong).

✳ You think there's too much blood; or there's more than usual (you have to change a pad or tampon more than every two or three hours).

✳ Your period lasts for more than seven days or less than three.

✳ You get pain that interferes with your life (you can't go to school or work or play sport).

✳ You have little bleeds or "spotting" between periods. It's very common in teenagers, but can also be the symptom of something you need treatment for.

✳ Your periods, after becoming regular, stop for more than two months. This can be a sign of body stress, too much exercise, not enough food, some illnesses or pregnancy.

✳ You forgot to take one tampon out before you put a new one in and you can't reach the old one. Don't worry, this will probably never happen to you – the vagina isn't very long so usually you can reach in and grab what you need to. If all else fails, a doctor will get it out without hurting.

✳ If you have the symptoms of **toxic shock syndrome** this is a medical emergency, so go straight to a doctor or hospital casualty department and say you need immediate help.

Toxic shock, a very rare infection, is caused by bacteria that can develop if you leave a tampon in for a long time.

Symptoms include a sudden very high fever, a rash similar to sunburn, vomiting, watery diarrhoea, confusion, muscular pain and headache.

Even if you don't use tampons, having those symptoms together means you need medical help absolutely immediately.

Always tell the doctor about any pills or medicines you have been taking, including herbal treatments and vitamin supplements.

Emergency clean-ups   If there's a lot of blood on your undies and you think it could soak through onto whatever else you're wearing, take off your undies, fold them up as small as you can and put them in a plastic bag to take home to wash. Clean between your legs with your baby wipes (or tissues or toilet paper). Insert a new tampon, or stick a new pad onto your emergency undies, and you're away.

> Why does everyone think that getting your period is embarrassing? Everyone will get it.
> Alisha, 14

Hiding bloodstains on clothes   Sometimes blood can soak through to your outer clothes. If you have a stain on your clothes that can't be privately or completely rinsed out, or you can't scoot home straight away to change, here are some possibilities:

- ☉ avoid wearing white or a pale colour on your lower half if you're expecting, or already have, your period
- ☉ wear a jumper or jacket tied around your waist and draped down at the back to hide the stain
- ☉ keep an old uniform in your school or work locker to wear as a spare
- ☉ see a school nurse or receptionist – they should be able to help you get sorted out
- ☉ ask a friend or another girl at school, or a woman if you're in a public place, to help you – most women have experienced this problem at least once or twice so they'll probably be happy to help
- ☉ adjust the long strap of your bag, if it has one, so that the bag sits over your bottom area until you make it home
- ☉ if you're at a friend's house, borrow something to wear or ask their mum to help.

Stain etiquette   If you see that someone else has a stain on their skirt or pants don't blurt the fact out in front of everyone. Talk privately and quietly to her. Help by lending her some clothes or giving her something from your emergency kit. Don't tell other people what's happened.

Make a pact with your friends that you'll keep on stain alert for each other, and that you'll tell each other discreetly. It's comforting to know that your friends are having the same experiences, and talking about them. And sharing information will help you deal confidently with the whole big deal of periods, and give you all an extra bond.

More info on periods

Your local doctor or the practice nurse at your GP's surgery can answer any questions about your period, and so can the NHS Direct health line (England and Wales), on 0845 46 47, or NHS 24 health line (Scotland), on 08454 24 24 24 (see "More info on body changes" earlier).

www.kidshealth.org/teen/sexual_health
A US health site with lots of articles written especially for teenagers about irregular periods, PMS, toxic shock syndrome, puberty, the female reproductive system and much more.

www.mum.org
A wacky online museum of historical products, names and attitudes about periods.

www.nimh.org.uk
The National Institute of Medical Herbalists has a list of practitioners which meet its educational and ethical standards. To find one near you, choose "About medical herbalists", then click on the link "Find a medical herbalist".

www.pms.org.uk
Tips for fighting PMS from the National Association for Premenstrual Syndrome.

[*At first it's*] scary, but after a couple of years it's actually normal. It's just like: "Another period, how annoying!" But it's no big drama.   Rachel, 15

I was actually 9 and a half when I got my period.   Jane, 18

Periods. Must. DIE.   Alice, 17

Periods suck!!!   Clare, 15

At the time, getting my period was a terrible and scary thing, and I was fully developed by the age of about 14. It's something we all go through, and nothing to worry about.   Caitlin, 17

Being 16, in the middle of my teen years, I can slowly see myself becoming a young woman.   Donna, 16

It's much less exciting once it actually happens to you. I can't believe I was so worried that it would never happen!   Gillian, 15

SKIN

2

Skin wraps us up; helps to keep us warm or cool; sends us messages about what we're touching; and occasionally checks our diary and sees that we have an important event coming up, then immediately erupts into an obvious, **throbbing** red spot the size of Argentina, which makes us want to scre-heeeeeeam the house down.

Most of the billions of pounds spent on skin cosmetics every year comes from women wanting to look younger (but without the spots). So your teenage skin is actually a **highly** fashionable commodity, dahling, I'll have you know.

The skin on your face

You've inherited your skin from your ancestors, which determines what colour it is and whether your face is prone to scarring, freckles, pimples, dimples or wrinkles. Cosmetics companies refer to skin "types" on the labels of their products to try to convince people they need special stuff (which is sometimes true).

These skin types are:

- ◐ oily (also tactfully known as "teenage", "troubled" or "problem") – shiny skin that may have larger-than-average pores (tiny openings in the skin)

- ◐ dry – lacks oil and moisture, and is more prone to flaking, rough, dry patches or eczema

- ◐ normal – no problems (possibly fictitious)

- ◐ combination – a mix of oily, normal or dry patches on your face

- ◐ sensitive – the skin tends to react, with a rash or redness, to cosmetic ingredients, heat, allergens and alcohol (skin products that are non-fragranced and "hypoallergenic" are usually best for sensitive skin)

- ◐ problem – prone to spots and blackheads. Products labelled "oil-free" and "non-comedogenic" (won't block pores) are better for skin that's prone to spots.

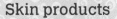

Skin products

Nobody needs to cleanse, tone and moisturise every day. You will probably just need to clean your face. You don't need a toner, and you probably don't need a moisturiser most of the time.

Cleanser   Wash your face morning and night. Some people clean their face with soap as well as water, but soap can dry out your skin because it washes off the natural oils that skin needs.

The sort of cleanser to buy is one that's:

- ◐ mild and non-perfumed (or a soap substitute), and specifically for the face, not a body wash
- ◐ oil-free, which will help cut down the oil on your face.

Moisturiser   A moisturiser is used to stop skin getting too dry. Your skin can become too dry if you over-wash it, have very hot baths, wax or shave, go out in the sun or swimming a lot, or spend most of your time in air-conditioned or heated buildings. And when that happens your body can be fooled into making more oil, causing blockages and spots.

A lot of people don't need a moisturiser for their face (or body). Many girls, especially those who drink lots of water and have enough oils in their diet from nuts and fish, or those who live in humid climates, probably won't need one.

When choosing a moisturiser for your face, buy one:

⊙ from a mid-range known brand, not a mysteriously cheap one from the £1 shop – but don't assume expensive is better than mid-range

⊙ with a sunscreen, of 15 or more SPF (sun protection factor), unless you have very dark skin (see the "Sun protection for all skin types" box a bit further on)

⊙ matching your skin colour if it's a tinted moisturiser

⊙ that's labelled for the face – body ones are more likely to block pores.

If you have very dry body skin you may need a body moisturiser: ask your doctor or chemist to recommend one.

Scrubs and exfoliators   These have crunchy little "beads", or particles, in them that are abrasive – rather like salt – so they scrub off dead skin cells. They're not good for skin that's sensitive. Most teens don't need to use one on their face: washing it twice a day, using a face wash or cleanser, should be enough to get rid of dead skin cells. Don't:

⊙ scrub too hard – it can make you go red and flaky

⊙ use a facial exfoliator more than once a week

⊙ use a body scrub on your face.

Toner   Nobody needs a toner (also called an astringent). Toners have chemicals to make your face feel briefly tingly or tight, but don't do anything to change or protect your skin. Some contain alcohol, which is drying. Toners can't make your pores smaller or improve your skin, and don't get rid of blackheads. Toners are just an expensive, stinging, useless liquid.

Beware of SCRUBS

Some days it feels as though the oil crisis could be solved by the amount

of oil on my skin.   Charlotte, 17

Cosmetics companies'claims

Companies are competing for those billions of pounds in cosmetics profits, so they have to spend big money on advertising and make huge claims about their products (next to a picture of a girl who's never had a spot in her entire life).

The more money a company spends on TV and magazine ads, the more they charge for their products – so the more expensive stuff isn't necessarily better for your skin.

Don't get sucked in by the companies' ridiculous claims. They can pretty much lie about what their products do because government authorities hardly ever bother taking them to court. I guess the authorities must be busy. Possibly getting their hair done.

There are a lot of ways in which big companies try to make you buy their products (see the Shopping chapter for the full lowdown). Here are some things to look out for in cosmetics ads.

Skin cream fibs   Skin creams can't change the way your skin grows, whatever the ads suggest. Stuff you put on your skin helps to clean it or to stop moisture evaporating, or makes the very top layer a bit moister, but there's no magic ingredient that can alter the nature of your skin. Any real changes happen from the inside (see the "Hints for healthy skin" box on the next page).

"Natural" claims   Some cosmetics companies sell "natural" products. This doesn't automatically mean they're good.

Potions made from natural ingredients may be less effective than some synthetic ones, or just be a cheap lotion with an added natural fragrance (which is still a chemical) or a natural ingredient that doesn't really do anything but sounds impressive and so they can charge more for it. Natural products usually need to have chemical preservatives added so they don't go "off" on the shelf. Many people are allergic to synthetic chemicals; others are allergic to common natural ingredients such as citrus, mint, tea tree and eucalyptus oils, and witch hazel.

"Scientific" claims   Cosmetics companies tend to bang on hysterically about how "scientific" their product is. If they'd really invented a cream that cured spots in a day, or prevented wrinkles, it would have been on the news. The "scientific breakthroughs" are almost always just a trick to get you to buy something new and expensive.

Most of the scientific-sounding ingredient names given in the ads are just completely made up by the company selling the skin product, like Enzyme B27 with Phyto-gel, New Dermfill Claro-spraunce with Cell-lift and… well, you get the idea.

Hints for healthy skin

✣ Eat well: good nourishment shows in your skin (more in the Food chapter).

✣ Drink lots of water: this helps your digestion and food absorption, and keeps your body and skin hydrated (although drinking more water doesn't stop spots).

✣ Exercise regularly: this increases blood flow to the skin, which helps clean up and repair any skin problems (see the Move chapter).

✣ Avoid cigarette smoke and smoking: they cause dull, discoloured skin and early wrinkles (see the Drugs chapter).

Exact percentages, kinda You can't measure whether skin is "86 percent brighter", or a product has "93 percent purifying efficiency" or is "71 percent effective on imperfections". This is just more advertising piffle. Sometimes I think three people stand in an elevator and make up numbers at random.

Claims you need a three- or four-step routine A magazine or website may tell you that you need a complex three- or four-step beauty routine, using lots of products, because it's keeping its advertisers happy. The advertisers would *love* to sell you all those products.

More info on looking after your face

www.paulaschoice-eu.com
Paula Begoun sells cosmetics but also gives product breakdowns and scam warnings; start with "Skin care facts".

www.thesite.org/healthandwellbeing/
appearance/skincare
Info on how diet and lifestyle can affect your skin, plus DIY beauty tips.

Spots and blackheads

As a teenager you can become so obsessed with looking at your new self, endlessly inspecting your body and face in the mirror, that you notice even a wee red dot and go through days of writhing torture thinking everyone is staring at your GIGANTIC SPOT: RULER OF THE UNIVERSE.

Some teenagers get just the occasional spot or blackhead outbreak (which some doctors call acne), or the odd zit here and there. Others have a really big problem that they have to face in the mirror every day (often called severe acne). Nobody has to put up with a terrible spot problem; there are ways of getting help.

These things DO NOT CAUSE spots or blackheads:

- ☾ greasy food
- ☾ not exfoliating your skin
- ☾ not washing enough or properly
- ☾ not drinking enough water
- ☾ dirt or germs on the skin
- ☾ chocolate
- ☾ bad karma.

Getting spots or blackheads is not your fault.

What causes spots and blackheads?

If you have spots or blackheads it's not because you're doing anything wrong, or failing to suck up to the Goddess of Clear Skin. You get teenage spots and blackheads because one of your grandparents or parents had a similar problem: you inherited it (some disappointment if you were hoping for a small French castle instead).

For a blemish (spot or blackhead) to form, you need a blockage in one of those tiny holes in your skin called a pore. Everyone has sebaceous (pronounced seb-aysh-us) glands everywhere in their skin, which pump out small amounts of oily stuff called sebum (pronounced see-b'm). Sebum protects us. It's why when we get in a bath or go swimming we don't fill with water and puff up like a sponge. Well done, sebum. Fine work. Just leave it there, thanks. Sebum? Down, sebum! Down!

Damn. During the teen years you have more of the hormone androgen, which overexcites your sebaceous glands, which then pump out too much sebum, which then blocks the pores, causing spots and blackheads.

Spots

When a pore gets blocked by extra sebum, bacteria can grow underneath, causing inflammation – the pore gets cranky and turns red. Then, as the bacteria builds up, white or yellow pus forms, which under pressure eventually rises to form a head on the surface of your skin. Now you have a spot.

Or you may get an under-the-skin spot (sometimes called a blind pimple): it looks angry and red but never comes to a point. A blind pimple stays under the skin and the pus is eventually absorbed by the body.

Spots can get worse during stressful times (such as before exams or a first date) because hormones caused by stress make inflammation worse.

Can you believe that we have the greatest number of sebaceous glands on the *face*? I mean, why not the stomach, where at least we could hide them? You can also get spots on your back, neck, buttocks, shoulders and chest. You know, just as a bonus.

Acne scars Spots can leave scars, particularly if you pick at them. Even under-the-skin spots, which don't come to a head, can cause puckered scars. Scars can be very hard to hide or remove, so it's better to prevent them if you can.

How bad the damage is can depend more on whether a person is prone to scarring than on how many spots there are or even whether they are picked. People with a tendency to scarring can include:

- those who get cysts (very deep spots)
- anyone of Asian heritage
- those who know from childhood experience that they scar easily
- some people with sensitive skin.

Anyone prone to scarring should see an experienced dermatologist – a qualified skin specialist – as soon as they start getting spots, and all scarring needs to be treated by one. Get a referral from your GP (and see "More info" at the end of this section). Never go to somebody who advertises – good dermatologists don't need to advertise – or who calls themself a "cosmetic surgeon" (they might not be a skin specialist).

Fighting spots There are a few things you can do to try to stop spots forming, or to hurry them along if they do arrive.

- Wash your skin every night to remove any excess surface oil and dead skin cells, which can clog your pores (but be gentle because too much washing and scrubbing can make your skin too dry, prompting your body to release more oil and irritate any healing spots). If your skin is very oily wash your face in the morning too.
- Make sure any gloop that goes on your face, whether it's make-up or a spot cream, doesn't clog pores (look for labels saying "non-comedogenic" or "non-acnegenic"; "oil-free" is also good).
- Wash sweat off after exercise or when it's very hot to avoid more blocked pores.
- Keep your hair clean and try to keep it off your face and neck, especially if you use "product" (such as gels and moulding wax).

- Try not to touch your face, or rest your cheek or chin in your hand, as you will rub off any spot cream you're using.
- Eat healthy food, which will help your immune system, which in turn will help your body fight bacteria (although it won't stop your sebaceous glands making the extra sebum). Eating oily or sugary foods doesn't *cause* spots, but it doesn't help your system either.
- Avoid cigarette smoke, which blocks pores.

Squeezing spots   Don't squeeze spots because that can cause redness and let in more bacteria, from the outside, making things worse, as well as increasing the likelihood of scarring. Ha! Easy for me to say. Sometimes it seems irresistible to squeeze.

If you absolutely have to squeeze, just gently remove a head that's already turned yellow. First wash your hands with warm water and soap, then use a clean tissue so you're not touching the skin with your fingers. Make sure you put a drying antiseptic cream on the spot afterwards. If the spot doesn't pop easily, stop – otherwise you will cause a bruise or redness that could last longer than the spot.

Covering up spots   Any foundation make-up used to cover spots should be oil-free and matched to your skin colour. "Cover sticks" made for adults are usually designed to disguise grey bags under the eyes so they're the wrong tint to hide red spots.

Complementary therapies   Complementary therapists and herbalists often suggest a vitamin supplement that includes B6 and zinc to reduce inflammation. Doctors say there's no evidence this helps. Herbal supplements and potions to regulate hormones must only be prescribed by a herbalist or therapist who is a member of the National Institute of Medical Herbalists.

Don't use a "colloidal silver" preparation because it doesn't work and can be toxic (poisonous). It's very important that you don't use vitamin A except in a spot preparation specifically prescribed by a doctor. Vitamin A supplements in the amount needed to attack spots are toxic and can damage your liver. The vitamin A medications prescribed for severe acne by doctors have had the toxic element removed.

Spot washes and creams   Spend some time in the supermarket aisle or at the chemist shop (pharmacy) working out which soaps, cleansers or spot creams could be right for you. Talk to the chemist (the professional behind the prescriptions counter) about your skin, and ask them to show you different products for your face in a range of

When my mum and sisters point out that I have a few spots it affects me a lot

because they are my sisters and mum.   Saskia, 16

prices. People go to the chemist all the time to ask for things to stick up their bum, so don't feel embarrassed asking about spot creams. The chemist may recommend a cleanser or other face wash, and a spot cream.

A **facial cleanser**, a **soap substitute** or a special **facial soap** is usually better than a traditional soap, which can be too drying, especially if you then put on another drying product such as spot cream. A gentle, oil-free cleanser is included in many ranges of acne products.

Wash your hands well, foam up the cleanser or soap in them, massage it gently into your face, then splash it off completely with a few scoops of warm or cold water.

Common ingredients in cleansers for skin with spots are salicylic acid, and alpha hydroxy acids (AHAs) such as glycolic acid. These are exfoliants, which help to loosen dead skin cells although exfoliants can irritate some sensitive skins). If you are using a cleanser for spots don't also use an exfoliator or scrub your skin.

> *I have some acne which I'm really touchy about. Even though nobody really cares, I do. People get like one spot and go on and on about how bad it looks and they talk about it to me and my face is covered in them!!*
> Sarah, 13

Spot creams can't do anything much to spots you already have. They work to prevent new ones coming.

Most creams use chemicals to dry out the spots already there, and have an antiseptic to kill surface germs that could cause further infection in broken skin. The drying ingredients include alcohol, sulphur, tea tree oil and benzoyl peroxide, which is believed to be the most effective agent because it fights extra oil, bacteria and the clogging of pores.

- ☻ Don't start thinking about using spot cream a couple of weeks before a special party: it won't have enough time to do its thing. Spots take about six weeks to form before you see the end result.
- ☻ Test a small amount on your face first to make sure your skin doesn't have a bad reaction to it.
- ☻ Don't mix spot creams or put different ones on at the same time: they can cancel each other out.
- ☻ Don't put too much on because all drying agents can cause flaking, peeling and dryness around the spots.

FACT

The girls in the spot cream ads with amazingly clear skin?

Take no notice of them. They've either never had a spot in their life – or they've had a "mouse makeover" by a digital "artist".

⑥ Apply it all over spot-prone areas, not just on the visible spots, because creams work to prevent new spots coming.

⑥ Make using the cream a daily routine because if you miss a few days the treatment won't have a chance to work properly. Use benzoyl peroxide in the morning because it can leave bleach marks on bed linen.

⑥ Continue using the cream once a day until you haven't had a spot for a month, then stop and see what happens.

> I've acne problems and the like. They're little, and I know they'll pass, but sometimes I look in a mirror and just feel hideous.
>
> Natasha, 17

Hang in there with the spot cream – it takes a number of weeks to see results. Not everyone's spot problem is solved with stuff from the chemist, though. See a doctor if, after six weeks of using a spot cream every day, there's been no sign of improvement.

Doctors' treatments for spots If you feel you're really losing your battle with spots, your doctor may prescribe some treatments or refer you to a dermatologist for specialist advice (although you may have to wait a while for an appointment, as there's a shortage of dermatologists in this country). Medical treatments for severe acne can take a few weeks to start working, and can include one or a mix of these:

⑥ antibiotic pills to kill the bacteria from the inside and calm the inflammation

⑥ antibiotic gels and lotions

⑥ vitamin A gel or cream to help unclog the pores, which is best put on at night and washed off in the morning because it can cause sun sensitivity

⑥ pills that reduce or counteract the amount of androgen, that pesky oil-producing hormone; a version of the contraceptive pill is often prescribed because the oestrogen in it suppresses androgen (if you need the Pill for contraception as well, see how to take it properly in the Sex chapter)

⑥ medication for a disorder called polycystic ovaries if you're diagnosed as having it – some cases of bad spots can be a sign that your ovaries are misbehaving

⑥ a strong vitamin A drug called isotretinoin, only prescribed for really difficult spot cases, which is available under different brand names, including Roaccutane. If you get pregnant while taking the drug, or in the month after you stop, it will severely damage the baby, so if there's any chance you'll be having sex you also need to be on the Pill and using a condom every time.

Isotretinoin causes side effects such as dry lips and sensitivity to sunlight, and you need family or friends to look out for any mood changes while you're on it (ask your doctor about these).

Blackheads

Everyone has tiny blackheads, most of which nobody notices (and whiteheads, which are only noticeable on darker skins). Blackheads happen in pores blocked by sebum when a skin protein called keratin turns black after it's exposed to the air. So even though the pores look black, it has nothing to do with dirt or not washing.

When do spots leave your life???
Shannon, 16

It doesn't last forever.
Former spot victim

🅖 Only try to pop a blackhead if it is really obvious (wash your hands before squeezing gently). The blackhead should then come out easily, but if it doesn't immediately, stop.

🅖 Scrubs may help, but you can't use them more than once a week. Exfoliators, toners and astringents do not cure blackheads.

🅖 Those sticky strips that you press on and rip off may or may not take a few blackheads with them, but they don't stop blackheads from forming.

More info on spots and blackheads

www.bad.org.uk
The British Association of Dermatologists; choose "Public resources" for all sorts of info about the skin, FAQs, patient info leaflets and advice on how to be referred to a skin specialist by your GP.

www.childrenfirst.nhs.uk/teens/health/conditions/a/acne.html
Info from Great Ormond Street Hospital and the NHS on teenage acne, including links to

skin tips for girls and questions from other teens suffering the same problems.

www.niams.nih.gov
US government health department site. From the home page choose "Health information", then "Acne" for a complete rundown.

www.patient.co.uk/showdoc/23068674
Independent info provided by GPs, funded by private companies, about the causes and treatments for spots (includes diagrams).

At the moment I am on antibiotics to clear my skin of spots. I am scared of my blackheads. Vanessa, 16

Common skin conditions

As if you didn't have enough going on with your skin when you're a teenager, you may have a common skin condition or rash, like eczema (pronounced ecks-ma) or psoriasis (pronounced sore-eye-a-sis). They're not caused by anything you're doing wrong with washing or eating, and they're not catching – but they are annoying. Here's what you need to know.

Eczema

Eczema causes patches of skin to go red, dry and itchy. If you have it, you might feel it must be incredibly obvious – but other people usually don't even notice. The other good news is that most people's eczema goes away, or gets much less severe, as they get older.

It often runs in families, and people with asthma or strong immune reactions such as skin sensitivities or allergies are more likely to have eczema.

A flare-up can be triggered by:

- any allergy (including dust, cats, washing powder, moisturiser or foods)
- using soap on the area
- very hot or cold weather
- any illness, which keeps your immune system busy
- getting your period, or coming up to your due date
- getting sweaty
- scratchy fabrics, especially wool
- being waxed
- very hot baths or showers
- stress
- pregnancy.

Ways to reduce eczema   Make sure you get a diagnosis from your GP so you know you're using the right treatments. You may not have eczema, but another kind of rash.

- Avoid skin irritants and allergens if you can (culprits can include perfumes, moisturisers and fake tan).
- Keep your skin moisturised: ask your pharmacist for a suitable moisturiser for very dry skin or eczema.
- Try not to scratch as this can cause infection. Try cold compresses and "wet wraps" (from the pharmacy), especially at night.
- Creams and pills prescribed by your GP. Steroid creams, although often used as a last resort, can be very effective.

Psoriasis

Psoriasis makes red, crusty, flaky patches appear on the skin, often on the knees, elbows and scalp. For some people it's itchy, too. Psoriasis is caused by your skin going into overdrive, replacing skin cells too quickly. It can make people feel self conscious and miserable.

Like eczema, it's probably linked to family history, and an immune system that's not quite behaving itself. A psoriasis flare-up can be triggered by stress, lack of sunshine, friction from clothes, scratches or scrapes to your skin, misbehaving hormones, alcohol and smoking.

Your GP or a dermatologist can prescribe treatments to help control psoriasis, including special moisturisers and ointments with vitamin A and D, and tar-based creams and shampoos. For more severe cases, you might be given steroid tablets or injections, or spend prescribed time in the sunshine or under an ultraviolet light (a treatment called phototherapy), which slows the growth of the skin cells (don't worry, it won't hurt).

More info on common skin conditions

www.britishskinfoundation.org.uk
Site of the charitable organization dedicated to skin research; choose "Skin information" for a complete A–Z of skin conditions, including eczema and psoriasis.

www.childrenfirst.nhs.uk/teens/health/conditions
Use the A–Z list on this NHS teen site to find out more about eczema and psoriasis, including treatments like phototherapy.

www.psoriasis-help.org.uk
Explanations, support and help, including a forum where you can "talk" online to other people with psoriasis.

Skin colour

Years ago it was fashionable in many countries to have "white" skin, to show that you were too rich and posh to have to work outside. Then it became fashionable to have a tan because it showed you were too rich and posh to have to do any work at all and could lie around in the sun all day or go away to expensive, exotic places on holiday. Then people realized the damage that too much sun can do to the skin, causing dryness, wrinkles and blotches, not to mention the whole skin cancer thing.

These days people realize it's cool not to have a tan – and to be whatever colour you were born, whether you have inherited the beautiful skin of people from Africa, Papua New Guinea and Aboriginal communities; the heavenly caramel skin of Polynesian Islanders; one of the gorgeous brown tones found in India, Pakistan and Sri Lanka; the attractive olive skin of folk around the Mediterranean Sea; the delicate prettiness of Asian skin; the moonlight-lovely pale skin and freckles found across Europe; one of the

Sun protection for all skin types

OK, we all know we don't get the best weather in the UK, but on those rare occasions when the sun does show it's face, you need to protect your skin – and it's just as important when you're on holiday somewhere hot or sunny. Here's what the experts have to say.

For people with pale skin

✷ Try to avoid going out in the sun at the hottest time of day (between 11am and 3pm).

✷ Wear a hat that shades the neck and face, and preferably long sleeves and long skirts or pants if you can't avoid being in the sun for ages. Clothes and shade give more sun protection than sunscreen.

✷ Use a sunscreen with a SPF (sun protection factor) of 15 or more. SPF 30+ gives you the best, maximum protection available.

✷ Apply sunscreen half an hour before going out to give it a chance to have the chemical reaction on your skin that will protect you.

✷ Slather on sunscreen every two hours (most people don't know they need to).

✷ Use a water-resistant sunscreen if you'll be swimming or sweating.

✷ Apply a toddlers' sunscreen if you have sensitive skin.

✷ If you get spots use a gel sunscreen, which is less likely to block pores.

✷ Don't use a sunscreen that's past its use-by date.

For people with darker skin

Some people actually need *more* sun than they usually get, especially in the winter. Girls with very dark skin (for example, those with two African parents) shouldn't use any sunscreen or wear hats. They, and girls who always wear scarves, veils and clothes that cover their arms and legs, need extra sun and may require a vitamin D supplement. (Pale, veiled girls will still need to avoid sunburn.)

much-admired skin colours belonging to South America; or any of the equally enviable variations that come from mixing them up with parents of different backgrounds.

All skin colours have their own beauty. To insult someone about the colour of their skin shows the very worst kind of ugly ignorance, and reveals nothing except the nastiness and embarrassing stupidity of the person who said it.

> The majority of people love that I'm Indian and brown. But u get some real a-holes that just don't know when to stop so, yeah, their comments can affect me. But usually I ignore it or give them the one-finger salute.
>
> *Vinu, 15*

The sun and your skin

We know too much sun is the biggest cause of skin damage, and also that melanoma skin cancer caused by sun exposure is the fastest-rising cancer in the UK. It is also the most common cancer in young people (aged 15–34). But a little bit of sunshine every day is good for you because it boosts your immune system and helps your body to heal and to make vitamin D, needed for healthy bones. People with naturally very dark skin need to worry less about sun protection, which is lucky because they need up to ten times longer in the sun than pale folk to make enough vitamin D.

Sunburn and skin colour changes caused by the sun are the things to avoid. The more times you are sunburnt, the more chance you have of later developing skin cancer – sometimes as soon as your late teens or early twenties.

Freckles Freckles are small, pale to dark brown spots seen mostly on the face and arms because those are the areas most exposed to sunlight. Freckles look fine – except to some girls who worry about theirs. Freckles seem to be the first and last thing they see when they look in the mirror; this time will pass.

People who get lots of freckles have skin that's likely to burn so they need to take extra care to protect themselves against the sun. Freckles can't be removed by exfoliating or home chemical treatments.

fake tans can look a bit carroty...

Wanting a tan

A suntan is evidence that the sun has damaged your skin. The tan is discolouration resulting from the skin trying to protect itself by producing more melanin (the chemical that causes pigment – skin colour). And a tan doesn't protect you from getting burnt.

Tanning salons: don't go there The British Association of Dermatologists warns that tans from tanning salons (also known as solariums or "sunbeds") are almost certainly far more damaging than sun-bathing, because the kind of rays they use penetrate further and can cause more damage, faster. Most skin experts agree that under-18s shouldn't legallay be able to use sunbeds.

At the least, going to a tanning salon will make your skin prematurely wrinkly, and at the worst increase your chance of skin cancer, which can mean large areas of your skin have to be removed, and in rare cases death. So if you see a friend going into a tanning place, follow them in there, stage a hysterical scene and drag them out by the ankle. If necessary you can tie them to a parking meter.

So-called tan "accelerators", "enhancers" and "magnifiers", sold as lotions or tablets (often by tanning salons), are claimed to boost the melanin in your body. A lotion can't do this, and it's very doubtful whether the pills can either. Using a tan accelerator won't protect you against sunburn or skin damage, and may cause blistering, nausea, headaches and itchy skin.

Fake tans A fake tan is a dye that is rubbed, sponged or sprayed onto your body. We've all seen those celebrities who have overdone it and look like beaming gigantic carrots wearing sunglasses. Although a fake tan is a berzillion times safer than a real tan caused by the sun or a scary tanning salon, it does have other risks – for example, looking like a stripy gigantic root vegetable.

Magazines mainly suggest you get a fake tan because the major cosmetics companies selling fake tan products spend millions of pounds a year on magazine advertising. The models in the magazines usually have a (professionally applied) fake tan: it's an easy way to get across the idea we should all look like that, so we need to buy one. A company might threaten to pull out their advertising money if a magazine article said that fake tans were unnecessary, or that you should make up your own mind about whether you want one or whether it suits you, or that some fake-tan products are ridiculously expensive and practically impossible to get looking right.

I would like to have brown skin.
Natalie, 17

How do you get rid of freckles and get a suntan?
[You can't.]
Jane, 13

As well as fake tans you apply yourself, you can get one sprayed on at a salon. This can be very expensive, and if sprayed on the face can block pores and cause spots. Spray-on tan has the same drawbacks as the stuff in bottles: it can smudge, stain and go streaky. It lasts for a few days, depending on how often you wash and what you wash with.

More info on sun protection

www.cancerresearchuk.org/sunsmart
Cancer Research's SunSmart campaign has tips about avoiding sunburn on holiday, covering-up and using sunscreen,checking your moles, and the dangers of sunbeds.

www.paulaschoice-eu.com
Specialist skin author's site. Choose "Sun essentials" under "Learn".

www.teenagecancertrust.org
The Shunburn campaign has competitions and fun stuff, as well as sun safety tips.

Skin marks

Everybody has moles, birthmarks or stretch marks – some people have all three. Some people have more than others, or larger or smaller ones, or a skin colour that means they don't show up as much.

Moles

Moles are usually brown or black dots on the skin that can appear anywhere, either alone or in groups. They can be flat or raised, smooth or bumpy. They mostly appear in the first twenty-five years of your life, and it's normal to have between ten and forty moles by then. (No, don't count them. How bored would you have to be?)

Moles can change over the years, or even disappear, but it's important to keep an eye on them. Have your doctor or dermatologist check them every year or so.

Most moles are not dangerous, but if you notice that one has changed – grown, become red or darker – or has edges that are itchy, bleed or have altered in some way, see a doctor immediately because misbehaving moles can lead to skin cancer. Moles that look as if they might be a skin cancer, or which get rubbed by, say, a bra strap, can be easily removed by a dermatologist.

Many people add a fake facial mole for glamour, using an eyebrow pencil or eye-liner. (It can be a little less glamorous when the real ones have hairs growing out of them – but if you like you can carefully pluck the hairs, using cooled sterilized tweezers.)

Birthmarks

A birthmark is any skin mark that you were born with or developed as a baby. Lots of people have them. Some of them go away as you grow older. There are marks that are blood vessels you're able to see under the skin, and others that happen because the body puts too much pigment in one area.

Birthmarks can range from small, light brown spots to a large area of pink or purple pigment. Most are harmless and there is no need to get them removed for health reasons, but it is always a good idea to get them checked out by a doctor.

People with a birthmark (or a scar) on their face can feel self-conscious. Some girls use make-up to tone them down, although others quite like them as a symbol of individuality. Some birthmarks are easily treated or removed; others aren't.

It's essential to see a dermatologist or a member of the British Association of Plastic Reconstructive and Aesthetic Surgeons or the British Association of Aesthetic Plastic Surgeons, not a "cosmetic surgeon" or "cosmetic physician", when you're seeking treatment, but you should still consult your GP first. And never just pop along to a "cosmetic centre" or "laser clinic" because some people who use lasers and other skin techniques don't have much experience or training.

Stretch marks

Almost everybody gets stretch marks. They're just the stripy lines left after your skin has had to stretch. They're most common on breasts, hips, thighs and tummies, and can happen when your body has a growth spurt or you put on a lot of weight quickly.

When they first happen they're often slightly raised and purply pink or red. Nothing – and no amount of rubbing with creams – will prevent them or make them go away. But the good news is they always fade to flat, silvery marks that blend with your skin colour and are often pretty invisible – or so faint you'd only notice if you were obsessing.

You usually don't notice them on other people: they're just not that obvious. Yet a lot of girls get self-conscious about them and hide their bodies. We're not used to seeing real naked bodies – just the computer-adjusted and make-up-slathered bodies of models in ads and magazines. (Yep, they use full body make-up to hide things like stretch marks.)

I have stretch marks on my breasts, upper thighs and so on. I get really self-conscious about it and have to wear less-revealing clothing, so my question is how do I get rid of them??   Ellie, 15

Does everyone get stretch marks and how do I get rid of them?   Paula, 16

More info on skin marks

See your GP for advice on whether you need surgery, and if so, where to find a highly qualified and experienced surgeon. (You will need a referral from your GP.) The NHS pays for some kinds of cosmetic surgery, but not all.

www.bad.org.uk
The British Association of Dermatologists. Choose "Public resources" for info on finding a skin specialist. You will need a referral from your GP to see a dermatologist.

www.bapras.org.uk
This organization covers reconstructive and plastic surgery for both medical and cosmetic reasons. Choose "Patient information" and then "Skin".

www.baaps.org.uk
The association has a focus on surgery for cosmetic reasons only. Click on "Find a surgeon" to locate a qualified professional in your area.

www.youngwomenshealth.org/facial_difference.html and www.changingfaces.org.uk
Non-profit sites for girls with a facial difference, such as birthmarks or scars.

Sweating

You've always been able to sweat, even as a little nipper. You probably haven't been aware of it, but the sweat from armpits, between legs or buttocks, and in other areas where the air can't circulate, has always stayed wet longer than elsewhere.

Now, in your teens, you're suddenly sweating more (although not as much as guys), because you've been developing extra sweat glands all over your body. And guess where in particular you've got extra sweat gland activity? Under your arms and between your legs. (Gee thanks, Mother Nature, you maniac.)

We do need to sweat: it cools us down if we get too hot because of the weather or exercise. And if we overheat we go purple and have convulsions. You'd probably prefer to sweat.

How much you sweat depends mainly on genetics. Some people just sweat less because that runs in their family, or because they're of Asian heritage.

You can sweat more if you're nervous. Extra sweat from nervousness often concentrates in your armpits and on your forehead, palms and feet.

Deodorants and antiperspirants

Not everyone needs an underarm deodorant or antiperspirant. Some people only use it before exercising or on very hot days.

✱ An underarm deodorant uses a chemical to help neutralize the smell of sweat, but it won't stop wetness. Most are perfumed.

✱ An underarm antiperspirant temporarily plugs or seals sweat glands, usually with an aluminium-based substance.

✱ Some products combine an antiperspirant with a deodorant.

✱ You may have to try different ones before you find the one that works best for you.

✱ If a deodorant or antiperspirant causes a rash or itchiness try another brand or type – maybe one that's hypoallergenic or unscented.

Things that make you sweat more include:

⊙ stress
⊙ undies, tights, socks, shoes and other clothes made from synthetic fabrics, which don't "breathe"
⊙ shoes worn without socks
⊙ hats – sunhats are cooler if made from cotton or some other natural fibre and are a light colour
⊙ very heavy skin-covering lotion or make-up, because the skin can't "breathe"
⊙ hair around your neck and ears on a hot day.

Smell

Everyone gets BO (body odour) when they don't wash sweat off every day. Now that you're a teenager, yours smells more than it used to because of the hormonal chemicals released in it. The longer sweat is left on the skin, the more it can change smell because of the build-up of bacteria. "Fresh" sweat usually smells fine.

Talcum powder, perfumes and body sprays don't stop or really disguise BO on bodies or clothes – washing properly is the only way to solve it.

You don't really need to feel too disgusted at the prospect of the teen years being leakier, oilier, sweatier and smellier (not to mention the whole once-a-month period palaver) because luckily you can be in control of it all.

And it could be worse. You could have been born in the Middle Ages, when there was no plumbing. You'd be lucky to have a bath once a decade, your mossy teeth would go a fetching shade of brown before dropping out, and you'd probably snuggle up at night with a rat or two on some nice warm horse poo, in your pyjamas crocheted from long grass and goat fur. Instead you've got toilet paper, so cheer up.

FACT

DIY "Intimate" sprays, vaginal deodorants, douches, perfumes, perfumed talc or other smelly stuff shouldn't be put on, or up, your girly bits. Your vagina is self-cleaning.

More info on sweating

www.sweathelp.org
The International Hyperhidrosis (excessive sweating) Society site. Choose "Teens".

www. hyperhidrosisuk.org
British support group for people suffering from hyperhidrosis.

Piercing and tattoos

Piercing and tattoos have become more ordinary, instead of new and exciting, because so many people have them now. (There wasn't a lot of eyebrow piercing or tatts in my granny's day, frankly.)

Piercing

It's possible, but not necessarily a good hobby, to pierce almost any area of the body. In the UK, there's no legal age limit for most kinds of body piercing, but many reputable piercing shops won't pierce anyone under 14, while those aged 15 or 16 will need their parents' permission.

Body-piercing facts

☾ It needs to be done by an experienced professional who uses a new needle, which is then thrown away, and who sterilizes all other equipment in a machine called an autoclave. This is the only way to make sure you and other people don't catch one of the serious and possibly fatal viruses – such as HIV (the AIDS virus) and hepatitis B – that can be spread by unhygienic piercing. Some equipment, such as the gun piercers that work a bit like a stapler, can't be properly sterilized.

☾ Make sure before you have a piercing that you're up to date with your immunisations, especially for tetanus and the hepatitis variations. There's no vaccine for HIV.

One of my friends just got her tongue pierced for a guy and she had to suck ice all week! DUMB, and to change for guys is wrong.
Salima, 17

ⓖ The British Dental Association advises against lip and tongue piercing. Dentists see some of the results: swollen tongues, causing breathing difficulty; infected gums; and teeth cracked, chipped or broken by the metal. Lip piercing can also cause speech problems, including lisping.

ⓖ The more chance there is for bacteria to breed, the more chance there is of infection: nose, mouth and (Ow! Ow! Oww!) girly bits are the most likely places.

ⓖ You should never pierce yourself or get a friend to do it: a home job is much more likely to become infected or look botched.

ⓖ Take extra special care after you have your piercing done. The practitioner should give you instructions on how to treat it until it has healed, including how to clean it properly.

ⓖ If there's infection, which is common, minor or major scarring can result. And if you no longer use a pierced hole it will close over but can leave a small scar.

ⓖ Know what the symptoms of infection are so you can get it treated by a doctor very quickly. These include soreness, redness, swelling and gunk coming out.

Tattoos

Before you get a permanent tattoo, you need to know some stuff.

ⓖ A tattoo is basically a wound that heals into a permanent scar. It hurts a lot.

ⓖ You'll need to go to a clean, licensed professional tattoo shop that sterilizes its equipment in an autoclave and uses a new needle for each client.

ⓖ If you're under 18 getting a tattoo is illegal. Good tattooists won't do illegal work, so that means if you're under 18 and a tattooist accepts you as a client you'll be getting inferior work by somebody without the right experience, equipment or skill. And if a tattooist doesn't observe the rule about asking you for ID proof of age, why would they observe the rule about sterilizing equipment?

ⓖ You'll need vaccinations against hepatitis and other blood-borne diseases (but you can't be vaccinated against HIV).

ⓖ The tattooist may do it crookedly, or start in the wrong spot.

WILL YOUR TATTOOS LOOK GOOD LATER?

- Most people who have a tattoo later have regrets.
- It's very much harder to remove a tattoo than to get one, it hurts more, it can cost several hundred pounds to remove and it leaves scars.
- The tattoo you want now may not be the one you'd have chosen five years ago. So would it be the one you'd choose in two, or ten, or twenty years' time? How do you think a tattoo looks on someone your mother's age or older?
- A tattoo is distorted if the part of your body it's on gets smaller or bigger. (Has your body finished growing? Will you ever be pregnant? Will your size ever change, permanently or temporarily?)
- A tattoo may not always suit the sorts of jobs you decide to go for, or your lifestyle later on.
- Many tattooed symbols turn out to mean something other than what people believed, and many are not spelt correctly.
- You don't need a tattoo to remember a friend, relative or event.
- The tattooist should give lots of information on how to keep the wound clean afterwards that you can easily follow.

The solution: temporary tatts   There are now lots of people, often at fairs, fetes, street markets and parties, and even at tattoo parlours, who can airbrush on a "temporary tattoo". This means you can change the design any time you like. You can also buy supplies online or at some tattoo shops so that you can stencil your own.

More info on piercing and tattoos

www.bbpa.org.uk
The British Body Piercing Association has a list of registered members who have to comply with strict hygiene and training requirements, and codes of practice.

www.childrenfirst.nhs.uk/teens
Search for "Body piercing" or "Tattoo" for all the latest advice for teens.

www.nhsdirect.nhs.uk/encyclopaedia
Search for "Body piercing" to get all the facts, including the law, the risks, recommendations and cleaning advice.

www.youngwomenshealth.org/
body-piercing.html
A non-profit US site with stuff on piercing problems to look out for.

3

HAIR

you HAVE tiny HAIRS
aLL oVER yOuR BoDY...

Hair insulates us from cold weather (though what a shame we're not as **furry** as brown bears in winter), it helps to stop dust or grit getting into sensitive areas, such as eyes, and it allows us to indulge in a number of mind-numbingly **ludicrous** and embarrassing hairstyles until we find one that suits us. And everyone ends up with **extra** hair on their head, legs, arms, face, armpits and private bits. It reminds us that we're descended from shag-pile-covered cave folk. Lovely. Let's move on.

Looking after your hair

Like skin, the hair on your head is often divided into types – oily, dry and normal (this doesn't mean more normal than the other types, just neither oily nor dry). Don't worry too much about which type yours is because it's usually not a problem. For instance, your hair might be naturally dry but probably won't be "too dry" (unless it's affected all the time by the sun, dyeing or hot hairstyling products).

FACT

Your hair's dead (sob)   Hair is made of the protein keratin (about ninety percent) and water. Every strand has an outer layer (the one we see, which is a protective surface); an inner layer that's made of keratin and gives the hair strength and texture; and a core of colour, which shines through the other layers. Hair is created in follicles under your skin's surface – but by the time it pokes out it's dead.

Shampoo and conditioner

Because your hair's dead, the shampoo and conditioner you put on it just strips out the oils ("cleans" it) and then adds a coating to make it easier to brush or comb and less frizzy or fly-away.

Two-in-one shampoo and conditioner combos are hopeless. A shampoo needs to get stuff off your hair; a conditioner needs to put stuff on. Combining them in the one bottle means you neither wash nor condition your hair properly.

Shampoo facts

- Crap shampoo from a £1 or discount shop is likely to be just coloured detergent, which will strip too much of the natural oil from your hair.
- You don't need top-of-the-range salon products. They're better for your hair than the really cheap shampoos because they contain gentler surfactants, the ingredient that makes shampoo lather, but there are products that are just as good at less than half the cost.
- Most people use far more shampoo – and conditioner – than they need to. Try using only a little bit and see if that does the job.
- Most shampoos recommend you lather, then rinse, twice to make sure your hair is thoroughly clean, but really you only need to shampoo once. You get a better lather on the second go because your hair's already clean.

Conditioner facts

- Most conditioners are just a coating that makes the hair shinier, and also smoother so that knots comb out more easily – they don't change the hair itself.

- "Leave-in" or "heat protection" conditioners usually have sealing chemicals to protect the hair from drying out too much when it's blow-dried.

- Sometimes conditioners cause a build-up of coatings, making hair look heavy and dull. To get these off you'll need a strong shampoo that doesn't contain "body" or other coatings.

- If your hair is the oily type, try conditioning it only once a week; use a conditioner labelled for oily hair; or just condition the ends.

Different hair

Because everyone's different and has a cocktail of genes that decide how their hair will sprout, there's an amazing variety of head hair. It can be straight, wavy, madly curly, bouffy, thick, thin, fine, red, strawberry blonde, black, dark brown, light brown, or dyed iridescent purple to scare your parents.

Many people who have blonde hair when they're little end up with brown hair as they grow up.

Curly or kinky A lot of people with wavy or curly hair want it to be straight. And you can temporarily straighten your hair yourself, with the right tools. Never try to iron your hair with a household

How to keep your hair looking good

✱ Eat lots of different healthy foods (see the Food chapter), and don't go on diets. Hair is affected by what you put, or don't put, into your body. Dieting and unhealthy food can make hair grow thin and weak.

✱ Wash your hair to get rid of dirt and any oil build-up: every few days is fine. Most people don't need to wash their hair every day unless it is very oily.

✱ Use a wide-toothed comb to untangle wet and freshly washed hair, and be gentle so you don't stretch and break the strands.

✱ If you need to use a hairdryer, stop before your hair is completely dry so you don't blast all the moisture out. If possible let your hair dry naturally.

✱ Wear a swimming cap in a chlorinated pool. The chemicals will make your hair drier, and could turn it swamp green, especially if you're blonde.

Label check

* Shampoos and conditioners with "natural" ingredients won't necessarily do anything better for your hair than ones with synthetic chemicals.

* Shampoos and conditioners that boast fruit or herbal ingredients usually just include chemicals that smell like the real thing.

* As with skin products, beware of "scientific breakthroughs" or "newly discovered" ingredients that have names made up by the hair product companies: "revolutionary new Pro-enz serum" may mean nothing.

* Shampoos and conditioners that claim they "thicken", "volumize" or add "body" are chemically designed to be sucked into the outer layer of your hair, making each strand look ever so slightly plumper.

* "Baby", "mild" or "hypoallergenic" shampoos usually have fewer chemicals known to cause skin reactions, but this is not a guarantee.

* "Moisturising" shampoos have moisture that is absorbed into the outer layer of each hair. This can be useful if you blow-dry your hair a lot.

* "Colour-enhancing" shampoos contain chemicals that help to prevent hair dye washing out. Sometimes they contain dye, but it isn't permanent.

* "Protein" conditioners are said to strengthen your hair, but really they just leave a coating on it.

iron. Seriously. It's a really quick way to sizzle your hair right off and cause burns. You need an electrical hair-straightener (the ones with ceramic plates are usually best), but good ones can be quite expensive. Most hair-straighteners end up abandoned in the bottom drawer. Borrow one for a while if you can, to see if using it regularly suits you and your lifestyle, and try to get a professional to show you how to apply it. Being straightened all the time (with straighteners or chemical products) will make your hair very dry and brittle, and may result in some of it breaking and falling out. If you do get your own hair-straighteners, it's best just to use them for parties and special occasions, rather than every day.

Straight While people with curly hair often want it to be straight, some people get bored with their straight hair and want volume, waves or curls. The best way to curl straight hair is temporarily. Don't get a perm. It's expensive, it uses a lot of strong, stinky chemicals and if it goes wrong you're stuck with it until it grows out or you cut it off. Instead you can experiment with cheap Velcro curlers: you wind damp hair around them and wait for it to dry. Or you can use heated curling tongs – but be careful not to burn yourself, and avoid repeated use because they'll dry out your hair. If you have a chance, get a professional to show you how to curl your hair, using your own tools.

Frizzy Some people straighten their hair to avoid frizz. Other people don't find frizz frazzling.

In the summer, hot, dry weather means less moisture and more static electricity, so hair has more volume or looks frizzier. (But when its hot and humid frizzy hair takes in moisture and has less static electricity, so the curls tend to flatten out.) In winter, wind and cold weather means less moisture, so hair can be dry and brittle, and wet weather can make curly hair frizzy and straight hair limp. Conditioners and sprays can keep the hair coated to try to beat weather effects.

Hairstyles You'll notice that lots of ads in the magazines are for shampoo, conditioner, hair-styling products and hair dye. Each year women worldwide spend billions (yes, you read that right) on their hair. So all the companies are competing to get you

everyone wants someone else's hair...

to buy their products. And all the magazines and websites are competing to get the hair companies to advertise with them.

The best hairstyle isn't the one the ads or magazines say is the most fashionable – you know, the one needing lots of hair-care products. It's the one that suits your face, the natural tendencies of your hair, your life and how much time you want to devote to faffing about with your hair. If you need to spend an hour to get your hairdo looking the way you want it, you won't be able to move, swim or go anywhere that has weather.

I find that my hair affects me a lot ... If my hair is looking especially bad and I know it the slightest comment on it can really darken my day.
Bryony, 16

Dyed hair Dyeing your hair – and maintaining it – costs time and money. And don't forget that results are not guaranteed. If you're certain that you want to do it, make sure you choose a colour that suits you, and that you understand how it will look as it grows out. You can get temporary hair colour that will wash out after

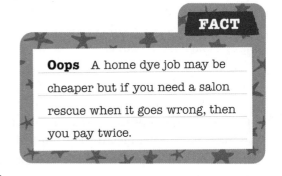

FACT

Oops A home dye job may be cheaper but if you need a salon rescue when it goes wrong, then you pay twice.

a few shampoos, or even one, which is probably the best way to start experimenting. "Permanent" hair dye usually penetrates to the inner part of the hair, and you're stuck with it until you can cut off the dyed bit or put another dye over the top (not always possible).

Some pretty hefty chemicals are used in hair dye. Avoid breathing them in. If you have a history of allergies make sure you do a patch test for a reaction before dyeing your hair, even in a salon.

If you dye your hair at home, from a packet bought at the chemist or supermarket, get someone older to help. Your 6-year-old sister, despite being keen, might miss a spot or dye your ears. Follow the pamphlet instructions absolutely exactly. Never dye your eyebrows or eyelashes yourself – you could permanently damage your eyes.

I'll bet you a million pounds the women in the hair dye ads didn't dye their hair themselves in their back garden, wearing rubber gloves and a garbage bag, so don't expect to look like the celebrity in the ad or the girl on the packet.

Salon hair colourists can usually do a much better-looking hair dye job than you, using several colours to give a more natural effect, but can charge loads, so always check the price first. Don't forget to ask how often you'll need a touch-up as it grows out.

Top six bad hairstyles

Avoid the latest celebrity hairstyle: it probably won't suit you, your hair or your wallet. And also avoid these six styles.

OVER-BLEACHED

Hair bleached to a hard white-blonde. Regrowth is quick and obvious, and the chemicals can make your hair break.

CUT BY AN AMATEUR

The DIY haircut or the one you let your untrained relatives give you. Just say no.

THE PERM

Fake, chemically tortured curls. Usually makes you look like a demented poodle.

THE MULLET

Short at the front and long at the back. Scarier than vampires and not controlled by garlic.

ASYMMETRICAL

Much shorter on one side than the other. Always looks like you fell into a blender, even if you paid for it.

BEEHIVE

A tower of "teased" and hair-sprayed layers. Perfect if you need to hide a hamster.

And don't get me started on bad dye jobs.

Dandruff

Dandruff is a skin condition in which dead skin cells keep flaking off your scalp, often causing itchiness. Sometimes people's eyebrows also get dandruff.

Everyone has a bit of a flaky thing happening, but with true dandruff dead skin cells are stuck together with sebum (skin oil) and so bigger, more noticeable flakes come off.

Treating it   First, make sure that you really do have ongoing dandruff, and that you're not just worried about normal bits of dead skin falling off.

- ⓖ Try washing your hair every day with a shampoo that says "gentle", "baby" or "mild" on the label, to keep the oil level down a bit.
- ⓖ Put conditioner only on the ends of your hair, not the scalp.
- ⓖ Avoid hair-styling products such as gels, mousses, waxes, serums putties or whatever else they're calling them.
- ⓖ Try a specialized dandruff shampoo and conditioner from your chemist or supermarket, and follow the instructions.
- ⓖ Don't change your diet because that probably won't have any effect on dandruff.
- ⓖ See your doctor for a referral to a dermatologist specializing in hair if your dandruff won't go away (see "More info on body hair" at the end of this chapter).

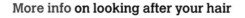

SHAKE FOR DANDRUFF

More info **on looking after your hair**

Most hair websites try to sell you stuff, but some have good info as well.

www.africanhair.com
For people of African heritage who want some tips on loving and dealing with their hair.

www.bbc.co.uk/switch/slink/fashion
The BBC's "Hair & beauty bible" for teens has style and care tips for all hair types, plus products and styling suggestions.

www.headzup.org.uk
Site for teenagers dealing with hair loss, run by the charity Alopecia UK.

www.ivillage.co.uk/beauty/haircare
Look past the ads to get bad-hair-day solutions, virtual makeovers, new style ideas and step-by-step how-to tips.

www.paulaschoice-eu.com
Choose "Hair care solutions" under "Learn" for stuff on how hair dye works, ceramic straighteners and hair-care tips.

www.virtualhaircare.com
Australian site with every problem or hair scare you can think of explained (or you can send in a query).

Body hair

Everyone has body hair. Fair-haired and fair-skinned people often have less notice-able body hair than those with darker hair. Some people, such as those of Asian heritage, have less than others. Girls of Italian, Greek, Turkish or Arabic heritage can have more body hair than some others.

An excess of facial hair can indicate a hormone problem such as the treatable condition polycystic ovaries (bad pimples are another symptom); if you feel it's really a bit out of control, see your doctor.

Downy hair can appear on the arms and back of girls who don't have enough body fat because they are starving themselves: it's the body's way of trying to keep warm.

me too

everyBody Has HaiRy Legs

Why do people remove their body hair?

Even though it is completely normal for girls and women to have body hair, there's a lot of pressure to remove it. Partly this is because of the idea that it makes us differ-ent from hairy men and therefore somehow more "feminine". But mostly it's because people make big money from selling us hair removal stuff. So the message girls end up getting is not "Make up your own mind about if and when you do anything to your body hair", but rather "You need to choose – right now – which product you'll buy to remove it or disguise it".

Some girls have been so affected by the pressure of advertising and a desire to be more "grown up" that they've started removing their body hair at a very young age. More than half the 13- to 15-year-olds in the Girl Stuff Survey plucked their eyebrows, and about three-quarters shaved their underarms and legs. This is way earlier than in past generations. In the older, 16 to 18, age group even more girls in the Girl Stuff Survey were removing hair: three-quarters plucked their eyebrows, and about 85 percent shaved their underarms and legs.

Most girls who remove body hair just do the legs below the knee and their underarms.

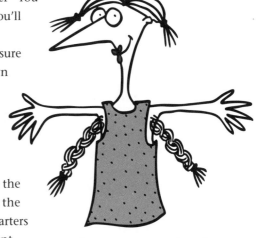

UNDeRaRM HaiR is usually pretty sHoRt

Some people never remove any. In the United States people can be almost fanatical about removing body hair.

It's part of wanting to look like the "high-maintenance" actresses, socialites and other rich, often idle women lurking in the magazine photos. (It costs tens of thousands of pounds a year to keep that look up.)

Pubic hair removal   Some people shave or wax the outer edges of their pubic hair to remove a few straggly bits that might otherwise show when they're wearing a swimsuit.

Removing all pubic hair was a fad for a while and is still done by a very small minority of women. But even if you use hair removal methods on other parts of you, let your pubic hair be free range. A little trim here and there with some carefully wielded nail scissors should keep you hiding your sprouty bits, or you can buy a less brief swimming costume.

If you really want the edges of your "pubes" waxed (called a bikini wax), don't do it yourself. Go to a busy professional salon, where they have a lot of experience, and be prepared for pain and expense.

Some areas where you may not have expected a furry visit

✱ Your forearms (below the elbow).

✱ The snail trail: you might develop a line of darker hair going from your map of Tasmania (the pubic mound area) up towards your belly button.

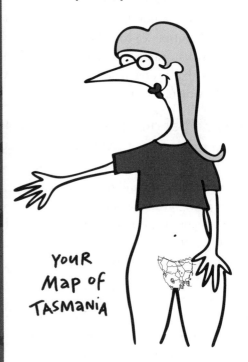

YoUR MaP of TASMaNiA

✱ Top lip: all women have a little moustache.

✱ Nipples: as you get older you'll probably get the odd hair around them.

✱ Your bot: it's quite normal to have a little bit of hair around your anus and on your backside.

Trying to remove all or lots of your pubic hair is a bad idea because it can result in:

⑥ big-time pain if you wax – it's a very sensitive area down there

⑥ irritation – shaving or waxing the pubic mound or hair between your legs can cause very painful rashes, redness and skin conditions that need treatment; many of the skin conditions of the labia and other girly bits seen by dermatologists are caused by the removal of this natural hair

⑥ uncomfortable, day-long itching (shaved hair can itch like mad as it grows back) and scratching – not a good look

⑥ ingrown hairs (when the removed hair attempts to grow again and is trapped under the skin, causing cysts or sores) – a sterilized needle or pair of tweezers can be used to relieve these, but pubic ones can be awkward or impossible to attend to yourself

⑥ embarrassment – do you really want a stranger looking at your girly bits that closely if they're not a doctor?

⑥ cost – because doing a pubic hair wax is not exactly a dream job for anyone, a full-on "Brazilian" is very expensive

⑥ a bad look – pubic hair trimmed into unnatural shapes can look weird

⑥ bald girly bits that make you look like a little girl – kind of creepy when you're not one. And as you get older it's extreeemely creepy if a man wants you to look like a little girl down there. If a partner wants you to remove your pubic hair you can just say no and ask why he needs his sexual partner to look like a 7-year-old girl. Or suggest he first get his scrotum, chest, arms, face, legs, back and bot-bot waxed for you. I don't think you'll hear much more about it.

SOME PUBIC HAIR IS SPROUTIER THAN OTHERS

Hair removal methods

All hair removal methods should just remove hair, not skin.

Shaving The most common shaving areas for girls and women are their underarms and their lower legs below the knee – mostly because they're easy places to reach and, in warm weather, the most visible. Shaving is cheaper than other methods, but the grow-back is really fast. You can use a razor, preferably with warm water and shaving cream, or a (more expensive) electric shaver.

Whatever "they" say, shaving does not make the hair grow back faster, slower, thicker or darker. Regrowth feels coarser and sharper because it has a recently cut end.

Many people only shave the day before a leg-featuring event because shaving every day, even if it takes only ten minutes, means more than an hour a week, which means more than three whole days a year! Bor-ing. Also stubble is always annoying.

Waxing, plucking and threading These are methods in which hair is pulled out by the roots so it doesn't grow back as quickly as when it's shaved.

With waxing, either hot or cold wax is poured on the region, then a strip of cloth is placed over the wax and ripped off, taking the hair with it. You can either do this yourself at home, using a product from the chemist or supermarket and following the instructions exactly, or have it done at a beauty salon by a professional, which is expensive.

Wax is most commonly used on the legs, armpits, eyebrows and upper lip. The upper lip area can be very sensitive and waxing anywhere can cause pimples and rashes. Never use hot wax near your eyes yourself – go to a salon. Waxing does hurt (sometimes a lot), and you'd need to do it somewhere between every three weeks and a couple of months. (Some girls only wax once a year, before summer.)

Plucking with tweezers and threading are methods of pulling out single hairs by the roots. In threading, a cotton thread is twisted around the hairs to pull them out.

When hair is pulled out by the root it can damage the hair follicle so not as much hair grows back or hairs become ingrown. The regrowth will not have a flat stubble end, like shaved hair, so will feel softer. (See also the "Eyebrows" section in the Clothes and Make-up chapter.)

Hair removal creams Depilatories are strong chemical creams or liquids that remove the hair by dissolving it so it can be wiped away. Even when used properly, creams can cause rashes and irritation, and you should do a patch test before using them for the first time. Never use them on your girly bits or anywhere else that has a body opening, including the eye and mouth areas. Ya-how! Sorry. Just thinking about it.

> Courtesy of my mother I have been so unfortunate as to receive the gorilla gene, and am nearly as hairy as my Italian boyfriend.
> Crystal, 18

you CaN wax
a MoustacHe

> Why is it expected of women to have plucked eyebrows, shaved underarms and waxed legs? It's painful and annoying yet we continue to do it. For men they have to shave their face (or not) and shower occasionally. One guy at school even found it appropriate to comment that I had forgotten to shave my legs. How dare he? Let's see him try ripping up his legs. Lucy, 14

Other methods You might have heard of electrolysis. In this method hair follicles are damaged permanently, so they don't produce any more hair, by inserting a needle into them one at a time and zapping them with an electric current (for god's sake, who discovered that?). It is generally only used for small areas of hair, such as the top lip. Electrolysis must be done by a professional beauty worker in a salon. (Ask what experience they have had with using it.) You need to have several appointments, it can take many hours, it hurts and it's expensive.

Laser treatment is also used to remove body hair. It destroys a hair follicle with high heat. It's not permanent, but it can take months for the hair to grow back. The regrowth will be finer and lighter coloured. You may need several treatments. It works best for dark hair or light skin. It's expensive, and if not done properly can cause skin discolouration and scarring. This is one that should be performed by an experienced, qualified dermatologist, not a "cosmetic surgeon" (see "More info" below).

It's not a removal exactly, but some girls bleach their dark body hair blonde so it's less noticeable on paler skin. You can get special body hair bleach at the chemist. Follow the instructions carefully and try a tiny bit first to make sure your skin isn't allergic to the stuff.

More info **on body hair**

Hair removal treatments are not usually available on the NHS, but your GP should be able to put you in touch with qualified dermatologists or plastic surgeons in your area.

www.bad.org.uk
The British Association of Dermatologists can also help you find someone qualified in your area.

www.hairfacts.com
A US consumer site on hair removal, with info on methods, side effects and dodgy products.

I hate being hairy. I have more facial hair than the average teenage boy. Not just a mono-brow and upper lip hair either – it comes onto my cheeks and jaw. It's really annoying having to pluck it. I also hate the fine black hair all over my belly and back as well. Natasha, 14

Although I do, and a majority of girls remove hair, I want it to be stressed that hair removal is unnatural and has nothing to do with becoming a woman. It really upsets me when women are labelled and harassed when they are seen as not going to all the extreme measures to be more "womanly" or desirable. Emma, 17

FOOD

4

You gotta eat! Otherwise you might not grow to the height you should (your skeleton size doubles in the teen years). Or **fight off** germs. Or stay **brainy**. Instead you'll spend the rest of your days stunted, sniffly and staring at the wall **wondering** how the tax system works, and what's the capital of Mongolia. (It's Ulan Bator.)

What you need

You're going to need to work out what food is healthy and eat it. (Unless you're the heir to a string of luxury hotels or a Hollywood starlet who, in between being photographed and sliding off nightclub couches into a pile of their own underpants, exists mostly on room service, narcotics and jelly babies soaked in gin by a personal chef.)

So here's the lowdown on the food you need, when you need to eat it, and how to make sure you don't miss out on any of the good stuff.

You need fruit and veg

According to the Department of Health and the Food Standards Agency (FSA) you need at least five portions of fruit and vegetables a day. (That's five in total, not five portions of veg *and* five of fruit.) They're packed with healthy vitamins and minerals and a great source of fibre. You should aim to eat a wide variety of fruit and veg – eating five bananas in one go doesn't count.

Can I eat too many vegetables? [No.]
Jess, 14

Are carbohydrates bad for you? [No.]
Rebecca, 15

One portion would be three heaped tablespoons or about half of cup of veggies such as peas, carrots, sweetcorn, cabbage, beans or lentils, or half a pepper, half a courgette or two spears of broccoli. Unfortunately, potatoes don't count because they're classed as a "starchy" food, and neither do chips, which are cooked in saturated oils and contain unnecessary fats.

A good way to get a mix of veggies is to have a bowl of steamed or stir-fried ones or homemade minestrone (veg and bean) soup, or a plate of salad or raw veggie sticks with a dip as a snack. "Snap" frozen veggies (like peas) are good for you as they retain lots of vitamins and minerals – unlike tinned veg. Try serving veggies different ways: with a splash of low-salt soy sauce, Asian-style; as a pasta sauce, Italian-style; or in a salad sarnie. Add flavour with chopped fresh herbs, garlic, grated lemon peel or lemon juice, and pepper.

One portion of fruit would be a whole medium-sized fruit, such as an orange, peach, pear, apple or banana; or two whole smaller fruits, such as a kiwi fruit, plum or satsuma; or a handful of grapes or berries; or one or two slices of a larger fruit like a melon,

FACT

Teenagers need more   Teenagers need more fuel than children or adults because of the growing they have to do. So listen when your body says it's hungry.

mango or pineapple. Different fruits have different vitamins, so go for a mix such as a fruit salad. Whole fruit gives you more fibre than juice or a smoothie, which your body needs (so you poo regularly), and it's cheaper.

You need starchy foods

This basically means stuff made from grains, such as wholegrain bread, (unsweetened) breakfast cereals, pasta, noodles, rice, cous cous and potatoes. (A sweet pastry is not a good grain food.) These foods are a really important part of a healthy diet. The FSA says they should form the main part of every meal and make up about a third of the food you eat in a day. Wholegrain versions are best because they're higher in fibre, so try to eat more brown rice, wholemeal bread and wholewheat pasta.

To avoid confusion, a perfectly fine amount of grainy things to have each day would be a big bowl of porridge or unsweetened cereal for brekkie, or a smaller bowl of porridge or muesli plus a piece of wholegrain toast; a sandwich or a filled roll or pitta for lunch; wholegrain toast with cheese and/or tomato for an after-school snack; and a bowl of pasta or rice with a sauce containing veggies and meat, fish or tofu for dinner. A jacket potato or some sweet potato mash could also make up the starchy part of your evening meal.

Grain foods are the biggest source of our most important energy nutrient: carbohydrates. They're the fuel that make us go, physically. And our brains need carbohydrates too. You may have heard that "low-carb" foods are always the best to choose. Ha. Low-carb diets are bad for you. Especially when you're a teenager.

spinach pumpkin mushrooms grapes banana plum

mix up your
≷ CoLouRS ≷

You need protein

Ever since we were faffing around in caves, trying to make a cute pair of knee-high boots out of dead squirrels, we've been meat eaters. The human body is designed to run on lots of protein, which is found in lean meat (meaning with the fatty white parts cut off), poultry (chicken, duck and turkey) and fish.

Eat the rainbow   Try to eat fruit and veggies every day from all the five colour groups: blues/purples; reds; yellows/oranges; whites; greens.

Recommended portions The recommendations about what teenagers should eat from each food group differ depending on which website or book you read. Many were written billions of years ago (well, a few), and in any case are a guide only. You don't have to be exact about it, or eat the same stuff every day.

Alternatives to meat include nuts, soya products, eggs and legumes (also known as pulses). Don't ask me what a legume is, I'll have to look it up. (Okay, it's beans and peas, including chickpeas, soya beans and lentils. For some startling reason, a peanut is also a legume, not a nut.)

The Food Standards Agency is a bit vague when it comes to protein portions, recommending "some", rather than "plenty" for carbs and fruit and veg. But the general consensus seems to be one or two portions of protein a day. That's two slices of roast beef or ham (about the size of your palm) in a sandwich; or two little lamb chops; or half a cup of bolognaise sauce; or up to 100 grams of some other meat such as a chicken breast or 120 grams of fish (a piece of fish a bit bigger than your palm). One portion also equals three heaped tablespoons (a third of a cup) of almonds, peanuts, seeds or legumes, or about half a standard-sized (400g) tin of beans.

You should have red meat about three or four times a week (beef, lamb, pork or … well, I doubt you'll be having venison, which is deer meat). Red meat is the best source of iron and zinc, which girls and women need lots of.

One egg is half a portion of protein (which makes a two-egg omelette one portion). A couple of eggs a week is plenty, but don't get hung up on counting exactly.

You need calcium

Dairy foods are a good source of calcium, which is important for your growing bones. They are made of milk from moo cows (okay, it's getting technical now) and you should eat three portions of milk, cheese or yoghurt a day.

One portion would be a glass of milk; or a couple of thin, sandwich-sized slices of cheese; or a small tub of yoghurt. If you

> People eat too much junk food from the tuckshop and don't eat their own healthy lunch. Lana, 13

don't eat lots of dairy stuff go for the milk with extra calcium added.

Some non-dairy sources of calcium include soya yoghurt, soya milk and rice milk, with added calcium; almonds; tinned salmon, with bones; and tahini (made from sesame seeds).

> I worry I'm going to injure or do some permanent damage to myself when I don't eat properly.
> Georgie, 17

You need fats and oils

You need to eat fats and oils to keep your skin and hair looking good and your hormones working properly, and to help some vitamins be absorbed effectively. This means making sure you eat useful fats, found particularly in some oils.

You need omega 3 fatty acids (oils) from fresh or tinned oily fish, such as salmon, trout, mackerel and sardines, and from fresh – but not tinned – tuna. But you should only have up to two portions a week. Other sources include some seeds and nuts. Other useful oils include canola, sunflower, rapeseed, corn and extra-virgin olive oil. Look for oils and spreads that are labelled "unsaturated", "monounsaturated", "unhydrogenated" and "polyunsaturated". Cooking or salad oils should be "cold-pressed" so they maintain their goodness.

You need water

Make water your main drink, not sugary soft drinks, fruit drinks or juices. Water keeps you hydrated, stops you from getting headaches, keeps your skin and hair looking good, and doesn't contain sugars that can cause tooth decay. The Food Standards Agency suggests you drink about 1.2 litres (six to eight glasses) of water a day. Aside from that recommendation, be guided by your own body and drink more when you're thirsty – for example, if you're exercising or if it's very hot.

You need vitamins and minerals

If you eat lots of fruit, veggies, protein and grains you should get enough vitamins and minerals. Many vitamins and minerals need other vitamins and minerals before they can be absorbed into the body – for example, calcium needs magnesium. Our bodies absorb vitamins and minerals more easily from real food than from supplements (such as pills).

To get the most vitamins out of your veggies it's best to eat them raw, stir-fried, lightly microwaved or steamed. The more you boil veggies, the more vitamins and minerals are lost (and you end up with gluey grey stuff).

If you think you need a supplement ask your doctor to check your health first, before paying out for one. If

MULTi VITAMINS &MINERALS

for people who have never heard of them

a supplement is necessary they'll be able to recommend the right one. Some girls need a zinc, calcium and iron supplement, which they can get in a "women's" multi-vitamin.

The way to go

Here are some ideas for a healthy way to eat, which will give you lots of energy.

Eat brekkie Oh yes, you can. Try unsweetened porridge made from rolled oats (cooked on the stove or microwaved with milk), and add sliced fruit or berries on the top; or wholegrain toast topped with banana or peanut butter (from the health food shop, with no added salt, sugar or oil). Even if you don't feel like eating a lot the moment you get up, or you're too busy rushing off to school, grab a piece of fruit or have a banana smoothie made with yoghurt to get you through until you can have a mid-morning snack.

If you skip breakfast it makes you crave sugary snacks or drinks during the day, means it's harder for you to concentrate, and causes shipping accidents and the raining of frogs upon the earth. Well, no. But have breakfast.

When time is the problem, get some things ready the night before. Soak some rice or oats for porridge, or lay out the bread and stuff you need next to the toaster. Mix some of the ingredients for a smoothie and store them in the fridge.

One of those high-sugar, high-fat, processed "cereal bars" is not the answer. (And they cost more.)

you NeeD BReKKie

Eat regular meals and snacks If you go too long without food your blood sugar level drops, and you can feel dizzy, tired and crabby. And if you let yourself get madly hungry you'll be more likely to grab something that is sugary or a fast food, which will only give you a quick burst of energy before you feel tired again. That's why eating three decent meals a day, with healthy snacks in between, is important.

The best snack foods create longer-lasting energy rather than a sudden "high" followed by a crash. These include dairy foods, soya foods, fruit and veggies, as well as rolled oats, beans and pulses, basmati rice and pasta. In second place for snacks are rye bread, brown rice and cous cous.

Snacks that travel well in a school bag or handbag include unsalted nuts (like almonds), seeds, carrot sticks and hard fruits such as apples.

not, you'll be surprised to know, a meaL...

Eat unprocessed food The least useful grain foods are the ones that have been over-processed, such as pastries and factory-made biscuits. They lack fibre, vitamins and minerals.

Packet breakfast cereals are usually so over-processed that most of the nutrients have been removed, and they're often packed with salt and sugar. Some nutrients have to be put back (sort of like sticking ground-up vitamin tablets into the cereal flakes) and are harder for the body to absorb. The independent consumer association "Which?" judged hundreds of breakfast cereals according to the Food Standard Agency's guidelines, and only recommended a few (see "More info on good eating" coming up). Look for cereals that are high-fibre, wholegrain and unsweetened.

Seedy multigrain bread is better for you than squishy whitey-white bread. Brown rice has more nutrients than white rice. Porridge is better than corn flakes. Know what you're eating, and choose wholegrain when you can.

this is not a meal. It's a ؟ SNACK ؟

Eat food close to its original form A fresh pear is better than sliced pears in a tin. Steamed veggies are better than a can of vegetable soup. Fish grilled at home is better than battered takeaway fish and chips or a packaged meal from the supermarket's frozen section. (Frozen veggies are fine.)

not a meaL

Learn to cook Because that way you get to eat more unprocessed, healthier, yummier, cheaper food. Your friends will want to eat with you, and return the favour. It's fun and relaxing, you learn heaps and it's something that's handy when you travel, are trying to impress somebody, live in a shared house or on your own, have kids or want a career in the hospitality industry.

↑ NOt LUNCH (oNe bite from sandwich)

FACT

Skipping meals People who skip meals usually don't lose weight – they just eat more stuff later.

I am not a meal. I am a jelly Snake

Vegetarians

Vegetarians don't eat meat, right? But what about vegans and all the other groups? Well, vegans avoid all food that comes from animals, including dairy (milk, cream, butter, cheese, yoghurt), eggs, meat (red or white) and fish. And pescatarians or pesco-vegetarians eat fish, dairy and eggs. And sorta-kinda-semi-vegetarians eat fish, dairy, eggs and white meat but no red meat.

Many people are vegetarian for moral reasons: they think eating animals is wrong. Some people think meat is unhealthy for them; some have religious reasons; and some are experimenting, just want something to talk about, or like rules about what they do.

> I asked my canteen at school why their menu wasn't more healthy, and the woman actually said this: "Pizza is bread based, Wotsits are cheese based, and pies are meat-based". How are teenagers meant to get to their right size when they can't order healthy and filling food?
> Rhianna, 16

Vegetarian and vegan special needs Many girls "go" vegetarian or vegan and then find they have no energy because they lack protein and minerals. Vegetarians and vegans need to find substitutes for the essential foods they've cut out. The "What you need" info earlier in this chapter gives good non-meat and non-animal alternatives.

- Ⓖ Vegetarians and vegans must replace meat each day with enough portions of other proteins.
- Ⓖ Vegetarians and vegans need an iron supplement because meat is the source of the most easily absorbed iron, which you need lots of. Some soya milks, cereals and breads have chemically added iron. Iron from vegetable sources is more easily absorbed by the body when combined with food or (sugar-free) juices rich in vitamin C,

Home movies When you're watching a movie at home with your friends, try snacking on bowls of fruit salad or plain popcorn (go easy on the butter and salt).

Food and feelings

You need to listen to your brain and body, rather than your emotions, when deciding what to eat and how much.

✱ **Recognize non-hungry eating triggers** Non-hungry "reasons" for eating can include being bored, sad or anxious; wanting a "reward" or treat; finding the food is just plain available; someone else is having some; or you eat stuff you like whenever you see it. Those responses need another solution, not food.

✱ **Eat when you're hungry** Most of the time you need to let yourself get hungry and then respond by eating, stopping when you're full.

✱ **Use your judgement** Experiment with what's a good-sized portion for you. How hungry are you? Do you need a smaller or a bigger size right now? Shops and takeaway joints often serve stupid sizes, with buckets of oily popcorn as big as a hatchback and muffins that could house a family of guinea pigs.

✱ **Have a relaxed attitude to food** Don't be upset if every meal isn't a perfectly precise balance of the right portions and measurements. It's not a good day if you have to weigh a mushroom.

✱ **Be adventurous** Food can be fun, not just fuel. Try new food and learn new ways of eating and cooking for yourself and friends. Try food from different cultures and new tastes. Sometimes you need to try something a few times to get used to it and to allow your tastebuds to change.

✱ **Don't ban foods** No food is "bad" or "naughty". If you say you can't have chocolate ever, you'll start wanting a whole block. Learn to have just a bit, or eat it only sometimes.

✱ **Share** Rather than eating alone, or in front of the TV, and rushing things, try to make your meals a chance to catch up with family or friends.

I only eat every 2nd hour in a month with a Y in it...

...and NO avocado before 7pm!

⇒ Strange food Rituals ⇐

such as red and green peppers, broccoli, blackcurrants, mangoes, kiwi fruit, oranges and other fruit.

🌀 Vegans (and vegetarians who decide not to eat dairy) need vitamin B12, which is only available in animal products, especially meat. Many soya milks and some other products have it as a chemical additive, and it is a common component in multi-vitamins and B-complex vitamins.

🌀 Vegans (and vegetarians who decide not to eat dairy) need good alternative sources of calcium. Certain foods, such as some juices and soya products, have extra calcium added.

It can be hard to eat right as a teenage vegetarian. A bag of chips that have been deep-fried in oil might be vegetarian, but it's not good for you. Having just veggies without protein when you're eating at someone else's house won't give you enough nutrition and energy. The more anyone restricts their food choices the more difficult it gets, and the more obsessed they may become with food and rules about food.

If you're determined to go vegetarian or vegan talk to your doctor or a qualified dietician first, and get informed so you can convince your parents that you'll be getting enough nutrition. Don't forget that as a teenager you have more nutritional needs than adults because you're still growing. Most info for vegetarians and vegans on the internet and in books and leaflets is for adults, and even the info for teens usually doesn't explain how much of the different foods you need.

> I am a vegetarian and any girls who think this helps you lose weight are VERY wrong!!! It's harder to maintain a healthy weight!!
>
> Bec, 16

you don't Have to CouNt youR food

More info **on good eating, and recipe books**

www.5aday.nhs.uk
Site dedicated to helping you get your five fruit and veg a day. Includes top tips, portion sizes and simple, healthy recipes.

www.bbc.co.uk/food/in_season
Info on what fruit, veg, fish and meat is in season (and therefore cheaper) throughout the year, plus recipes from the BBC.

www.bda.uk.com
The British Dietetic Association has info on finding a dietician, but it's best to go to your GP first. Click on "Food facts" for fact sheets on healthy eating, food labels and fad diets.

www.childrenfirst.nhs.uk/teens/health/healthy_eating
Teen site covering all the basics about food groups and healthy eating, plus diet and weight FAQs and info about the digestive system. You can also ask questions on the "Dear Doc" page.

www.eatwell.gov.uk
The best place to start for info about healthy eating. Choose "Healthy diet" for the lowdown on nutrition, food groups and eating well. Choose "Teens" under "Ages and stages" for sample menus, recipes, quizzes, tips and practical advice.

www.which.co.uk
On the independent consumer association site search for "Breakfast cereals" to find out how healthy your favourite cereals and cereal bars really are. Also check out "Food and drink" for loads more.

Complete Perfect Recipes by David Herbert, Penguin
More than 250 short, easy, classic recipes that are great for a beginner.

Cooking up a Storm: The Teen Survival Cookbook by Sam Stern, Walker Books
Tasty, simple, yet healthy and sophisticated recipes written for teenagers by a teenager. This, and the sequels *Get Cooking* and *Real Food, Real Fast*, can inspire both boys and girls.

not a meal (no, really)

Many girls who are maybe a little overweight complain, but when you look at their diet, the majority is junk food. Rather than complain, they should accept some responsibility, but still realize thin does not necessarily equal beautiful.   Lauren, 18

Growing up, my mum had an eating disorder, and because I watched her not eat I never thought it was unusual or unhealthy. When I was a perfectly healthy child my grandma ridiculed my weight a lot, so that nowadays I don't have the confidence to eat in public.   Tess, 18

What you don't need

The body saves any sugars and fats it doesn't need as extra weight. In the past it was hard to get fatty and sugary foods (you couldn't exactly go out with a spear and hunter-gather a packet of crisps, a gigantic muffin and a fizzy drink), but now they're available all the time, everywhere, and they're cheap.

People have got into the habit of eating more sweet, fatty food than they need, and not doing much activity. And if they don't get out of this habit they end up at an unhealthy weight.

You may be amazed at the amount of fat and sugar in processed, takeaway and fast food. One takeaway hamburger or portion of fried chicken, or pre-packaged creamy curry from the supermarket, can be more than half or two-thirds of your whole day's energy needs, without providing much nutrition that your body can use.

If you want to eat this kind of food find out what's in it – and what's not in it – so you're informed.

FACT

The fuss about weight   There's no "perfect weight" for your height or your age. There is a healthy range for each individual. If you follow the guidelines in this chapter and the Move chapter (about physical activity) you should stay in your healthy weight range. The Shape chapter helps explain about sizes.

You don't need much sugar

Our bodies are designed to love the taste of sugar (it's even a pain reliever). The human body assumes, from its experiences in the tough old cave folk days, that sugar is hard to get so it craves more.

We used to have to make our own cakes from scratch to have something sweet. Now we can get sugar hidden in nearly every packaged and processed kind of food, so most of us eat way more of it than we need.

High-sugar products include cakes, biscuits, muffins, many breads, sweets, chocolate, ice cream, bottled fruit drinks and juices, cordials, fizzy drinks and alcohol.

'health bars' can be just 'Fat'n'Sugar Bars'

Cakey things Sometimes seen as treats or rewards, high-sugar and high-fat foods are okay occasionally – say, once or twice a week – but not every day.

If you put a teaspoon of sugar on a bowl of processed breakfast cereal you're probably adding another one to the perhaps five teaspoons of sugar already in the cereal. Honey's the same as sugar so don't add it to everything either. Sugar is also a major cause of holes in the teeth.

Label check

⊙ Sugars can be listed as glucose, fructose, lactose or maltose.

⊙ If a label has sugar in the first three or four ingredients listed, that usually means a high sugar level.

⊙ There are 4 grams of sugar in a level teaspoon, so if the label says one food serving has 12 grams of sugar in it, that's three teaspoons.

⊙ Check out the fine print on the labels of foods you mightn't think would contain sugar.

⊙ Look for things labelled "no added sugar".

⊙ Don't drink products labelled as "sports" or "energy" drinks (they're usually really high in sugar and caffeine) unless an accredited sports coach tells you to.

You don't need unhealthy fats and oils

You often hear about "bad fats", as if there are tiny evil fats trying to take over the world and going "Nyahahaha" in high, squeaky voices. "Bad fats" means saturated fats, trans fats and hydrogenated oils, which have no health benefits in large quantities and can eventually cause big health problems.

Unhealthy fats are mostly the ones from animals, and they are mainly found in cream, butter, hard cheese and full-fat dairy products, fatty meats (especially the white bits on red meat and the skin on chicken), biscuits, cakes, pastries, pies and other processed foods. They're also found in coconut cream and the oils used to make takeaway food, especially fried food.

FACT

Weird but true   The fatter the chip, the less fat it has absorbed, so traditional thick-cut chips are usually less fattening than thin fries. Very few takeaway joints seem to have taken any notice, so yuo're better off cutting up potatoes to make your own chunky chips.

A little bit is okay, but eating high-fat takeaways or fast food every day or several times a week can quickly take you above your healthy weight and put you at risk of diseases such as diabetes. They make your body do all the work of turning them into fat or poo without it getting anything useful on their way through.

> This girl at my school, all she eats is junk food and a lot of it. Seriously I have never seen her eat anything healthy.
> Natalie, 14

Label check

- ⊙ Check the labels on packaged food: anything with 20 grams of fat or more in a 100-gram serving is considered high fat.

- ⊙ Food that's labelled "low-fat" or, say, "95 percent fat-free" usually has heaps of added sugar to make it taste better. Any extra sugar you don't need will be converted to fat in your body.

- ⊙ Look out for the "traffic light labels" now found on lots of different foods. They show you at a glance if the food you're about to buy is high, medium or low in fat, saturated fat, sugar and salt. It's really very simple. A red "light" or spot means it's high in something unhealthy, so you should only eat that food occasionally; an amber light means it's medium, so you can eat it some of the time; and a green light means it's low, so its a healthier choice and you can eat it more often. Try to choose foods with mostly green lights. (See "More info on fast food, additives and labels" coming up.)

LeaRN to ReaD LaBeLS

You don't need fizzy drinks and sweetened juices

Most fizzy drinks (except unflavoured fizzy mineral water) and fruit drinks have an unbelieeeevably high amount of sugar in them: up to about six to eight teaspoons each. Juices in bottles or cartons usually also have a really high sugar level.

Juice bars sell drinks that are hellishly expensive for the ingredients actually used, and sometimes claim that the additives in their juices could give you energy, help you lose weight or boost your immune system when this isn't true or proven.

Don't make a habit of drinking fizzy or sweetened fruit drinks: try for none, or one a week, or only occasionally. Processed fruit juice is okay now and then, but as a daily habit could be way too sugary and cost you heaps. Go for plain water.

Label check

- ◉ Fizzy drinks that are labelled "low-fat" could still have high sugar levels.
- ◉ "Diet" versions are just expensive water that has been flavoured with chemicals.

FACT

Hard to believe By drinking one sugary drink a day you could convert the unwanted sugar to 6 kilos of extra body fat by the end of a year. Hold 6 kilos of potatoes and you'll get the idea.

You don't need too much salt

Salt, like sugar, is something the human body has evolved to crave because in the past it was hard to get. (Cave folk didn't have packaged food or a salt-shaker.) To survive, your body needs a little bit of salt every day, but not a lot. Too much salt can make you dehydrated, bloated and tired, and put you at a higher risk of heart disease and other health problems.

There's way too much salt in most tinned, packaged and processed foods. Savoury biscuits (especially rice crackers), bread, microwave meals, bought sauces (especially soy and barbecue) and spreads often have high levels. Even most processed sweet foods contain salt.

Label check

- ◉ Watch out for sodium or sodium chloride listed as one of the first or major ingredients (sodium is the scientific name for salt).
- ◉ "Brine" on a label means salted water has been added, so buy canned fish in just spring water (or oil) instead.

⑤ Choose "no added salt", "reduced salt" or "low-salt" versions of foods.

⑤ Choose foods with the green "traffic light" symbol for salt, rather than red or amber.

Ways to reduce salt

⑤ Don't add salt automatically when you're cooking, or sprinkle it on food after it's cooked.

⑤ Use herbs, spices and other condiments to brighten food up if it seems too bland without added salt, and wait until you're used to the new tastes. This may take some weeks, but after that when you taste salty foods you'll be shocked.

⑤ Go for unsalted chips, popcorn and nuts.

You don't need too much caffeine

Caffeine gives you a buzzy, more awake and energized feeling, but it can also make you restless and jittery, cause headaches and keep you awake at night. It makes your heart beat faster, your blood pressure rise and your body wee more.

The highest levels of caffeine are in filtered or shop-made coffee, then energy drinks, then instant coffee, then cola drinks, then tea, then chocolate (that's why little kids go berserk at Easter).

A one-gram dose of guarana (in "energy" drinks) is usually about as strong as a medium cup of coffee. Work out how many grams are in the amount you drink.

One weak coffee a day shouldn't do you any harm.

4th → long black

THERE IS SUCH a THING as too PERKY

Label check

⑤ The "recommended serving" on the label may actually be only a third of the can, and the number of grams in a serving will apply to that, whereas you'll usually drink the whole can (three servings).

Finding out what's in processed foods

Most manufactured foods and drinks have to have a label telling you what's in them. Labels show a food's energy content in both kilojoules (kj) and kilocalories (kcal) and its weight in grams (g) or volume in millilitres (ml). They list its protein, total fat, different types of fat, carbohydrate, sugars, sodium (salt) and any other relevant ingredients.

If there were labels on unprocessed foods they would look something like this:

- **Small apple** 114g (weight), 226 kj/54 kcal (energy), 0.34g protein, 0.11g total fat, 12.31g carbohydrate, 11.74g sugar (fructose and glucose), 0.23g starch, 97.01g water, 2.17g fibre.
- **Cooked lamb chop (trimmed of 75 percent of its fat)** 36g (weight), 312 kj/75 kcal (energy), 9.86g protein, 3.89g total fat, 2.02g saturated fat, 1.44g monounsaturated fat, 0.07g polyunsaturated fat, 22.1g water, 0.86mg iron.

Being healthy isn't always about what size you are or what other people think. Being healthy is when you feel comfortable with yourself, eating right, and feeling fit.

Kaz, 17

Tricky claims on labels

- The law doesn't define "Light" or "Lite", so these could just mean the product is a fine, not thick texture: it doesn't necessarily mean it's low in fat or sugar (or "energy").
- "Barn-reared" or "farm-reared" doesn't mean "free range". Any big building can be called a barn or a farm. Free range means animals are able to move around outside.
- The serving size can be misleading; for example, a manufacturer can decide a can of diet cola has 1.88 servings so that they can say it has "only one calorie per serving".
- "Natural" or "no added chemicals" doesn't mean organic. Organic means no chemicals are added to the soil or in the growing or feeding cycles when the food is produced.
- If an item claims to be, say, "93 percent fat-free" it means it contains 7 percent fat, which is not considered a low percentage in food (3 percent is considered a small amount).
- "Baked not fried" sounds healthier, but the food may have been baked in just as much fat.
- "Fresh" means the product hasn't been preserved by freezing, canning, high temperature or chemical treatment. But it may have been refrigerated, processed and transported weeks ago.

Changing habits

If your family eats unhealthy stuff maybe you could suggest you all get together to plan how you can change your eating habits. Perhaps you could show your parents the websites in "More Info on good eating" earlier in this chapter; or see if you could go as a family to a dietician for advice about how to change the way you shop and eat.

Some parents are so busy you might need to:

- ☺ help them to make fresh meals, when you can, rather than relying on takeaway or frozen meals or high-fat, -sugar and -salt options

- ☺ make a list of healthy food choices and go shopping with them

- ☺ suggest that it becomes one of your jobs to check that the fruit bowl is always filled with a variety of fruit, and the same for veggies in the fridge

- ☺ ask if you can have your own supplies, and make your own breakfast and lunch, and even cook a simple dinner for yourself, if your family really can't stop eating takeaways most nights

- ☺ keep talking to them about healthy eating, and learning together, rather than slagging them (and your siblings) off about their choices.

Top ten hints for enjoying food

1. Eat food with fresh ingredients.

2. Make it for friends and/or family.

3. Prepare and cook it with friends and/or family.

4. Eat it with friends and/or family.

5. Don't watch TV or read while you're eating.

6. Don't stand up and walk around while you're eating.

7. Eat slowly instead of "bolting".

8. Don't diet.

9. Don't think of some foods as "forbidden" or "naughty".

10. Try lots of different foods.

HINT

Out and about Go for a salad and meat or veggie wrap and a water instead of a hamburger and a fizzy drink.

More info on fast food, additives and labels

See also the sites recommended in "More info on good eating" a few pages earlier.

www.actiononadditives.com
Campaigning site from the non-profit UK
Food Commission listing foods and drinks
which contain additives that are thought
to have a negative effect on children's
behaviour.

www.bbc.co.uk/food/food_matters
Covers all the hot food issues of the day,
plus info on labelling, trans-fats, salt,
choosing healthy food, packaging, organics
and fairtrade.

www.chewonthis.org.uk
This interactive site by the Food
Commission Research Charity covers
food labels, advertising and marketing
tricks, and all the weird stuff in food – from
artificial flavours and chemicals to colours
and sweeteners.

www.eatwell.gov.uk/foodlabels/
The Food Standards Agency helps you to
understand all the gobbledegook on food
labels, from organic and lactose-free to
E numbers. Choose "Traffic light labelling"
to get the scoop on those red, amber and
green labels on different foods, and how
to use them to avoid eating too much
unhealthy fat, sugar and salt.

MOVE

5

Physical activity can ☾ make you feel good ☾ make you feel strong ☾ make you happier ☾ guard against depression ☾ make you like yourself more ☾ maintain your body in good condition ☾ **be fun** ☾ give you more energy ☾ help you fight off illness ☾ help to repair and heal your body ☾ help you feel like you **belong** (to a team) ☾ give you a sense of calm aloneness ☾ help you concentrate better ☾ help you get to sleep ☾ help you make **friends** ☾ spice up your day ☾ help make strong bones and muscles.

Physical activity

The point of physical activity is to be healthy. If you don't do any you'll become unfit and feel stiff and heavy, cranky and tired; you'll be unhealthy and not able to fight off colds and other illnesses; and you won't burn up any extra sugars and fats as energy.

Why activity makes you feel good

When you do something active, especially suddenly (for example, running from a standing start), your brain releases "good mood" chemicals such as endorphins and serotonin (see the Brain chapter).

Probably the simple reason exercise makes most people feel good is because the body is doing what it's supposed to do – moving around, pumping blood, getting oxygen in and out. And anyway, what's not to love about dancing? (Especially with the lights out and the door locked.)

dancing fights stress

The amount you need

Health experts suggest kids and teenagers should be doing an hour of physical activity a day. It's something to aim for, not a rule to get upset about. Health guidelines also say teenagers should:

- ❻ have no more than two hours a day of combined screen time, which includes watching TV, playing videogames and using computers (but not time spent doing homework on the computer)
- ❻ be active every day in as many ways as possible

> Doing a little bit of exercise a day makes you feel better about yourself.
> Grace, 14

⊙ try to do some moderate exercise every day (moderate means you're moving your body but not necessarily getting a much faster heart rate and faster breathing)

⊙ get some regular vigorous exercise for at least twenty minutes three to four times a week. Vigorous exercise makes you "huff and puff" – your breathing is quicker and it's hard to speak normally.

> I always feel better after exercise. You feel like you've accomplished something.
> Jharna, 14

> I feel horrible if I don't exercise.
> Gemma, 15

Moderate huff-and-puff activity includes walking above a strolling pace, going on a long bike ride, skateboarding, playing rounders or volleyball or another game in which you spend a bit of time standing still or waiting for your turn – that sort of thing.

Vigorous huff-and-puff exercise is stuff that keeps your heart rate up for a while: playing basketball, hockey or football, swimming laps, running, walking fast, dancing full on.

> Exercise is a great way to stay healthy and meet new people.   Katie, 14

> I really ought to exercise more. That's probably one of the reasons why I'm so short. [*No it isn't.*]
> Sian, 15

walk to meet friends...

A–Z of exercise

abseiling ✻ aerobics ✻ aikido ✻ aqua aerobics ✻ archery ✻ athletics ✻ badminton ✻ ballroom dancing ✻ basketball ✻ belly dancing ✻ bobsledding ✻ bodyboarding ✻ bowling ✻ British bulldog ✻ building a tree-house ✻ building fences ✻ canoeing ✻ capoeira ✻ carrying, not pushing, groceries ✻ circus skills ✻ cleaning vigorously (music helps) ✻ climbing trees ✻ contemporary dance ✻ **cricket** ✻ croquet ✻ cross-country skiing ✻ curling ✻ cycling ✻ dancing on your bed with the door locked ✻ delivering newspapers or pamphlets on foot or wheels ✻ digging holes and planting trees ✻ diving ✻ dog training ✻ elastics ✻ fly-fishing ✻ folk dancing ✻ football ✻ Frisbee ✻ Frisbee golf ✻ fruit picking ✻ gardening ✻ get up out of the chair ✻ gliding ✻ **going the long way round** ✻ golf ✻ gym machines ✻ gymnastics ✻ hapkido ✻ hiking ✻ hockey ✻ hopscotch ✻ horseriding ✻ ice hockey ✻ ice skating ✻ in-line skating ✻ Irish dancing ✻ javelin ✻ jogging ✻ **judo** ✻ jujitsu ✻ jumping ✻ karate ✻ kayaking ✻ kendo ✻ kite boarding ✻ kite flying ✻ lacrosse ✻ lawn bowls ✻ leaving the train/tube/bus early and walking the rest of the way ✻ line dancing ✻ long jump ✻ lunchtime walk ✻ marching ✻ modern dance ✻ mowing the lawn ✻ mucking around in water ✻ netball ✻ non-contact boxing ✻ orienteering ✻ Paralympic sports ✻ petanque ✻ Pilates ✻ **playing catch** ✻ polo ✻ power walking ✻ power shopping ✻ pushing a pram ✻ quoits ✻ rock climbing ✻ rollerblading ✻ rounders ✻ rowing ✻ rugby ✻ running ✻ sailing ✻ salsa dancing ✻ scuba diving ✻ sheepshearing ✻ shooting hoops ✻ shot-put ✻ skateboarding ✻ skiffle boarding ✻ skiing ✻ skipping – on your own or in a team ✻ sledging ✻ snorkelling ✻ snowboarding ✻ softball ✻ squash ✻ stacking shelves at work ✻ stair climbing ✻ stationary bike class ("spinning") ✻ stretching ✻ surfing ✻ **swimming** ✻ synchronized swimming ✻ table tennis ✻ Tae Kwon Do ✻ tag ✻ tai chi ✻ taking the stairs, not the lift ✻ tennis ✻ touch football ✻ training ✻ trampolining ✻ treasure hunting ✻ using a swing ✻ underwater hockey ✻ vacuuming ✻ volleyball ✻ walking club ✻ **walking the dog** ✻ walking to work ✻ water polo ✻ weightlifting ✻ whitewater rafting ✻ windsurfing ✻ woodchopping ✻ wrestling ✻ yachting ✻ yoga ✻ Zorro-style fencing with swords (well I had to have a Z).

bounce!

Finding your own activity thing

Most girls try a few different sports or activities before they find the right one for them. Don't stick with something you hate or find boring. Sometimes it takes a while to find one you really love and are good at.

You might want a sport that's related to hand-to-hand fighting so you can scream a lot, or to belong to a team that believes winning is important. Or you might just be the sort of person who likes a "hit and giggle" with friends, or a long walk listening to music. (See also "A–Z of exercise" box opposite.)

Choosing an activity near home makes it quick and uncomplicated. Your local council's sport, leisure and recreation department can tell you about teams and clubs, dance groups, yoga and other classes, and bike and walking tracks in your area. You can also ask around or look in local newspapers, at shop and leisure centre noticeboards, in youth clubs and community centres, or on the internet. Many teams and classes don't cost much to join.

Meet or take a friend so you motivate each other to keep going. Joining a group activity is a good way to catch up with old pals and to make new friends.

Team sports can be fun but may not provide a lot of activity, depending on where you're positioned on the court or field (unless they have really active training sessions). So, if you find that you're spending a couple of hours per game standing still in the outfield, you'll need to do something else that's actually active as well.

> Tae Kwon Do is GREAT exercise. Plus it teaches you great self-defence and body control. I would highly recommend it!
> Michelle, 13

Getting active

For some people doing any kind of physical activity seems like a huge challenge – maybe they've never had good sports skills, or they've always felt clumsy, or they're embarrassed about people seeing them exercise. Other people like the idea of physical activity but just don't know where to start, or they need help to see how to fit it into their schedule.

Of course it's important to remember that if you're unfit, or above your healthy weight, you may get out of breath very easily, or certainly quicker than someone who plays an hour of non-stop hockey every other night. Oddly, doing no exercise can make you feel tired so it can be harder to get started (but you will feel better after you do).

Some hints for starting

⚙ Do more than nothing: do *something*, even if you don't feel you can do the recommended hour a day.

⚙ Start slowly, perhaps with a 10- or 15-minute walk each day, then build it up by 5 minutes each time to 30 minutes, and finally by 10 or 15 minutes to an hour. It gets easier.

⚙ Don't do the hour a day in one go. Try walking for half an hour in the morning, 15 minutes at lunch, 15 minutes to and from the bus stop, and around the block a few times with the dog when you get home (unless your block is a 20-acre farm).

⚙ Look for any opportunity to be active: walk to the local shops; get off the bus a stop or two earlier and walk the rest of the way; walk round to a friend's house to say hi instead of sending them a text; go the long way home.

⚙ Keep in mind that everyday stuff is activity too: hanging out the washing; doing the vacuuming; walking to work or school; dancing; mucking around with friends outside; doing work such as heavy gardening or delivering pamphlets.

⚙ Choose an activity you like so you don't get bored. Or vary the activities.

> Exercise doesn't have to be a big workout or anything, just something that you enjoy that's active. I always like music to get me motivated.
> Lou, 15

> I do lots of exercise because I enjoy it.
> Sarah, 14

circus skills

HINT

Stre-e-etch Always stretch before an exercise session to warm up a little and help prevent injury, and afterwards to improve your flexibility. Ask an accredited trainer, coach or school sports teacher to show you some good stretches.

◎ Try exercising before homework and before tea or dinner, and not too close to bedtime: between 4 and 6pm is a good time.

◎ Work out an exercise plan with your doctor if you have a medical condition such as asthma. (Asthma shouldn't stop you from being fit and active: some champion swimmers have it.)

◎ Set targets, if that will help you get started, such as joining a team that has regular practice and playing times, or doing an hour's brisk walk four times a week. You can keep charts or reward yourself with flowers, a movie or nice undies (when you reach the little goals as well as the big ones).

◎ Walk with a group of friends.

◎ Combine walking with someone and going somewhere you both want to go: chatting while you're strolling round the park, or talking and, say, window shopping are ways of being active without feeling it's a compulsory chore.

◎ Listen to music – it makes the time go quicker, if that's what you want. But don't use earphones if you're cycling on the road or crossing streets or driveways because music tends to distract you and block out other sounds (see the "Hearing" box in the Body Maintenance chapter).

The lone mover

Some people prefer to do physical activity by themselves. If you're one of those people, options that might work for you include:

✱ swimming laps, hitting a tennis ball or golf ball, or practising archery rather than taking up a team sport

✱ exercising at home – you can rent or buy DVDs for aerobics, yoga, Pilates and other disciplines

✱ going to yoga or a dance class or another activity where you don't have to know anybody or chat

✱ doing vigorous housework or gardening

✱ walking or jogging in the park, along the beach or around your neighbourhood. If you don't want to be seen, go early in the morning or evening – maybe with a dog for protection.

🕝 Learn circus or dance skills – they can open up a whole new world.

🕝 Keep a box or basket of fun stuff – bats, balls, helmets – on hand by the door or in the garage. Don't store your bike in a hard-to-get-at place (such as the attic).

The goal is to make activity the normal part of your day that your body expects it to be.

And let's say it again: the point of activity is to be healthy. It's not to be thin. Naturally thin girls who don't move their bodies around much and exist on jam doughnuts and coffee will not be anywhere near as healthy as heavier girls of the same height who eat well, are robust and full of energy and like to move their butts. (And the rest of their bodies. Just moving your butt would be weird, like one of those tragic girlies in music videos.)

Many girls think of exercise as a chore, something they have to do to "work off" a chocolate biscuit. Exercising isn't a short-term "fix" for anything or a punishment for eating. Think of food as fuel for all the things you need to do with your body, such as move it around, make cells and grow bones.

If you think of activity as something that's natural to the body and makes you feel good, you'll save yourself from a lifetime of grumpy, resentful exercise, and be able to enjoy mucking around with friends and having a walk in the fresh air.

When it's hard   When you haven't done much exercise for a while, or you're very unfit, it can feel as if you'll never get there, as if you'll never be fit. This is when self-discipline comes in: it sounds boring, and it can be, but the results are amazing. You'll feel proud of your achievement and healthier than you've ever been.

🕝 You may have to try a little longer, get active a little more often than other people you know, and go a bit harder. Gradually your body will get stronger and more resilient, but it may be a while before you notice a difference.

🕝 Don't overdo it; and if you do, rest the following day.

🕝 Don't be cross with yourself if you miss a day: think about why you did and how you can change that, then try again tomorrow.

🕝 Find a public pool, have a couple of swimming lessons if you need to, and then try some laps – being in water can make you feel lighter and more graceful, and puts less strain on your ankles and knees than some other activities.

🕝 To check you're exercising in an efficient way that won't cause injury, work out a programme with an accredited trainer or school PE teacher.

More info **on finding your own activity**

For any sports, martial arts or dance styles you're interested in, use your web search engine or contact your local council to find the nearest club or lessons.

www.sportengland.org
The official Sport England site. Choose "Get active" to find out about clubs, teams and sports activities in your area.

www.sports-council-wales.org.uk; www .sportni.net and www.sportscotland.org.uk
Find out about sports news, activities, clubs, teams, funding and special projects in the rest of the UK.

www.clubsforyoungpeople.org.uk
A UK-wide network of clubs, projects and activities for young people in their local communities. Choose "Do somethin'".

www.everydaycycling.com
Click on "Where to ride" to find cycle routes and events all over the UK.

www.wsf.org.uk
The Women's Sport and Fitness Foundation aims to get more girls and women doing physical activity.

www.yoga.co.uk
Search for a yoga class near you, or find out about yoga events, holidays and training.

Since I started playing rugby I have become more confident. I'm not so shy any more and I can now talk more openly to my friends and family. I have also built more confidence for when I talk to/approach guys.   Lauren, 17

My father comments about my weight. He started calling me fat when I was about 10. I had puppy fat but before that I was really active and sporty. Then I became really self-conscious about my body and refused to wear shorts or run because I thought I would jiggle. I've started jogging now but it took a long time.   Isobel, 17

It is essential to being healthy and happy, and beneficial to yourself, in that it increases your confidence and all good things like that.   Jess, 15

It's good for you. I like running because I feel the wind. It's required in my life or else I would be wired and would be bouncing all over the place.   Naomi, 13

Physical activity by real girls

Girls aged 13 to 18 in the Girl Stuff Survey said that this is what they do for exercise:

football, cricket, sports in general ✻ walk sometimes, go for rides, OCCASIONALLY go to the gym ✻ Pilates and sumo wrestling ✻ netball, basketball, dancing and water polo ✻ jogging, swimming in the morning ✻ swim, walk, row, play basketball, want to start tango lessons ✻ school sport coz its mandatory, though I walk a lot ✻ netball, ride my bike, play footy and stuff ✻ football, go for walks ✻ run, walk ✻ dancing, netball, football ✻ tennis, netball, go skiing ✻ walk dogs (part-time job), kung fu, surfing ✻ walk, dance around to a song, stretch ✻ sports at school ✻ school sports ✻ sport, go for runs ✻ occasional bike ride or run, hula-hooping, using our treadmill ✻ walk ✻ sport, swim, go for a bike ride, go for a walk ✻ netball, walk to and from school ✻ PE at school, skateboard a bit ✻ school sports, horse riding ✻ swim ✻ PE, sports training and matches, a lot of walking ✻ netball, sport, bike riding ✻ hockey, run, other sports, snowboard ✻ run ✻ walk everywhere, shopping, school sports, netball, surf, football ✻ dance, Tae Kwon Do ✻ walk, bit of sport for fun ✻ run, walk the dog ✻ basketball ✻ netball, school PE ✻ morning paper round ✻ run, walk, bike ride ✻ dance, running, crunches ✻ kick a football around ✻ dancing after school ✻ netball training ✻ rowing, swimming, basketball, hockey ✻ none ✻ ballroom dancing, hockey, netball, softball ✻ walking, swimming, playing badminton ✻ power walking, netball ✻ athletics, running, hockey, swimming, surfing ✻ cross country ✻ softball ✻ hockey, tennis, softball, golf, football, cricket and more ✻ jog twice a week, do sport with school ✻ cardio boxing ✻ walk, hockey, netball, dancing ✻ mini-exercises in my room ✻ frequent long bike rides ✻ gym, go for runs ✻ Irish and Latin dancing, hiking ✻ aerobics ✻ Pilates, walking, laughing ✻ jogging with friends ✻ a lot of exercise in everyday life because I am bouncy ✻ 30-minute walk every night (if I get time) ✻ cardiovascular workouts (in dance class) ✻ outdoorsy things ✻ refereeing ✻ dance around my room to rock music mostly ✻ ride my bike to school ✻ weights, badminton ✻ starting to do sit-ups and press-ups, running, skipping ✻ walks with mum and dogs ✻ exercise bike and various toning exercises ✻ treadmill (walking) ✻ run every day ✻ gym ✻ run, stretch, walk fast ✻ tennis and netball training, games ✻ shop for hats ✻ walk a couple of blocks to school/home ✻ two laps around the track, walk at lunchtime ✻ run or play with my dogs, sport ✻ gym at least three times a week after school, volleyball ✻ run, jump on my trampoline ✻ kick boxing ✻ rhythmic gymnastics ✻ football for school ✻ Tae Kwon Do, exercise on my rollerblades ✻ karate, basketball, swimming, dance ✻ sometimes randomly dance in my room ✻ martial arts ✻ run, row, rollerblade, bike ride, PE ✻ star jumps ✻ kicking the ball, running with my bros ✷ tennis, golf ✷ **rock climb** ✷ walk with friends ✷ occasional rock climbing ✷ ice skating ✷ touch football, ballet ✷ tae bo, walk a lot ✷ netball, walk home every day ✷ any type of sports I can ✷ walk home every night, do dancing ✷ skipping ✷ running, jumping ✷ swimming, walking ✷ dance, Tae Kwon Do ✷ basketball, orienteering, running ✷ **sail, karate** ✷ water polo ✷ canoe, surf, swim, walk ✷ tennis, skipping, running ✷ netball, tennis, touch rugby, walking ✷ run around the block, ride my bike ✷ school sports training, club netball ✷ walks to the park with family, sometimes sit-ups and push-ups ✷ run around the block, play energetic sports like netball, football, etc. ✷ run on the spot ✷ walk to and from the bus stop ✷ go to gigs and jump around ✷ yoga ✷ squash ✷ just stretching ✷ **because my mum doesn't have a licence we walk a lot** ✷ mowing the lawn ✷ archery ✷ hip-hop dancing ✷ run around and be happy!!! ✷ Pilates ✷ cricket ✷ lots of stairs ✷ walking, swimming, yoga, Pilates ✷ run around the park ✷ umpiring, swimming, dancing, gym ✷ running, tennis, netball, orienteering, dancing ✷ walk everywhere ✷ Tae Kwon Do, other martial-arts training, fencing, archery ✷ bike riding, swimming, walking, cricket ✷ dance a lot ✷ in-line hockey, run, swim, PE in school ✷ lots: netball, tennis, swimming, rowing, athletics ✷ walk to school from the train station, and home ✷ rollerblading, tennis, netball ✷ run, row, ski, play football ✷ **belly dancing** ✷ athletics training ✷ go for walks, dance, aerobics, sports ✷ play basketball, running, walking, walk home from school each day ✷ jog in the nearby national park ✷ jump on indoor trampoline ✷ tap dancing, running, netball, hockey, tennis, bike riding ✷ gym, soccer, swim, jujitsu, run, sail, walk ✷ Irish dancing ✷ walk – it's lovely to have the wind in my hair ✷ walk the long way to my bus stop ✷ walk round the shops ✷ walk with the family ✷ **Tae Kwon Do, hockey, jogging, chasing after small children** ✷ windsurfing ✷ walk the dog with family, go on exercise bike ✷ sprinting ✷ ride my bike 8km to work, and 9km back ✷ play the drums ✷ waitressing: continuous walking around ✷ aerobics at night ✷ cardio-Pilates ✷ work on the farm with dad ✷ line dance ✷ climb masts on a boat ✷ train my football team ✷ compulsory school sport ✷ body jam ✷ highland dancing ✷ Rugby Union ✷ **I'm an acrobat** ✷ dance aerobics video ✷ Latin dance ✷ netball, swimming, cross-country, triathlon ✷ shopping ✷ dance like a mad thing in my lounge ✷ apprentice chef: on my feet for up to 12 hours a day ✷ 150 skips (skipping-rope) a night ✷ bodyboarding ✷ dance in front of mirror ✷ competitive aerobics, jazz, hip-hop ✷ Tae Kwon Do, stretching, balintawak (Filipino martial art) ✷ table tennis ✷ rugby training ✷ **tennis with mates** ✷ taking my daughter for walks ✷ working at a store cleaning ✷ walks in the forest ✷ body-combat class ✷ swing dance, walk, modern ballroom.

Activity problems

Some physical activities have downsides that you
need to know about. Avoid:

- ✆ over-training – such as several hours a day
- ✆ any sport that has coaches or parents
  who shout at you
- ✆ something that often makes you feel
  like crying or think that you're a failure
  when you lose or you're never good
  enough
- ✆ any activity that causes repeated injury, especially in the same
  part of your body
- ✆ a sport that overheats you – choose sports and times carefully in hot weather and
  don't let yourself become dehydrated (drink water before and during exercise,
  whenever you feel thirsty)
- ✆ sports or activities that encourage you to lose weight or to stay
  at a certain weight or size. These include some ballet,
  gymnastics and modelling disciplines; although many
  kids are picked because they are naturally smaller or
  thinner than others, normal puberty and growing
  up can "get in the way".

  Athletics and other sports practised at an elite
  level can impose severe and unhealthy weight
  controls. If you're told to weigh yourself as part
  of your sport it's probably time to get out. It's
  physically and mentally unhealthy to fight your
  natural body changes. It's not your body that's the
  problem; it's the attitude around you.

Exercises

Exercises and stretches are good for keeping your
body flexible and your muscles strong. It's really
useful to work the abdominal or core muscles,
which help keep your back strong and supple: yoga
and Pilates have these kinds of exercises or "poses".

> Whatever I do I seem to have no time for it with
> all my schoolwork.   Tanya, 14

> I don't do any exercise as my
> mum can't be bothered driving
> me to places. She tells me to
> exercise around the house
> (no idea what that means).
> Keeley, 14

hockey one

A lot of gyms and fitness magazines provide specific exercises, done with or without equipment, to build up the muscles in certain areas, such as the arms, stomach or legs. That's fine, but daily exercises for a "firmer bottom" or a "flatter stomach" can have you obsessing about something that isn't a problem. If you're already fit and healthy your body is basically its natural shape.

yoga...

Gyms can be expensive and intimidating places, but you don't have to join one to get fit or to do gym-style exercises. You can do exercises at home, perhaps with a hired or a bought instructional DVD and some basic equipment. Another option is to check whether your local council has a nearby youth or leisure centre with cheap classes or gym equipment that you can use for free or a small fee.

I think a lot of us don't try because we're scared of what we look like when we do – guys don't do that. It's not feminine to be competitive or actually sweat. If we forgot about all that crap, it's so much fun, and so worth it!
Dakota, 17

Screen time

People now move their bodies much, much less than people did in the past. (Compared with a hundred years ago or more, we're practically as active as a building. I mean, do you know any hunter-gatherers?) What with homework, computer time, sitting-around-chatting time and getting-driven-around time, a lot of people miss out on physical activity (not to mention thinking and creating). TV- and computer-watching are probably the biggest munchers of the time that used to be spent being active.

It relieves you from stress, and yoga/Pilates is really good to just clear the mind and relax and enjoy life without really thinking about it. Lisa, 15

Changing habits

Your family might not have a tradition of doing physical activity or exercising. This means you will probably have to work a bit harder to develop new habits. Here are some ideas on how to do so.

- Call a family meeting and start a discussion about whether family members would like to be fitter and healthier. You don't need to talk about anybody "having to lose weight" or being "overweight" as this can seem like an accusation. Ask everyone for suggestions. Who can exercise together? What games or walks could you try together? Which activities would be good for weekdays and which for weekends? Where's the Frisbee?
- With family members, or by yourself, start doing half an hour's activity each day if you can, and then build up to an hour, even if it's in two or three lots (and check out the section "Some hints for starting" earlier in this chapter).

Suggestions for watching less TV

- Make a decision about how much you can watch a day. Maybe set a limit of one show a day, or two a week – one to two hours is a lot of TV time, even if it's less than normal for you.
- Cut down progressively: watch half an hour less a day for a week, then an hour less a day, and so on.
- Look at a TV guide to work out what you really want to watch instead of flicking through endless crap, hoping something good might come on – it usually doesn't.
- Record shows you like and watch them later, without the ads.
- Don't watch TV in the morning – take the time to leave home earlier and walk further to school or work.
- Do an experiment – don't watch the TV for a week! Throw a rug over it, and see what you do instead.

FACT

Lost years If you watch TV for an average of two hours a day and have since you were 4, by the time you're 70 you'll have spent five and a half years of your life in front of the screen.

❻ Talk to your parents and teachers about what can be done to allow you to exercise your human right to exercise. If your life is too busy for exercise, then there is something wrong and it needs to be fixed.

If nobody in your family wants to change, or can commit to the change, don't let that be an excuse to hold you back from a healthier and more energetic life. It's up to you.

Do it! Just do it! It makes you feel refreshed and it helps you keep fit and you may even meet a cute guy!   Jodie, 14

I think exercise is the perfect medicine. If you are upset or depressed, it releases endorphins, making you feel slightly more alive. If you are confused about something, a quiet walk can clear your mind.   Holly, 18

I finished school and I was soooo fit, and then all of a sudden I just had no exercise routine and I put on like 10kg and realized how much I actually did at school. So I had to get motivated to start getting involved again and realized how much I missed it and how much better it made me feel about myself and my health.   Sally, 18

you Look **FINE**, girl

6

SHAPE

Be your own Best friend

Heaps of girls are unhappy with how they look. Large girls are unhappy, thin girls are unhappy, girls with **wide** hips feel afflicted, girls with **slim** hips feel short-changed, girls with **big** boobs are dissatisfied, girls with **little** breasts are crestfallen, girls with **curly** hair are disgruntled, girls with **straight** hair are troubled, **tall** girls feel peeved, **short** girls want a refund. And some girls are convinced their earlobes are wrong.

Your body shape

The "ideal body" admired in the media is the shape of a very tall, thin girl aged about 10 but with big breasts. Very few girls or women are that shape. This means they tend to think there's something wrong with them. "Why don't I look like that?" they ask, instead of "Why is that shape supposed to be the only good one, anyway, and who says so? And, by the way, shut up".

You're the shape you are because of your genes. You could take after your mum or dad, or look like someone else in the family – possibly cousin Yuri. Or maybe auntie Lorraine, who has spectacular sideburns.

A lot of girls have a negative body image, meaning they don't like the way they look. But there are billions of people on earth so it doesn't make sense to think there could be only one "perfect" kind of body. Instead there are heaps of different kinds of beautiful.

Body types

According to some people who follow the theories of a twentieth-century American psychologist, there are three basic body types:

- ⑥ ectomorphs (Oh, what a charming word, I don't think) – long, lean and lanky, with narrow hips and waist, more angles and fewer curves
- ⑥ mesomorphs (another delightful word) – tending to be muscular and athletic looking, with broad shoulders, narrow waist and wide hips
- ⑥ endomorphs (get a grip) – more heavy boned than the other two types, with a rounder body.

There are really many more variations than these basic three, but you can see just by looking around that some people inherit genes that make them tall, lean professional basketball player types, while others are built like short, cuddly… amateur basketball players.

After you're fully grown, your size can be slightly affected by what you eat and how much you move your body around, but your shape will always be essentially the same. It isn't based on your star sign or any other ancient made-up system, or on the latest theory from someone trying to sell a new diet book. That's all piffle.

As well as different inherited body types, people also have different metabolic rates: some of them burn up fat as energy quicker and more easily than others.

Your weight

In the Girl Stuff Survey 38 percent of girls aged 13 to 15 said they didn't feel that they were at a "comfortable, healthy" weight. Among the 16- to 18-year-old girls this had risen to 43 percent.

There are two possible reasons for this: some girls have a false concept of their bodies because they're so confused about what's healthy and what being "fat" is; and some girls are dealing with the uncomfortable feeling of being above their healthy weight range.

What's healthy?

Healthy means having a body that lets you do all the physical activities you need and want to do, and one that is able to fight off illness. So when the term "unhealthy weight" is used it means there's too much weight – or not enough weight – for the body to be able to function well, and too much strain is being placed on organs and other parts of the body, making injury and illness more likely, now or in the future.

Since it's obvious that there can't be one exact healthy weight for you or anyone else, a healthy weight should always be expressed as a range of possibilities, based on several factors.

You need body fat

We female folk have to get over our unrealistic expectations about what's normal and natural when it comes to fat. Girls need to be putting on body fat as well as muscle during their teens – it's a natural part of becoming a young woman. It's healthy for fit, gorgeous mature girls and women (say, from the age of 16) to have 25 to 30 percent of their body as fat. It's not a dirty word. It doesn't mean *too* fat; it means *necessary* fat.

We usually need about 17 percent of our body weight as fat to be able to have any periods, and at least 22 percent as fat to have them regularly. Speaking in averages, a 10-year-old girl needs and has 10 to 15 percent more body fat than boys of the same age. A grown woman has 10 to 30 percent more fat than a man.

This girly padding is mainly around our breasts, hips and tummy, and basically it's there to help our bodies in case we ever want to have a baby. If this body fat falls below a healthy level it can result in periods stopping, difficulty getting pregnant

hmmmm

have a think about
why you NEED
some body fat...

What's your healthy weight range?

If you answer yes to all the following questions it's likely that you're within your healthy weight range.

- Do you feel healthy and comfortable?
- Do you feel fit, strong, flexible and able to do any physical manoeuvres you might want to?
- Do you usually get some real physical activity every day? (See the Move chapter.)
- Are you eating from a wide range of healthy foods? (See the Food chapter.)
- Do you eat when you're hungry or at the usual times each day – rather than either ignoring your hunger and rigidly policing your food intake, or eating when you're bored, upset, already full or not hungry?

or breastfeeding, damage to bones (which can result in serious fractures) and other problems, including lifeless hair, bad teeth and dull skin.

"Cellulite" Cellulite is a made-up word for dimples on the skin of thighs, bottoms and sometimes stomachs, caused by the natural fat underneath. Everyone has it, even thin people. It's not caused by toxins, it's caused by being female. No "firming" or other type of cream, no amount of scrubbing or seaweed wraps or sweating, will get rid of it. Cellulite is just something cosmetics companies would like us to obsess about so we buy useless expensive crap. The only cure for cellulite is not to care about it.

Being thin

You don't have to have big bosoms or wide hips to be a real woman. A lot of girls are genetically programmed to be small and thin or tall and thin. People can make rude and thoughtless comments (who loves being compared to a stick?) and even suggest that you have an eating disorder.

Thin girls are just as beautiful as girls with more curves. But if you feel that you're underweight and it's affecting your health and energy levels, ask your GP to refer you to a dietician for advice.

If you're worried that you (or a friend) may be losing too much weight or obsessing about food, see the "Eating disorders" section in the Mind Health chapter.

Assessing yourself

You can't judge yourself by:

- whether you look thin or not – having more fat than some other people doesn't necessarily mean you're unhealthy. And being thin doesn't automatically mean you're healthy.

ⓖ whether anything wobbles. Next time you're watching an elite athletics race and the women runners are getting ready, notice how they wobble their muscles and skin – and they have even less body fat than is healthy. Everyone wobbles. If we didn't, we'd be skeletons.

ⓖ doing a Body Mass Index (BMI) calculation – it's no good for anyone who hasn't finished growing (which sometimes isn't until you're 18 or so) and ignores many possibly relevant factors, such as how fit you are, how much of your weight is muscle (which weighs more than fat) and whether you're healthy.

And don't judge yourself by:

ⓖ weighing yourself – weight gain can be natural because your bones are getting bigger, or be caused by your body making extra muscle (that's good), while weight loss may be caused by having a stomach bug for a couple of days (that's not good). Even once you've stopped growing, you don't want the bathroom scales ruling your life. Getting on them every day is misleading – everyone goes up and down a little depending on daily factors.

I have a "normal build", and I found at secondary school most girls define this as fat. Abby, 13

Comments people shouldn't make about weight

"You're getting fat. You need to go on a diet."

Try not to be influenced by these comments. They can hurt your feelings (particularly if they come from your mum or dad), don't help you to change even if you need to, and are often just plain wrong.

And be careful not to make these kinds of comments yourself. Many girls say such remarks started them on the road to an eating disorder, when they were a healthy size to begin with.

"You look great. Have you lost weight?"

People mean this as a compliment, but actually it's just as intrusive as "You need to lose weight". And it makes you think, "What – did I look terrible before?"

So don't link someone's looks to their weight: again it can hurt feelings and even trigger an obsession with getting thinner. Just compliment somebody on their hair or their clothes, or say they look pretty.

◎ consulting a weight-for-height chart – these are often outdated, based on men's measurements or ignore the fact that muscle weighs more than fat. They aren't scientific or individual enough for you to judge from.

◎ doing a fat-pinch calliper test. Sometimes gym instructors or coaches use a little set of tongs to pinch some fat, often at your waist, and measure it. It's invasive and humiliating, it doesn't tell them anything useful scientifically, and is often used as a tool to intimidate you into buying a gym membership, or into feeling you have to achieve a certain set of numbers on a chart. Don't bother.

> There is so much conflicting information about what is a healthy weight for certain heights. It's hard to know which one to believe.
> Sheree, 17

◎ relying on your clothes size, because sizes differ a lot. Girls' clothes sizes are supposed to be related to age (11–12, 13–14, and so on), but vary wildly from brand to brand (and besides, all 13-year-olds aren't the same size). Women's clothes sizes (8, 10, 12, 14, 16 and so on) are supposed to be based on a series of measurements taken a gerzillion years ago, but they vary wildly too, depending on shop and brand (or label). You can be a size 10 in one brand and a 14 in another, or a different size on the top and bottom.

And you absolutely *mustn't* judge yourself by:

◎ "going up a size" – healthy girls need to get bigger during the teen years. Going up a size when you're a teenager doesn't mean you have to lose weight. If you're a size 12 and suddenly you need a size 14, you're not "getting fat".

◎ comparing yourself with other people – your height and hair colour are different from a friend's, and your weight will be too (unless the two of you are clones in a science-fiction movie, and you eat exactly the same foods and move your body exactly the same number of centimetres every day and have the same metabolism).

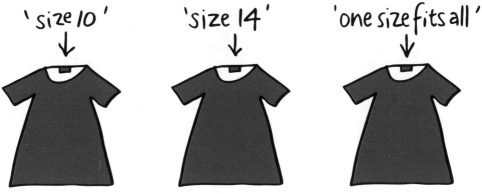

'size 10'   'size 14'   'one size fits all'

LaBeL sizes don't mean MUCH...

Things to say when somebody comments on your size or shape

"Go away, you're boring me."

"I'm the right shape for me."

"Mind your own body image."

"Oh, get a grip."

"Who made you the Body Police?"

"Don't worry about *me* changing my size – can *you* change your attitude?"

"Here, read this chapter."

My shape is not your business

6 comparing yourself with the fashion models. They are unusually tall, unusually thin women with unusually wide shoulders (they're more like hangers that the clothes are draped on), and some have fake breasts. As the saying goes, "The only people who look like models are models".

6 comparing yourself with the models in clothes ads. Many are pre-teen girls who haven't gone through the natural body changes yet. In other words, they're children. Advertisers are saying to teenagers and grown women, "This is the body shape you should want, and you need to buy our product to help you get it". (You can supply the evil-cackle sound effect yourself.) If most women were shaped like a stop sign, with a big head and a pole-thin body, the advertisers would be selling strap-on bottoms, special pens to draw dimples on our thighs, spray-on hips and supplements to make us look bigger.

Magazine HELL

🌀 comparing yourself with famous actresses – they exercise for hours and have full-time teams of trainers, minders and chefs to care for them. A lot of them are bored and hungry. And look like Bratz dolls. It's a miracle they don't take a bite out of their own agents.

🌀 what a relative or anyone else says, even if it's your mum – these comments often come from ignorance about weight and eating, or from the person's own problems or bad feelings about food and body image. And I think we all know how mean brothers and sisters can be. Bullies too can be very good at finding something to say that they think will freak you out (but which isn't necessarily true).

QUOTE

"Change your mind, not your body."
Positive body image slogan

Being too heavy

Some people are above their healthy weight, and this really restricts their life. We're not talking here of being big and healthy or naturally curvy and fit. We're talking about being too large to feel comfortable a lot of the time.

Girls who are very much bigger than they need to be can find it hard to bend, stretch and be flexible, their fitness levels may drop, and it could limit their choices of hobbies and career. They could also face a number of health problems that range from diabetes to finding it hard to get pregnant when they want to have a baby. People who are above their healthy weight range can also find it hard to buy nice clothes that fit.

It can seem as if the whole world thinks you're lazy and have no "willpower", and that it's okay to hurt your feelings. You can feel, wrongly, that it's your fault and you're less worthy than other people, and get sad and depressed.

Obesity Being "obese" means being at a much higher weight than you need to be. There's no magic line you cross, although many doctors use charts of heights and weights or weight ranges to work out whether you're a lot heavier or a little bit heavier than is healthy for you.

The word "obese" was originally used by scientific researchers to describe a section of the population. Like "fat", it can sound insulting applied to individual people and make them feel bad about themselves. We don't need to use these words about ourselves or anybody else.

I would love to be healthier and to lose about 20kg. At the moment I am 120kg. I would like my hair to grow out and be its natural colour again. Izzie, 18

Seeing a doctor about a suspected "weight problem"   If you're worried about your weight, check out the box "What's your healthy weight range?" a few pages back. If you answer no to most of the questions it could be a good idea to see your GP – that's the only way to know for sure what you're dealing with. The doctor will probably weigh and measure you (which, as you can imagine, is not the most fun you're going to have that week). They should explain nicely what the healthy weight range is for you personally – not for your age group in general – and whether you're above it.

> People calling me "fat": even if they're joking it hurts. And body image is like a huge thing these days – calling someone fat does not make it any easier.
> Lisa, 16

Changing to a healthier life   If you need to change:

⊙ ask your GP whether this means you need to lose weight – maybe instead you can stop gaining weight and stay the same until, when you've become taller, it's a healthy weight for you (you've "grown into it").

⊙ ask a school nurse for advice, or your GP to refer you to a dietician, who will talk with you about the food you eat, the usual size of your food portions and the reasons why you eat, and about how to choose healthier food.

⊙ see the Food chapter for hints about food and eating, and the Move chapter to find a physical activity you like – no weight-maintenance or weight-loss programme makes any sense unless it involves increasing your physical activity as well as decreasing certain kinds of foods.

⊙ don't "diet" (see the "Dieting" section below), and don't take "weight-loss tips" from magazines, websites, well-meaning relatives or friends.

⊙ contact one of the eating disorder groups given in the Mind Health chapter if you feel that you can't control the amount of food you eat, that you binge-eat or that you can't stop eating even when you're not hungry – they have many people with the same problem in their support groups and can recommend counsellors and strategies.

⊙ accept that changing your life is going to take effort and work – it can be mentally challenging, and sometimes physically hard going.

⊙ give yourself regular rewards (think about ones that aren't food, such as pampering sessions, new clothes, money towards a holiday) – you deserve them for all your hard work.

⊙ try to be as kind and understanding to yourself as a best friend would be.

⊙ go slowwwly and gradually – any successful and lasting change has to become part of the way you think and feel. Don't get furious with yourself if you stray from the path – just step back on, don't wander further off into the distance.

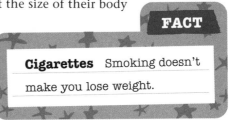

don't worry if you step off the path occasionally...

Losing weight means you're still you, but a healthier you with a lot more energy. One of my favourite stories is about a girl who had been over her healthy weight for years. After months of hard work she changed her life and lost the weight she needed to. A guy who had been her friend for many years made a pass at her and wanted her to be his girl-friend. Instead of feeling grateful and thrilled, she told him where to go. "If he wasn't interested in me before," she said, "when he knew me just as well, then he wasn't going to really love me for me." That is a great girl with the right attitude.

Dieting

It can be confusing when people talk about "your diet". That means the sort of foods you usually eat. A "diet" or "going on a diet" or "starting a diet" usually means some-thing else: a short-term diet people put themselves on to try to lose weight, which is a Very Bad Idea. This section isn't about a healthy diet. It's about "dieting" – meaning the diets that people "go on" to try to lose weight.

People go on diets because they don't know that these don't work. They want to lose weight because they think looking thinner will make them happier. It's hard for them to realize that happiness isn't about the size of their body but about what's happening in their head. And they go on diets because magazines, books and weight-loss companies promote diets as a way to lose weight.

> **FACT**
>
> **Cigarettes** Smoking doesn't make you lose weight.

Short-term diets are guaranteed to fail you, while making you feel that you're the failure. If you go on one, or stop eating much for a couple of days, you will lose weight. So it will seem to be "working". The catch is – it can't last. The weight you lost will go back on, plus more.

Why don't diets work?

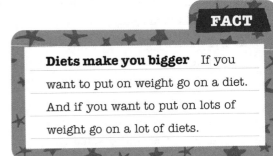

FACT

Diets make you bigger If you want to put on weight go on a diet. And if you want to put on lots of weight go on a lot of diets.

- When you severely restrict food the body thinks you are in starvation mode, so it starts conserving fat to create an emergency supply. It does this by making it harder for you to burn fat during exercise. It allows your body to lose water, but not fat. Your metabolism slows down, meaning you need to exercise more to burn the same amount of energy as you used to. And it starts sending you signals saying "Feed me!" It's a survival thing.

- By saying, "I will never eat a doughnut", you pretty much guarantee that that's all you'll think about. So you get cravings, go off the diet and overcompensate by eating too much.

- Dieters feeling sad and deprived of comforting food are far more likely to binge eat than other people. Then later they feel guilty or depressed about "failing".

- Diets are almost always too hard to stick to. They can require people to devote masses of time and brain space to counting, measuring, weighing, following instructions, having strict shopping lists, buying foods that aren't in season, and eating things they don't like or which are expensive and not suited to family meals.

- Crazes or fashionable diets that suggest that being overweight is caused by cheese, indigestion, mucus, eating the wrong things before 11am, eating certain combinations of foods, your blood group or your body "type" never last long because they are too faddish, and dieters get sick of them. There's absolutely no scientific basis for them. You may as well base a diet on numerology, your horoscope, your hair colour or your favourite football team.

- Virtually no short-term diets are designed for an individual, so they don't suit anyone perfectly. They're too inflexible: the diet says you must eat fish and a salad tonight, but it's cold and you feel like chicken risotto.

- We're social beings whose world is arranged around eating together. Dieters have to slink off or aren't able to join in fully, and it can feel lonely and isolating.

Don't starve yourself. Monica and Charlie, 14

Believe me the diets aren't working. Siobhan, 14

Why you shouldn't diet

✴ Dieting can stunt your growth and delay your development – fad diets that restrict you to only one or a few kinds of food deprive your body of the nutrients it needs.

✴ Dieting can cause hunger, tiredness, crabbiness, forgetfulness, inability to concentrate, headaches, constipation, muscle cramps, weak bones, vitamin and mineral deficiencies, dull hair and skin, bad breath and dehydration.

✴ Dieting is a known cause of depression – the more you diet, the more severe the depression can be.

✴ Dieting is a known trigger for eating disorders (see the Mind Health chapter).

✴ Most diets don't factor in exercise as a must-do part of a healthy life, or provide enough energy for you to exercise without becoming exhausted or sick.

✴ Dieting can lead to futile "yo-yo" dieting – a diet doesn't work so inevitably you try it again or try another one (lose some, put more on, lose some, put even more on).

✴ Dieting can set you up for a lifetime of feeling sad, bad, mad and out of control about food.

✴ Dieting makes you gain weight.

Some don'ts

◎ Don't diet with a friend or through a club, magazine or website. It can result in shared obsessions and competition about how much weight is being lost. (Everyone is different and competitions are dangerous.) It's especially unhelpful to go on a diet with an adult (such as your mum) because you have different needs. Share food, not dieting.

◎ Don't diet for an event, such as a wedding at which you're a bridesmaid, or your school leavers' ball.

◎ Don't fast (have no food or fluids, or very little, for a day or more): it's dangerous and damaging for teenage girls. (Some people are required to fast for religious reasons, but religions will make exceptions and other arrangements for children, teens, pregnant women and women who are breastfeeding.) Never participate in charity diets or fasts. Show your support another way.

'If you eat an egg half an hour before fruit, you'll get cellulite on your left leg...'

THe coNfused FooD PoLice

⑥ Don't take diet pills. Most of these are a form of "speedy" drug that makes you less hungry, or not hungry at all, and may make you feel buzzy, unable to sleep, cranky or faint. You could do damage to your adrenal system and become deficient in basic nutrients.

⑥ Don't take laxatives (drugs or herbs used to cause diarrhoea as soon as possible after eating). They don't result in any weight loss whatsoever, because food is still absorbed on the way through. Taking laxatives a lot can lead to you not being able to control when poo comes out. Bleeding from your bottom and dehydration are other results.

⑥ Don't take meal "replacements" or "supplements" (usually a powdered drink or a biscuit). No fun, not social, hard to stick to and just plain weird.

⑥ Don't try patches or gels that are claimed to release a "fat-burning" or "fat-melting" substance into your system. They don't – there is no such thing. (Damn. You've been totally ripped off.)

⑥ Don't over-exercise because it can get out of hand, and too much can cause many health and mental problems: your period may stop, stress fractures of the bones are common, and repeating one type of exercise, whatever it is, can cause permanent physical damage.

Blame the diet

Girls tend to blame themselves when a diet fails. They think they didn't have enough willpower and that they just needed to stick to it – even when sticking to it is illogical and makes them unhappy. Blaming themselves means that they're likely to feel even sadder. And that can be a trigger for eating to feel comforted, instead of when they're hungry.

Don't blame yourself – blame the diet.

Diets make you farty

Diets, in my opinion, are wrong. A healthy eating scheme and exercise plan are much better. It gets me REALLY pissed off if my grandmother tells me about diets. Erin, 18

More info on avoiding diets

For websites on healthy eating, see the "More info" sections in the Food chapter.

www.teenweightwise.com
British Dietetic Association site to help teens manage their weight safely and without yo-yo dieting. Includes a health quiz and loads of recipes, plus info about eating habits, being active, safe weight loss, food labels, fast food and eating out.

If Not Dieting Then What? by Dr Rick Kausman, Allen and Unwin
The books and website (www.ifnotdieting .com.au) of Dr Rick Kausman, the Australian eating behaviours expert, help people develop a good relationship with food and their body.

The last time I went on a diet was at the beginning of December for a major eighteenth party, where this boy I like was going to be. I lost about 5 kilos in two weeks and I'm still recovering from it and I've actually gained 10 kilos – currently I'm trying to do it slowly and one step at a time.   Grace, 17

In year 9 I only ate dinner [*not breakfast or lunch*] because my parents were there and now as a sort of "rebound" I suppose I've put on about 10 kilos. I do try to stay fit and healthy now, the proper way!   Sophia, 17

Diets girls have tried that **didn't work** for them long term

Girls who answered the Girl Stuff Survey said they had tried:

stupid starvation diets ✽ eating and spewing!! ✽ stopped eating ✽ eating less carbs and fat ✽ currently attempting a high-exercise, low-junk-food diet – I am also failing miserably ✽ anorexic diet ✽ junk-free ✽ **one with mum** ✽ no wheat, meat, dairy, sugar, salt ✽ stupid one where you didn't eat much at all, but still junk and stuff – that's soooo stupid ✽ just lettuce ✽ starvation diet ✽ starving, bingeing, purging ✽ ciggies and diet coke ✽ apple and water – it is very draining, and made up by the girls at school ✽ Slim-Fast and it was horrible and didn't work at all ✽ **not eating lunch and brekkie** ✽ think I have tried every one!!!! ✽ hardly-eat-any-food kind of diet ✽ Eat Right 4 Your Type, starve yourself ✽ just salad ✽ Weight Watchers, Atkins ✽ soup diet, but that didn't last very long ✽ fruit and yoghurt, lots of water ✽ a blood-type diet for my eczema, many other diets ✽ not sugar, only vegetables and very little meat ✽ meal-replacement shakes ✽ bulimia ✽ South Beach ✽ **only eat what fits on a small plate** ✽ only eating fruit and plain bread ✽ water only, dinner only, one piece of fruit a day, six meals a week, breathing in when eating ✽ not eating for days and then pigging out (bulimia) ✽ **low GI one – it was working but I couldn't keep going** ✽ Fat Blaster Lite, Easy Slim, Slim-Fast, Optislim ✽ make up my own really: no bread, detox diet, only fruit ✽ wouldn't eat anything except dinner ✽ a kind of not-eating-and-throwing-up diet ✽ everything from tablets to starving myself ✽ didn't eat for a while ✽ **starving** ✽ ate vegetables and fruit for three weeks ✽ anorexia and bulimia for the past two years; also binge eat a lot ✽ low-calorie ✽ no-fat foods, but it didn't really work out ✽ just a diet my family put together ✽ stupid one I made up that would be skipping meals or cutting down the portions I ate ✽ tablets ✽ soup and fruit ✽ **strange, self-invented ones** ✽ only allowed to eat some stew ✽ crazy unhealthy one that made me lose too much weight ✽ liquid diet ✽ what sort have I NOT been on?!?!?! ✽ mostly salad and only tiny amounts of carb diet mum once put me on ✽ only green things, no bread, extreme water, lots of chocolate ✽ Ultra Slim ✽ **made up my own! – starving usually (very silly)** ✽ some diet my mum had ✽ mainly starvation diets or throwing up after every meal ✽ tried to cut out carbohydrates – it didn't work! ✽ blood type ✽ detox, no sugar, brown bread ✽ starve myself ✽ **fat-free options** ✽ food-combining diet, and under 1500 calories a day ✽ dinner-only diet ✽ used to cut out breakfast and lunch, but had no energy and used to faint regularly ✽ eat one piece of fruit or veg a day ✽ no bread.

Not liking your bits

When you spend a lot of time obsessing about how you look (otherwise known as The Teenage Years) you can develop wacky ideas about one of your bits. Some people hate their ears; others their nose. Some are convinced their ankles are the first thing everyone notices about them because they're the first thing about themselves *they* see when they look down or in a mirror.

And yet if you asked a stranger to guess which bit you hated they'd probably never get it. Likely comments would include "Your knees? What the hell's wrong with your *knees*?", "But you've got GREAT hair!", "Huh? I've never even noticed your ears".

Wanting cosmetic procedures

Talking through a body image problem with a trained psychologist is more likely to make you feel better than assuming you need to be "fixed".

Cosmetic surgery   The number of teenagers having cosmetic surgery in the US is rising every year. It's not so common in the UK, but certainly more girls here are thinking about it, wanting it and, in a small number of cases, having it.

Although the British Association of Aesthetic Plastic Surgeons doesn't have an official policy on surgery and teens, its website says it's generally not a good idea unless there are medical reasons or special circumstances (such as really big breasts that are making life uncomfortable and difficult).

Some cosmetic procedures that a plastic surgeon may be happier to perform on a teen include removing large birthmarks or moles, and pinning back ears that stick straight out from the head. The operations that most reputable plastic surgeons wouldn't touch for a teenager include "nose jobs" (rhinoplasty), liposuction and breast enlargement.

Who can do cosmetic surgery?

It should only be done by a plastic surgeon – a specialist with more than eight years of study and

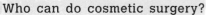

COSMETIC SURGERY IS PROBABLY NOT the ANSWER

experience on top of a medical degree. To repeat a Skin chapter warning: never respond to an ad from a "cosmetic surgeon" or "cosmetic clinic". A "cosmetic surgeon" could just be a GP who's watched a training video on using lasers. The primary concern of cosmetic clinics is making money, not necessarily why you're having the treatment or whether there's a better solution for you.

A plastic surgeon is someone who is legally entitled to have the initials FRCS (Plast) (Fellow of the Royal College of Surgeons) after their name. Most other letters you see after someone's name are irrelevant, and sometimes the result of weekend courses.

Some revolting characters in the cosmetic surgery business have been convincing women they need surgery on their girly bits. These creatures prey on girls and women who are worried that their vulva area and labia look untidy, lopsided, odd or too big.

Girls and women can worry about theirs because usually we don't get to see each other's girly bits, so we have nothing to compare ours with. (What you see in pornographic magazines is no help because everything about those girls has been faked.) You can rest assured that your girly bits are both as individual and as normal as anybody else's, but if you're really worried ask your doctor to have a look and reassure you. You may feel more comfortable with a woman doctor.

The downsides and dangers of cosmetic surgery

The downsides and dangers are rarely discussed when magazines and TV shows talk about cosmetic surgery. If you are under 18 your parent or guardian will have to approve the operation. Surgery isn't something to be taken lightly – as if it's just a quick, easy nip 'n' tuck.

✻ It is usually very expensive and, unless it's a procedure done for a medical reason, like a breast reduction, it probably won't be covered by the NHS or any health insurance policy.

✻ The risks include complications under general anaesthetic (people have even died).

✻ Many operations involve breaking bones, the rearrangement of facial features and massive bruising. Recovery time and pain can be the same as for car accident injuries.

✻ Some mistakes made by surgeons are impossible, difficult or painful to fix, and the repair work needs to be attempted by a qualified plastic surgeon.

Injections   Some ludicrous people are claiming Botox injections in your twenties are a good idea to stop lines from forming. Botox is simply a toxic substance that paralyses areas where it is injected, for up to three months. Each "unit" of Botox is a measure that's enough to kill a mouse. Injections to paralyse an area such as the forehead can be up to sixty units – in other words, a lot of dead mice. You can see the effect of Botox on many actresses – the ones who can't move their foreheads or have a natural facial expression; the ones whose faces look like giant boiled eggs. Botox side effects can include a droopy eyelid for several weeks or months, not to mention the weird alien effect of not being able to frown.

How can I get rid of my boobs?   Fran, 17

My weight is good, I just don't like being tall!

But that's OK, I guess...   Rosie, 13

I wish I had an ass.   Angela, 18

You are what you are.   Keira, 15

I don't like my thighs.   Jasmine, 14

Be grateful for what you have, not what

you don't have.   Letisha, 16

I hate the shape of my legs. They seem huge. Apparently they're not too bad but I still worry. I've been told there's nothing wrong with it and there isn't really anything to do about it. But I would like to know if there is something.   Leah, 14

My body is what it is. I'm extremely glad

to be me.   Kirsty, 17

There's this one coach at my gym club that puts some of us down, particularly me, saying that I'm fat and overweight, when I know for a fact that I'm not, I'm in a healthy weight range, I eat good food (most of the time) and I exercise regularly.   Vera, 18

I am a skinny girl and I get called stick, paper and anorexia.   Róisín, 13

I feel upset when people comment on my body. It's not theirs so why do they have to say anything?   Freema, 18

I have to say that I get annoyed when girls my age complain about their belly mound – because it's NATURAL for all girls to have it! And I wish we could all stop being so self-conscious of it!
Natalie, 17

I know I'm not fat but I still feel that I am sometimes.
Bonnie, 15

I want to be smaller but my friends say I am perfect.
Sam, 15

How come even though I'm thin I haven't got a fantastic figure?   Simone, 14

Why can't I put on any weight?
Erin, 14

I hate seeing girls in magazines (you know, the ones in bikinis on the front of fashion magazines or FHM). I get fidgety and anxious because I worry that I'm not good enough because I don't look like them. I know my boyfriend loves me but I still have this constant feeling that I have to look like a supermodel. It makes me sick.   Shaz, 17

I don't feel confident about my body – my mother tells me that I'm fat, but I'm only a size 10 (and 180cm tall). I know that I'm not fat, but I still don't have much confidence.   Ally, 16

Whenever I go shopping with mum and I need a size bigger, she always tells me I'm fat. Because I'm a size 14 and I need a 16 sometimes, it makes me feel really awful.

Anna, 14

I think everyone feels that there is something wrong with their body at one time or another.   Maddy, 15

I know I am not fat because people always comment on my thinness, but I want to be skinnier – I think it looks better. People always say how hot models are.   Amanda, 17

What is the right size?

Paige, 15

I have a bit of trouble putting weight on. It does not help me to want to put weight on when girls constantly compliment me on my skinniness.

Lola, 15

Sometimes being abnormal is the normal and being the normal is the abnormal.

Kerry, 17

If somebody says something about my body or appearance I get quite upset. I know in myself that I'm not "fat" but sometimes it hurts to be called that all the same.

Prashanti, 15

My parents, mainly my mum, have been telling me since I was 13 that I should go on a diet despite being in the healthy weight range. It's screwed my thoughts on dealing with being healthy and maintaining a good weight and diet. Sometimes parents don't know what's best.

Callie, 18

I'm not very sure whether I'm overweight or underweight or anything.   Victoria, 16

There's an insane amount of pressure put on girls to be thin, but most of it comes from themselves.

Taylor, 17

Growing out of obsessions

Generally feelings about hating your bits tend to get less as you grow into your body, and as you get older you don't obsess so much. And of course until you stop growing you don't know what your body is finally going to look like anyway.

Most obsessions that result in a girl wanting cosmetic surgery or some other physical treatment are actually cured by non-surgical methods: learning to like yourself the way you are; growing to realize your "flaw" is quirky and attractive, or something that you hardly think about any more. One day soon you'll look back at yourself in a photo and think, "Damn, I looked good, and I didn't even realize it at the time!" Or at least, "That was an awkward stage but it's all turned out fine".

> Just don't take what people think too seriously – they're saying it because they're jealous that they aren't that confident with their own bodies.
>
> *Nikki, 16*

Mirror, mirror, mirror, mirror, mirror… that's enough now

✱ Think about putting any full-length mirror on the inside of a wardrobe door, rather than somewhere in your bedroom where you can stare at yourself all the time.

✱ Have a mirror in the bathroom, but not on your desk.

✱ Avoid magnifying mirrors – they are really quite the evil item. Nobody ever sees you up that close.

✱ Don't spend ages looking into any mirror. You can always find something to worry about if you look long or hard enough.

Take a compliment

When someone pays you a compliment – "You look great", "I love that skirt" or "That haircut really suits you" – smile and say thanks.

Don't say anything negative about yourself or deny the compliment – none of that "Aw, I look terrible", "But what about this gigantic pimple?" or "Shut UP, I so do not look okay".

HOW TO TAKE a COMPLIMENT

More info on body image

www.adiosbarbie.com
Fights stereotypes and has a "feed the supermodel" game.

www.bodypositive.com
A US site about being happy whatever size you are.

www.completelygorgeous.com
Cartoons, hints and games about body image based on my (out-of-print) book *Real Gorgeous*. Good links page.

www.thesite.org/healthandwellbeing/ wellbeing/bodyimageandselfesteem
This site run by the UK charity YouthNet has all sorts of articles about distorted body image, cosmetic surgery, self-esteem and coping with embarrassment.

Body Outlaws: Rewriting the Rules on Beauty and Image **edited by Ophira Edut, Seal Press**
A multicultural collection of personal tales from the US by young women talking about body image and identity (www .bodyoutlaws.com).

The Body Snatchers: How the Media Shapes Women **by Cyndi Tebbel, Finch Publishing**
A book by an ex-women's magazine editor who lost the fight with advertisers who wanted thinner models. She explains the body image pressures.

I wanna lose weight but my friends think I need to gain weight.   Lexie, 13

I think it would be nice to see some normal-sized girls being promoted and I don't mean a feature story on "love your body" or whatever, I mean just spread through everything. The mags say they are about promoting good body image but in reality it's very token.   Ellen, 18

I want to try marijuana but I'm scared I'll get addicted.   Lucy, 14

Hello,
I'm
me

If anything gets too overwhelming I just ask myself, "Will it even matter in five years?" If the answer is "No" I let it go, if "Yes" then I try to figure out a way to solve whatever the problem is.

Michelle, 16

I think it's important to be with friends who will look out for you if you decide to drink or do drugs because if something happens then they will be there.   Anna, 17

HEAD →

PART 2

BRAIN

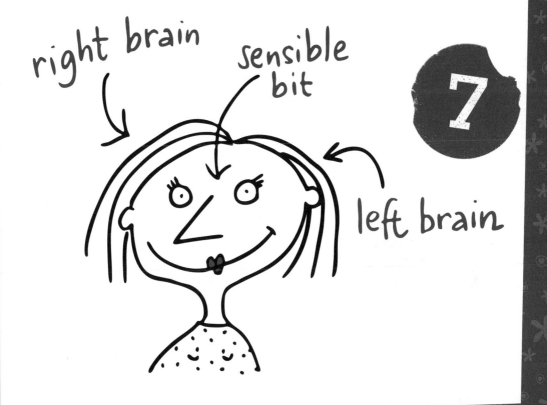

right brain

sensible bit

left brain

7

Brain researchers are perpetually **blowing their own minds** with what they're finding out. Experts used to think that our brains were fully formed by the age of 12, and that they knew everything about how our minds work. Now they know that there's still **lots** to find out. But they do know what can scientifically be defined as "some stuff". And here it is.

What we know about the teenage brain

We know that a teenager's brain is not as fully developed as an adult's. You're more likely to have mood swings, react emotionally, not recognize other people's feelings, and get into an argument with someone who's telling you what to do. When you're a teenager the part of your brain that handles assessing risks, making judgements and decisions, and planning and organizing still needs some work.

The upside of all this is you have a big excuse for doing dumb things: "It's not my fault – my brain's not finished yet".

But if you use that excuse your parents and teachers can say that's why they can't let you make important decisions for yourself: "Until your brain is finished, I can still treat you like a kid".

Hmmm. Let's see if we can get around this.

Use it or lose it

Between 0 and 3 years old your brain does most of its growing. By the time you're 6 your brain is already just about adult size, although the contents aren't finished yet.

Right through childhood and the teenage years your brain is making new connecting pathways so that your ideas, memories and conclusions can bounce around more quickly and efficiently, and work together to help you plan and assess things. So the more you challenge your brain, and the more you have to think about different things, the more your brain needs to keep its pathways open and to make more pathways.

As a teenager your brain is busy spring-cleaning and decluttering to make room for new stuff – destroying any connections it thinks it won't need. (Experts call this "pruning". Ouch.) So brain researchers now have a "use it or lose it" theory: they reckon that if you don't use your brain and you, say, spend all day smoking weed or watching bad TV, it will shut down bits you don't seem to need. In other words, you can make yourself more stupid or you can make yourself smarter.

Guy and girl brains

Guys' brains are likely to be bigger than girls' (by about ten percent), but this doesn't mean guys are smarter than girls. Girls' brains develop more quickly than guys', but that doesn't mean girls are necessarily smarter either – just less likely to take risks.

We're really in the very early stages of understanding the common differences between the male and female brain: we know that boys are more likely to have brain-related conditions such as attention deficit disorders, autism disorders and dyslexia (a brain problem that makes it harder to learn reading and spelling).

Many people believe that, because of their different brains, women are better at understanding and dealing with emotional situations and negotiations, while the typical male brain makes it easier for men to understand systems and how they connect. But of course it also depends on an individual's genes, abilities, personality, skills and education.

What's in your brain

Everyone's brain has a left and a right side to its main part (the cerebrum – pronounced serre-brum). The left hemisphere controls all the movements you make with the right side of your body. The right hemisphere controls your left side.

Here are some of the main brain bits.

- ⑤ **Frontal cortex**   This is your sensible bit. You use it to work out what's important and logical, and to decide and plan. In a teenage brain it's not so well developed yet. It's the frontal cortex that guys are not using when they staple their scrotum to a fence to see what will happen. (They cry.)

- ⑤ **Corpus callosum**   This is a big cable connection of nerves linking the left and right hemispheres. The better the connection the more creative you can be, and the better the solutions you'll think up. If it could light up it would go on like a light bulb when you had an idea.

- ⑤ **Amygdala** (pronounced a-mig-d'lar)   This sits in the middle of your

I may look like I'm staring into space, but I'm pruning my brain...

brain, underneath the corpus callosum, and is the emotional, reactive part that teenagers tend to use more than the logical frontal cortex. It plays a role in risk taking, mood swings, decisions based on sudden "gut reactions", and the difficulty many teenagers have when trying to recognize the emotions of other people. Researchers think girls use the frontal cortex more than guys, who rely more on the amygdala.

☉ **Hippocampus**   This little bit of your brain, right next to the amygdala, is the memory centre – it would light up, if it could, when you smelt coconut sunscreen reminding you of a beach holiday. It's also the bit that your brain rummages through to remember an answer for your science exam.

☉ **Cerebellum** (pronounced serra-bell-um)   This is at the back of your brain above your spine. Scientists used to think it was only used to run your muscles and physical movements, but now they think it also influences how you coordinate your thoughts. It's believed to be not fully developed until your early twenties, meaning that it could be responsible for some scatterbrained teenage thinking.

Is it your fault or your brain's?

So can you blame your teenage brain when you do risky or dumb things? Well, maybe.

But what excuse do adults have when they behave like idiots? And there are lots of adults who tend to panic and dramatize things, always using a gut reaction instead of a logical one.

If you're going to take risks and not think things through, try to:

✱ restrict those times to actions without life-or-death consequences – such as cooking experiments, fights with your family and trying out orange eyeshadow

✱ access your fast-developing frontal cortex when deciding important stuff such as whether to drink alcohol at a party, whether to try a drug and how you're going to get home.

After all, you're not stupid. You're a teenager. There's a very big difference.

Brain chemicals   Brain chemicals zoom about between nerve cells, making lightning-quick electrical connections and helping to control your moods, your body and your actions. The chemicals include:

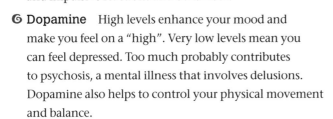

- ⑥ **Serotonin**   The right amount, or a bit extra, of this keeps moods even and helps you to feel calm and able to make judgements, and to go to sleep. If you haven't got enough serotonin, you're more likely to have depression, anxiety and impulsive reactions and behaviour.

- ⑥ **Dopamine**   High levels enhance your mood and make you feel on a "high". Very low levels mean you can feel depressed. Too much probably contributes to psychosis, a mental illness that involves delusions. Dopamine also helps to control your physical movement and balance.

- ⑥ **Endorphins**   These are pumped around your brain during vigorous exercise, childbirth or a trauma – whenever your body needs to override stress or pain and create a kind of high.

Looking after your brain

You've got to look after your brain to make sure you don't end up with the mental powers of a demented guinea pig.

Keep your brain healthy

Luckily there are lots of things you can do to keep your brain healthy.

- ⑥ Eat "brain foods" such as fresh fruit and veggies, fish and other sources of healthy omega 3 fatty acids (oils), and lots of protein (see the Food chapter).

- ⑥ Exercise. Moving yourself about, whether doing organized sport, dancing or whatever, will release your feel-good brain chemicals (see the Move chapter).

- ⑥ Relax. Stress and depression give you brain strain and make it harder for your brain to develop. Get help if you live in a stressful home situation or often feel anxious or scared (see the Feelings chapter).

- ⑥ Get regular sleep (see the sleep info coming up below).

ⓖ Avoid brain injuries. They can sometimes be improved, but not always cured. Wear a helmet if you're doing fast or high-impact sport or riding a bike. Avoid high-risk vehicles: tractors, motorbikes and "quad bikes".

ⓖ Don't let a coach or parent put you back into a game after a head knock or injury: go straight to a doctor.

ⓖ Protect your brain from outside chemicals. The most dangerous time to use alcohol or drugs is while your brain is still developing – that's now (see the Drinking and Drugs chapters).

Protect your Brain

Give your brain plenty of sleep

At this time of your life your body starts making more of a hormone called melatonin, which "sets your body clock", telling you when to be sleepy and when to be awake and alert.

You have more melatonin zapping about your body in the morning than adults and less late at night, which means you're likely to feel awake late at night and tired in the morning, as if you had jet-lag. If you don't get enough sleep you can feel cranky, irritable and a teensy bit dull-witted.

Why you need sleep   Between the ages of about 12 and 18 you are having growth surges, and most of the action happens in your deepest phase of sleep. (Yes, you *can* kind of grow a bit in the night.) If you don't get enough of this deepest phase of sleep you won't achieve your height potential.

If you're sleep deprived you're going to find school and work harder, and are more likely to get depressed and anxious. It also means you might be tempted to use caffeine to stay alert, which makes it even more likely that you won't sleep, setting up a vicious cycle and possibly damaging your health.

Keep your brain exercised

Maybe in the future there'll be a pill or a slot-in brain card to keep us smart. In the meantime keep using your brain for thinking and creating instead of just letting it hang out up there between your ears.

Here are some suggestions for making your brain work better.

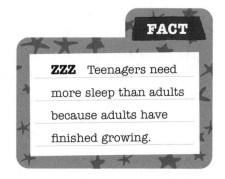

FACT

ZZZ Teenagers need more sleep than adults because adults have finished growing.

⊙ Play memory games, learn an instrument or a language, read books, play chess or card games, do crosswords and other puzzles. Don't play the same games every time.

⊙ Try not to totally specialize in school subjects or hobbies until later in your teens. Do a little bit of lots of things, instead of all science or all swimming. (I can tell you from personal experience that if you don't use the maths pathways in your brain they become overgrown with brambles, like the ones outside Sleeping Beauty's castle. No prince is ever going to come along and teach me what nine times eight is.)

dREAMS are not REAL.
Sometimes we dream in symbols

⊙ Daydream: it's creative, not a waste of time. Think about ways to solve the world's problems – both social and physical. What would you do if you were the ruler of the world/stuck down a pit without a ladder/born with green skin? Make plans for hypothetical events or overseas trips, design your dream home, imagine what you'd do if you were trapped on a deserted island and which five things you'd want to have and why.

Be proud of your brain

Some girls pretend to be stupid, thinking that it will attract guys. It's a shame these girls don't realize that only dumb guys would want dumb girls, and who wants a dumb guy?

FACT

How much sleep is enough? Teenagers need at least nine or even ten hours a night for their brain and the rest of their body to develop properly. That means that if you have to get up at 6am, for sports training or to travel to work or school, you really should be asleep by about 9 at night. And if you have to get up at 7am to do chores, you should be gently snoring by 10pm.

Some ideas to help you in the night-time snooze department

✳ Sorry, I know it's truly appalling, but you should probably have a bedtime to aim for. Record any TV show that's later than that and watch it the next day (without the ads).

✳ Go to bed before you get overtired – people who fall into bed when they're nearly dead on their feet find it the hardest to sleep.

✳ Turn off the TV, screen games, computers and mobile phones ideally at least an hour before bed so you begin to wind down from all that stimulation.

✳ Listen to relaxing music (not thrash metal) in the hour before bed, and turn all music off before you go to sleep.

✳ Do sport, exercise, yoga or dancing often as they will help you to fall asleep easily – but finish at least a couple of hours before bedtime or you'll be too alert.

✳ Try not to eat heavily just before bed or have anything with lots of sugar or caffeine (yes, that means chocolate). And don't drink a huge glass of water, as you'll be getting up too many times to wee.

✳ Try not drinking any coffee, cola, or "energy" or guarana drinks during the day.

✳ Make sure you won't be disturbed by a pet in your room – or trying to get in.

✳ See if your daily schedule needs adjusting – trying to fit in a part-time job with schoolwork, for instance, can make it hard to squeeze in all the hours of sleep you need. When you readjust your daily schedule don't suddenly change your bedtime by an hour: gradually move it by ten or fifteen minutes a day.

✳ Check that your bed is warm enough – being cold can make it hard to fall or stay asleep.

✳ But make sure your bed isn't too hot either – dreams can be weird and intense if you're overheated.

✳ Make your bedroom as dark as you can – any light (a street lamp, an illuminated clock face, a left-on TV or a night-light) tells your brain it's not time to sleep. (But don't turn off a night-light if you get scared in the dark.)

✳ Don't take sleeping tablets: they're not good for the teenage brain, and can make you groggy the next day. Repeated use can result in addiction and liver damage. You shouldn't take sleeping tablets prescribed for anyone else, even a family member.

Can you pay back a "sleep debt"? No. "Sleep binges" only confuse your body clock. Have an extra hour or two of sleep on the weekends if your body wants it, but avoid "marathons".

While you're pretending to be dumb you may really be getting dumber, switching off brain pathways and making it harder to get smart later on when you want a high-paying job or to work out the best way to get that fabulous trip overseas.

Smart people can pretend to be dumb, but dumb people can't really pretend to be smart. Or not for long. Smarter is always going to work better for you, throughout your whole life, no matter what you decide to do. I'm not saying you have to be brilliant at exams and schoolwork. Or a whiz with words, or a physics genius. Some other ways to be clever include being:

- ☾ a practical problem solver
- ☾ good at building and making things
- ☾ creative and artistic
- ☾ able to understand other people and their needs and motives ("emotional intelligence")
- ☾ able to make and stick to a plan to achieve or escape something
- ☾ an observer who learns from watching others
- ☾ good at physical or mental games.

Your brain is one of the cool, positive things about being a teenager. It helps you get better at stuff you love doing, and at understanding what's happening in your life or why somebody behaves the way they do. It can make you feel confident, optimistic and full of energy. Your brain helps you figure out how you can change the world.

You're young and, if you choose to, you can still get smarter and more interesting every day – take that, adults.

Lack of sleep can make you ₹ CRANKY ₹

More info on your brain, and sleep

For chill-out and relaxing music or meditation CDs to listen to before you go to sleep, try big music stores and download sites, which usually have a good range.

www.brainconnection.com
Click on "Library" to browse loads of articles covering how the brain works, development, learning and memory, sleep, adolescent brains, the effects of alcohol and caffeine, and more, or choose "Brain teasers" for a mental workout.

www.pbs.org/wgbh/pages/frontline/shows/teenbrain
A special on the teenage brain from the US Public Broadcasting Service show *Frontline*: interviews, research and diagrams.

www.sleepfoundation.org
US hints for a better night's sleep.

www.vu.edu.au/teenagesleep
Download "Teenage Sleep: Understanding and Helping the Sleep of 12 to 20 Year Olds", an Australian e-book by Professor Dorothy Bruck, for info on individual sleeping patterns, finding it hard to sleep, dreams, what happens when you stay awake too long, how important deep sleep is, and common sleep problems. Includes a blank diary sheet for you to work out your own sleeping habits.

Why the Toast Always Lands Butter Side Down: The Science of Murphy's Law by Richard Robinson, Robinson Publishing
A fun explanation of brains and the senses, and why we make mistakes.

Blame My Brain: The Amazing Teenage Brain Revealed by Nicola Morgan, Walker Books
On teenage brains, why teens take risks, sleep deprivation and more.

everyone's BRAINY at something...

FEELINGS

There are some days when a mood ring on a teenager would be flashing about 273.5 colours for **different moods**, and you'd have to carry around a dictionary-sized textbook to decode every one from awkward but charming, through vivacious but proud, to brave but slightly baffled. Not to mention giggly, creative, clever, annoyed and dying to lie down in a hammock.

A lot of the moods described in this chapter involve **negative thoughts** and feelings because those are the ones you might need help with, such as being worried or embarrassed. But being a teenager usually means lots of great moods too.

Moods

Adults get moody too (especially supermodels and socialites, who throw shoes at their
assistants), but teenagers have a reputation for moodiness because it's a contrast
to the more even, little-kid years (not
counting toddler tantrums).

Reasons for being moody

There are several possible reasons for feeling up and
down and all over the place.

- Your brain hasn't had enough sleep – this can make you cranky.

- The brain's chemicals are out of whack, which can happen during the teenage years. They need to be in balance for you to feel calm and happy.

- Teenage hormones – up and down moods are often blamed on these. For instance, higher oestrogen in girls and women can trigger extra dopamine (that brain chemical that makes people feel happier), but when the oestrogen falls, as part of the monthly cycle, the dopamine does too and they can suddenly feel less happy. High levels of progesterone, just before and during a period, make some girls feel flat, tired, grumpy, tearful or anxious (see PMS in the Change chapter).

- You're thinking too much about your own problems.

- The stressful stuff that can happen when you're a teenager – moodiness can be a logical response to all that.

bewitched...   bothered...   bewildered...

Feeling embarrassed

The level of embarrassment you suffer between the ages of 12 and 18 pretty much goes through the roof. (It's crashed back down to earth by the time you get to old age, when you're quite happy to go shopping wearing a hairnet and socks with sandals, singing show tunes at the top of your voice and hitting annoying people with an umbrella.)

> I worry about embarrassing myself in front of people.
> Emily, 13
>
> I blush.
> Lily, 14

You can be so freaked out wanting to be perfectly normal that falling over, or blurting out something during a silence, can seem sooooo embarrassing you have to move to another country and live in a tree for the rest of your life.

Part of the embarrassment is that during these years you're intensely self-conscious and always super-aware of what you're doing and how you might be seen. Actually nobody else is noticing you as much as you think they are – they're probably too concerned with how everyone else is seeing *them*.

All you can do in the face of hideous humiliation is apologize, if necessary, hold your head high and move on gracefully, then get behind a closed door, cry, think about it 1,647,474 times and get the embarrassment out of your system. You'll remember it long after everyone else has forgotten it (in about ten minutes).

Blushing A common side effect of being embarrassed is blushing. This is because the stress triggers the release of the hormone adrenaline, leading to blood being pumped rapidly to all parts of your body (so that you're ready to run away from a woolly mammoth if necessary). The extra blood close to the surface of your skin makes you look redder. (The adrenaline can also cause you to suddenly sweat more, especially on your palms, and make your mouth go dry.)

I wonder if my head will explode?

Handy recovery lines for an embarrassing situation

"Maybe I'll take my foot out of my mouth."

"This might be a good time to move to Iceland."

"Or I could actually say something far less embarrassing. I'll get back to you on that."

"But now I must go and find my identical twin [*insert your own name here*], who never gets herself into a situation like this."

"Did I just say/do that? I guess I've been possessed by that damned alien again."

"Somebody press rewind."

"Does anyone have a hole in the ground I can get into now?"

Laugh. Blush. Be embarrassed. Then move on.

As well as going red with embarrassment, you can blush because someone has accused you of something (not that blushing is ever proof that a person is "guilty"), or they've given you a fright or even just looked at you. You can also blush when you're angry, self-conscious, nervous or surprised. Most people won't even notice that you blushed, even though you're super-aware of it.

There was a time when I was afraid of walking around the school because I was scared of getting embarrassed – but then I thought I'd try something different. If something embarrassing happened to me that wasn't insulting or anything, just cringe-worthy (eeek!), I would laugh it off. I felt so much better and the next time something embarrassing happened it just came naturally to me and I was admired for it! Now anything can happen to me and I don't feel like I'm going to fall over and die! Of course if the embarrassing thing just isn't funny I tell the person and they usually get the message. Kirsty, 15

Feeling angry

Girls can get the idea that they're not allowed to be angry, that it's not ladylike or it's too disruptive. Not admitting you feel angry, and bottling it all up inside, can lead to more stress and random outbursts that don't seem related to what you're really cross about. (You're angry with your parents but you take it out on your little brother.) If you don't acknowledge your anger and talk about it, it will still be there.

Sometimes, though, teenagers don't realize that what they're experiencing is anger. Writing down your thoughts and feelings can help you recognize your anger. Talking to someone is also a good way to work out what's going on inside you.

It really is okay to be angry, and some of us need help with expressing anger – but also sometimes with managing it.

More info on feeling angry

If you're having trouble with angry feelings, ask your GP about counselling services and anger management courses in your area. See also the info on family abuse in the Savvy chapter.

ChildLine: 0800 1111
If you would like to talk about a parent's or friend's anger, or your own, call this free young person's helpline from anywhere in the UK. See also www.childline.org.uk.

www.youngminds.org.uk/publications/all-publications/feeling-angry
Download this booklet on feeling angry, dealing with anger and getting help from the charity Young Minds.

Sometimes when people say things that hurt you it has nothing to do with you, but how they feel about themselves. Figuring that out helped me brush off nasty comments. Hannah, 17

I find sport the best way to relax and you can let all your anger and frustration out without hurting the people close to you. Layli, 15

Dealing with anger

Try these useful ways to handle anger:

✳ work out the feeling behind the anger – is it a sense of being unfairly treated or ignored, or is it a reaction to seeing a general injustice such as racism?

✳ admit it when you're not sure why you're so angry, and talk about it

✳ talk about how a situation has affected you ("I feel…" or "I had trouble understanding why…" rather than blaming or accusing – "You did this to me" or "It was your fault")

✳ explain that in a discussion you need to have your turn, even with parents

✳ allow yourself to "come down" from the brain chemical high that anger causes, before you make any important decisions

✳ do something really physical – sometimes running, dancing or playing sport can help dissolve angry feelings (see the Move chapter)

✳ think and talk about ways to avoid the situation that caused the anger, and about having a more positive response to the situation if it happens again

✳ ask a calm, sensible friend or relative for advice about how to handle a problem – don't feel you have to tackle everything on your own

✳ take a quiet moment (or even days) to collect your thoughts before trying to resolve a problem with somebody so that you're not confrontational

✳ admit a mistake or say sorry – this makes it easier for others to do the same with you

✳ follow the old saying "Living well is the best revenge", which means that when somebody does the wrong thing by you, get on with enjoying your life instead of brooding or plotting against them.

Try to avoid anger that's only negative, which can make you (and others) feel worse and won't fix anything. Unhelpful responses include:

✳ refusing to speak

✳ breaking or damaging things

✳ shouting or swearing at somebody

✳ ignoring or snubbing somebody

✳ being mean or bullying someone

✳ being constantly sarcastic

✳ damaging yourself (self-harm)

✳ being violent

✳ focusing on "punishing" whoever you're angry with.

Feeling anxiety and stress

Anxiety is the feeling of nervousness, worry, concern or fearfulness about things that might or will happen. In severe cases it can lead to panic attacks, in which you feel terrified or "frozen". Severe anxiety needs to be treated (see the Mind Health chapter).

Stress is the feeling that you can't cope with or control everything you have to do, or live up to your own or other people's expectations. Although stress is more about feeling under pressure, while anxiety is more about being worried, sometimes they feel kind of the same.

As well as these feelings, you can experience physical symptoms with anxiety and stress, which can include a faster than normal heartbeat, sweating, trouble sleeping, and lots of colds and infections because your body's too busy with the anxiety or stress to keep up a healthy immune system. Some girls get headaches, stomach pains or nausea (feeling squirgly, as if you might throw up).

People often go to great lengths to avoid anxiety-making or stressful events, such as facing a bully.

Beating anxiety and stress

Here are some good ways to tackle anxiety or stress:

- ☾ talk about your feeling with mum, dad, friends, your auntie, a doctor or nurse, a friend's mum, a counsellor or teacher, or anyone else you feel comfortable with
- ☾ do some physical activity each day – it can help you be a calmer person
- ☾ drop something (not a priceless vase) – a part-time job, school subject, or one of the three sports you train at each week, or a friend who teases you and causes anxiety
- ☾ distract yourself – instead of staying home all afternoon thinking about your problems, see a movie with friends
- ☾ analyse how you can get out of the stressful or anxious situation, and try to avoid it happening again (What's the worst thing that could happen? Who can help you with that?)
- ☾ read the Confidence chapter

I have a lot of trouble with standing up in front of groups of people, no matter how big or small. I sweat, shake and stutter. My breathing speeds up quite significantly and I have become physically sick on a number of occasions.
Anna, 16

◉ avoid caffeine (in coffee, cola and "energy" drinks) – it tends to make you hyper and more jittery

◉ get more sleep, which will help you cope better with everything

◉ breathe slowly – this is a quick, simple way of calming down. Breathe in for a count of six (or four, or whatever you can manage). Pause, then breathe out for a count of six, if you can. Repeat for a minute or so. Learn yoga to find out more about the deep relaxation possibilities of breathing techniques.

Talking to someone   The girls who answered the Girl Stuff Survey said they find it helpful to talk to people about their worries. Many girls spoke to lots of different people: about two-thirds spoke to their friends, and about a third spoke to both their parents. About a quarter of the girls talked to their mum but not their dad, and a handful of girls only talked to their dad. Other people who girls talked to included sisters, brothers, aunties, uncles, cousins, grandparents and God. Some girls suggested speaking to a psychologist, a school counsellor, a favourite teacher or a doctor; chatting to internet friends, writing a journal or a blog (but be careful about your privacy); and telling a pet.

Sadly, nearly one in ten girls said they didn't talk to anybody about their worries. Whatever you do, pick somebody to talk to.

it HeLps to talk aBout woRRies

CHANGE. It's the one thing that scares me. Change always seems to take over and make

people and life different and sometimes more difficult. Amelia, 16

What girls worry about

Here are some of the things that the girls in the Girl Stuff Survey said they worried about:

boys, love, friendship, grades, the usual stuff ✱ whether my mum, who got breast cancer last year, will die ✱ exams ✱ **change, and hurting myself** ✱ money shortage and my family ✱ whether it's going to rain on my school shoes 'cause then my socks will get wet and I will have to walk home in soggy socks ✱ being attacked by random people in the street; animals that are kept in tiny cages; our family not having enough money ✱ **I'll never be healthy** ✱ people and friends seeing me as a slut or a skank or thinking that I try to be popular ✱ now I am 15 I am seen as an adult and I feel as if my childhood is over ✱ my friends, my appearance, school, what others think of me – so much stuff ✱ I might get pregnant at the age of 15 ✱ what's going to happen to me at school today – am I going to fall over in front of everyone or do something embarrassing? – and my brothers because they both do drugs ✱ **my mum drinking too much** ✱ my school leavers' ball ✱ everything (catching the train, going to parties) – there's just so much to worry about, and I worry about forgetting something important I should be worrying about ✱ Am I pretty enough? Am I fat? Why am I different to everyone else? Is my family wealthy enough? Do I have cool enough clothes and are they expensive? ✱ my father killing me and my mother ✱ my grades and assignments; disappointing people; having fights with friends; ending up alone; SPIDERS; people not taking me seriously so I look like an idiot; people not liking me ✱ nothing much ✱ what I'll get for my birthday/Xmas/Easter/any present occasion ✱ global warming; money and my parents running out of it coz of me ✱ my parents finding out interesting facts about me that they didn't know! ✱ **I don't get over 95 percent in my tests** ✱ BAD HAIR DAYS ✱ what's going to happen to this country – I have already seen a huge increase of racism just in my school ✱ everyone else liking the same bands as me, and that my acne won't go away ✱ death, my stomach (it could be flatter I think – but it's okay, I guess) ✱ going somewhere new because I fear that I will not be accepted ✱ just about everything, but I pretend I don't really care about anything ✱ falling for someone hard and them never having the same feeling back ✱ my parents – I know they are both depressed, have money issues and will probably get divorced soon ✱ mum finding out all the naughty things I've done ✱ boys, clothes, and that huge zit that always pops up before a big night out ✱ **Mum finding out about my boyfriend** ✱ my bizarre-looking toes; the amount of time it takes to straighten my hair ✱ my son's father, because I'm scared he will want to take him away, and whether my baby will be okay when he's born, and if I will be able to take care of him properly ✱ pimples.

More info on feeling anxiety and stress

Your GP can refer you to a counsellor experienced in techniques for avoiding anxiety and stress. Or you can contact Childline (0800 1111; www.childline.org.uk) or the Samaritans (08457 90 90 90; www.samaritans.org.uk) if you'd just like to talk to someone.

www.thesite.org
This charity website covers all the issues that often cause teenagers stress and anxiety, from exams, school and work to health, family and relationships. Search for "Stress" or "Anxiety" for more info.

Too Stressed to Think: A Teen Guide to Staying Sane When Life Makes You Crazy by Annie Fox, Free Spirit Publishing
The author also has a US website to answer questions from girls about their feelings, at www.heyterra.com.

Feeling down

"Feeling down" covers different emotions such as grief, sadness and depression.

Normal grief reactions

Grief is the word used for the intense feelings caused by a severe emotional loss, such as a death; a family or relationship break-up; the upheaval and separation resulting from war or another trauma; the departure of somebody; or a life-changing illness.

Different people grieve in different ways – even those in the same family or group who lose someone they all love.

Ten things to avoid when you feel down

1. Thrash-trash-death-puke metal or country music.

2. Eating 56 Kit Kats.

3. Tragic movies that make you cry so much that snot comes out.

4. The news.

5. Staring at yourself in the mirror.

6. Wearing clothes that are the wrong size.

7. Deliberately avoiding sleep.

8. Documentaries in which animals eat each other's head off.

9. Asking someone if your bum looks big in whatever you're wearing.

10. Cutting or dyeing your own hair.

The swirling feelings of grief can include lots of responses.

- **Crying**   "Every time I think about our old life I start crying", "I haven't been able to stop crying since dad left."
- **Denial**   "She didn't really die. She'll walk in the door tonight."
- **Questioning** (to make sense of the loss)   "Why did this happen?", "Why us?"
- **Anxiety**   "How will I cope?", "What's the right thing to do?", "What's the best way to behave?"
- **Self-blame**   "If only I hadn't said/done that, maybe mum and dad would have stayed together."
- **Anger and frustration**   "How could you leave me to cope by myself?", "You've never lost anyone so how could you possibly understand what it's like?"
- **Loneliness**   "I'm the only one who really understands how this feels to me."
- **Depression and loss of interest in life**   "I'm not getting up and going to school today", "Whatever. I don't care what we do."
- **Sadness**   "I wish my mum was here for my birthday party", "I don't think I'll ever see my homeland again."

As well as these reactions, many grieving people experience physical symptoms, including headaches, an upset stomach, tiredness, trouble sleeping or sleeping too much.

In the early stages of grief it's totally okay just to think about what to do in the next hour, or the next day. You don't have to sort out everything right away, or even soon. Everyone who grieves needs some help and other people to talk to. Taking each day as it comes, one step at a time, and getting help is a good way to move forward.

You just hit "one of those days" and you're down for no apparent reason.   Danielle, 17

I'm sad when I am tired.   Lisa, 18

Nobody should expect you just to "get over it". You need time to grieve properly, and you then need find a way to take your sadness with you into the next phase of your life where you can feel more positive, without having to forget someone or pretend an important event never happened.

Sadness

Grief is an extreme, not an everyday, emotional experience, whereas sadness can be a less intense feeling that you might have quite often, about many things.

Depression

Like sadness, depression isn't only experienced in times of grief. "Being a bit depressed" usually means a temporary mood: feeling rather flat after a big excitement has ended, being "blue" for a couple of days, or having "a good cry" here and there after something rather sad happens. It's part of everyday life.

Clinical, or major, depression is different: it's a constant crushing feeling of blankness, nothingness and hopelessness that seems as if it will never, ever lift – there's more on this in the Mind Health chapter later in the book.

More info on grief and loss

www.rd4u.org.uk
This charity site is for young people who have suffered a death in the family or among their friends, and it's put together by young people who've been through it. Their helpline is only open on weekdays during work hours, on **0808 808 1677**, but you can also read their helpful info, join online forums or ask a private question by email.

www.suicidegrief.com
To chat with people who have had the same experience, if you have lost somebody through suicide.

www.winstonswish.org.uk
Charity for young people who have lost loved ones; includes info, FAQs and a forum where you can talk to other teens in the same boat.

Motherless Daughters: The Legacy of Loss by Hope Edelman, Da Capo Press
A book about living without your mum: the feelings and practical things.

www.riprap.org.uk
A site for young people whose parents have cancer; has real-life stories and info about cancer, and offers support and advice.

Give yourself a reality check when you feel one comment or incident wearing you down. Mentally list ten things that make you special, beautiful, desirable, different.   Chloe, 17

Don't say "It's too hard, nobody can help me, I'll be like this forever". Try this: "It will get better, and I can help myself." Because as soon as you can admit to yourself you're on the way up, people can help again.   Katie, 17

Feeling optimistic and strong

Almost everyone goes through bad patches, experiences moody phases and has times when they feel down. Some have the ability to "bounce back" quickly. They're optimistic: they expect that things will, or are likely to, turn out well. If that's not you, you'll be relieved to hear that you don't have to be born with optimism – you can learn it. You can also learn resilience: the buzz word that means you are strong; a survivor who can face hard times and come through it all okay; the sort of person who can take a disappointment, instead of going off to brood for days or weeks.

Sometimes I'll sit in front of my mirror and I play my iPod and just sing some of my favourite songs, and because a lot of the songs are meaningful, something about them just makes me feel beautiful and loved.
Chelsey, 15

You can *learn* not to let the pain of a rejection stop you from making new friends. You can aim to be a girl who doesn't take crap from anyone, the kind of girl who, when "one door closes" in their face, will kick down a few more. Or at least think about knocking politely.

Getting strong

Here are some ways to get strong.

- Ⓖ Like yourself. If you try to be a good person who isn't mean and nasty, then you can feel good about yourself. When a bad thing happens you'll know it's not your fault.

- Ⓖ Have a support team. It could be family or friends or both. Being part of a team, club or neighbourhood helps.

- Ⓖ Have a list of people, activities, DVDs, books and music that cheer you up.

- Ⓖ Think about great times you've had. Think about bad times you went through that got better.

- Ⓖ Recognize that sometimes things don't get better by themselves – you may have to take action or ask for help. Sometimes you have to persevere before things improve.

- Ⓖ Face fears and hard times because they do have a positive side. You'll be more experienced at solving problems, feel braver, perhaps get to know yourself and your limits, and be better prepared for other obstacles in your life.

Happy, happy happy!

Ten things to help you cheer up

1. Laughing – with friends, at a movie or a show. If necessary, have a water or pillow fight.

2. Fresh air and light – proven mood lifters.

3. Affirmations: use a diary, sticky notes, posters or your own thoughts to remind yourself of your good points and the things you enjoy or want to achieve.

4. Exploring your creative side – express your feelings in writing, drawing, music, performance, cookery.

5. Having things to look forward to. Check your schedule this week: is there any time for fun? If not, start to schedule it for coming weeks.

6. Taking time out – try to get some time all to yourself. Just lie there in silence or listen to some soft music.

7. Doing "good works". This could include helping to look after an animal, or volunteering some time or money to a charity (see the Caring chapter).

8. Telling someone you love them – and doing them a favour.

9. Having a big clean-out of your room: chuck out stuff you don't want that's cluttering your space, rearrange things the way you want them and start afresh. If it's too big to tackle all at once, do one bookshelf or one wall at a time.

10. You choose. Some people want to spend every spare moment with other people, liking to be "kept company", but others prefer to have some time on their own.

- Try to be realistic. Instead of saying "Nothing will ever change", set an achievable goal.
- Don't be a catastrophiser – that's a person who turns the smallest problem into a catastrophe by panicking, shouting, being a drama queen or complaining to everyone. Save your energy to deal with real problems.
- Stand your ground on fixing the big things, even if they're not big to someone else.
- Even while you are dealing with a problem, make sure you have breakfast and two other good meals a day, and that you keep up your general grooming (no need for elaborate hairstyles with a tiara, but don't stop showering for a week).
- Check just in case there's a funny side to the problem you're dealing with.

One of my friends is a cricket coach and says that when a guy misses a catch he'll usually blame the state of the ground, the sun in his eyes, or even that "my pants are too tight", but then he'll try harder for the next catch: "I'm gonna get this one!" My friend finds it frustrating that when most girls miss a catch they blame themselves – "I'm hopeless at this", "I never catch anything" – and don't try as hard the next time, leading to even more dropped catches and an even more pessimistic attitude.

Girls often focus on their weaknesses, the bits of themselves that "need work" or "could be better". How about your strengths? Can you make a list in your head, or on paper, of your good points? If not, you either need to think harder or to cultivate some (see the Confidence chapter for hints).

More info on feeling optimistic and strong

See also "More info on self-confidence" in the Confidence chapter.

www.centreforconfidence.co.uk
Choose "Positive psychology resources" and then use the menu to get all sorts of info about happiness, optimism, resilience, motivation and confidence from the Scotland-based Centre for Confidence and Well-being.

A for Attitude by Julie Davey,
Times Editions
A little book of bite-sized positive mottos and "inspiration and encouragement".

Don't Sweat the Small Stuff for Teens by Richard Carlson, Hodder & Stoughton
Self-help advice on simple ways to keep your cool in stressful times.

Positive Thinking (Essential Lifeskills) by Susan Quilliam, Dorling Kindersley
Agony aunt and psychologist Susan Quilliam gives simple tips and practical advice on how to have a more positive, confident and happy life.

If my sister and me bake cookies together I forget my problems and have fun.   Sara, 13

9 DRINKING

Some people have this image of a whole generation of wasted girls rolling about in their own wee on the floor of the nearest house where the parents are out, or performing upside-down sex acts, hanging from a light fitting by their underpants, after knocking back a six-pack of ready-to-drink fizzy, raspberry-flavoured vodka, and throwing up in hot pink. The **truth** is a little more complicated.

Most teenagers drink at some stage. A lot of teenagers will have a drink or two but don't get drunk because they **don't like** the out-of-control feeling. Some can get drunk a couple of times and then stop. Others will drink every day, hurting their brain and their body. Many girls "binge drink". Some teenagers develop a psychological dependency on, or a physical addiction to, alcohol (doctors can use either word to describe someone who **can't** or won't stop drinking). Some teenagers aren't interested in drinking at all.

Things you need to know about alcohol before drinking

Alcohol, like other drugs, uses natural or manufactured chemicals to cause a mind-altering effect (see also the Drugs chapter, next). It affects the body too. Selling alcohol is big business, and the drink companies are very sophisticated these days so their products generally taste better than rancid turnips mixed with paint. (Good marketing move.)

Alcohol is a legal drug – but not because it's necessarily safer than other kinds of drugs. The companies that make alcohol are immensely rich and very powerful and can influence governments on the rules. The alcohol industry in the UK is worth tens of billions of pounds a year, so the national government makes billions from it in taxes. Those taxes help pay for the cost of some of the health and social problems caused by alcohol abuse.

What alcohol is

Alcohol is the liquid that results from controlling the way chemically treated fruit or vegetables go mouldy (ferment) over time.

> People say they get drunk all the time but sometimes I think they're just showing off.
> Lizzie, 14

> Half of my friends have, half haven't drunk alcohol.
> Jessica, 14

Alcohol percentages   The average percentage of alcohol in different drinks is:

- ⓖ beer or lager (made from fermented grain) – 4 to 6 percent
- ⓖ cider (made from fermented apple juice) – 4 to 6 percent
- ⓖ low-alcohol beer, lager or cider (but only if it is low-alcohol; "light" and "lite" can mean low-calorie or light in appearance or taste, not necessarily low-alcohol) – 2 percent
- ⓖ super-strength beer, lager or cider – 9 percent
- ⓖ alcopops or "designer drinks" (flavoured alcoholic drinks that taste like soft drinks) – 4 to 6 percent
- ⓖ wine (made from fermented grapes, and includes red, white and sparkling) – 10 to 14 percent
- ⓖ fortified wine (heavy, more concentrated wine; for example, port and sherry) – 17.5 to 20 percent
- ⓖ spirits (concentrated, distilled alcohol; for example, whisky, vodka, gin and rum) – 38 to 40 percent
- ⓖ liqueurs (highly flavoured, extra-concentrated spirits; for example, whisky and cream, or brandy and coconut) – from about 15 to 60 percent or more

❻ cocktails (a mix of one or more spirits with flavourings, liqueurs and sometimes fruit juice) – about 40 percent.

How alcohol affects the body

When you have a drink the alcohol is taken very quickly into your bloodstream from your stomach. Within an hour nearly all of it has been absorbed by your body (which is why you're still drunk even if you throw up).

Alcohol travels all around the body but a lot of it hangs about in the brain, liver and kidneys. The liver and kidneys try to process it and get the waste elements out of the body.

Teenagers have smaller livers than adults so they get drunk quicker on the same amount of alcohol and process it more slowly. It's now thought that a teenager only needs to drink half as much alcohol as an adult for it to have the same effect. Yet teenagers take longer than adults to become sleepy or clumsy when they're getting drunk, so they may not recognize the early warning signs.

Alcohol is a depressant, not a stimulant – in other words it's more of a downer than an upper. It affects people differently: it's impossible to say exactly how much will be a danger to an individual.

Oddly, given it's a liquid, alcohol causes your body to dehydrate. This can become a life-threatening problem in extreme cases.

> My mum lets me drink, as do most of my friends' parents. The only rule is that I have to drink only what she buys me. However, that doesn't usually happen.
> Annabelle, 16

> Hangovers suck.
> Alison, 15

no, really I'm fine..

FACT

The legal age for drinking   The legal age for buying alcohol or drinking it in a pub or other public place in the UK is 18. It's not illegal for you to drink before then (but that doesn't mean it's a good idea to start early and go hard). If you're 16 or 17 you can drink beer, wine or cider with a meal in a restaurant, but only if you're accompanied by an adult.

How much alcohol is in one unit?

In the UK, the alcohol content of a drink is measured in "units". One unit is surprisingly small: it contains 10ml or 8g of pure alcohol. Almost all glasses of wine or champagne poured at home or in a pub, all alcopops and all average cans of beer have more than one unit in them.

The list below shows how many units are in some "standard" drinks – everyone gets a surprise at how little makes a single unit for the different alcoholic beverages. Binge drinking for adult women is sometimes described as having six units or more in any one day – that's two large glasses of wine, two pints of beer or one strong cocktail.

the number of units in a drink can vary A LOT...

The number of units in average-strength drinks are:

* one standard glass of wine (175ml) – 1.75 to 2.5 units

* one large glass of wine, poured as standard in some pubs (250ml) – 2.5 to 3.5 units

* one measure or shot of vodka, whisky or another spirit (25ml) – 1 unit

* one "double" vodka, whisky or another spirit (50ml) – 2 units

* one small, individual-sized bottle of an alcopop or flavoured "designer drink" (275ml) – 1.4 units

* one bottle of normal-strength beer, lager or cider (330ml) – 1.3 to 2 units

* one can of normal-strength beer, lager or cider (440ml) – 1.8 to 2.6 units

* one pint of normal-strength beer, lager or cider – 2.3 to 3.4 units

* one standard measure of sherry or port (50ml) – 1 unit

* 1 average-sized pub or party cocktail, depending on specific ingredients and number of shots added – 4 to 5 units, or more.

cocktail= 4 or 5 units, maybe!

How alcohol affects the teenage brain

Research has revealed that alcohol works more quickly and has more effect on a teenage brain than an adult one, because it's still developing up to the age of 20 and beyond (see the Brain chapter). And when a teenager is really pissed, the alcohol probably does more damage to the areas of the brain that controls vocabulary, memory, judgement and the ability to learn things.

New research shows that a teenager is far more likely than an adult to develop a dependence on alcohol.

> I often can't remember the night before, and for a while I didn't know if I was a virgin.
> Stella, 16

> I once drank champagne by myself, without eating much before. I have never thrown up so much in my life.
> Alana, 18

The right age Many experts say that the more they find out about alcohol's effect on a developing brain, the more they think teenagers shouldn't drink any alcohol at all until the age of 18 or even later, and that they should try not to get drunk before their brain has finished developing, say, after 20.

That's probably pretty unlikely to happen, so what they say is: don't start drinking until you're at least 16, and then try not to get drunk. The most important thing is not to binge drink (drink to get drunk), which definitely risks damaging your brain.

Why girls tend to be more affected by alcohol than they planned

Girls tend to be more easily affected by alcohol than they planned to be for heaps of reasons, which are to do partly with their bodies and partly with the way they drink.

- ☉ Girls naturally have more body fat and smaller livers than guys, and this means that they almost always get drunker on the same or a smaller amount of alcohol than guys. The more body fat percentage you have, the more susceptible you are to alcohol. But even if you're a thin girl you still have a different percentage of body fat from guys and a smaller liver. The simple fact is that if you're female your body processes alcohol at a different rate.

- ☉ Teenage girls can soon get beyond the low-risk level of alcohol without realizing it (see the "What's the right amount?" box opposite).

- ☉ In some groups girls tend to have drinks with higher percentages of alcohol, like wine, spirits and alcopops, while guys tend to drink beer. If you're drinking vodka mixed with a fizzy drink and you're not measuring your units, you could be having two or three drinks to his every one – which means that, being female, you're going to be four or five times drunker than he is. (Not a good look.)

What's the right amount?

There is no recommended amount of alcohol for teenagers.

Because it's not known what the safe level is for a brain that is still developing, it's never going to be recommended that you drink early, often or a lot.

"Officially" adult women should have no more than two or three units a day, and no more than fourteen units a week. Having more alcohol than that is dangerous, and six or more units in one day is considered to be even more dangerous "binge" drinking. Female bodies are not supposed to have alcohol every day – you need several alcohol-free days a week, even as an adult.

Experts now believe that this recommendation for adult women should be halved for teenage girls – but they still won't recommend that because they believe teens shouldn't have any alcohol at all.

If we take that halved figure for teenage girls it means the most you should ever drink in a day – taking more than two hours to drink it – is only one or perhaps one and a half units. That's only about half a glass of wine.

There's no recommended safe level of drinks during pregnancy so girls and women are advised to stay off it completely through pregnancy and until they've finished breastfeeding.

- ☻ If they are drinking bottled or boxed wine girls often have their glass refilled before it's empty – this makes it harder for them to keep track of how many units they've had.

- ☻ Bubbly alcoholic drinks affect people quicker than "flat" ones because the high oxygen content takes the alcohol to the brain faster. This is risky for girls, who often choose "bubbly" not realizing they'll get horribly drunk quickly.

- ☻ Most wine and champagne glasses hold much more than a standard drink. Each glass of wine could actually be three or more units, not one or two.

- ☻ Because many alcopops and premixed drinks are sweet, girls drink them faster.

Other reasons girls get drunk quicker than they meant to are:

- ☻ cocktails look pretty, but because one cocktail can have up to four or even five units in the one glass they are way, way over the safe limit

- ⑥ many more alcohol ads are now aimed at young women
- ⑥ once anyone has a couple of drinks they start to lose their judgement, so they're more likely to keep drinking
- ⑥ some girls drink a lot, quickly, because they want to get "out of it"
- ⑥ teenage girls often haven't experienced the different factors that can affect how drunk they get; drinking on an empty stomach, drinking quickly without leaving time between drinks, and not alternating alcohol and water – all these things can greatly increase the effects of alcohol
- ⑥ some girls under the legal pub or club drinking age drink in parks, on quiet streets, or at someone's house when the parents are out or don't care what their kids are doing. This means there's often no experienced person around to say, "I think you've had enough".

> **FACT**
>
> **Alcohol and a healthy weight**
>
> Alcohol is high in sugar so people who drink a lot often put on unwanted weight, as well as having other health problems.

More info **on alcohol**

www.truthaboutbooze.com
The Drinkaware Trust's teen site covers the law, the effects of alcohol, young people's stories, useful links and FAQs.

www.thesite.org
YouthNet's site on the key issues affecting young people. Choose "Drink & drugs" for info on responsible drinking, hangovers, binge drinking and alcohol problems.

www.knowyourlimits.org.uk
Government campaign site which has real-life stories, as well as lots of info on staying safe on a night out.

www.units.nhs.uk
This NHS website has info on the number of units in various drinks, how alcohol affects health, cutting down and alcohol in pregnancy, plus a drinks diary, FAQs, alcohol myths and a drinking quiz.

A few friends have had their stomachs pumped and I've been arrested for over-intoxication and possible harm or damage to myself and others. Jen, 17

My best friend had a massive go at me when she was drunk. We didn't talk for two months after as I was so hurt. We are back on track now, I think. Kim, 16

My friend's dad tried to crack onto me while I was drunk. And my friend spewed on me once. Natalie, 16

I enjoy getting drunk. It's my choice and any "consequences" I can deal with. Farah, 15

I absolutely hate alcohol and can't even bear the smell so I don't go near the stuff – not even at parties! Emily, 15

I think it's sad to watch all the smart people I know slowly be dumbed down by alcohol and drugs. As far as I can see they're spending all their money so they can act like arseholes, throw up a lot and then have a really bad headache. Wow. Top night out. Maddison, 17

Guys blackmailed me by sending photos of me drinking and snogging a friend to my parents. Kelly, 17

My friends get happy and start dancing and then they just fall asleep. Jodie, 13

I used to have a group of friends but now I don't like hanging out with them. They are too shallow and immature. All they do is go to parties and drink. I'd rather do my own thing now.
Tess, 17

I usually have really good experiences when I'm drunk cos I get really happy and fun. A friend always gets depressed, and finds something to talk about, and the majority of my friends act like hussies and blame it on the alcohol the next day. Sarah, 17

My friend was an alcoholic when she was 11, but she got help. Lisa, 13

I got very drunk and ended up getting very sick at the end of the night. I felt horrible and had the worst hangover the next day. I was yelling things at people and flashing older disgusting guys… Leyla, 14

Deciding whether or not to drink

A large percentage of teenagers don't drink.

Before you have a drink, ask yourself why you want it. Here are some common reasons – not necessarily good ones – that teenagers give for drinking: they think it will make them more grown up; to help them relax; because they're allowed to drink; because they're not allowed to; everyone else is drinking; someone just gives them a drink so they have it; they don't know how to have fun without a drink; they think you have to drink on every possible occasion; they want to "wipe out" their feelings temporarily; they have a dependency problem – any teenager who drinks every day, or gets drunk every week, has a serious alcohol problem, whether or not they admit it (there's more on this later).

QUOTE

"One reason I don't drink is that I want to know when I am having a good time."

Lady Astor

A sneaky strategy for not drinking

If you're going somewhere and feel worried you'll get hassled about not drinking, or that you'll lose control, here's a trick to try:

✻ get your parents or another adult to buy you a couple of mixed alcoholic drinks in screw-top bottles

✻ carefully unscrew the tops

✻ pour out the contents and replace them with lemonade, flavoured mineral water or cordial (whatever looks the same as the original)

✻ screw the tops on again

✻ take the bottles with you as your "personal drinks".

non-alcoholic

Things to say when you're not drinking (even if you're fibbing)

going to THROW up...

"No thanks."

"I don't feel like it tonight."

"I'm not feeling too good."

"I'm allergic to the preservatives in alcohol."

"One's/two's my limit."

"I'd rather have water, thanks."

"My parents are picking me up."

"I don't like being drunk."

"I can't – I promised my friends I'd stay sober to keep an eye on them."

"That's not my drink, thanks."

"Yuk, sorry, but I hate the taste of those."

"I usually like to stop before I fall over and wee my pants."

"I'm taking it slow tonight."

"I like a water in between."

"Not for me, thanks."

"No more for me, thanks."

"I've had enough."

"I have this test/game/family thing early tomorrow morning."

"My mum is going to call me soon."

"Maybe later."

"I like to know what language I'm speaking in."

"I have to call my dad every hour and let him know where I am."

"I'm not in the mood."

"I'm off it at the moment."

"I need to have a blood test tomorrow and I don't think they like it when it's half vodka."

"I'm not drinking tonight/this week."

"I had a few before I came."

"Not unless you want me to be sick all down your front."

"I hate throwing up on my hair and I haven't got a scrunchie."

Being drunk

Roughly speaking, drunkenness follows certain stages, although not everyone gets drunk in the same order after the same number of drinks, or continues until they pass out.

Stages of drunkenness

If you keep drinking, the stages go more or less in this order.

Up to and past the legal driving limit of 0.08 percent blood alcohol

- ⑥ You feel good – warm, relaxed, confident, friendly, chattier and less inhibited than normal.
- ⑥ You have less judgement and control, and your mental and physical reflexes are slower – you're clumsier.
- ⑥ You may not be noticing any of these changes.

All of the above only more so

- ⑥ You have emotional swings, possibly becoming affectionate or aggressive: "I love you", "Shut up".
- ⑥ You lose judgement about what's a risky behaviour or a dumb idea ("Why don't I photograph my breasts and email the picture to my ex! Wheee!").
- ⑥ You're excitable and loud.
- ⑥ You don't listen and you keep repeating yourself.
- ⑥ You're having a real problem with balance.

Body and brain really not working properly

- ⑥ You're confused and sleepy.
- ⑥ You're dizzy and staggering, and your speech is slurred.

- ⑤ You're having very big emotional swings or extremes – you're sloppily affectionate or more aggressive or violent – and no one can reason with you.
- ⑤ You're not seeing straight – your sight is blurred.
- ⑤ You can hurt yourself and not notice the pain.

Horribly drunk

- ⑤ You can't manage the simplest physical tasks, such as getting a key in the door or walking.
- ⑤ You don't respond to pain, prodding or voices.
- ⑤ You could be vomiting, weeing or pooing.
- ⑤ You fall asleep or become unconscious.

Unconsciousness

- ⑤ Your body temperature and blood circulation are lowered and your breathing is repressed.
- ⑤ You vomit, wee and poo without knowing it.
- ⑤ You could progress to coma and, if you'd drunk a really stupid amount, even death.

> One of my friends went home drunk and then threw up on her dad at their front door.
> Bobbie, 14

> I'll never forget when I drank so much wine I threw up all over my best mate's house, IN FRONT OF MY CRUSH, and then passed out.
> Tori, 15

The risks of being drunk or being where others are drunk

Sometimes you don't even have to be horribly drunk for something bad to happen, such as an accident, but you increase the risk by being drunk or being with drunk people. Alcohol is also involved in most of the drug-related deaths of young people.

An average-sized 16-year-old who drinks solidly (one drink after another) could damage herself very seriously within an hour.

People who are drunk take more risks. You're more likely to do or say something that you don't mean, or that you'll regret, or that will be an embarrassment. You are also more likely to be assaulted, or otherwise in danger.

Unwanted sex   Drunk girls are vulnerable to sexual experiences they don't choose or fully agree to. (They are also less likely to use contraception or to make sure the guy uses a condom as protection against sexually transmitted infections.)

My friend got drunk at a party and passed out in a bed and was raped. I'm the only one she's told but she still drinks.
Jo, 14

Many girls do things (or have things done to them) that they don't want and would never do when sober and safe. Many regret that their first sexual experiences were drunken encounters that they can barely remember, with people they didn't really like or who didn't respect them.

In the answers to the Girl Stuff Survey a lot of girls aged 13 to 18 said that they or a friend had been raped when they were drunk – often by somebody they knew. It might have been that there was no hitting but force was used, or the girls were not capable of stopping the guy even though they didn't want to have sex.

Cars   Alcohol is involved in many, if not most, serious car accidents. It's safest not to drink *any* alcohol if you need to drive a car because it's hard to guess your own blood alcohol level. Police can test your breath or blood at any time.

If you are over the legal limit (0.08 percent, or 80mg of alcohol per 100ml of blood) that result will be used against you in court. Penalties include heavy fines, losing your licence and jail.

Getting in a car with a drunk driver, or a driver who has been drinking, increases your chances of injury or death by a huge margin. It doesn't matter if a driver says they are not drunk or if they don't seem drunk. If they have been drinking, don't get in the car. Call an adult who has agreed to come and pick you up no matter what time it is (see the "Your emergency contacts" box in the Savvy chapter).

Drink spiking   Some people at pubs, clubs or parties have had drugs (or extra alcohol) added to their drinks, which make them woozy or even unconscious, and they have then been taken elsewhere and assaulted or raped. Although this is rare, it's a good idea never to let your drink out of your sight and never to accept a drink from someone you don't know and trust. Some girls who think their drink was spiked have probably underestimated how quickly and severely they got completely "out of it" on the alcohol alone.

you're more likely to accidentally get too drunk than have your drink spiked...

Drowning Many drownings, whether at the beach or in a pool, lake or river, involve alcohol. If people are drinking don't let them go into the water, especially at night. (Guys in particular tend to want to do this.)

Violence The more alcohol drunk, and the more guys present (especially ones who don't know each other), the greater the risk of violence at a party, festival or other event, or on a camping weekend or holiday. Added elements may be previous tension and hot or humid weather.

> If you're drinking at a party make sure you know where your friends are and that you look out for one another.
> Jacqui, 13
>
> I was lucky not to have any real damage done.
> Maeve, 17

Drunk people

Sometimes things can go very wrong when people are drinking. If you can see a potential problem, or at the first sign of ugliness – big talk, threats, pushing, shoving, someone leaving and threatening to get revenge (and perhaps returning with reinforcements), rumours of lots of gatecrashers – leave, and take your friends with you. What seems exciting and dramatic in theory is actually nasty and terrifying in real life.

Coping with a drunk person The first rule is to keep yourself safe. If doing any of the following – or any of the actions outlined in the "When to call an ambulance" box – means that you are at risk of injury yourself, then your first priority is to keep clear and call for help from somewhere else.

If the drunk person is conscious but very drunk and out of control:

- 🟢 don't leave them behind or alone, or believe them when they say they'll be fine or can get home on their own
- 🟢 take them to a safe place where there is no alcohol available (home, for example) or take all alcohol out of their reach (basically, remove them from the party or remove the party from them)

> **FACT**
>
> **Why does alcohol make you throw up?** Your body recognizes an excess of alcohol as poison and tries to get rid of it by throwing up, weeing a lot, sweating, having diarrhoea, or all four (for an extra-classy bonus).

When to call an ambulance

Call 999 and ask for an ambulance if the person has:

�֍ not responded to you trying to wake them up by nudging or pinching them a few times and shouting at them (but not shaking, punching or kicking them)

✶ blue lips or face

✶ eyes rolling back into their head

✶ foam on their lips

✶ stopped breathing

✶ anything else that doesn't seem normal and is scaring you.

Waiting for the ambulance

If the person is lying down and has vomited or is vomiting, or is unconscious, make sure you quickly clear any vomit out of their mouth and throat with your fingers and move them onto their side so they don't choke to death. Put them in a safe place; for example, off the road.

✶ Don't leave the person alone. They could wander off later, or otherwise put themselves in danger.

✶ Keep watching the person until the ambulance arrives, unless you are in danger, and ask an adult or a sensible person who hasn't been drinking to help you.

✶ Ask if anybody knows what the person has been drinking and any details about what drugs they may have taken, whether legal or illegal (what, when, how much or how many), so you can tell the paramedics (ambulance medical staff). They will need to know what has been drunk or taken so that they can save the person's life – they're *not* interested in telling anybody's parents or the police. Treatment varies according to the kinds of drugs or alcohol, and the quantities.

Ⓖ don't try to reason with them – if necessary lie and tell them you are taking them to a place where they can get another drink

Ⓖ if you feel you can't control the situation, find a responsible person who has not been drinking or call your emergency person to come and get you

Ⓖ before you leave the drunk person at the safe place to "sleep it off", make sure they're only asleep and can be roused, not unconscious.

FACT

Hospitalization   Most people who are badly poisoned by alcohol need to be put on an intravenous drip, with vitamins and minerals, to rehydrate their body. A minority have their stomach pumped, which involves the person being held down by hospital staff while a tube is put down their throat: nurses dread it and it's a really bad experience for the patient.

More info **on help with alcohol problems**

Your GP can give you more info about alcohol or refer you to alcohol services, free support groups and counselling in your area, or you can contact one of the organizations below. See also "More info on drugs and help with drug problems" in the Drugs chapter.

England and Wales
Drinkline: 0800 917 8282
www.alcoholconcern.org.uk

Northern Ireland
Health Promotion Agency: 028 9031 1611
www.drugsalcohol.info

Scotland
Drinkline Scotland: 0800 7314 314
www.knowthescore.info

www.alcoholics-anonymous.org.uk
Help and info for anyone dealing with drinking problems. Choose "Region & local websites" or "Meetings" to find support in your area, or call 0845 769 7555.

www.al-anonuk.org.uk
Al-Anon and Alateen support families and young people affected by other people's drinking problems. Contact: **020 7403 0888** (England and Wales); **028 9068 2368** (N. Ireland); **0141 339 884** (Scotland).

I've had an uncle who was an alcoholic (he's recovered now) and I saw him mess up my family's life. I never, ever want that to happen to me.   Mary-Anne, 13

I don't like it when my dad gets drunk because he promises things to people like my little sister and then doesn't keep these promises as he doesn't remember. My sister then gets really upset and Mum ends up getting blamed.   Amy, 15

I've had to look after people who are throwing up and/or passing out. They have done stupid things and regretted them the next day, or not remembered them at all. Yet they still continue drinking. This has added to my reasons for being uncomfortable about drinking.   Shelley, 14

A drinking problem

Some people are more likely to develop a dependency on, or an addiction to, alcohol than others. Signs that someone has a problem include:

✳ drinking has caused problems but the drinking continues

✳ drinking every day

✳ getting drunk once a week or more, or regularly (but getting drunk at all risks brain damage for a teenager)

✳ anger if it's suggested they need to cut down or they might have a problem

✳ dark moods, sarcasm, abuse, a bad home atmosphere or violence associated with the drinking

✳ drinking to forget or wipe themselves out temporarily

✳ drinking alone

✳ drinking at every social gathering

✳ drinking more and more

✳ drinking secretly or hiding alcohol.

If you think that you are experiencing any of these signs – or that a parent or friend is, which can be very scary – you need to speak to an adult you trust or ring an anonymous helpline about what you can do (see "More info" on the previous page). The treatment options suggested can include counselling, finding strategies, a withdrawal programme, support groups and sometimes medication prescribed by a doctor.

With a dependency or an addiction, giving up alcohol or even cutting down is not really possible alone – everybody needs help with the "how to", no matter how good or determined a person they are.

Taking control

Some researchers say that teenagers drinking at home with their parents learn to drink alcohol responsibly; others think that's sending the wrong message and is more likely to lead to problem drinking. Probably it has more to do with the way your parents use alcohol.

Think about how alcohol is used in your family: maybe a parent has a glass with dinner a couple of times a week. Or perhaps drinking is the only way your parents know how to celebrate or wind down, or they drink to get wiped out, which are more dangerous ways to use alcohol.

If your parents don't limit your alcohol intake you will need to do it yourself, unless you want to get regularly sick and embarrassed.

Make your own drinking rules

You can vary the rules on different nights, but here are some examples you could think about.

- Don't drink at all until you're at least 16 – 18 is better.
- Don't feel that because you started early you have to keep drinking – leave it alone for a couple of years.
- When you do start to drink, set a limit.
- Work out how many units are in whatever glass, bottle or can you are drinking.
- Have no more than half a unit an hour.
- If you lose count or control assume that you've had more than two units and stop drinking.
- Don't drink every day.
- Don't aim to get drunk.
- Ask for help if you have a problem.

A safer drinking environment

Some people are going to get drunk. They will do more damage to themselves and others if they don't choose to do it in a safe environment.

- Stay in a house or other environment where sober friends, parents or other people are within reach. Don't go out for a drive, down the road to a park, or to another house or party.
- Always go out in a group.
- Organize to have a couple of friends who'll stay sober and look out for you, or do the same for them.

designated sober person

- Don't get split up from your group so that you are in a different room or place with strangers or with people who are not close friends. (Most sexual assaults are carried out by someone the person knows, not a stranger.)
- Don't aim to get drunk. (This is likely to result in you getting so drunk you can't speak or move properly.)
- Make sure you always have a working phone or are with a friend with a working phone, and that you have the number of an adult who will come and pick you up at any time (see the "Your emergency contacts" box in the Savvy chapter).
- Don't accept a drink that you didn't ask for or from somebody you don't know.
- Don't mix taking any kind of prescription, non-prescription or illegal drug with drinking alcohol – the combination can cause unexpected and dangerous reactions, including coma or death.
- Don't ever get a lift with somebody who's been drinking, even if they say they're fine to drive. Call your emergency contact instead.
- Never leave anyone behind, even if they are too drunk to move. They will be vulnerable to assault, injury or arrest.
- Make sure that no drunk person is left unconscious on their back or in any other position in which they could choke to death on their own vomit.

How to drink slowly and carefully

- Eat a full meal in the hour before you drink.
- Start with a non-alcoholic drink so you're not thirsty. Being thirsty means you will probably drink alcoholic drinks too fast.
- Eat substantial food while you're drinking, even if it's just nibbles and snacks, but try to avoid the salty ones as they'll make you more dehydrated. If the nibbles and snacks are salty and you get thirsty, drink something non-alcoholic.
- Work out how many units are in what you're drinking and how much will be within your safe limit (see the boxes "How much alcohol is in one unit?" and "What's the right amount?" earlier in this chapter).

dRiNK WateR in Between aNy aLcoHoLic DRiNKs

⊙ Never drink alcohol with bubbles on an empty stomach, or quickly.

⊙ Always finish your glass before putting more in it: that's the only way you can measure how much you have drunk. And stop someone else "topping you up" from a jug or bottle.

⊙ Stop when you get to the limit you set yourself no matter what anyone else says.

⊙ Take your own water because it may not be available. To cut costs, refill bottles from the tap at home.

Always stay in a group...

⊙ Don't touch the party punch – some idiot always throws in a vat of vodka.

⊙ Dance – then you don't have to stand around for hours with a glass in your hand. Drink water when you get thirsty.

⊙ Dilute your drinks with water, melting ice, soda water or juice.

⊙ Have water or another non-alcoholic drink in between alcoholic drinks.

⊙ Drink low-alcohol drinks.

⊙ Stick to one kind of alcohol: beer OR wine OR the same spirit with the same mixer.

⊙ Don't get involved in buying rounds of drinks as it means someone will buy you another drink when you don't want it (and you end up spending more money).

⊙ Don't get involved in drinking that's a contest, a bet or a game.

⊙ Don't "down" drinks in one go, or encourage others to.

⊙ Don't gulp down alcoholic drinks. They're supposed to be sipped.

⊙ Don't drink liqueurs – they're too ridiculously alcoholic.

⊙ If you're given a drink you don't want, get a non-alcoholic one and ignore the alcoholic one, or walk away and "lose" it, or pour it out on the ground (if you're outside).

⊙ Don't hang out with people who hassle you to drink more.

There should always be one person who doesn't drink who can keep their eye out

for the others and to drive. Milly, 18

DRUGS

10

Some herbal and chemical compounds can do **amazing things** – stop pain, help healing, prevent an anxiety attack, cause an anxiety attack, block or boost certain hormones, put you to sleep, make you feel wide awake. Nearly every culture has fiddled with nature to create substances that will make them feel more relaxed, dreamy or excited. But none of it comes for free. Every drug has **risks and side effects**. The more drugs you take, whether legal or illegal, the more you risk damaging yourself. The most common drugs you'll come into contact with are cigarettes and alcohol. We've just had the full bottle (sorry) on drinking, so here's what you **need** to know about tobacco and other drugs.

Cigarettes

Why do people start smoking? They probably have their first cigarette to be rebellious because it seems wrong and forbidden. Many girls have their first cigarette because they're with older guys who smoke – just as many girls give up when they fall for someone who doesn't like smoking.

Why does almost everyone *keep* smoking? Because they're physically addicted. The essential ingredient of cigarettes is nicotine, one of the most addictive substances ever discovered. Even more addictive than mobile phones and chocolate.

> **FACT**
>
> **What's in cigarettes** As well as the nicotine they contain more than forty cancer-causing chemicals and burning agents.

Things you need to know about cigarettes

Smoking can seem fun because it often gets associated with taking a break or partying, but there is no upside to its effects on your brain and body. Here's what it does.

Straight away

SMOKERS SMELL

- Your hair, clothes and breath smell of smoke.
- Your sense of taste and smell is reduced.
- Your brain and nervous-system activity is stimulated for a short time.
- If you feel temporarily calmer that's because you're already addicted.
- You possibly experience dizziness, nausea, watery eyes, increased acid in the stomach and a sudden urge to poo (because the body wants to get the poisons out of your system).
- Your lungs are damaged by every cigarette you smoke.
- If you're pregnant, your unborn baby "smokes" too (through the bloodstream) and their health is damaged with every cigarette.

After a little while

- You're addicted.
- Your skin, hair, breath and clothes smell strongly of smoke – although you can't smell it any more.

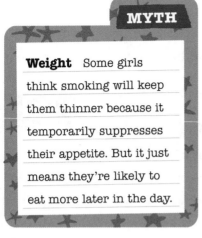

MYTH

Weight   Some girls think smoking will keep them thinner because it temporarily suppresses their appetite. But it just means they're likely to eat more later in the day.

- Ⓖ Your sense of taste and smell is suppressed.
- Ⓖ You develop yellow or orangey stains on your fingers and teeth, and drier skin.
- Ⓖ You are short of breath and have a cough – regular or heavy smoking causes lung damage that may not be reversible.
- Ⓖ You find it harder to walk, run, play sport, go upstairs or dance without feeling unfit.
- Ⓖ You get more colds, coughs and chest infections, and take longer than non-smokers to recover.

Long term

- Ⓖ Your hair, breath, hands and clothes constantly stink of smoke.
- Ⓖ Your skin develops "smoking" wrinkles.
- Ⓖ You may suffer from a disease called emphysema (pronounced em-fiz-eema), which starts as shortness of breath and progressively makes

Things to say when you don't want to smoke (even if you're fibbing)

"Not for me, thanks."

"My mum/dad always smells it on me."

"No thanks, I've given up."

"No thanks, I'm trying to cut down."

"I'm in a netball/hockey/football team and need all the lung power I can get."

"I sing/play the saxophone and need all the lung power I can get."

"No thanks, I don't like it."

"I can't – it gives me asthma."

"I hate menthol/rollies/filters/ unfiltereds."

"I can't because it gives me a lung infection."

"No thanks, I've never been into it."

"No thanks, it's not my thing."

"I already have seven bad habits and I need to concentrate on those."

"No, I only smoke Cuban cigars." (Okay, that might be a bit hard to make convincing, but you get the picture.)

"No thanks, I was addicted and I don't want to go there again."

"No thanks, I'm sick of it."

Stuff the cigarette companies don't tell you

✳ Smoking causes more damage to women than men. Researchers are not yet sure why.

✳ Low-tar cigarettes are not better for you – they still contain as many damaging chemicals.

✳ "Light" or "mild" cigarettes contain as many damaging chemicals too.

✳ Menthol cigarettes are not better for you.

✳ Roll-ups are not better for you – in fact they may be worse.

✳ Cigars are not better or worse for you than cigarettes.

✳ Herbal cigarettes are not good for you.

✳ You can have all the ill-effects of smoking by breathing in the smoke from other people's cigarettes when you're in a house, car or public place with them (this is called passive smoking).

✳ Cigarette companies make huge, huge profits – in the billions of pounds – even though almost 80 percent of each packet's price goes to the government in taxes.

breathing harder until you need an oxygen mask or you can't get enough air to survive.

🌀 You may develop cancer: smoking is a proven cause of, or contributing factor in, many cancers, including those in the lungs, throat, mouth, bladder, kidneys, pancreas, cervix and stomach.

🌀 You may have a stroke or a heart attack, or have to have your toes, feet or legs amputated: smoking is a big cause of these because it narrows the arteries and veins, restricting blood flow.

Giving up smoking

The best way is never to start. Because it's way addictive it's really hard for some people to give up "on their own". Stopping smoking causes cravings for cigarettes (because the person is addicted), possible weight gain (only short term) and grumpiness.

ask for HELP

Getting drunk helped me start smoking.   Amy, 16

You will need one or some of the following while you are giving up smoking:

- ⓖ a reason to stop, such as liking a guy (or girl) who doesn't like smoking; finding that smoking is affecting your sports performance or general fitness; fighting an illness; being pregnant, breastfeeding or not wanting smoke to damage your baby; being frightened of getting cancer later in life
- ⓖ advice and support from a GP or a helpline (see "More info" below)
- ⓖ friends and family who help and encourage you
- ⓖ goals such as saving the "cigarette money" for a big treat or trip instead
- ⓖ hypnotherapy
- ⓖ nicotine gum or patches
- ⓖ a smoke-free environment (stay away from people who smoke)
- ⓖ determination and mental strength.

More info on smoking

Smoking helplines
England and Wales: 0800 022 4332
Northern Ireland: 0800 85 85 85
Scotland: 0800 84 84 84

www.nhs.uk/gosmokefree
NHS website to help you stop smoking. Has contact info for local support services.

www.quit.org.uk
UK charity offering a step-by-step guide on giving up, exercise programmes and support by phone, email and text message. Quitline: 0800 00 22 00.

www.quitbecause.org.uk
Aimed at young people, this anti-smoking site has scary photos and videos.

Most of my friends are smokers. I don't smoke because my dad is dying of lung cancer and it kind of puts you off the idea. However, we all drink and smoke pot simply because it is part of our social culture, a way for us to relax. We're just imitating what we see our parents and the rest of society doing. Zoe, 16

I've smoked before but I only have a puff at parties. The taste reminds me of parties and makes me feel a bit rebellious coz I know my parents would hate me doing it Rachel, 16

Legal drugs

Apart from the main legal drugs – alcohol and cigarettes – there are heaps of prescription drugs, and stuff you can buy without a prescription at the chemist and even the supermarket, that are very dangerous if not taken in the right way or by the right person. Nicotine is the most addictive drug but other legal ones are right up there, including not only alcohol but also some prescription drugs.

Almost everybody I know drinks, smokes cigarettes and weed, and takes different medications to get high. They steal prescription drugs all the time.
Jen, 15

   Just because a drug is legal doesn't mean it's safe for you – in fact it almost certainly won't be unless it was prescribed specifically for you by a doctor or suggested by the pharmacist (not a shop assistant). Some over-the-counter drugs (meaning ones that don't need a prescription) can only be sold to you after a pharmacist has explained them to you.

Problems with legal drugs

You should never take more of a drug than the dose prescribed by your doctor for your age or weight and written on the chemist's label on the packet. And always read the manufacturer's information given in the leaflet inside.

   Most prescription medications are for an illness or symptom that is specific to one patient – this means if you take someone else's drugs you may not know what you've really taken, and you won't know how it is going to affect your body and brain.

   Some people may "only" take two or three pills, but that's more than their particular body can handle. Don't accept any prescription pill or medicine not prescribed for you, even if you think you've got the same symptoms as someone else, and even if it's a family member offering it.

   If not used correctly, many common, supermarket-bought painkillers can cause massive damage to internal organs, such as lungs, heart, liver and kidneys.

   The results of taking more legal drugs than you are supposed to include brain damage, incontinence (not being able to control when you wee or poo), and being wheelchair bound from then on.

   Mixing alcohol with either prescription or over-the-counter drugs makes them more dangerous.

See the box "When to call an ambulance" in the Drinking chapter for some of the signs and symptoms that mean someone needs emergency help and info on what to do while waiting, and ring 999.

If you are worried that you, a friend or a family member may have a psychological dependency or be addicted to a legal drug, see the section "How to help somebody with a drug problem" at the end of this chapter.

I take drugs. No one knows and I don't hang around many people who do, other than my dad. Missy, 14

Pot ruined my friend's life. Now he is schizophrenic. You never know what it can do to you. Parminder, 14

I took E. Nothing much really happened. Maybe it wasn't what they said it was. Louise, 17

I'd like to know where you can get drugs. Leah, 14

I used to want to try cannabis but now I am going to wait for a few years. Gina, 15

Smoking is just as bad as any drug and I'm really glad neither of my parents ever smoked. Liv, 17

My friend the daughter of the teetotaller school guidance officer has done every mood-altering drug known to mankind. Tegan, 15

Some of my friends have overdosed and even died from drugs. Judith, 17

Illegal drugs

The most common illegal drugs include cannabis, methamphetamine, ecstasy and heroin (see the "Illegal drugs" chart coming up for more info).

Teenagers are not the biggest users of drugs – people in their twenties and thirties are – so you may not see or be offered any for a while, or ever. But it's probably a good idea to be prepared just in case you are, so that you'll have some idea of what the drug is and whether you think it's wise to go ahead.

Things you need to know about illegal drugs

Despite the scary-pants stories, taking a drug once isn't going to make you addicted, and smoking a joint won't lead you directly to harder drugs and a heroin "habit". But it is true that things can go very badly wrong even the first time.

The upside of taking illegal drugs is that they can cause you to forget any troubles for an hour or two, feel high and happy, or floaty and out of it, and experience a different way of thinking. The reverse side is that individual brain chemistry produces different reactions. Some people who smoke cannabis (weed) get terrified and worried instead of giggly; some people who take heroin throw up instead of feeling floaty; some people who take cocaine don't feel high and chatty and smart – they feel paranoid (sure that everyone, or someone, is out to get them). Other problems can include feeling down the next day after a high; running out of money because you're spending it on drugs; and seeming like a loser who's only interested in drugs.

There are some really big downsides to drugs. Immediate ones, even the first time you take a drug, can include suddenly getting so out of it you can't protect yourself from sexual assault; and an accidental overdose causing a medical emergency, brain damage or death.

Longer term downsides if you're a regular, repeated or heavy illegal drug user include not being able to keep up with schoolwork or sport; the development or sudden onset of a severe mental illness; several serious physical illnesses; "ruining your looks" because of the side effects; dependence and addiction; losing friends or boyfriends because you've developed a drug problem; and legal difficulties (such as being arrested).

Many girls find they need to break up with a guy when he gets involved in heavy or regular drug use, especially of cannabis, and becomes incredibly boring and doesn't want to do anything.

The risks of illegal drug use   The only way to avoid risk with illegal drugs is not to take any. Because everyone's brain and body are different, even the same batch of a drug will affect people in different ways. While a friend may have a good time on a drug, and

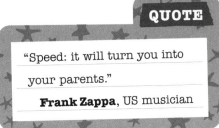

QUOTE

"Speed: it will turn you into your parents."

Frank Zappa, US musician

encourage you to use it, that doesn't mean you'll have the same result, even if it's the same batch and dose. Illegal drugs aren't like prescription ones; they don't come in accurate doses, so you'll have no idea how much you're getting. In most cases when you're deciding whether or not to take or smoke something, it will be impossible to know precisely what's in it, its strength or its likely effects.

If you have any predisposition to mental illness, including depression and psychosis, illegal drugs or misuse of legal drugs can trigger episodes of the illness. Having a relative (especially a parent) who has or has had a mental illness makes a predisposition more likely, but it is not something someone can know beforehand (because it's something locked in their brain, not something they can see); the first time their mental illness shows itself may be triggered by their first drug use.

For many people common results of drug-taking are vomiting, stomach cramps, sweating and diarrhoea, all symptoms of the body trying to get rid of the drug as soon as it can. More severe reactions can include convulsions (jerking and foaming at the mouth), unconsciousness, coma and death.

> **FACT**
>
> **What's a safe dose?**   There's no known safe dose for any illegal or unregulated drug – that's why the "Illegal drugs" chart coming up doesn't go into details about how to take a drug, or in what dose.

Many problems, emergencies and overdoses happen because people combine drugs with alcohol or other drugs or take them within a day of each other.

Please read the whole of this chapter and see the "More info" section at the end, as well as the "Illegal drugs" chart a few pages on, to be fully aware of what you're dealing with.

Travel and drugs

The laws of other countries can differ hugely from the UK's. Prescription drugs that are legal in the UK can be illegal in some countries, so take your GP's original prescription with you and check with the Foreign & Commonwealth Office (www.fco.gov.uk) before you travel.

Many countries have mandatory (automatic) life sentences or death sentences for using the smallest amount of an illegal drug; having any amount on your body or in your pockets, handbag, rucksack or a room where you are or have been; and selling or trafficking. For example, Malaysia and Singapore enforce the dealth penalty for drug-smuggling, and prison sentences in Thailand can be as long as 49 or 99 years.

An offence such as cannabis possession in the UK might result in a warning or a fine – in another country it could mean you never come home again. There are around 1200 Britons in prisons abroad for drug offences at any one time – it just isn't worth the risk.

✳ Never travel with drugs on a plane, whether on an internal flight or overseas. If you don't get caught the first time, your risk gets bigger each "next" time.

✳ Never go somewhere unknown with a stranger to buy drugs. (Strangers can act friendly to win your confidence.)

✳ Never assume the British government can get you off a drugs charge in another country – it can't. It can only advise you of available lawyers, and it won't pay for them.

drugs

DRUGS

HOW NOT to tRaveL

The legal risk Penalties vary, but generally the lowest are for using or growing a small amount of cannabis, and get more serious for possession, dealing (buying and selling drugs, or sharing them with your friends) and trafficking (taking them from one place to another). Penalties range from a warning or a fine to a short or very long jail sentence. What gets you a warning or a fine in the UK may mean jail or something even worse in another country (see the "Travel and drugs" box earlier).

> Why let something take control of you? What could happen whilst you are "tripping"? Who knows? That thought scares me.
> Julie, 15

In the UK, illegal drugs are divided into three categories – Class A, Class B and Class C. Class A drugs are considered the most harmful, and possession, dealing or trafficking of these drugs attracts the highest punishments. The "Illegal drugs" chart coming up tells you the "class" or category of each of the most common drugs.

Postal services regularly screen for drugs in letters and packages. Police can search your car if they stop you on the road, but they must say they have "reasonable cause" (which could be the smell of drugs or someone with a drugged appearance).

Drug-driving is illegal, just as drink-driving is, and the police can stop you on the side of the road and make you take a "field impairment test" to see if you're unfit to drive. They can then arrest you and take you into the station for blood or urine tests, which can detect some drugs in your system hours, days or even weeks after you've taken them. Penalties for drug-driving can include a fine, loss of your licence and jail, and you could be charged with drug offences.

Deciding whether or not to take drugs

Most people don't take drugs. The reasons given by those who do – not necessarily good reasons – include wanting to feel relaxed; wanting to feel nothing; trying to cure or help an illness; curiosity; not wanting to be left out; boredom; being rich enough to afford drugs; feeling indestructible; wanting emotional or physical pain to go away for a while; not realizing, or denying, the risks; pressure from a friend or group of so-called friends; a dependence or an addiction.

Before you decide to take a drug, think about why you want to. Is it because you want to fit into a group or impress somebody? (Because that's a bit tragic.) Is it because you want to get

WANTING to feeL NoTHINg MeaNS you Need HeLP...

or keep a friend? (Because, even if that works, it's not a good basis for a relationship.) Are you sad and hoping it will wipe out your pain? (Because the pain will still be there a few minutes or hours later, and there are other ways of making sad feelings go away – see the Feelings chapter.)

Get informed before you decide. See the "Illegal drugs" chart coming up, and some of the websites recommended in "More info" at the end of this chapter.

> Pot should be legalized. It's so cheap and easy to get already it's not like it would make a difference.
> Kayla, 16

> Friends that were smoking weed felt isolated even when surrounded by friends.
> Erica, 16

Not taking drugs Reasons not to take drugs include:

- ☯ different brains have different reactions to drugs
- ☯ some drugs are known to trigger mental illness in somebody with a predisposition, but nobody knows beforehand if they have a predisposition or not
- ☯ all drugs have side effects and some of them are major
- ☯ it's impossible to tell how strong or pure the drug is just by looking at it – this means you are more vulnerable to a bad reaction or an overdose
- ☯ you can become dependent or addicted
- ☯ by being a drug consumer you are part of an industry that exploits, cheats and kills
- ☯ some illegal drugs are very expensive because people take risks to get them to you without being caught by police
- ☯ it's illegal.

If you think you'd feel embarrassed or seem uncool refusing drugs, see the list in the Drinking chapter of things to say, and also the one in the "Smoking" section earlier in this chapter. If friends seem to be going in a direction you don't want to follow, you may want to see the Friends chapter for ideas on ending a friendship and finding a new group.

> Don't do drugs: they can't take your pain away permanently. Rhiana, 13

> My uncle died from a drug overdose. Jane, 14

Illegal drugs

The known facts about the drugs listed here could change, and some drugs aren't included, so check out "More info" at the end of the chapter for websites that can keep you up to date. There are no details below on how to take a drug or in what dose, because there's no one-size-fits-all safe dose of any illegal or unregulated drug. All illegal drugs can damage an unborn or breastfed baby.

Cannabis

Class C   Also known as dope, weed, marijuana, grass, pot, blow, puff, draw, gear, skunk, hash, ganja, wacky backy, and a reefer, joint or spliff.

What is it?   Cannabis is a depressant drug with possible hallucinogenic effects (causing weird visions and delusions). It comes in various forms, all from the cannabis plant. The most common form used in the UK is the resin from the plant (hash). It comes as a browny-black lump and it is usually smoked in a hand-rolled cigarette (joint) or in a pipe or bong (water pipe). It's also baked and eaten in cakes or biscuits (this creates a greater overdose risk). Herbal cannabis (grass or weed) is the crushed leaves (the least potent part of the plant) or the stronger buds and flowers (heads), and it's usually smoked in a joint, pipe or bong. "Skunk" and "sinsemilla" are newer, extra-potent forms made from artificially created, or hybrid, plants. They can be two or three times stronger than the other forms. Cannabis is the most common illegal drug. Many teenagers will come into contact with it and about a third will try it. In some areas or friendship groups most people will use it.

Why do people take it?   It can make them feel calmer, floaty, temporarily less shy, and like laughing. A puff of a joint can be enough to feel "stoned".

Side effects and problems   Effects depend on how much you take and which part of the plant is used. Many people believe cannabis grown with chemicals is more likely to cause problems. Side effects include red eyes, enlarged pupils, hunger and sleepiness. Cannabis is far from a "harmless" drug, and is particularly damaging to a teenage (still-developing) brain. Regular use is now firmly linked to disordered thinking, memory problems, depression and serious mental illness. Heavy use can cause panic attacks, severe depression, paranoia and psychotic episodes. Regular or heavy cannabis users tend to seem boring and antisocial. The smoke damages the lungs and other body parts in the same way cigarettes do.

Dependence and addiction   Some people become psychologically dependent; and some become physically addicted, despite what was once thought.

Speed and crystal meth (methamphetamines)

Class A (Speed is Class B, unless prepared for injection) Speed is also known as sulph, whiz, billy, amphetamines, uppers, phets, amphs and dexies. Crystal meth is also known as ice, glass, yaba, Christine, Tina and crank.

What is it? Speed, as it sounds, is a stimulant, which speeds up the activity of the central nervous system. It comes as a powder, which can be off-white, yellow, pink or brown, and other chemicals are usually added as filler to make it go further. Crystal meth is a much purer, more powerful, more addictive and more dangerous kind of speed that comes in crystal form. (Crystal meth is up to ninety percent pure; speed is up to twenty percent.) It looks like transparent rice grains or tiny glass shards, sometimes with a yellow or brown tinge. Speed and crystal meth are usually snorted through the nose, eaten, smoked or inhaled as the powder is heated, or possibly injected.

Why do people take it? To try to block feelings of hunger or tiredness (it's often used by people who want to stay awake) or to feel a sudden "rush" or high.

Side effects and problems Side effects for both include jittery feelings, aggression, exhaustion, feeling invincible, blurred vision, dry mouth, fast breathing, enlarged pupils, headache, nausea, anxiety, "high" mood, talkativeness and repetitiveness. Regular or heavy users tend to become paranoid and confused, which can lead to mood swings, depression, extreme anxiety, severe mental illness (psychosis) and sudden violent acts.

Crystal meth has especially nasty side effects. It's more physically damaging than speed and has more extreme effects on behaviour, health and lifestyle. It badly damages the skin and hair, and causes teeth to rot and fall out.

Speed or crystal meth mixed with filler chemicals can be poisonous if injected. Injecting puts you at more risk of diseases, vein damage and overdose. Some users end up turning to crime or sex work to pay for the drug, which also puts them at risk of violence, exploitation and jail.

Dependence and addiction Regular or heavy users will become addicted. Crystal meth is *extremely* addictive (much more so than speed) because of its purity. Inhaling, rather than injecting, is associated with faster addiction.

→

Ecstasy (methylenedioxymethamphetamine – MDMA)

Class A   Also known as E, XTC, X, pills, tabs, party pills, brownies, disco biscuits, love drug and by various "brand" names that change regularly.

What is it?   Ecstasy belongs to both the stimulant family (like speed) and the hallucinogen family (like LSD). It comes in tablet or capsule form, in all sorts of colours and designs, (or occasionally as a powder): most of the tablet could be filler or other drugs (such as speed). It is usually swallowed, but some users poke the tablet up their anus.

Why do people take it?   Because it can temporarily heighten the senses, boost energy and create feelings of belonging, social confidence, closeness and a "happy high". It's often taken at clubs or dance parties, where it can intensify music and light effects.

Side effects and problems   Faster heart rate, raised body heat, possible jaw clenching, shaking, nausea, anxiety and sweating. In the days afterwards: feeling down, cranky, listless and unable to concentrate. Ecstasy is associated with anxiety and panic attacks, and with depression, possibly in people who have an unknown predisposition.

We don't yet know the long-term effects of ecstasy, but we do know it can change and harm your brain. Accidental overdose or mixing it with other drugs or alcohol can cause convulsions, hallucinations (seeing or hearing imaginary things), brain damage and heart failure (death).

Ecstasy shouldn't be taken by anyone with their own or a family history of brain problems, heart disease, high blood pressure or mental illness, or by anyone taking prescribed drugs. Some teenagers have died after taking ecstasy, either because of an underlying medical condition they didn't know they had or from an accidental overdose. See the information about drugs and drinking water which follows this chart: some ecstasy users have become dangerously dehydrated or have accidentally drunk a life-threatening amount of water.

Dependence and addiction   From what we know so far, it appears most users don't become physically addicted but may develop a psychological dependence.

GHB (gammahydroxybutyrate)

Class C   Also known as GBH (Grievous Bodily Harm), liquid ecstasy or liquid E (although in fact it isn't like ecstasy, which is a stimulant).

What is it?   A depressant, GHB comes as a clear liquid with no smell and just a slightly salty taste. It is swallowed or, rarely, injected.

Why do people take it?   It can cause a "rush", then calm.

Side effects and problems   Has a reputation as a drink-spiking drug sometimes used in sexual assaults because it's almost tasteless and it can really knock you out. Can include sleepiness, calm, nausea, headache, intense sense of touch, dizziness and memory loss. Heavy use can cause extreme vomiting, worry and confusion, muscle stiffness, breathing problems, coma, convulsions and death. The difference between taking enough to get an effect and enough to kill you is very small. A "safe" dose of GHB is very hard to calculate: accidental overdose causing death is a very high risk.

Dependence and addiction   Regular or heavy users will become addicted.

LSD (lysergic acid diethylamide)

Class A   Also known as acid, blotting paper, blots, dots, tabs, trips and Lucy.

What is it?   A hallucinogen, LSD usually comes in small squares of paper with pictures on them (similar to postage stamps), which you swallow.

Why do people take it?   To try to heighten their senses and see what perceptions the mind will have. The brain may have uncontrolled "flashbacks" to the LSD reaction some days, months or even years later.

Side effects and problems   Whether the "trip" is pleasant or scary can depend largely on your state of mind when you take the drug, and depends on the individual. Effects can include nausea and stomach cramps. LSD is particularly dangerous for those who are predisposed to mental illness (which they may not be aware of). Because each "batch" is a different strength it's hard to tell how much you can "safely" take: one dose can be enough to cause permanent brain disorder.

Dependence and addiction   LSD is probably not physically addictive, but people can develop a psychological dependence on it.

$\rightarrow$

Cocaine

Class A   Also known as coke, Charlie, snow, blow, dust, white, toot, sherbert and Percy.

What is it?   Cocaine, derived from the coca plant, is a stimulant. It's a white powder that's usually arranged in a "line" and "snorted" up the nose. It can also be smoked but this is rarer, and known to cause quicker and more dangerous dependence, and it can sometimes be made into a solution and injected. "Crack", also known as rocks, stones and freebase, is a form of cocaine made into small lumps or rocks about the size of a raisin. It is usually smoked in a pipe, glass tube, plastic bottle or off heated foil.

Why do people take it?   To try to get a fast high, and to feel buzzy, super-alert and confident. Cocaine also makes them talkative. It blocks hunger, but users always eat later.

Side effects and problems   Can include fast heartbeat, raised body heat, enlarged pupils, anxiety, wild behaviour, aggression, sleep problems, paranoia, severe mental illness (psychosis) and heart attack or heart failure (death). Long-term use is linked to depression, eventual permanent destruction of nose tissue, panic attacks, possible heart problems and brain damage. People with their own or a family history of heart or mental problems should avoid it.

Users can't tell by looking how pure the cocaine is, or whether it has been "cut" with other white substances (such as baking soda or talcum powder) to make it go further. This can mean an increased risk of accidental overdose.

Dependence and addiction   Known to cause heavy dependence and addiction.

Solvents (gases, glues and aerosols)

Unclassified   Also known as glue sniffing and volatile substance abuse.

What is it?   The fumes of chemicals (often glue, paint, petrol, gas lighter refills and various aerosols or household products), which are inhaled, causing a depressant effect.

Why do people take it?   They want to feel numb or "wiped-out".

Side effects and problems   Inhaling can cause nose bleeds, sore eyes, nausea, flu-like symptoms, stinky breath, stains around the nose and mouth, stumbling, zombie-like staring, vision and hearing problems and passing out. Ongoing problems can include lack of energy, confusion, crankiness and serious eye, organ or brain damage. Some users have died when they inhaled before physical activity. Others have suffocated.

Dependence and addiction   Can cause psychological dependence.

Heroin

Class A   Also known as smack, skag, gear, junk, Henry, horse and brown.

What is it?   It's a depressant and painkiller chemically derived from the opium poppy. Pure heroin is a white powder, but the kind found on the streets is usually dark brown, yellowish or off-white. Most commonly it's dissolved in water and injected into a vein. It's also heated and smoked ("chasing the dragon") or snorted.

Why do people take it?   Because it can give them a floaty feeling that temporarily wipes out bad feelings. But most continue to take heroin because they are physically addicted to it.

Side effects and problems   Can include feeling sick and vomiting, sweating, itching, feeling dizzy and weeing a lot. Heroin slows the breathing system, blood pressure and heartbeat: users can doze off. As with crystal meth, some users end up turning to crime or sex work to pay for the drug, which also puts them at risk of violence, exploitation and jail.

Medical problems include self-neglect, malnutrition and needle infections (including hepatitis C and HIV/AIDS). The overdose risk is high because the dosage is hard to estimate. Most heroin overdoses are linked to using pills or alcohol at the same time. Almost all drug deaths involve heroin.

Dependence and addiction   A hugely addictive drug, both physically and psychologically.

Minimizing the harm

If you have decided to take a drug:

- ⑥ never take it when you're alone
- ⑥ take too little rather than too much – this is always better because you can never know exactly what's in the drug
- ⑥ never take anything without telling a friend what you're taking, and how much or how many (also always find out exactly what your friend has taken, and how much or how many)
- ⑥ always have at least one designated sober person (no drugs and no alcohol) – this is really important. You need someone on watch who's completely together. Talk to your friends about what they should do if things go wrong.

aargh!

HaVe A PLAN SO you DON't PaNic if THiNgs go WRONg...

Drinking water All party and club goers need to drink about 250 ml of plain water (not a sports drink) an hour if chatting, and about 500 ml an hour if dancing – not less, and not lots more. Too little or too much water combined with some drugs can cause serious damage to your body or (rarely) death. Take rest breaks and don't dance non-stop for hours.

Reaction and overdose

If someone has an adverse reaction or overdoses on a drug it's really important that they receive professional help as soon as possible. A quick response can save their life.

See the box "When to call an ambulance" in the Drinking chapter for some of the signs and symptoms that mean someone needs emergency help, and for info on what to do after calling 999.

How to help somebody with a drug problem

Many people with unlimited access to a drug they like will develop health problems and an overuse or dependency problem (although they will often deny it).

One time my friend became paralysed and started throwing up.

It really scared me. Marg, 15

FACT

Some don'ts   People who have taken drugs certainly shouldn't drive, swim, look after children or operate machinery because of the risk of an accident or of being unable to react properly in an emergency.

◎ Listen to what they have to say, and be there for them, but don't compromise your own decision, values or safety.

◎ Friends (and relatives) can be angry, even mean, if you raise the subject of their drug (or alcohol) problem. Share your worries with a trusted adult, or with a friendly doctor or a counsellor on one of the anonymous helplines listed further on in "More info" (they're not interested in telling the police – their job is to help the person).

◎ Have some information on hand, such as the helpline numbers and some fact sheets on drugs from one of the websites found in "More info", so that in a crisis, or when the person is ready to seek help, you've got something useful to give to them.

◎ Accept that unless and until they want help there's nothing more you can do. Their drug problem is not your responsibility and you can't fix it. If it starts to affect your own enjoyment of life, step back and distance yourself (while assuring them you'll be there when they need you to help them tackle their drug problem).

addiction is like Being in a cage: you Need HeLP To get out

◎ If a parent or family member's drug problems are putting you in danger or causing you physical or emotional harm, concentrate on getting help for yourself (and any brothers and sisters), rather than trying to help your parent. Speak to your GP, a teacher or another adult you can trust, or call one of the helplines listed in "More info" on the next page.

More info on drugs and help with drug problems

If you think you may have a drug problem, your GP should be able to offer confidential advice and support and refer you for specialist treatment. Otherwise you can contact one of the organizations below or call ChildLine on 0800 1111.

National drugs helpline: 0800 77 66 00
The government's "Talk to FRANK" helpline offers free, confidential drug advice 24 hours a day, and can help you find support services in your area.

www.talktofrank.com
The Talk to FRANK website has a complete A–Z of drugs info (including magic mushrooms, "poppers" and other drugs not mentioned in the "Illegal drugs" box), plus young people's stories, the latest news and FAQs. You can also ask questions and get confidential help and advice by email.

www.addaction.org.uk
Specialist UK charity offering treatment to people with drug problems and support to their friends and families.

www.adfam.org.uk
Adfam is a national organization that helps families affected by drugs and alcohol. Click on "Help and info" to search for support groups and to read real-life stories.

www.drugscope.org.uk
The independent charity Drug Scope has heaps of info, articles and links. Choose "Resources" for their DrugSearch encyclopaedia, FAQs and the D-World site for 11–14 year olds.

www.knowthescore.info
The Scottish government's drug info site. You can also call their drugs helpline on 0800 587 5879.

www.positivestories.org.au
Australian site with real-life stories about people who've beaten drug problems.

www.thesite.org/drinkanddrugs
The YouthNet site has mountains of useful info, from drug safety, the law and how drugs affect your body to peer pressure, drug-driving and addiction.

I believe that MOST people will try drugs/alcohol at least once in their life and I think that if you are going to try them make sure you are with/around people that you can trust and are going to look after you if it gets out of hand.   Tash, 18

I have had ecstasy about four times. On my second time I OD'd. I could have died. I regularly take speed and smoke bongs. I also have been smoking cigarettes since I was 11. My ex-boyfriend also is currently doing this thing where he is staying high for two weeks.   Kath, 16

11

CONFIDENCE

Confident people believe, "I'm okay, and it doesn't really matter whether you agree". **Real cool** has nothing to do with fashion or money: it's a head thing.

Nobody expects you to have total confidence, or to get it all at once. But it's something to work towards. The more you can laugh at yourself, the more you don't care what you look like all the time, the more you don't obsess about what other people think, the freer and **happier** you'll be – and the cooler you'll seem.

Not feeling confident

It can be hard to feel self-confident when you're a teenager because:

- 🌀 you usually haven't worked out everything about who you are, what you're good at and what you love doing (secretly lots of grown-ups haven't either)
- 🌀 you may not want to be seen as special and different – some girls want to blend in and not be noticed
- 🌀 it can be tough not caring about what other people say about you, even when they're just being mean.

> I guess what affects my self-confidence negatively would be myself, really, because sometimes it's hard to turn off that inner voice telling you something isn't good enough.
> Hannah, 18

What girls don't feel confident about

Some of the girls in the Girl Stuff Survey said these things made them feel less confident:

people thinking I was a fool or an idiot – this makes me extremely self-conscious when I meet new people and prevents me from being myself! ✳ other people's expectations ✳ going to parties and being around others who are drinking or doing drugs ✳ being a bit shy ✳ my ability to have or get a boyfriend ✳ what I am going to do after school ✳ the opposite sex ✳ my body and how others see it ✳ spots ✳ body image ✳ when I learn someone's name – I don't feel confident about saying it, just in case I get it wrong ✳ being around guys ✳ my place in the world ✳ going up to people and introducing myself – I absolutely hate that ✳ feeling as if I must please everyone – I hate that about me ✳ meeting new people ✳ the way others perceive me, especially how the opposite sex sees me ✳ standing up to people – can't do it, never could ✳ public speaking, speaking my mind, doing things by myself ✳ singing, dancing, performing, speaking in public ✳ exams! ✳ talking in front of groups ✳ my height ✳ talking to strangers ✳ I don't feel confident about being taken seriously by my mum ✳ meeting people for the first time – I always put my foot in my mouth ✳ putting forward ideas that could be cut down ✳ pretty much everything ✳ my appearance, my "coolness" and some of my school results ✳ I feel a bit awkward around some people – guys mainly ✳ my friends.

Getting confident

Being confident means life opens up, you try new experiences and you have a more interesting time. Having self-confidence means wearing an invisible suit of armour against people who try to put you down, criticize or tease you.

Things you can do

Here are some steps on the way to feeling good about yourself and your strengths, talents and capabilities.

> If you have no self-confidence here is a little trick that helps me when I wake up in a bad mood: look at yourself in the mirror and find at least ONE thing you like about yourself (it doesn't have to be big), and tell yourself that it looks good, GREAT even.
>
> Kristen, 18

Get some basic body confidence

- Stand up and sit up straight (seriously – it makes you look more confident).
- Let yourself be recognized – don't hide behind a hairstyle that covers your face, or in baggy clothes.
- Stop being fussed about whether something's in fashion – wear what *you* like.
- Wear comfy clothes that are not about to trip you up, fall off, expose a nipple or show any underpantery.
- Realize that, although right now your changed body is new, you have a lifetime to get used to it. Keep reminding yourself that you really will adjust and feel comfortable "in your own skin".

do you want to hide, blend in, or stand out?

Encourage yourself

◎ Go easy on yourself: don't tell yourself you're hopeless if you make a mistake or do something others laugh at. Be your own best friend. What would you say to others to make them feel better about themselves? Tell it to yourself.

◎ Be content, knowing that for you, and for everyone around you, "me" is a work in progress. It takes time to discover who you are and what you're going to be. Nobody is allowed to rush you. "I don't know" is a perfectly fine answer to a lot of questions.

> When people say something nice to you appreciate it and take it on board because it makes you feel better about yourself. When you are having a bad day you can think about the things that are good about you.
>
> Jessie, 18

◎ Be still for a while. It's hard to work out what you think or how you feel if you're always with other people, watching TV, listening to music or on the computer. Sit or walk by yourself and give yourself time to think.

◎ If there's something you don't like about your personality, ask yourself how you can come to terms with it; or, if it's something you really hate, how you can change it.

◎ Know that there are ways to become more optimistic (see the Feelings chapter).

◎ Keep in mind that it doesn't matter if someone doesn't like you. Not everyone has to like you. Some people liking you is enough.

◎ Know that you can move away from friends who say mean things, and find new ones (see the Friends chapter on how to do this).

◎ Trust that you will find Your People – people who think like you and who like the same things. You just may have to wait until you leave school or move out of home. It's a much bigger world out there, beyond your school, your suburb, your town – there is a rightful place for you in it.

Do something that makes you feel better about yourself

◎ If you live in a family where there is a lot of sarcasm, where nobody ever says "I'm proud of you" or "You did really well", it can be very hard to feel proud of yourself – but it can be done. First tell your family members, or a parent, how the put-downs are making you feel. If that doesn't work, you need to look somewhere else for validation: talk to friends, a teacher or another trusted adult.

⊙ Don't be embarrassed or apologetic about your pastimes or hobbies – find a group or club that has the same interests, or websites that let you know there are other people out there who like the stuff you do (just don't decide to go out and meet "Great Guy, 19" from the chatroom – he'll probably turn out to be "Desperate, Creepy and Pathetic, 46").

⊙ Do something for others – it will make you feel useful and that you're doing something important (see the Caring chapter).

⊙ Find something you really like doing and get better at it.

Practise being confident

⊙ Role-play situations you might find yourself in: go over in your head things you could say, and practise them with a friend or parent, or on your own.

⊙ Practise being strong, even if you don't feel so inside – real courage is doing things even though you're scared.

⊙ Experiment with ways of walking, standing up straight, looking people in the eye and saying things such as "I'd like to do it this way instead".

> I don't care what anyone thinks. People at school think I'm weird because I listen to punk/rock/emo/hardcore music but I don't care. I think it's funny they're teasing me when they're the ones listening to the crappy music. Fay, 13

⊙ Exercise your right to try new things. As long as it's fun, give sports, arts, music and other hobbies a go, even if you're not good at them straight away.

⊙ Don't mind too much when you make a mistake. It's just an investment in a more confident future.

⊙ Defy any labels or reputation put on you. You can change if you want to. Don't accept labels, such as "not smart" or "mean" or "slut". Show with your behaviour that you are your own person regardless of what's happened in the past or what people have said about you.

⊙ Do public speaking or some kind of performance art – if it's too embarrassing to do it at school find somewhere out of school hours. Learn how to use confident body language, and how to project your voice suddenly for effect.

> Don't listen to the people that put you down. The only ones that matter are the ones that make you feel good. Holly, 16

Be assertive For some people being assertive doesn't come naturally. It means being able to stand up for yourself and what you believe in. It means being able to say no as well as yes. It means being able to make the right decision and act on it, even though the right decision is often not the easiest or most popular one. (It *doesn't* mean being loud and bossy or imposing yourself and your ideas on other people.)

- ✆ Ask adults to listen to your problems and help you. Don't let them say, "Just ignore it". Tell them that doesn't work.

- ✆ Read the Drinking and Drugs chapters to find out how you can make your own decisions, and to get reasons – and excuses – for saying no.

- ✆ Don't agree to something just to impress somebody else. Walk away if you need to (see the Friends chapter for ideas on finding a new group).

- ✆ Don't behave in ways that disrespect your own beliefs and intelligence – even if other people are pressuring you to. Leave rather than give in.

- ✆ Learn how to complain, protest and hassle your local media and politicians when you feel strongly about an issue (see the Caring chapter).

Some ways to say no

"No."

"Nope."

"No thanks. It's not really my thing."

"I'm pretty busy right now."

"I'm not allowed."

"I can't – I'm supposed to be home in ten minutes or my mum will kill me."

"I've got something better to do/ somewhere better to be."

"Maybe another time."

"I've got too much on at the moment."

"I'll let you know later/tomorrow/next week." (This gives you time to think.)

Being less shy

When you're shy almost any social situation can seem excruciating and embarrassing. Many people are shy with those they don't know. Even if your natural tendency is to be shy, life can become a lot easier with just a little extra confidence and poise. People used to do "deportment" classes in which they would be taught how to confidently and slowly sit, stand, walk and eat – a good start. You can practise these yourself.

> I think acting confident is the best way to feel confident. If you do something for long enough it tends to become who you are.
> Keisha, 17

Be polite, but feel free to remain quiet until you've seen how you could warm up and be more outgoing, or how the social rules work in an unfamiliar situation. (You can dance on the table later if that seems like a good idea – although having two beers can make it seem like a good idea when it really isn't.)

A lot of people use tricks and confidence boosters to overcome their shyness. Try:

- ☯ pretending to be yourself, only a more confident version
- ☯ getting drama or voice lessons to learn how to speak and move in front of other people without being embarrassed
- ☯ joining a drama, debating, performance, sports or any other group in which people are brought together by a shared goal or interest.

Actually I think the most annoying part of being shy is when adults point it out. As if you've never noticed.

Cool

Being confident isn't being up yourself, or thinking you're better than every-body else, or that you can put other people down. Real cool is not caring too much about what's in fash-ion or what other people think. What's cool right now will be uncool pretty quickly. Real cool lasts.

And then one day, I realized all the people in the 'cool group' behaved like chimps...

I don't usually care if other people don't like me because I like myself the way I am and I'm not changing who I am. Jade, 14

I hate it when I say something that I think sounds really stupid and that means everyone must think I'm a freak, only to find out the next day that nobody remembers and I feel even more stupid because I made a huge deal of it. Salima, 13

Don't just rely on your looks, and don't compare yourself to other people.
Rebecca, 18

If someone says I'm bad at something I take it personally, and then I get really nervous about the next thing I do. Lizzie, 13

When you don't feel confident about something but you do it, and you feel good, and then someone says something to destroy that new-found confidence – you don't want to try [again] for fear you will be made fun of.
Kristen, 16

All it takes is one look from someone who doesn't like me to send my confidence level plummeting.
Amber, 15

Mostly comments from my friends or my mother affect my self-confidence.
Elise, 17

When I'm at home I stay in my room and don't do anything 'cause it's so tiring faking all the time. Moira, 14

I meditate. Not the whole yoga meditation but I try and stay as still as possible and as quiet as possible and I ask myself questions like "Am I happy? Why/why not?" or "What do I want to be like?" Sometimes I don't like the answers that I get, then I look at whether or not I want to change those answers and how I can go about that process. Kate, 17

Girls are expected to like but not love themselves, and not complain but still worry about what they look like. We are expected to change personalities to suit different people. Clare, 15

Self-confidence is something that you will achieve only when you find that what others think of you is not the be all and end all.
Sarah, 16

When people give me compliments I don't take them in. I say thank you or whatever but it sort of goes in one ear and out the other. When I give someone else a compliment I genuinely mean it. Don't know why it's like that.
Chrissy, 18

If you want to build up self-confidence you should find a talent and improve it. Other than that get friends that appreciate you.   Chandi, 16

I think that teenagers need to stop looking at magazines full of supermodels! Some magazines even say they are showing "real girls" but it looks like they have had makeovers and photo enhancement. It's hard to teach someone self-confidence – maybe you should get all your friends to write a list about the good things about you and make sure you read it every day to remind yourself how important you are.
Ange, 18

Adults being patronizing – makes you wonder why you went through the whole toilet-training saga if only to be seen as a child.
Emily, 16

Don't listen to what people say, and don't believe the photos in magazines. Value you. Value what you have to offer to the world as a human being, not as a pretty face. There is more to being alive than spending a life on the scales, or in front of a mirror. No one else has the right to judge you for the importance or adequacy of your contribution to the world. And if they think they do, prove them wrong.   Nicola, 16

Avoid negative thought patterns and remember life is what you make it, and not everything is always about you – no one is constantly taking notice of what you are doing.
Anonymous, 18

Really cool people don't need to feel better by criticizing others. People who desperately want to be cool are the most judgemental.

Things that definitely aren't cool   These can include:
- G trying hard to be popular and fashionable
- G being mean to other people so you can get into or stay in the "cool group"
- G being cruel to other people because they're different
- G being rude to staff in shops or cafes
- G sneering at everything, and everybody else
- G being a snob.

The "cool group"   This group always flounces around, acting cooler than everybody else. It's probably not much consolation at the time, but here is the news: the cool group is usually exactly the same bunch of people who, at the school reunion ten years from now, turn out to be the biggest losers of all time. Still stuck-up, of course, but with absolutely NOTHING to be stuck-up about. You realize they're such a bunch of has-beens you wonder why you ever cared, for a microsecond, about what they thought or did.

More info **on self-confidence**

See also "More info on feeling optimistic and strong" in the Feelings chapter.

Too Soon Old, Too Late Smart: Thirty True Things You Need to Know Now by Gordon Livingston, Mobius
If you don't have a family whose wisdom helps you along in life, try this guy.

Kiss My Tiara: How to Rule the World as a Smart Mouth Goddess by Susan Jane Gilman, Time Warner
Funny book about being strong, feisty and your own self.

Who are you?

As you grow from a kid into an adult you start to ask questions such as "Who am I?", "Why do some guys have feet that smell like mouldy cheese?" and "How come I'm not an international movie star with my own island?" But let's start with that first one.

> Being yourself can be hard. But it's a lot of fun. Once you have learnt about yourself, that's when it's easy.
>
> Billie, 13

What do I know for certain?

You can say these things for certain:

- ⑥ "I'm a good person."
- ⑥ "I have as much right to life and happiness as anyone."
- ⑥ "I am an individual and I am okay."
- ⑥ "Nobody is perfect. I don't have to be perfect."
- ⑥ "I don't have to settle for something I'm not happy with."

If it helps, you can say these affirmations to yourself regularly.

Is there a role model who would suit me?

A role model – somebody you admire – can be a useful person to learn from or to feel inspired by. But it can be hard for girls to find role models in a culture that mainly celebrates women for what they look like rather than for their achievements.

You may just have to look a little harder. You'll need to seek out some women you can admire for what they've done – not whether they're rich enough to lie around getting fake tans and being photographed in four-inch heels, with weeny, bald dogs.

Think about women politicians; sports people; song writers and musicians; writers; businesswomen; actresses; brainy girls; kind girls; political activists; mothers; racing-car drivers; scientists; philosophers; grandmas; interviewers; paramedics; teachers; engineers; aunties; journalists; percussionists; artists; photographers; designers; comedians; small-business owners; chief executive officers of major corporations; political leaders; environmental activists; social workers; acrobats; councillors; builders; nurses; doctors; TV producers; farmers; daredevils; trailblazers; good girls; naughty girls; brave ones; feisty ones; ones who don't care what their hair looks like while they're getting stuff done.

Some thoughts on role models

- ⑥ Don't get so involved you want to be them, not you.
- ⑥ Don't set them up as a saint or a goddess who's oh-so-perfect and then get disappointed when they try to break into a bar at 4am with no knickers on.

A role model may be good at acting, but not so good at dignity.

- ☉ Don't let regard for one role model blind you to other people and other options. It's good to have other role models too.

- ☉ Don't settle for role models who are being pushed in your face. Search outside the mainstream film, TV and sports stars. Who else is doing something interesting? Important? Different? Out there?

How can I find out more about myself?

To discover more about yourself why not try the "Who Am I?" quiz opposite. (If you find the answers are depressing, or confuse you, talk to a trusted adult about it.)

You can photocopy the quiz first so you can do it again every few months. Maybe you'll be surprised at the things that change, and the things that don't. Keep the filled-in quiz sheets in a safe place such as your diary or a secret hidey-hole, and look back to see how you and your life change as time passes and how much confidence you've gained.

Blend in or stand out?

One of the confusing things about being a teenager is that:

✱ in some ways you want to be just like everybody else – "Don't notice little ol' me, I'm just going to blend in with the back wall here; in fact I'm going to paint myself beige".

✱ yet in other ways you want to be so special and different that you can hardly stand it – "Hey, check it out, I'm going to be FAMOUS!"

"When I was little I felt embarrassed about being different. Later I learned that the things that make you different make you special."

Kylie Kwong, chef, restaurateur, author

Who am I?

My name: _____

Date: _____

What do I love doing? _____

What interests me? _____

What am I good at? _____

What makes me happy? _____

When do I feel the most confident? _____

What do I believe in? _____

What are my biggest problems right now?
_____

What am I afraid of? _____

What qualities do I like in people/friends?
_____

Who are my closest friends? _____

If I wasn't in this group of friends,
would I be different? _____

How do my friends treat me? _____

I need to find friends who are interested in:
_____

I'll always love: _____

How am I like my parents? _____

How am I like my siblings or cousins? _____

In what ways am I different from my parents?
_____

In what ways am I different from my siblings
or cousins? _____

What's special about my family? _____

What makes me feel good about myself?
_____

Who can I confide in with total trust? _____

What have I changed about my life? _____

What would I like to change about my life?
_____

What would I like to stay the same? _____

What are my short-term goals? _____

What are my long-term dreams or
ambitions? _____

What girls feel confident about

Here are some of the things the girls in the Girl Stuff Survey said made them feel confident or that they feel confident about:

my sporting ability ✱ my morals and personality ✱ my hair ✱ I'm good at acting so even if I don't FEEL confident I act as though I am ✱ I'm not bad looking; I know I can make people laugh; I can walk in heels ✱ that I am a good person, that I am intelligent and healthy, and not too ugly ✱ my friends ✱ speaking in front of my class mates! ✱ Um… everything basically ✱ not much ✱ nothing ✱ my intelligence ✱ being able to enjoy myself ✱ doing school work and playing sport ✱ drumming ✱ answering teachers' questions – sounds stupid, I know, but people think I do that well ✱ that I can walk the streets at any time of day and feel that if I am attacked I will be able to defend myself ✱ I'm a good listener; I live to help friends and I'm confident that in some ways I can help ✱ how I look when I am wearing clothes my mum says suit me ✱ talking to people ✱ my reading/writing ability; performing ✱ don't really feel confident about anything, I just love to give everything a go ✱ sports ✱ nothing – but I can deal with nerves okay ✱ I try to look and feel confident about everything ✱ my image, my friends, meeting new guys ✱ that I am going to be happy and successful in whatever path I choose to follow in my life ✱ my face ✱ my family loving me no matter what ✱ my swimming and my legs – love my legs! ✱ that I can look after myself and young children ✱ my personality and those who I can trust ✱ my dancing ✱ asking for assistance; talking to adults; ability to do well at school; trying new things ✱ outdoor stuff ✱ people always say I'm a nice person ✱ I can always make my friends laugh ✱ I am good ✱ playing wing defence in netball, and making a fool of myself for a laugh ✱ my family loving me ✱ my life, and I am doing the best I can to live life to the fullest ✱ mixing with new and different people ✱ I'm not popular and I don't want to be so I can just be myself because my friends accept me for who I am ✱ sailing, and having a laugh ✱ art ✱ being around my friends and my family ✱ everything ✱ my calves ✱ my Tae Kwon Do abilities ✱ wearing what I feel comfortable in ✱ my hair (sometimes) ✱ everything except public speaking and talking to guys ✱ getting where I want to be ✱ I have a larger vocabulary than my friends 'cause I like to read – this makes me feel special ✱ who I am on the inside ✱ I am good at netball and people like me (most of the time!) ✷ my fringe ✷ that I can talk to strangers now ✷ basically everything but my appearance ✷ **my attitude** ✷ being gay ✷ making new friends and not caring about what people think or say about me ✷ everything – I'm an overly confident person ✷ cycling ✷ cooking, and standing up for my rights ✷ designing! ✷ **helping people sort out their problems** ✷ acting – it's when I can be a different character, not me any more! ✷ my intelligence ✷ my personality ✷ being myself; trying hard at everything ✷ I am a good person ✷ I'm able to hide my insecurities from myself and others so that I may be confident ✷ riding motorbikes ✷ singing ✷ when I am in a group of people ✷ my mum – we have a good relationship ✷ **my image – I'm different and I like it** ✷ showing people the movies I make; talking to little kids ✷ my smile ✷ my clothes ✷ I feel that I am very good at science and I'm the best in my class ✷ I want to become a journalist and I'm confident that I will become one ✷ **everything** ✷ I feel confident when I am laughing ✷ karate and music and school ✷ my strength ✷ that I will go somewhere in life and succeed ✷ **that if anything bad happens there will always be someone to support me** ✷ looking after my siblings when mum and dad go out ✷ my long legs because I spent most of my life hating them and got sick of it so I made myself love them!! ✷ I believe that if you're good at something, you don't need to say "Oh, I really suck" ✷ my abilities to listen, be a good friend, sing ✷ kickboxing ✷ speaking my mind ✷ my choice in fashion ✷ my family will always love me no matter what I do or what I look like ✷ **my fashion – I know most girls my age are afraid to wear some things that I do** ✷ my water-skiing and my artwork ✷ that my pets will always love me even when I make mistakes ✷ my organizational abilities ✷ parenting; labour ✷ being able to help people in most circumstances; and telling people how I feel ✷ **my health** ✷ talking to people and dealing with customers; most of myself; being able to handle any type of horse ✷ **my academic abilities** ✷ my artworks ✷ my face ✷ **I can cook!** ✷ saving my money ✷ speaking different languages ✷ my ability to have interesting conversations with older age groups (55 plus) ✷ work (only part-time but still) ✷ being silly – I can laugh at myself and really not care ✷ **working and earning** ✷ one of my friends always looks confident and I think it is due largely to how she walks so now I try to walk confidently! ✷ **the way I think**.

I'm a middle child so often I feel insignificant.   Ruby, 16

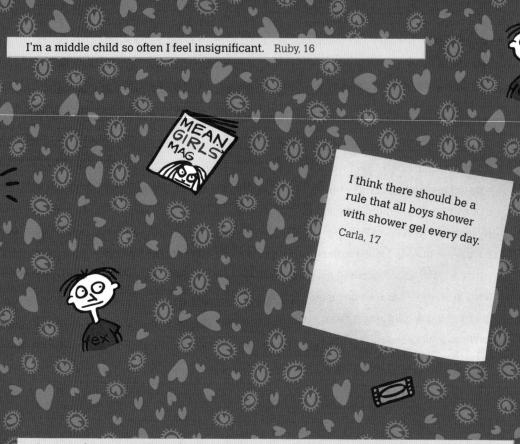

MEAN GIRLS MAG

I think there should be a rule that all boys shower with shower gel every day.
Carla, 17

I want to know everything there is to know about sex, really.   Bridget, 14

When I'm with my friends I get this weird courage so that I can do loud and exciting things.

I exude this confidence that I just don't feel.   Kath, 15

PART 3

HEART →

FAMILY

12

Some families are happy havens where you go when you need help and cuddles. Others are sad or bad, and you spend most of your time trying to avoid them.

When you're little you think that **all families** are the same – that all parents do what yours do, and that all families eat the same food and have the same problems. As you grow up you start to realize that families can be very different, and that your parents may not be as smart as you thought – or as stupid.

tHeRe aRe MANy Kinds of famiLy...

Happy families

Happy families seem to share some of the same elements. Not every family can achieve these, but working towards them can make family life happier.

In a happy family people tend to:

- ⑥ love each other and show it
- ⑥ like and respect each other
- ⑥ communicate honestly and openly with each other
- ⑥ spend time together
- ⑥ solve problems together
- ⑥ get through bad times together
- ⑥ not have serious stresses such as mental or physical illness, drug or alcohol abuse, war or a history of distressing events
- ⑥ have an okay financial situation so that they are not worrying about money all the time – this is not necessarily about how much money a family has, but its attitude to money
- ⑥ be willing to find ways to get on better together.

> We've had some great and awful times. But we've always pulled through them together. No matter what happens I know they'll be there for me. I love them.
>
> Cassie, 13

Getting on with a parent

If you get on with a parent everything is easier. Letting them know you well is an important part of this. Tell them what you think about, what your hopes and worries are. Tell them when you find something difficult, when you're trying your best, when you're happiest. And tell them that you want them to be proud of you.

Try to be honest. If you let them know how you feel they won't have to guess (and maybe get it wrong): "I guess I feel angry because I really, really wanted to go". Let them know that when they start panicking or yelling as soon as you tell them worrying stuff (such as someone offered you drugs) it makes you feel you don't want to tell them anything.

You don't have to tell a parent everything – you are entitled to your privacy and your own thoughts – but it will help you to get on better if they know how you think and feel.

It also helps if you make an effort to understand where *they're* coming from

(which can be hard to do if your parent or parents are away from home a lot or otherwise busy or distracted).

How to get to know a parent

- Offer to go out for a walk with them some days, before or after they've been to work. It will give you a chance to chat.
- Help to get the evening meal, and sit down together to eat it.
- Take the time to get to know the parent you spend less time with (even if you have to do this by writing messages, emailing or texting).
- Go on family outings and holidays together (you can trade these for other occasions when you want to do something on your own or with friends).
- Show support by offering to help them when they're going through a rough time.
- Go to their work or sporting events if they want you to: this makes it more likely they'll return the favour when you need it.
- Let them know that you appreciate what they do for the family and that you're proud of *them*.
- Accept apologies from them as you would want them to accept yours. You're old enough to know that your parents aren't perfect: they make mistakes and can handle things the wrong way.

When a parent isn't there for you

- Ask for their attention, in a nice way. Try a suggestion like, "mum/dad, can we do something together soon, such as make a cake/see a movie/play Frisbee?"
- Explain that you understand they're very busy, but you don't want to turn into one of those kids who only gets attention when they do the wrong thing. That'll scare 'em.
- If they're busy, or in the middle of a temporary project, ask to make an appointment with them to do an activity or have a talk later on and stick to it.

> I can talk to my mum about anything and I know she won't judge me.
> Hayley, 17

◑ If they're always busy, ask them when they think that might change, or what you could do to help change it.

◑ Wait for the right moment to talk to them. Don't interrupt them when they're on the phone or in the middle of something else (including a busy junction).

◑ Learn a few parent-friendly phrases such as "I'd really like your advice", or "I think you could help me with this", or "Can I come with you and help?"

◑ Try arranging a regular "appointment" with a parent – such as Sunday brunch or a Friday-night walk.

Family rules

Most families have rules about safety, schoolwork and responsibilities, and ones to avoid fights and to let kids know how to behave. A lot of people think the rules are the same for all families, but they're not. One girl who wrote to the Girl Stuff Survey was amazed somebody had even asked what her family's rules were: "Duh, the usual rules – no horses in the house". This will come as news to folk who never thought of popping a pony in the pantry.

It seems to some teenagers that their families are nothing but rules, with laws laid down on even what opinions they're supposed to have. (And if parents live apart there may be a different set of rules in each house.) Others think their family has hardly any rules at all, leaving them to find their own way to adulthood with not much more than a tin opener and a couple of pairs of socks provided.

Conversation starters with a parent

Ask them:

✳ what they loved doing when they were your age

✳ what naughty things they did as teenagers

✳ whether their life turned out the way they thought it would

✳ what makes them happy

✳ what makes them sad

✳ what they'd still like to accomplish in life

✳ what their ideal holiday would be

✳ what they have to do at work and whether they like it.

Dads shouldn't make stupid comments about their daughters' looks. It affects them and families should remember to tell each other you love each other and that you are proud of each other.
Gabriella, 18

Common family rules

- No hitting.
- No disrespectful talk or swearing.
- Everyone must sit down together for the evening meal.
- No going out wearing a skirt smaller than a packet of crisps.
- No TV until homework is done.
- No more than two hours' screen time a day (including videogames, TV and surfing the web).
- Everyone, except the adults, must keep their room tidy.
- No wet towels to be left on the floor.
- Kids must put their dirty clothes in the washing basket.
- Half an hour of phone time a night.
- Parents should always know where the kids are.
- No alcohol before you're 18.
- No illegal drugs.
- Kids must be home before dark or call to say they're in a place the parents are happy with.
- Kids will be grounded when they lie.
- Kids must do household chores to earn their pocket money.
- Kids must pay for their own mobile phone calls.
- Kids must be in bed by a set time but can then read for half an hour or an hour.
- No stealing granny's wig.

> ★
> **famiLy RuLes**
> 1. no undies on heads
> 2. feed the ferret

Negotiating rules   If you want a clearer understanding of the rules that seem to be operating at home, or you'd like fewer rules or some input into them, ask if the family can have a meeting.

- Ask your parents to write down the important rules – or perhaps you can do it together.
- Ask politely for the reasons behind the rules ("Could you please explain why my brother is allowed to do something, but I can't?"), and show that you appreciate some of their concerns: "I understand that you're trying to protect me".

> I'm shocked to see how different my friends' families are to mine. Usually the kids get whatever they want, yet have no close relationship with their parents and just think of them as a free meal. It makes me really value my own family.
> Phoebe, 14

FACT

Training parents You can train parents to treat you more like a grown-up by proving you can act more like a grown-up.

Mum and dad work 24/7 so I have to cook tea and look after my sister and I hate it.
Erin, 14

My parents give my younger brother privileges I wasn't allowed at his age.
Laura, 17

🌀 Ask them to explain what will happen if you break the rules: "Will I be grounded, or yelled at, or what? And will the consequences be the same if I break the rule accidentally?"

🌀 Ask if any of the rules have exceptions or are open to interpretation. (To you "Keep your room tidy" may mean you know where everything is. To them it may mean there has to be nothing left on the floor.)

🌀 Tell them if you don't think a certain rule is fair and why: "I think this rule is fair, but that one doesn't seem to be because… [give reason]", "I'm feeling frustrated because none of my friends has that rule in their family".

If you feel a rule is too strict or unfair, but your parents won't change it, perhaps there is a relative, a teacher or one of your parents' friends who could talk to them about loosening up a little (with or without you being there).

Changing the rules Most families have fewer rules as you get older – parents love it when you show them you can be trusted.

Here are some possible ways to get rules changed or relaxed.

🌀 Get acceptable marks at school.

🌀 Always be reliable when you say you'll call or you'll be home at a certain time.

🌀 Don't lie to them about where you're going or where you'll be staying.

you SO have a point

HOW to tALK TO PARENTS WHEN you WANT SOMETHING

I've learned that parents aren't always right.   Faith, 16

- Have sensible friends, who they can get to know.
- Do a self-defence course or martial arts training so you won't seem so vulnerable.
- Drop any bad toddler habits, including tantrums, rolling your eyes and saying, "What . . . ever".
- Ask them for their advice on how you could have made a situation better: "How could I handle something like that next time?"
- Tell them what you think you learnt from a mistake or an experience, good or bad.
- Talk about the difference between rights and responsibilities. (You have the right to be treated respectfully; you have the responsibility not to frighten them by staying out all night without telling them.)
- Say in a reasonable voice that you think you're ready for more independence: "Can I tell you why I think things have changed?", "I think I can act responsibly because… [give reason]", "What can I do to reassure you that I'm ready for… [whatever it is]?"
- See if you can reach a compromise – if the rule is you can't go out at night, how about only Friday or Saturday as long as you're home by a certain time and they know where you are?

> I had no rules. My mum never asked me where I was or what I was doing. I could disappear for days and walk home in the middle of the night. It was like she just didn't care what happened to me.
> Jessica, 17

Brothers and sisters

How you get on with your siblings (brothers and sisters) can depend on your ages; personalities; interests; whether one needs more health care than the others; and whether you are seen as both equal *and* individual (you may not be treated the same, but you can be treated with equal fairness and love).

Good things about brothers and sisters

- They understand where you are coming from.
- They can be an ally against your parents.
- They can be loyal friends when you need them.
- They can give you a feeling of belonging.
- You can share lots of secrets and memories.
- Younger ones look up to you.
- Older ones can look out for you.
- Older ones do some of the hard work with your parents on gaining freedoms before you have to.

I used your lipgloss

SIBLING CRISIS

What girls say are the strict rules in their family

Here are some of the responses from the Girl Stuff Survey:

mum won't let me go to parties unless she calls the parents first ✳ every day 24/7 we must show respect to our older relatives, and rebellion is as bad as murder ✳ if a boy sleeps over they cannot sleep in the same bed ✳ sensible actions. Think ✳ no dog upstairs, no games before homework, no going out on the streets after dark ✳ don't skip school or get pissed ✳ no chat rooms ✳ I am not allowed to shave my legs or buy *Sugar* magazine ✳ I can't have a boyfriend ✳ I have a curfew for using the phone: 8pm ✳ my dad is in charge – don't annoy him ✳ I'm not allowed to tell anyone we are on the dole ✳ I can't date, go to parties where there are boys, sleep over at friends' houses, wear miniskirts or low-cut tops ✳ no slamming doors, no saying shut up ✳ nothing with preservatives to eat ✳ don't eat meat ✳ no parties!!!!! It is the WORST rule! And no make-up ✳ not allowed on the net during the week ✳ can't go out on school nights ✳ no mobiles till you're 18, can't leave church till you're 18, no dating till you're 16, can't leave home till 18, can't dye your hair till 18 ✳ I have to do maths for one hour every day ✳ call if you are running late home ✳ always tell mum where I'm going and when I'll be back and who I'm going with ✳ no kissing the rat too much and no tormenting the rat ✳ no cat on the table ✳ don't go in cars with drink drivers, or friends with their learner or restricted licence. No drugs, drinking ✳ whenever dad makes up rules he forgets them a week later. Ha ha ✳ NO BOYS IN THE BED (except when my parents don't know and they are SLEEEEEEPING!) ✳ my parents have a lot of faith in my brother and me. We do what we think is right, and if it isn't they put us back on the right path ✳ my mother just says no to everything ✳ to tell my mum if I have sex ✳ no wearing heels with a miniskirt ✳ my parents say if there are no parents where I'm going, or they can't speak to them beforehand, then I CANNOT GO. They are good about most other things but usually places I go are unsupervised so it means a lot of sneaking around them and lying! ✳ I'm only allowed to take two alcoholic drinks with me to parties ✳ don't dress like a man, don't have short hair, don't discuss Muslims, Christians, the economy, feminism, gay rights. Don't speak to dad unless you're spoken to, don't talk back to dad, don't disagree with dad. No parties, no short clothes, no boyfriends or boy friends (girlfriends for boys okay) ✳ no rules.

6 You don't usually stay mad with each other for long.

Annoying stuff about brothers and sisters

6 They can seem the favourite.
6 You may have a personality clash.
6 They may take your stuff.
6 They're in "your" space (or face).
6 People assume you're the same.
6 People expect you to "follow in the footsteps" of an older one.
6 People expect you to take responsibility for the actions of a younger one.
6 People assume because of your position in the family you'll have a certain personality.

> I absolutely ADORE my little brother.
> Jade, 15

> My mum expects me to be as good as my sisters.
> Madison, 15

> How are you meant to cope when you share a room with your sister who leaves her mess all over the floor and cleans it up about once a month and I like my room clean?!?!?!
> Annette, 15

> They're my step-sisters. They're mad! They are so much fun!
> Alex, 14

> I don't think of them as my half brother or sisters but as normal brothers and sisters. Theresa, 14

Not-so-happy families

Every family has its tensions, its secrets, its roles for each member (the clown, the peacemaker, the responsible one, the naughty one), and some families are dysfunctional (don't work properly) and full of tension and strife. Many families, though, can learn how to turn fights and arguments between generations, or between siblings, into (reasonably!) calm discussions.

> My mother and I don't talk and haven't for nearly a year.
> Nic, 17

> My parents aren't around much.
> Alana, 14

Dumb things to say in an argument

The following statements will either make a parent (and anyone else) even more furious, or will make you seem like a little kid who can't argue on a grown-up level.

"That's not fair", "You're so unfair".

"You hate me."

"I hate you."

"You never let me have any fun."

"Piss off."

"You suck."

"You don't have a clue."

"You're trying to ruin my life."

"It's different since you were a kid."

"Everyone else is going."

"You are so…"

"Shut up."

"You can't make me."

"Anyway, nerny, nerny, ner ner."

"What would *you* know?"

"I *said* sorry." (That doesn't suddenly make it okay.)

"That haircut makes you look like a baboon's arse."

Unhelpful "body language"

Also avoid speaking in a shouty or defensive tone of voice, or using body language that could make a parent (or anyone else) even crosser. (It may be entertaining, but it won't help you get what you want.) Try to steer clear of:

* "closed poses" such as crossing your arms, lying rolled up in a ball, turning your back, refusing to make eye contact, shrugging or turning your body away

* grunts instead of replies (which are so Neanderthal and non-verbal as to be almost body language)

* aggressive or hostile poses such as standing too close to someone, or looming over them if they're sitting down; clenching your fists; making violent movements; putting your hands on your hips; or staring in a challenging or angry way.

UNHELPFUL
BODY
Language

Useful things to say in an argument

Give yourself an advantage by sounding responsible and smart, and showing that you're able to listen and take in what a family member is telling you. Saying something like the following will help:

"I disagree, but I don't think it's worth fighting over so we'll do it your way." (Save your energy for an argument you really want to win.)

"Let me get this right: what you mean is…"

"What are you feeling?"

"Are you angry, or worried, or both?"

"I didn't know that's how you felt."

"I hear you."

"I never thought about it that way."

"Can we talk about this later, after I've had time to think about what you've said?"

"Could we please sit down and talk about this because I'm confused."

"Let's talk later when we're not upset. Maybe after school?"

"Is it my turn to speak now?"

"I'm sorry."

"Can we try and work it out together?"

Taking the heat out of arguments

Perhaps your family can agree to a few guidelines that will help calm a disagreement. Here are some examples.

- Anyone can make an appointment to discuss something with another family member or call a family meeting.
- No interrupting. Everyone waits their turn to speak and listens respectfully.
- No one is allowed to end a discussion without hearing everything the others want to say – but a discussion can be suspended until everyone has calmed down.
- No shouting or insults.
- No physical hostilities.
- No pouting, sulking, flouncing, theatrical sighing or slamming of doors.
- Discussions must be conducted without sarcasm, mimicry or other meanness.

If it feels as if a discussion is getting off track, try to get the family to refer to this plan: somebody raises a problem, then everyone talks about their ideas on how to solve it and the possible drawbacks they see to each solution, and finally everyone agrees on a solution together.

Tension breakers for yourself (and other family members)

- Scream into a pillow.
- Do something that makes you laugh.

⑤ Have a bath.

⑤ Go for a walk.

⑤ Dance madly in your room for fifteen minutes.

Conflict between partners

All partners have arguments (even if they try to keep them from you). It is a natural part of a relationship and doesn't necessarily mean they are going to break up. But it can be horrible for you to hear your parents or other family members having arguments, especially if they sound mean or they're violent.

Maybe you Have a PaReNt WHo is stRessed ←

If the fighting does upset you, try explaining to the grown-ups (when they're not fighting) how it makes you feel. Ask them to make an effort to argue when you are not around.

Sometimes the fights involve the children of the family as well. When conflicts never get resolved, family counselling services can help. Many talking therapists (counsellors) specialize in getting families together and helping them to find solutions to their problems and better ways of listening to each other.

When parents are hopeless

Not everyone has kind, generous or useful parents. Some parents do not know how to properly look after and care for their children – or even how to show love. Many parents were themselves brought up in sad, cold, abusive or violent homes, and some don't know how to change. If you need to avoid home, try to find another family that you can go to for relief and to see people relating in healthier ways.

It can be comforting to know that lots of people who have been brought up in a bad home situation eventually form new "families" with groups of friends. You may not have met yours yet, but one day you'll be out of there and can go off to find them.

In the meantime you can get advice on how your family life might improve by calling ChildLine (see "More info" coming up soon).

Family abuse   Family abuse can include emotional, physical or sexual abuse. Some families are so dysfunctional that almost everyone abuses everyone else, although of course the children are always the most vulnerable. Abuse can be by a dad, mum, brother or sister, or a relative from outside the home. The person being abused can be a child, a parent or a grandparent.

Abuse is wrong and never the fault of the person being abused, even though it can feel that way. The Savvy chapter has info on how to recognize and stop emotional, physical and sexual abuse.

More info on not-so-happy families

ChildLine: 0800 1111

www.childline.org.uk
On the Childline site, choose "More info"
and then "Home and families".

www.relate.org.uk
The charity Relate provides counselling
and support for families, couples and
young people.

www.theinsite.org
US teen site. Choose "Relationships
unlimited", then "Parents", "Siblings",
or whatever else you're interested in.

www.thesite.org
On YouthNet's teen site, select "Sex &
relationships" and then "Family & friends"
for articles on dealing with family holidays
and dinners, problematic and clingy
parents, and a sibling survival guide.

My mum is a judgemental person, so I don't feel comfortable sharing personal details with her, as much as she'd like me to. Cassandra, 16

I think we have the funniest moments together, especially when we go on holidays, camping. Hannah, 13

Families are freaky, weird things! Everyone thinks only their families are the most dysfunctional, but there's always one out there that tops you... And there's no such thing as a perfect or totally happy family, even if it seems that everybody else's family is more together than yours. Heather, 16

My mum acts like she doesn't even like me sometimes, and she acts like I do and say everything wrong. Tess, 13

I hate the thought of moving away from my mother even though I know it is a normal thing to do. Amelia, 18

I don't live at home because my dad assaulted me, so I live with my best friend's family. Alex, 16

My dad makes me sad. He doesn't realize how much what he says affects me. I've tried to tell him, but he chooses not to hear it. Bethany, 17

When families break up

Lots of teenagers have parents who separate or divorce (the legal version of separation). Often the people separating are very sad, and sometimes also feel angry with each other, guilty about the break-up of the family and worried about the future. There might be another adult involved because one of the partners has started a new relationship, but sometimes the two people separating just don't want to be together any more.

Family breakdowns can happen really quickly, and you might have had no idea that anything was wrong before you we're told. This can make it hard for you to understand why your parents want to separate, or make you believe that it isn't necessary, but usually adults have thought long and hard about it before making the final decision.

Sometimes former partners stay friends, even taking holidays together as a family. Sometimes the parents don't like each other any more but, because they respect each other and their kids, they're always polite and never criticize each other in front of their children. But sometimes the conflict, hurt or anger between them is so strong that they say bad things about each other and continue to fight, or refuse to communicate.

If the parents can't agree on how to share the parenting, a mediator will try to help them sort things out. If that doesn't work, there may be a case at a family court where a judge will decide where you will live (Residence) and how much time you will spend with the other parent (Contact). Because the court's main aim is to do what's right for the kids, you may be asked to see an independent official called a "Children and Family Reporter" who works for Cafcass (the Children and Family Court Advisory Support Service), to talk about how the conflict is affecting you, and how you can divide your time between the two parents or which one you'd like to live with. It's their job to listen to you and to make sure your views are heard in court.

Talking it through

There are a lot of important things you'll want your parents to discuss with you about the separation. You can:

- ask them why they have agreed to stop living together – they may have decided not to discuss this because they're afraid it will upset you to talk about it, but you may want to hear the answers even if it is upsetting (have these conversations at a calm time, not when they're having an argument)
- say you prefer them not to go into the details of what they fight about, or what one "did" to the other or didn't do
- tell them you can't take sides

> My mum is my best friend and I never fight with my dad. Although my parents are divorced, I see my family life as more stable and healthy than a huge percentage of my friends' families whose parents are together.
> Alice, 17

Things to know about separation and divorce

✿ Separation or divorce is not caused by you, even if your parents sometimes argued about your behaviour. It's caused when adults don't want to be together any more, and that's never a kid's fault.

✿ You have a right to be upset about such a huge change in your life, which you did not ask for or cause.

✿ You shouldn't be asked to "take sides" by either parent.

✿ You have a right to ask one of your parents not to criticize the other one in front of you.

✿ Your parents are separating from, or divorcing, each other but they will always be your parents.

✿ You have a right to continue to see both parents, and both sets of grandparents (and other relatives), if you want to.

● make it clear you won't be the "messenger" between them, or pass on info about what the other partner is up to

● ask them not to say anything negative about the other one when directly talking to you, or where you can hear it.

Speak up if you're not happy with the living arrangements they've decided on or if you'd like to spend more or less time with one of your parents. You don't have to make a decision suddenly or quickly: you can just say that you'd like the arrangements to be for a month or so, and then talk about possibly changing them later.

Often after a separation or divorce one or both of the parents will have less money. One may give you presents and money to reassure you they still love you, but a parent who can't afford lots of presents still loves you.

Go easy on yourself as this isn't something you just get over immediately. Your parents are upset, and you're upset. You're not in control of the situation, and it's normal to feel angry and to grieve for what life used to be like (see the Feelings chapter). It will take time to adjust to the new situation, but it can help to talk about how you feel.

I get very upset about not seeing my dad.
Flick, 13

I think my dad is a jerk and I don't really want anything to do with him.   Rosie, 15

I can always rely on mum to understand me, and dad to give me stuff.   Natasha, 13

The upside of separation

- ☺ Your parents will probably be happier apart.
- ☺ Your parents may be more honest with you.
- ☺ Your home life may not be so stressful.
- ☺ You may get a better understanding of your family and yourself (talking therapy can help).
- ☺ It can be a reminder that, no matter what the family goes through, your parents still love you.

More info **on when families break up**

All this info is also helpful for parents who are separating or have separated.

www.cafcass.gov.uk
The Children and Family Court Advisory Support Service. Choose "Info for teenagers" to find out about family courts, Children and Family Reporters (remember that's a person the court employs to be your "voice"), adoption and what will happen to you if your parents live separately.

www.divorceaid.co.uk
Divorce Aid is a support organization for parents and young people dealing with a family break-up. Click on "Teens" for info on your feelings and the law or to download useful leaflets.

www.itsnotyourfault.org
Support and practical info for children, young people and parents going through a family break-up, from the children's charity NCH.

My parents divorced when I was 5, and what really shits me about society is how they think divorce is SO terrible. They rarely understand that in a lot of cases divorce is a very, very good choice to make.   Alex, 16

My mum has been divorced from a rude bastard.   Libby, 14

My parents fight all the time even though they don't live together any more.   Sky, 13

It can be heartbreaking when you finally realize that mum and dad are NOT getting back together.   Lauren, 14

The thing that makes me sad is having to go to my dad's house and my mum's house on set weekends. I don't like having two different houses to go to.   Stella, 14

Different family combos

I think you'll get the idea from the box overleaf: there are nearly as many kinds of family as there are families.

Single-parent families

For some or all of your life you may have known or lived with only one parent. It may be because your other parent died or can't come to this country; but sometimes it may be because one parent decided from the start that they didn't want to be involved in a family, or they drifted away after a separation or divorce.

Some parents don't want to be in their kid's life. This is never the kid's fault. Some adults can't handle the responsibilities of bringing up children or never learnt how to make a good family. It's okay to be angry and to feel let down by one of your parents, but it helps to talk to someone about it. Be proud that you're part of a successful team with one parent.

Being adopted

Finding out suddenly that you're adopted can be confusing. It's usually easier when your adoptive family is open and honest about it from the start.

If you feel you want to find your birth parents you may decide to wait until you've left home because you don't know how to talk about it with your adoptive parents and don't want to hurt their feelings. Legally you are not entitled to see your birth certificate and adoption records (which will give you a starting point in trying to find your birth parents) until you are 18 (or 16 in Scotland).

The agencies that reunite you are not allowed to give your contact details to anyone searching for you until you give your permission, and you can choose not to be contacted by a birth relative if you prefer.

Some reunions with birth parents are successful, and some aren't, but it might be easier to deal with if you can talk to your adoptive parents and get their support. There's a lot to think about, and no way to predict the outcome. You may want to have a continuing relationship, or you may just want to meet once.

"Partner parade"

When your parents are no longer together you can often have their temporary (or ongoing) new partners in your life.

FACT

Gay parents The main problem with having a gay parent is having to explain it about 96,573 times to people: "Yes, mum has a girlfriend. No [sigh], it doesn't seem weird to me".

Any of these combos can make a family

mum and kid

dad and kid

mum and kids

dad and kids

mum and kid and "weekend" dad

dad and kid and "weekend" mum

mum and dad and kids

mum and step-dad and her kid

mum and step-dad and his kid

mum and step-dad and her kids

mum and step-dad and his kids

dad and step-mum and her kid

dad and step-mum and his kid

dad and step-mum and her kids

dad and step-mum and his kids

mum and dad and his kids and/or
   her kids and their kids together

mum and mum and kid

dad and dad and kid

mum and mum and the kids of both

dad and dad and the kids of both

mum and mum's boyfriend and her
   or his kids

dad and dad's girlfriend and his or her kids

mum and mum's girlfriend and kids

dad and dad's boyfriend and kids

granny and grandkid

grandma and granddad and grandkids

kid living with an auntie or uncle

kid living in auntie's or uncle's family

kid and adult brother or sister

kids living with a friend of the family

kid living with their friend's family

mum and grandma and kid

mum and grandma and kids from
   different dads

dad and grandma and kid

mum and dad and pop and granny
   and kids and great-auntie Fanfaronada

mum or dad and kid or kids, with
   various other relatives and a bunny

And I wouldn't be surprised if there
   was a family with a step-bunny.

Some parents have a series of partners who come, then go. A new partner can be very hard for you to accept, especially if you don't like the person, feel they're in your space or don't respect you, resent them taking your other parent's place, or really like them but fear they'll put you through another break-up.

You have a responsibility to be polite and to behave well towards new partners, but you also have the right to ask your parent:

- to keep the details of their love life, particularly their sex life, to themselves
- whether their partner is allowed to tell you what to do, or whether that's your parent's responsibility alone
- for the privacy and space you need, and an assurance that you won't have to deal with a shared bathroom that doesn't have a lock on the door
- not to expect that you'll consider the partner your new parent or call them mum, dad, auntie or uncle. First names, used respectfully, are perfectly fine.

"Blended" or "step" families

Most parents who separate will make new families straight away or within a few years by getting together with a new partner – and sometimes that partner has their own kids or will have a baby with your parent. So there'll be a "blended" or "step" family situation – with all kids living in the same house all the time or moving between their different parents' houses.

Getting your head around the idea of a new family is a pretty big project, especially if it happens before you've absorbed the shock of your original family coming apart. Sometimes it's the upsetting point at which you really understand your own parents will never get back together.

Before you become part of a step-family   You need to discuss with your parent the issues outlined in "Partner parade" above, and also talk about:

- what your parent expects of you
- who will tell your other parent about their ex's new relationship
- where each person will live
- what will happen if you don't like the new family members

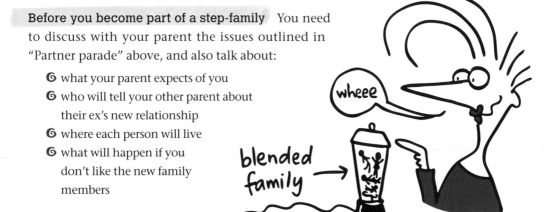

blended family →

wheee

I love my family. Even though it's small, it's great.

My mum is a champion, and she does a wonderful job as a single parent.   Emily, 15

The ups and downs of step-families

Downside

✱ Your other parent might be jealous and angry about the new family and ask you questions or say mean things about it, or make you feel disloyal.

✱ It might be hard to adjust to a new family and/or a new house.

✱ You might feel you're missing out on your parent's attention as they try to make the new relationship work and welcome the other kids.

✱ You might feel left out, especially if there are more of "their gang" than "our gang".

✱ You might have to share a bathroom with more kids, which is especially difficult if one is a guy who's the same age or older.

✱ It takes time to get used to your parent being affectionate to someone new.

✱ It's confusing if your parent is acting differently with this partner from the way they acted with the previous one.

✱ Try as you might, maybe you won't be able to like your parent's partner or their children.

✱ You might resent your new step-parent telling you what to do.

Upside

✱ There can now be more people in your family gang who will be loyal to you and look out for you.

✱ It can be fun to have "new" brothers and sisters.

✱ Your parent will probably be happier and there is now someone else to love and look after them, which can take pressure off you.

✱ It can give you another opportunity for a happy family life.

✱ The cost-sharing can mean there's a bit of extra money for fun things.

✱ You can share thoughts on the situation with step-siblings.

✱ Your new step-parent loves your parent so they will want this to work. With luck, they'll want to be your friend, while understanding they're not a replacement for your other parent.

✱ More presents!

- ⑥ what will be the response if any of the new family members are mean to you
- ⑥ who your parent will side with if you have a disagreement with their partner
- ⑥ whether you will have to change school or move house
- ⑥ whether you will have to share a room with anyone
- ⑥ whether you will have new responsibilities such as looking after younger step-siblings
- ⑥ what will happen if this partnership breaks up too.

You do have to be reasonable and you can't deliberately sabotage your parent's new relationship. Your parent will appreciate you making an effort to give it a go.

You also shouldn't "spy" on the step-family for your other parent.

But you don't have to adjust to the idea of a new family the first time it's suggested. You need time to get used to the idea. And you do have rights that need to be respected, including the right to have any new rules or responsibilities explained.

You may even end up being connected to two new blended families, one with your mum and one with your dad, and find you've suddenly got a lot of instant step-relatives. (And if the new partners were to break up you'd end up with a lot of ex-step-relatives.) Don't even start on what happens at Christmas. But then Christmas can be a pretty full-on time for any family.

More info on step-families and adoption

www.bbc.co.uk/parenting/family_matters
Choose "Stepfamilies" for all sorts of info on step-families, extended families, new babies and same-sex families.

www.stepfamilyscotland.org.uk
Provides support and info for step-families, including info about legal issues and adoption. Click on "Publications" for a range of leaflets on "Living in step-families".

www.adoptionsearchreunion.org.uk
This website run by the British Association for Adoption and Fostering is the best place to start tracing birth relatives, locating adoption records and getting support.

www.afteradoption.org.uk
This charity offers support for everyone affected by adoption, and runs a national helpline for young people: 0808 808 1234.

I don't mind living in a two-house family at all. Since my elder brother moved out to live with my dad, I like the female energy mum and I have in our household.   Denise, 17

Being adopted can be a good thing. I love the way mum told me and my sister we were adopted young so we've always known.   Kelly, 16

I hated my step-mum at first but then I realized she wasn't there to take my mum's place, she was there because she and my dad were happy.   Mel, 14

FRIENDS

13

good friends can make
you laugh 'til you cry...

Like the old nursery rhyme says about the little girl with a curl right
in the middle of her forehead, when friends are **good** they are very,
very good and when they are **bad** they are HORRID. The hardest part
of school for many people isn't about working out complicated maths
equations, or even worrying about exams. It's about friends – trying
to work out who's a **real friend**, what happens when friends are mean
to you, how you make new friends, whether you have to be in a group
and whether you need a best friend.

Good friends

Having friends can make life so much easier and more fun. It means laughing so much you nearly wet your pants (or you actually do wet your pants – but enough about me). It means hanging out together, and having secret codes, words and private jokes that only you understand. It means writing songs or plays together, borrowing each other's stuff, going places together, being there to help each other through bad times, having someone you can blather on to about absolutely anything.

I can rely on my best friends for everything. It doesn't matter if I make a total idiot of myself with them because I'm confident that they will always be there for me.
Steph, 15

It's about having a safe place to go, except that the safe place is a person or a group of people.

You choose

Just by being yourself you will often attract people who like the same things. And sometimes you "click" with somebody without really knowing why (although you can't always tell when you meet someone for the first time whether they are going to become a good friend).

But don't sit back passively, waiting to be chosen. You're better off "toughing it out" for a while until you find a good friend, rather than letting yourself be chosen by someone who's too bossy, boring or not nice to you. And don't go to all the bother of pretending to be different in an effort to be liked by someone – it's too hard to keep up the act. (The section "Making new friends" later in this chapter has tips to help you.)

Sometimes somebody you choose won't be interested in being friends with you. That can be hard, but you have to move on. It's still heaps better than just waiting there, like a box of muesli on the shelf, for somebody – anybody! – to pick you.

Not everyone has to like you or be your friend. A couple of friends are enough.

What makes a good friendship?

Real friends:

- ♂ genuinely like each other
- ♂ can be themselves when they're together

NOT A
GOOD
LOOK...

- keep each other's secrets
- like doing some of the same things
- make time for each other – and not just when it's convenient for them
- really listen and try to understand each other's feelings
- are loyal, stick up for each other and never join in when others are being mean
- accept that friends have different opinions, clothes and interests.

a good friend doesn't blab your secrets

More info on good friends

For hints about finding friends safely online read the Savvy chapter.

www.thesite.org/sexandrelationships/familyandfriends/friendship
The YouthNet UK site has stuff on making new friends, being a good mate, surviving rows and improving your social life.

www.reachout.com.au
The site of the Australian Inspire Foundation for teens. From "The issues" choose "Friends & Relationships" for info on friendships and getting along.

I feel confident about my relationship with my friends. Surround yourself by a good group of friends. They always see the good bits, the important bits.   Kat, 16

My closest friends remain my closest friends. I feel confident that I am loved for who I am, and that I am the most comfortable with them, which gives me confidence that I'm doing something right!   Jane, 18

I just want lots of good friends, not a best friend.   Maddie, 14

I often feel like it's hard to make friends because I am quiet. People don't give me time to open up and instead they write me off straight away.   Megan, 18

Guy friends

Some good things about guy friends

✤ They can be just as loyal as girlfriends.

✤ They're like your secret agents in Guy Land – they can tell you how guys think and what they're saying.

✤ They help you to be less nervous around other guys.

When you have a guy friend

✤ Be yourself – don't suddenly be girly or flirty, or all tough and sporty, if that's not the usual you.

✤ Don't treat him as a substitute boyfriend who gets dropped when the "real thing" comes along.

✤ Don't expect him to hang out with your boyfriend, but don't ever let a jealous boyfriend tell you who you can't have as a friend.

✤ Don't touch him in a girlfriend way: no kissing on the lips or lingering hugs.

✤ Don't ever expect a gay guy to "turn" for you and become your boyfriend – it's a waste of time and offensive to try to change somebody's sexuality.

✤ Be totally honest with yourself about whether you really do want to be "just friends". One way to tell is to imagine him full-on going for it, kissing another girl, and see if you wish that girl was you.

✤ Be kind but honest if he wants to be more than a friend and you don't. Say that you don't feel that way about him, but that you'd like to stay friends (and try not to act weird around him afterwards). If you find he can't be just friends you'll need to take a break (but never, ever tease him about his feelings or joke that you might change your mind).

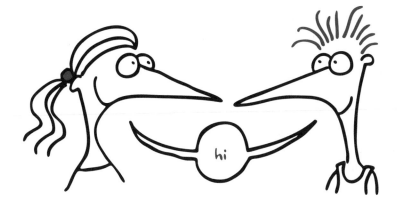

Changing a friendship

No one should stay in a bad friendship. Some friendships are good for a little while, or even for a long time, but then it's best to move on. Sometimes you need to decide if a good friendship has gone bad, or if it has just been damaged but can be repaired.

When a friendship goes bad

The giveaway signs are that the "friend":

- 🔄 makes you feel used
- 🔄 treats you differently at different times, depending on who else is around
- 🔄 doesn't keep your secrets and confidences
- 🔄 dumps you when they get a boyfriend or a "better offer" from another friend
- 🔄 makes you feel uncomfortable, nervous or frightened
- 🔄 is possessive or clingy – always jealous of your other friends and insisting on being with you
- 🔄 makes you feel you are being controlled or manipulated to do what they want
- 🔄 promises a lot of things but doesn't come through
- 🔄 gossips and judges a lot, creating a negative atmosphere
- 🔄 thinks only of themselves
- 🔄 seems to compete with you all the time.

In our early teens kids can be so cruel, it's hard to remember you are beautiful. Surround yourself with positive, supportive people.
Liz, 17

It's time to let a friendship go instead of trying to patch it up when:

- 🔄 a friend has let you down so badly that you don't feel you can trust them again
- 🔄 you don't really want to make up – you're just avoiding conflict or being polite
- 🔄 the other person doesn't really want to make up (although it can be really hurtful, you have to accept rejection and move on)
- 🔄 you can forgive, but you don't want to be close again
- 🔄 it's only other people who want the two of you to be friends again
- 🔄 you'd only be agreeing to be friends again to stop the tension of constant fighting. A relationship in which one person has to give way all the time isn't really a friendship.

The problems I have experienced with friends are that they are

self-absorbed little...   Jen, 17

Fixing a friendship

A friendship is worth saving if you:

- ☺ really want to be friends again and the other person does too
- ☺ can forgive them, or want them to forgive you
- ☺ want it to be okay between the two of you, even if you know it won't ever be quite the same
- ☺ understand that you expected your friend to be perfect and that wasn't realistic
- ☺ accept that you were blaming your friend for everything, but perhaps should share some responsibility for what happened.

> Hang around with friends that don't make you feel like you have to conform or act in a certain way.
> Joey, 17

> My best friend often ditches me for a boy.
> Jasmine, 14

How to fix a friendship   Make a few attempts to talk through whatever is making you or your friend mad or upset, and see if you feel there is a friendship worth saving. If there is, invite your friend somewhere, or suggest doing something together, and see what the reaction is. Spend a little more time together and gradually you may find the friendship is back on.

Sometimes it's just time that hammers out the dents left on a friendship by a mis-understanding, a bad mood or a mad moment of meanness. Friendships can be up one week and down the next, or even on different days.

How to leave a bad friendship

The following suggestions may make it sound easy, but ending a bad or unsatisfying friendship is always hard. The whole thing can be very messy and upsetting. It can make you feel anxious, give you tummy aches and cause tears. One way to get through it is to focus on what you really want, such as new friends who don't tease you, or friends who do stuff instead of just sitting around gossiping. Keep reminding yourself that the pain you're going through is worth it because your life will be so much better.

Doing the drift   You can just let a friendship wind down by gradually spending more time on other things and with other people.

- ☺ Explain nicely to the friend you want to leave that you have a new hobby, lunchtime theatre rehearsals, something to study in the library, sports training or whatever.

> **Actually my friends don't really like me.**   Andrea, 13

◔ Get a parent to say you're not allowed out so often, or you have to make a wider group of friends. (If you want, one of your parents can contact one of theirs.)

Stopping right now You can't just stop talking to someone and walk away whenever they approach, because that's mean and unfair.

◔ Say things such as "I'm sorry, but I just don't want to be close friends any more. I don't like the way you talk to me", or "I don't want to fight with you any more so let's take a break from seeing each other out of school", or "I think I'm going to sit with different people at lunchtime for a while".

◔ If you end up in a huge fight try to stay calm enough to say the things you want to, such as "I was so hurt when you told people my secret. I just feel I can't trust you again", or "You yelling at me like that is one of the reasons I don't want to hang around with you any more".

Saying sorry

If you're the one who has behaved badly in a friendship, you need to apologize sincerely, not just with a "Yeah, sorry". Show that you know what you did and the effect that your actions or words caused: "I'm so sorry. I did the wrong thing and I can't take it back. I hope you can forgive me or at least give me another chance".

One solid apology should be enough. You don't have to grovel, but you do have to accept that if you let your friend down again (or a third time) they will be wise to move on. And you too can have a two-or-three-strikes-and-you're-out policy.

If you're on the receiving end, accept a genuine apology gracefully by saying something like "Okay, then. Thanks for saying sorry", and either patch up the friendship or choose not to.

Making new friends

Making new friends can be hard, especially if you're shy. (And who isn't a bit shy and slow to warm up around someone new?) The most obvious place to make friends is at school, but there are plenty of other places too.

I just kept my head down and rode it out. Found some new friends that I'm still best friends with today. Kathryn, 18

Starter sentences

Here are some ways to kick off a conversation with someone new.

"Mind if I sit here?"

"Did you have any idea what that science experiment was supposed to do this morning?"

"What are you listening to?"

"Help! I don't know anyone else at this party and I'm about to talk to the pot plants."

"Hi. Where'd you get your shoes? They look great." (Don't overdo this or it will sound like you're sucking up to them. One compliment a conversation is plenty.)

"Hi. Have we met?"

"Can we talk? I've been texting all day and I don't know if I remember how to have a conversation any more."

Getting started   Making friends usually involves some effort. Unless you're the sort of person who can set up a booth with a sign saying "Apply Here to Be Friends with Me: £2" and wait for a customer, you'll need to develop some "small talk" skills. The best thing is to quickly hit on something that you're both interested in and get chatting about it (see the "Starter sentences" box for some suggestions).

Making good friends, rather than acquaintances (people you know but aren't close to), takes time. Don't go telling people your deepest, darkest secrets when you first meet them, or asking them really personal things, as this could scare them off. ("Hi. Ever had a sexually transmitted infection? Hey, where'd everybody go?")

Where to look for new friends

- Is there someone you see around but have never got to know? It could be someone you've seen at the bus stop reading a book you love.
- What about your local neighbourhood? Can you reconnect with kids you knew at primary school who went to different schools?

friends don't Have to be tHe same ...

⑥ How about cousins or friends of friends, or the kids of your parents' friends who you haven't seen for a while?

⑥ Is there a part-time job you could take that would mean meeting new people as well as learning new skills?

⑥ Can you think of a sports team, band, youth club, film-making course, or circus-skills, art or karate group that you could join? (See the Caring chapter for heaps more ideas.)

In year 7 my "best friend" decided she didn't want to hang out with me any more. I can easily say that was the biggest grief I had ever had to deal with. The loss of that comfort zone was devastating.

Zoe, 18

I spent six months alone when I left a mean friend. Sitting on benches, reading. Now I have a best friend and other friends. I don't need her any more, and I don't need to feel bad when she sneers at me or makes up more rumours. I'm strong now.   Julie, 13

A girl used to swear at me and I felt sad and left out because she was in our group and everyone was on her side. Can you still be someone's best friend when you don't like them?   Kathy, 13

I would like a best friend who I can share all my thoughts with and who would be able to share her thoughts with me. Not having a best friend makes me feel kind of lonely.

Lee-Anne, 15

I'm always scared to show them the real "me".   Caz, 13

When I'm with my friends I get this weird courage so that I can do loud and exciting things. I exude this confidence that I just don't feel.   Kath, 15

I completely changed friendship groups, which was the hardest and best thing I have ever had to do. You worry about what the people you were leaving behind will think, and whether the people in the group you want to be a part of want you there. I am so glad I changed friendship groups.   Vicky, 16

Groups

Some people love the sense of belonging so much, or feel so attracted to an image or lifestyle, that they join a group that almost has a uniform, code of conduct and head-quarters. This "tribe" might be the goths, nerds, emos, skaters, cool group, art gang, musos (musicians) or whatever else is going at the time. These small worlds can give you a strong sense of belonging and being among friends who understand you – but they can also make you feel like you're living in a little box.

Other people choose to be friendly with lots of people rather than joining one group: they're natural diplomats who don't need intense friendships. Not everyone is like that, but even when you're someone who wants a spe-cial group of friends it's good to be able to get along with other groups or different people outside your own circle.

> I have never really fitted into a particular group anywhere. I'm friends with lots of people in different groups.
> Tracey, 15

> My friends always bitch about each other. It makes me wonder what they say about me!
> Lauren, 17

Fitting in

It's great to feel you fit in, but you should be able to do so without having to be exactly the same as everybody else. If you hang out with positive people who don't mind your little differences or eccentricities, it makes you feel more positive too.

In a good group of friends you should be able to:

- ☺ feel proud of your own interests
- ☺ keep (or change) your opinion even if it's not the same as everyone else's
- ☺ choose your own clothes and how you look
- ☺ admit to feeling unsure about something
- ☺ feel as if there isn't a group leader who makes the rules for everyone else
- ☺ make your own decisions about where to go and what to do
- ☺ feel confident your friends won't ridicule you.

"Peer pressure"

"Peer group" is a term that can mean a particular bunch of people of similar age, back-ground and interests: say, the drama group at school. (It can also mean all people of similar age and experience – teenagers, for example.) Sometimes being in a group means

> Sometimes I get a little too much pressure to follow their rules, and to have to look
> a certain way to fit in, but my friends are really the best!   Lucy, 15

all the members deliberately or unconsciously start doing the same things and looking alike (lots of piercings, blonde with a fake tan or whatever).

Bad peer groups make you feel as if you have to do and say the "right" things or you'll get frozen out. Being seen hanging out with the popular mob may not be as much fun as it looks. In fact it may be like being a puppet in hell.

I worry that when I am myself my friends won't like me, because I don't like to act immature all the time like my friends.
Smita, 17

"Peer pressure" is the pressure you feel to change your behaviour, your appearance, your interests or what you have to say because you want to impress your friends or be accepted by them.

Peer pressure can be:

- **Direct**   Somebody orders you around.
- **Implied**   You know that if you don't wear what the others are wearing people will mock you or be cruel to you.
- **Manipulated**   Advertising and other kinds of marketing make you feel that if you don't have the latest thing you won't be cool (see the Shopping chapter).
- **Internal (comes from within you)**   Because you're unsure of yourself, you copy others to feel you're more likeable and doing the right thing.

Peer pressure can give you logic-fade. Remember when you were little you could get into soooo much more trouble if you were with a friend, brother, sister or cousin than if you were on your own? Because when you were together something could seem irresistible: decorating the sofa cushions with mashed banana, "borrowing" mum's lipstick, or feeding the dog beer. The same thing can happen to you as a teenager, or even when you're grown up. "It seemed like a good idea at the time" may be completely true, but it isn't the brainiest philosophy of all time.

How not to be controlled   Always have a few good comebacks ready for when you're being pressured into something you don't want to do or say. In the Drinking and Drugs chapters there are lists of things to say that can be useful in other situations. The Confidence chapter has ideas on how to feel strong and good about yourself, and ways to say no.

HINT

Dodgy sales pitch   If you get pressured to do something RIGHT NOW, then it's probably a good idea to say no. Give yourself time to think.

Moving groups

If you're in a group that's pressuring you to con-
form, if you're threatened by, frightened of or
being frozen out by people in the group, or if
you feel restricted, or that you can't be yourself,
or that you don't like what they do, consider
moving groups. Have a look at the tips on how
to end a friendship given in the "Changing
a friendship" section earlier.

The breakdown of your relationship
with a group is a really confusing and upsetting time, and can make you feel like hitting
somebody with a plank or hiding in the
library forever. And the changeover to a new
group can be difficult and take a while, but in
the end you'll have new friends who are
more fun to be with.

> I think that it is about year 9 when people begin to realize who you are (and there
> was some nastiness). I knew I had to move on. I am now in a group with 6 other girls
> (I also have friends from other groups) and I love them all.   Mia, 15

Meanness

Have you ever spoken to an adult about somebody being mean to you and the adult has
replied, "Oh, just ignore it"? If this happens to you again, ask the adult, "Who was the
mean kid in your year at school?" I'll bet they can remember the person's whole name
and everything else about them. It will remind the adult that mean stuff sticks with
you. It's not trivial, and they need to take your problem seriously.

Meanness is the flip side of friendship, and it can even come from someone who
claims to be your friend. Being mean is something that can be done carelessly or
deliberately. It's nasty to say something cruel to somebody's face, and it's cruel to say
something nasty behind their back.

Ignoring meanness is hard: it doesn't always make it go away, and it doesn't stop
it hurting. Even if you walk away or don't show a reaction, of course you can still feel
crushed or furious.

Meanness (and bullying) is seen to be at its most horrible during the late primary and early secondary school years, although it can go on way before then and way after. Some people just stay mean all their lives, so it's good to know how to deflect their meanness. (Because leaping at them from trees and trying to strangle them is apparently illegal. I checked.)

When you're the mean one

In the replies to the Girl Stuff Survey, about seventy percent of girls aged 13 to 18 said they had been mean to somebody else, although many also said they regretted it. (I can remember being mean to a girl at my school, and I still feel bad whenever I think about it.)

Bad excuses for being mean

- ✪ "I was just telling the truth."
- ✪ "I didn't do it on purpose."
- ✪ "I was just joking – they should get the joke."
- ✪ "Everyone does it."
- ✪ "They were mean to me so I was mean back."
- ✪ "It's what girls do."

That last one's the biggest bad excuse of all. Lots of girls and women support each other, as friends and in the workplace, and it's not fair or true to say that all girls and women are mean to each other.

The main reasons people are mean

- ✪ It makes some people feel powerful to be able to affect how someone else feels.
- ✪ Everyone else was being mean and they wanted to fit in.
- ✪ It makes some people feel better about themselves to make others feel bad.
- ✪ By accusing someone of being uncool or wrong they hope to seem more cool or better by comparison.
- ✪ Some people get bored and don't have enough going on in their lives so they stir up drama to entertain themselves.
- ✪ Some are just not very nice, and they've got away with being nasty all their lives.
- ✪ Others are frightened or feel challenged by people who are different in any way – those who have different-coloured skin or different ideas – but can make themselves feel superior by putting those people down.

Gossip and rumours

Gossiping can be a way of catching up with friends' news; a way of keeping in touch. But nasty gossip can do terrible harm to somebody's reputation and self-esteem. People often make a rumour sound more likely by claiming to have a close connection with

How to stop being mean

You need to stop being mean because you'll get a reputation as a "bitch" – which means guys as well as girls won't trust you and will start to avoid you. And because it's more fun to have real friends.

✱ Stop and think before you speak. Is there any point, apart from being mean, to what you're about to say? (Be honest with yourself.)

✱ Make a pact with friends not to do it. If one of you starts, say something like "Bitching alert!", and stop.

✱ Get busy. Have some activities to do with friends so you talk about the movie you just saw, or how your team's doing, or something else.

✱ Get happier. Mean people are often unhappy. See what you can do about your life to improve your mood (see the Feelings chapter).

✱ Get out of the mean group (see "Changing a friendship" earlier in this chapter).

it – their cousin "saw it happen" or a friend of a friend was involved.

Unless you know for sure that something is true – *and* you have a real reason for telling somebody else about it – you're better off ignoring it and not becoming part of the gossip chain.

Why you need to avoid mean gossiping and spreading rumours

⊙ The gossip you're passing on may be a lie.

⊙ Making up a rumour is not only wrong, in some cases it's illegal.

⊙ Cruel gossip hurts people, even if they're not there to hear you.

⊙ It makes people feel it's fair enough to gossip about you.

If you get caught gossiping you should apologize sincerely. Don't make it worse by making excuses.

If the gossip is about you   The gossip could be a made-up rumour about you, or a secret of yours that somebody has told. You have several options.

⊙ Ignore it by remaining "above it all". Instead of an Invisibility Cloak, you have the Invisible Cloak of Dignity.

⊙ Distract yourself. Get on with whatever you're doing. Don't drop everything to investigate and brood.

⊙ Deny it, and just stick to your

I've excluded people and insulted people, although mostly jokingly.

Chrissie, 15

story. Everybody knows that
people can have their own
reasons for making up stupid
or hurtful stuff. Rumours get
distorted or more complicated
as they pass from person to
person, so usually at least some
of it's wrong. This can make it easier
for you to deny it.

a Gossip

☉ Confront the original source
or the spreaders of the gossip,
alone, if you can find them. Tell them to stop it.

☉ Tell a parent or a teacher who you think could help you.

☉ If the rumour or gossip is about something that's true and that can't be avoided
(such as you're going to have a baby, or you have a new boyfriend called Thor and
you're moving to Lapland), take the sting out of the gossip part. Just shrug and say,
"Yeah, what's the big deal? Why are people gossiping about it? I'm not trying to
hide anything".

More info on being mean and gossip

The Big, Fat Bitch Book for Girls by
Kate Figes, Virago
All about gossip and bitching: how to stop,
how to protect yourself, why girls do it.
Flip the book halfway through for the adult
version.

The fun movies *Clueless*, *Mean Girls*,
Girls Just Want to Have Fun and (for older
teens) *Cruel Intentions* (all on DVD) also
have something to say about gossip and
bitchiness.

Friends can make pretty harsh comments and tell you that they're only doing it
because they are your friend. They call it being "brutally honest", but sometimes I feel
that some comments should be kept to yourself. Pip, 16

I have a girl who thinks she's my friend, but I find her really difficult, because she
always makes fun of me, 'cos I'm smart. She does this stupid voice and imitates what I
say if I use a big word, and it makes me feel really bad about myself. Pru, 13

The Intentional Freeze-out

Most people will go through a freeze-out at least once – at some point they get left out of a group.

Of course sometimes it happens accidentally: for instance, people forget to save you a seat. But sometimes you can be hit with the ugliest of mean tactics, the Intentional Freeze-out. You know the kind of thing: people turn their backs or walk away when you arrive, ignore what you say, give you dirty or cold stares, make sure you catch them whispering about you.

The central point of the Intentional Freeze-out can be that nobody will tell you why they're freezing you out. And if you ask, "What did I do?", the answer is, "You KNOW what you did".

It can go on for a lunchtime, a day, a week, or in rare cases even longer. Of course all the time the group is careful not to let adults see what they're doing. What they're doing is bullying you.

There can be any number of reasons for the Intentional Freeze-out:

✱ the Head Bully (or "Queen Bee") of the group is testing her muscles by ordering the action (possibly you have angered Her Majesty by being more interesting than her, or by standing up to her)

✱ maybe there's a rumour going around about you

✱ you said something and now everybody's mad

✱ you didn't say anything, but somebody's boyfriend said they liked you

✱ some girl decided Thursday was International Intentional Freeze-out Day.

Don't ask, "What have I done wrong?" It could be *anything*. Or nothing. Ask yourself, "How can I find some nicer friends?"

If you're doing the freezing out

The least you can do when you're mad at someone is have the decency to tell them why. And make an agreement with your friends that it's no way to treat anybody in the group – otherwise you could be next.

Bullying: way beyond unfriendly

Bullying is ongoing meanness. It could be regular, often or constant, or organized. Bullying is a big cause of sadness, depression and self-harm in teenage girls. Some who are targeted even think about taking their own life, as a number of girls told the Girl Stuff Survey.

The types of bullying include repeated:

- ✿ nasty comments and insults
- ✿ teasing
- ✿ mean "jokes", such as telling you the wrong room to go to
- ✿ rudeness when you're talking (rolling eyes, sighing, sarcastic comments, whispering, mimicking, mocking or smiling in a mean way as if they're laughing at you)
- ✿ the Intentional Freeze-out (see the box earlier on)
- ✿ intimidation – following you, looming over you, staring at you
- ✿ threats
- ✿ sexual comments, rumours, insults or pornographic pictures shown or sent to somebody
- ✿ damage to your things
- ✿ physical violence.

About two-thirds of the girls aged 13 to 18 who responded to the Girl Stuff Survey said they had been bullied, although when they described what had happened the behaviour ranged from awful, repeated bullying that had lasted for years to someone saying a mean thing once. When the charity Bullying UK carried out a National Bullying Survey recently, 69 percent of the girls and boys who replied said they had been bullied, with each one saying they had suffered an average of six different types of bullying at school.

Who are the bullies?

Bullies can be loners or part of a group. They can be someone your own age, or older, or sometimes even younger. Bullies can include your friends, a family member, a boyfriend or girlfriend, a teacher or a boss.

Some reasons (not excuses) for their bullying

- ✿ They don't care about other people's feelings.
- ✿ They want to make themselves more powerful in a group.
- ✿ They may have been bullied themselves, perhaps at home, and developed low self-esteem. This often leads them to become Assistant Bullies who attach themselves to a Head Bully.
- ✿ Many bullies, particularly Head Bullies, just enjoy feeling powerful. They're not insecure and they have a high opinion of themselves.
- ✿ Their parents never stopped them from doing it.

Other reasons (not excuses) for bullying could be:

- ⑤ they get away with it because nobody in authority knows they're doing it (and they can get worse the more they can do their stuff in secret and the more they're not stopped)
- ⑤ they're jealous, ignorant or stupid, or freaked out by anything different
- ⑤ they're bored
- ⑤ they're just in the habit of bullying.

The main reasons people give for joining in on bullying include:

- ⑤ "She made me."
- ⑤ "I had to show that I was in the cool group."
- ⑤ "I had to take down the threat to me."
- ⑤ "No one stopped me."

It doesn't always matter why they do it. You don't have to understand a bully, but sometimes it will help you work out the best way to make them stop.

> You have to work really hard to keep their antagonistic voices out of your head.
> Sandy, 17
>
> I started acting tough.
> Suze, 16

Getting back-up

Dealing with the feelings bullying creates and turning them around to a positive can be very hard – especially when you feel that you're alone.

Asking for help isn't a sign of weakness: it takes courage. You could have a friend with you when you tell an adult about what's been happening. It can be useful to write down each time you're bullied and how, and bring this with you – it will help with the "evidence" against the bully.

MEAN GIRL   ASSISTANT BULLY   FOLLOWER   OVER IT

Cyberbullying

This is being mean, threatening or cruel to somebody, using phone calls, text messages, emails, instant messaging, photos or videos sent by phone, and chatroom, website or social networking site postings. (It can also be known as phone, computer, online, electronic or "e" bullying.)

Using a phone or computer for threatening or obscene purposes is a crime.

How do you stop it?

✱ Try to keep your email address and phone number private – only give them to friends, and always keep your phone in your bag or pocket unless using it. Turn on Caller ID and only answer calls from numbers you recognize. You can change your number or email address by calling your service provider – the company you pay the phone or computer bills to.

✱ Show any obscene or horrible messages to a trusted adult so they know what's going on and can support you.

✱ Tell the bully in person, when they're alone or with their parent, to stop sending you messages. If you have to tell them in a message, make it unemotional, impersonal and clear: "Any further messages/emails from you will be reported to the authorities and your phone-user access may be blocked."

✱ Keep the messages sent to you and, if your phone or computer doesn't record the time and date they came in, keep a list of those details. This information can be used later as evidence.

✱ If it's unwanted calls, not texts, that are giving you a hard time, get your mum, dad or big sister or brother to answer the calls. This can give the caller a fright, especially if your parent says calmly, "I know what you're doing and I will speak to your parents/the police if this happens again", and hangs up without abusing them.

✱ Turn your phone or computer off to give yourself a break, and keep your phone in another room when you're asleep.

✱ If the person is from your school or another one and they are using school equipment, or sending the messages during school time, tell the school, which should have a policy of stopping these actions.

✱ If the harassment continues you can "block" messages from particular email addresses or people on social networking sites, and some mobiles allow you to block certain phone numbers. If that doesn't work, inform your service provider who can investigate and take steps to stop the harassment.

✱ The person harassing you can be formally warned by the service provider in a letter that sets out the legal penalties if they continue.

✱ If this doesn't work, or if from the start the messages are threatening or

obscene, you can contact your local police directly and they'll investigate the complaint.

See the Savvy chapter for hints about online safety.

If you're the one using a phone or computer to be a bully

✱ You'll be caught, even if you're using a false name, because investigators can track where calls and emails come from: history that can be used as evidence.

✱ You can get a permanent record with phone and computer companies, and they will refuse to issue you with a service.

✱ You may be suspended or expelled. Many schools have a policy of doing this to students who use phones or email to harass people.

✱ Making abusive phone calls is a crime, and under phone and harassment laws you can be fined or sent to jail for harassing someone.

If the first person you tell is a bit hopeless, keep trying until you find someone who can make things happen.

Who you can tell about bullying

◐ Brothers and sisters, cousins and friends: they can help you by sharing problems and talking things through.

◐ Older students: some bullies are more likely to listen to them than to teachers, and to be spotted by them if they keep bullying you.

◐ Your mum or dad: try to make them understand how you feel. Explain that ignoring the bullying doesn't work, and ask them to help you work out what to do. (Many parents need help to understand the depth of suffering bullying can cause and how to support their daughters. There are special ideas for parents on some of the websites given in "More info" at the end of this chapter.)

◐ Teachers: it depends on the teacher, doesn't it? A lot of girls

I'm ashamed to say that I used to be the one doing all the bullying. I had this friend who was really mean. I was willing to do anything to make her think better of me. So I turned into a really mean person. I feel so bad. I probably made more than one person's life hell. Lucy, 17

Changing the feelings caused by bullying

Bullying can cause stress, fear, low self-esteem, illness, physical injury, loneliness and depression. But some of these feelings can, in time, be turned around. Instead of each of the common thoughts below, try the ones in bold.

"It must be my fault somehow."
"No, it's not my fault."

"It's never going to stop."
"There are things I can do to try to make it stop – and I'll start right now."

"I have to face it alone."
"No, I must talk to an adult who can help – and I can find one."

"Nothing can help me."
"There are lots of people and strategies that can help."

"Nobody likes me."
"I need to find some of My People. These are not My People."

"I don't fit in anywhere."
"This is not a place where I would want to fit in. But somewhere there is a place where I can be different and still fit in, and I can find it."

"I should try and change the way I look."
"I don't need to change myself to get their approval. Even if I changed they might still pick on me about something else."

"I should hurt myself so I can keep control of that hurt."
"Their bullying shouldn't cause me to want to hurt myself. There is help available to turn these thoughts around."

who responded to the Girl Stuff Survey said there was no point in telling teachers because they didn't seem to be able to do anything, but others said that when the bully was told off by a teacher and watched, the problem stopped. Your school should have a proper anti-bullying policy that tells teachers what to do when you make a complaint.

- ☉ A school counsellor or nurse: if your school has one, they should be trained in handling these situations. Or, you can talk to another trusted teacher, or the deputy head teacher or your head of year – they often know more about anti-bullying policies than class teachers and might be more able to help.

- ☉ A helpline counsellor: you can call ChildLine to talk and get advice (again see "More info").

I get teased and put down all the time. Occasionally I get threats of physical violence – it really scares and worries me. Rain, 13

"I should give up the thing I like that they're teasing me about."

"If I give up the thing I like I'll be even sadder, I'll feel like they've won, and they might still pick on me about something else."

"I feel rejected and depressed."

"I need to find some friends and get some help so I don't feel rejected and depressed. It will take some time, but I will start feeling better and be back on the way to happiness."

"I should pick on someone else so that they do too, and leave me alone."

"I refuse to let them turn me into one of them."

"I need to pretend I'm fine and make lots of jokes."

"I don't have to pretend that what's happening is okay. It's not a joke if only one side laughs."

"I'm scared to go to school or where the bullies are, but I can't escape."

"I can escape: I need to get some help to stop this, or move to another school."

"I'm ashamed of myself, my family and my culture."

"I'm proud of myself, my family and my culture. It's the bullies who have the problem."

Common suggestions for dealing with bullies Sometimes these tactics work, but sometimes they don't. It depends on the bully. I know some of these methods won't work in all situations, or on some bullies. (I mean, how can you "avoid them" if they're in four of your classes every day?) You may have to try a few methods until you get one that seems to work.

- Try to ignore them. Don't react, don't reply, walk away.
- Have a special mantra to repeat inside your head – "You're a pathetic worm, you're a pathetic worm, you're a pathetic worm" – instead of listening to them.
- Be assertive: stick up for your opinions and beliefs.
- Fight back by saying something smart or sarcastic to show they haven't hurt you. (The opposite of "ignore them".)

Maybe I'll try to stop … I think I will … It's harder to be nice, but more rewarding. Mary, 17

I was in a group at school and thought everything was fine, then one day they all just literally stopped talking to me, and now they are talking to me again and I asked why but no one ever gave me an explanation.   Ruby, 17

You don't realize how much it hurts until it happens to you.   Lulu, 14

I am in year ten and have just found a couple of people who I can really connect with.

Nic, 15

You need to surround yourself with people who love you and can keep you really positive about every situation you get in. They will keep telling you that you can do it and help you to become a strong person.
Chelsea, 18

I used to try and "fit in" and do everything "right". Right clothes, act the right way, talk the right way, do the right stuff. But I was unhappy, and when I learned to be the true green-loving freak that I am, I was so much happier, and found friends who like me for me, not what I'm trying to be! BE YOURSELF. Try not to worry about what people might think of you. Be proud of who or what you are!!

Jamila, 17

The group I was hanging around was the popular group, and one girl decided that she didn't like me so like sheep … the rest follow. I felt not wanted and like no one cared.   Danni, 14

I got teased & bashed up. Felt like no one cared about me any more. Just felt like I was nothing.   Anonymous, 14

I have stood by and watched someone being mean to someone and I could have stopped it but I was too scared to.   Alanna, 17

Sometimes I worry that people must talk about me behind my back as the people I do it to are so oblivious it could be happening to me too.
Annabelle, 15

There has been a lot of bitching in my life but I left that clique. Now I don't have to worry about walking away for a few minutes and have the whole group bitching about me, it's great! Ashley, 16

I just can't find a friendship group that suits me. I have had at least five different friends groups during my life. Alicia, 13

Do something outside of school so you make friends away from your school groups and stretch your comfort zones. Try things u never thought u would try.
Phoebe, 14

There was one main ringleader and she always caused trouble for me. I was never good enough, I felt worthless and I didn't have anyone to be close to. Suzie, 17

I was bullied for three years, people stole my things and called me names, they wouldn't let me sit with them and the boys often beat me up.
Bronwyn, 16

I tend to make fun of people to make myself feel better.
Emma, 16

I made a pact and said that next school year I'm getting out of this group even if it means I'd be alone for a while. I made loads of awesome new friends and am really happy.
Katherine, 13

These two girls decided to pick on me for some reason – they humiliated me publicly and no one did anything to stop it. It feels really disorienting, you start to question your self worth. You wake up fearing the day and go to sleep planning revenge.
Meena, 17

- Stay positive: when the bully is saying bad things, focus your mind on people who love you, good times you've had and all the things you like about yourself to help build up your confidence.
- Try to avoid the bully. Find safe zones such as the library, go to a friend's house after school, or get a parent to pick you up at the school gate for a while.
- Try to hang around with other friends so the bully doesn't get you alone.
- Confuse or toy with the bully: say something nice to them; speak in another language; sing; turn up at school with your Uncle Spike, who is six foot tall and covered in tattoos, and introduce them.
- Threaten to tell an adult, to scare the bully into stopping.
- Learn a self-defence martial art so you feel more physically confident about defending yourself.
- Move groups or schools.

> Ignore comments from those peers who don't have two brain cells to rub together: ie the majority of the "popular" people at school.
> Jo, 16

Some people might tell you that being bullied is part of the "real world" and that everyone has to put up with it at some time in their life and everyone survives it. But everyone has the right to live without harassment and discrimination. No one deserves bullying, and no one "asks for it".

Why most people aren't mean or bullying

Most people aren't mean to each other, and don't take part in bullying. This is because they:

- don't have a bullying personality
- can understand and sympathize with other people's feelings
- know it's wrong
- want to have good friendships, not to be involved in nasty situations
- would feel ashamed if they were mean or bullying
- are scared a teacher or parent would find out
- don't need to suck up to, or try to impress, a Head Bully
- have got better things to do and aren't bored.

Most people know it feels better to be kind and that it's a lot more fun having real friends to share things with.

> That's why I have way more guy mates.   Clare, 15

Standing up for somebody else

Never join in malicious (nasty) laughter or name-calling. Being a bystander who doesn't say anything means you're part of the problem. Bullies can gain strength from an audience who don't protest. They take silence for approval. And a lot of bullies stop as soon as the "victim's" friends speak up.

Standing up for somebody being bullied is not only the right thing to do, it makes you feel good about yourself. And it helps stop bullying from spreading or getting worse. A Head Bully might try to pick on you instead, or as well, but the more that people stand up against them, the more the bullies will have to retreat.

Some schools now have "telling" policies that say it's a bystander's duty to tell a teacher if they see somebody being bullied, and that they won't be accused of telling tales or being a "snitch".

Some ideas

✱ Get together a group who will help – several people confronting a bully can be more powerful than an individual.

✱ Walk away, and take the person being bullied with you. You don't have to be best friends forever – the point is to do the right thing at the time.

✱ Make it uncomfortable, difficult or embarrassing for the harasser or not worth their while to keep bullying. Ask them, "Why are you doing this? What would your parents say if they knew, or your sister/brother?" Or say something along the lines of "Stop embarrassing yourself. You're behaving like a 10-year-old", or (to the person being bullied) "This is so boring and pathetic, let's go".

I'm sure you can think up some good things to say yourself. Keep it short and simple as if you can't be bothered with the bully and they're not important.

It can be useless to try to make a bully realize the hurt they've caused to someone's feelings – because they already know and they don't care, or because that's exactly what they want to happen.

More info **on bullying**

ChildLine: 0800 1111

www.antibullying.net
The Anti-Bullying Network (based in
Scotland) has areas for parents, schools
and young people (choose from the menu
on the left), and info sheets on racist
bullying, discipline, peer support and more.

www.connexions-direct.com
Connexions Direct is a government-run
support service for young people; choose
"Relationships", then "Social life" for articles
on bullying at school and at work, and tips
on dealing with bullies. Also has useful
links, and tells you how you can talk to a

personal advisor by phone or in person in
your local area (England only).

www.need2know.co.uk/beatbullying
Get info on beating the bullies, read about
the personal experiences of other teens,
and find helpful contacts and people to talk
to about bullying.

www.thesite.org
On the YouthNet site for older teens,
search for "bullying" to get the lowdown on
bullying, discrimination and harassment.

yp.direct.gov.uk/cyberbullying
Government site for young people with facts
and tips about dealing with cyberbullying.

Ignorant guys/girls make comments about me being in a wheelchair and being able
to walk. They call me a fraud and yell out stupid comments about me.   Kate, 13

I was being controlled by a person and the person wouldn't let me make any other
friends.   Deena, 13

I have tried to exclude girls I don't like from entering my group of friends at school.
Sarah Jane, 14

I am often a bitch to people before I actually know
them.   Georgina, 16

Girls started rumours about me because they
thought it was funny. It got out of control and we
stopped talking for a while. It's sorted out now,
though.   Francesca, 13

I can be bitchy. I feel really
sick afterwards. I'm trying
to be nice now and just
being an all-round nice
person to everyone makes
you feel better inside.
Liz, 13

Bullying resources to tell your parents and teachers about:

www.anti-bullyingalliance.org.uk
The Anti-Bullying Alliance has lots of useful resources and documents to help teachers develop anti-bullying policies and tackle bullying in schools.

www.antibullyingweek.co.uk
Activities, resources, events and info for schools that want to take part in National Anti-Bullying Week, held each year in November.

www.besomeonetotell.org.uk
The Parentline site has message boards, Q&A and info on bullying for parents who think their child is either being bullied or bullying others.

www.bullying.co.uk
This charity website has sections for young people, parents and schools, and covers everything from bullying policies and helping someone being bullied to cyberbulling, abusive phone calls and "happy slapping".

www.direct.gov.uk/en/Parents/
Yourchildshealthandsafety
Parents should choose "Dealing with bullying" for government info on bullying.

www.teachernet.gov.uk/wholeschool/
behaviour/tacklingbullying
Teachers and schools can sign up to the "Anti-bullying Charter" and download the Department for Children, Schools and Families (DCSF) official anti-bullying guidelines called "Safe to Learn: embedding anti-bullying work in schools".

www.teachers.tv/bullying
TV programmes, articles and resources on tackling bullying.

Queen Bees and Wannabes: Helping Your Daughter Survive Cliques, Gossip, Boyfriends and Other Realities of Adolescence by Rosalind Wiseman, Piatkus Books
An American book that tells parents what goes on and how to support their kids if they need to.

Odd Girl Out: The Hidden Culture of Aggression in Girls by Rachel Simmons, Harcourt Brace International
Another US book that explores why girls can be mean and what to do about it. Helps parents understand and support girls.

I talked about people behind their backs and made fun of them to their faces but as it happened to me also I realized I was really hurting people. I am now much more careful about things I say.
Felicity, 17

14

LOVE

Is it gastro, or love?

Imagine a little alien has landed on your shoulder and asked you to explain **love** on your planet. "Well", you might begin, "I really **love** avocado on toast, and I **love** this guy who's the lead singer of my favourite band but I've never seen him – I just **love** his music and the way he looks and everything about him – and I **love** my goldfish Martine and, well, obviously I HATE my parents because they won't let me go to Dylan's party on the weekend, but I sort of **love** them, but I'll never **love** my little brother, but I guess I kind of do, and I **love** purple, and sunsets, and my friends, but not Mel because she told Ashley what Jake said (did I tell you I'm in **love** with Jake?), and obviously I **love** Grandad, even though he died, oh and I **love, love, love** having my ears tickled and – hey, where are you going? Alien?"

Different kinds of love

Family love

"They drive me crazy." (But you probably love them anyway.)

Pet love

"I love all my pets, but I love Sparky best." (It's usually easier to love a dog than a fish. Why is that?)

Friendship

"I *love* my friends." (Until they're not your friends any more.)

Fair-weather friendship

"Some of my friends only seem to love me when they need something." (So not really friends then.)

Attraction

"Hmmm, he's cuuuuuute. I don't even know his *name*. Am I blushing? I'm blushing."

Celebrity crush

"Oh, my GOD. I'm cutting a picture out of a magazine."

Real-life crush

"There he is. He's still there. Now he's moved his left foot slightly. I think I'm going to throw up. In a good way. No, that's not good."

Unrequited love

"I love you, but you don't love me." (Or the other way round. Bummer.)

Romantic love

"I'm so happy I could SING it from the rooftop. But that would be weird. But I don't CARE."

Lust

"I *really* want to do things with this person when the lights are off. Or on. I'm not interested in lighting."

Relationship love

"We've been together six months. I don't know if we'll be together forever, but right now we want to be with each other and we have heaps of fun."

Lasting love

"I've loved this person for years. We get along well and have similar ideas about some important things, and we're comfortable together and I never seem to want anyone else."

Falling in love

You'll probably have heaps of relationships in your life, particularly since girls these days generally wait longer to settle down and have kids (or even to move out of their parents' house). In your romantic life you'll get dumped, you'll do some dumping, you'll have some so-so relationships, make some bad choices, break someone's heart, have your heart broken, think you've found The One, be betrayed, betray, get over it, make mistakes, and then fall in love again.

Attraction

What makes us feel attracted to certain people? Nobody really knows. Different theories say it's all about:

Don't rush in. They have to be a friend not just a partner.
May, 16

I think I'm getting more fussy.
Sara, 16

- ☉ **Genetics**   This idea says we're programmed to choose people who we want to have stronger, cuter children with. It doesn't explain why some people prefer short brunettes with big legs, and others are crazy for nerdy-looking guys with glasses.

- ☉ **Sexuality, or gender preference** (even though you may not have had sex yet)   Most girls are heterosexual: they're attracted to guys. Some find themselves more romantically interested in other girls (they're gay – homosexual). And some are attracted to both guys and girls (they're bisexual).

- ☉ **"Type"**   The first guy who was ever lovely to you was a tall redhead with hairy knees. Ever since then you've been a sucker for big Scottish chaps with a furry middle leg area.

- ☉ **"Me want pretty one"**   It's like wanting a shiny toy. You choose a good-looking one, whether or not they have any brains or are useful as well as decorative.

- ☉ **Repeating what you know**   You pick someone who somehow looks or acts like your dad or someone else in your family.

- ☉ **Playing nursie**   You pick people who are in trouble or need looking after, or who have no energy and need some of yours.

◎ **"Some day my prince will come"**
You want the whole romantic package. If
somebody agrees to take care of you while
you stay at home and file your nails,
then your work is done.

◎ **Finding your comfort zone**   Some
people just "fit right" – like an old
security blanket or your favourite pair
of tracky bottoms.

◎ **"Danger: falling person"**   "Oooh, some
people are just so exciting! They make stuff happen!
You never know what to expect! Take me with you on that adventure!"

◎ **"Danger: falling expectations"**   "Oh, pick me, because I'm getting desperate.
I'll settle for anyone."

◎ **Getting conned**   You'll take anyone who can talk you into it because you just
want to hear those sweet nothings.

◎ **Physical messages**   Mysterious hormones and scents called pheromones
(pronounced fare-em-owns) attract you to a guy without you knowing why –
it's almost a subconscious decision.

> A lot of my boyfriends have
> been sort of unsure about what
> they are supposed to be doing,
> and it seems they only "make
> a move" because their friends
> keep hassling them.
> Denise, 17

Symptoms   Falling in love symptoms can include a racing heartbeat; sweaty palms;
flushed cheeks; tingly bits; nausea; enlarged eye pupils; not being hungry; wild feelings
of happiness and crushing disappointment; utter self-
consciousness; knowing exactly where
the person is, even if you're pretending not to notice; not being able to
think about very much else; an inability to concentrate.

Of course these symptoms also apply
to a fleeting attraction, a crush and several
tropical diseases.

crush
crush
crush

Crushes   Getting a crush on someone means you are
attracted to them but don't necessarily ever do anything
about it: you just admire them from afar, blush when they

> I lost my best friend of all my life because I'm a girl and he's a boy. He got a girlfriend,
> and that didn't bother me, but his girlfriend didn't like us being friends.
> That ruined our friendship. Helen, 17

come anywhere near you – and then get a crush on someone else one day.

Most girls get at least one crush on someone they don't know. Usually the crush is on a celebrity such as a singer, sports person or actor. The "celebrity machine" (magazines and newspapers) makes this easier for you by writing stories and publishing pictures of "pretty guys" who are likely to become crushes.

Guys

Now we pause for some stuff about guys. (If it's girls you seem to be romantically interested in there's something on that later in this chapter – and all the dating and relationships info coming up is for you too.)

Bonus facts about guys

✱ Guys your own age are probably more immature than you are. (But that doesn't mean you should go out with a 30-year-old instead.)

✱ They're going through their own body changes, insecurities and self-esteem struggles.

✱ Guys are all potential friends, not just potential boyfriends.

✱ Guys are not aliens. Most of them like doing the same stuff you do – going to the cinema, watching TV, playing sport, eating, breathing.

Stuff to know

◌ There is no perfect person for you, no Mr Right. There are lots of Mr No Ways, plenty of Mr Approximates, quite a bunch of Mr Okay For Nows, a small gang of Mr Nearly Rights and a handful of Mr You'll Do Me, Sunshines.

◌ If you change your personality to impress a guy, and he starts spending time with you, you won't be able to keep up the act. (Be yourself. If he likes you, yay. If he doesn't, bzzzt. Move on.)

◌ If you judge a guy by looks alone, you may end up with a creep.

◌ Don't give up your girlfriends or spend all your time with a boyfriend.

◌ Don't fall for a guy who is with someone else, especially a girl you know. Try to have a radar that will only go into full-on Possible Boyfriend mode if he's single.

Guys to avoid

◌ **The racist, rude or otherwise stupid guy**   Life's too short to hang out with an idiot with a small brain and a big mouth.

◌ **The arrogant strutter**   A guy who thinks he's "it and a bit" will never respect you because in his own head he's king.

◌ **The stud**   He acts as if he's made a conquest instead of just being somebody's boyfriend.

◌ **The blabberer**   Who needs their private business broadcast everywhere?

Hints that a guy might be a good one

- He asks you about yourself and what you want to do.
- He likes his mum.
- He doesn't change his behaviour towards you depending on who else is around.
- He makes you laugh.
- He's never mean to you.
- He's not mean to other people to try to impress anyone.
- He admits that he finds some things scary and doesn't know stuff.
- He doesn't blab about things you tell him.
- He doesn't try to pressure you into doing stuff that you don't want to do.
- He uses deodorant and otherwise looks after himself, without thinking he's a movie star.
- Other girls like him as a friend.
- He's generous.

HINT

How to make a guy like you For this you will need to study the ancient discipline of hypnotism. You will need about six years of study time, plus various trinkets to give as bribes (such as shiny baubles, large-screen televisions and vehicles with sound systems the size of a fridge). Oh, and a guy.

HINT

How to catch the guy Many methods can be used, such as acting stupid, doing everything he says, or shooting him with a tranquillizer gun.

HINT

How to keep the guy A nice strong cage ought to do. Make sure you change the shredded newspaper at the bottom of the cage every day.

- **The mean guy**   Maybe he has a hard home life. That's sad, but it's not your responsibility to fix it, or to take abuse from him of any kind.

- **The risk taker**   He'll always love the risk/drink/drug more than you, and you can get damaged if you are drawn into it with him.

- **The little boy**   He can come back when he's grown up. Gross jokes and uncontrollable giggling ain't that entertaining.

- **The vampire**   Look out for the tragic soul who'll drain your energy and make you feel tired just from being around him.

Let's talk about all my problems again...

tHE VaMPiRe

- **The boy who wants a trophy girlfriend**   Yes, he thinks you're pretty, but does he listen to you or just show you off like a new toy?

- **The trophy boy**   Yes, he's handsome and cool and used to go out with that popular girl, but you're really just using him for show, aren't you?

- **The mummy's boy**   This guy's mother does everything for him and is always hovering over him like a helicopter.

- **The friend's boyfriend**   Out of bounds.

Hooking up, dating, or going out with someone

If you like teen magazines you've probably already read about a gazillion words on going on dates. Here are some more, briefly, before you lose consciousness from boredom.

- Going on a date, or going out with a group and pairing off with someone, doesn't mean either of you are in love, or will have sex, or anything else. It just means you go out.

- You have to communicate about this stuff. When you ask someone out make it clear whether it's a date or if you just want to be friends (studying or going to band practice together).

- Think about making a first date going out somewhere in a group (unless you don't want other people watching you) and maybe to see something (a movie or music gig) so that you don't have to talk for hours. If you like how it went you can go for a second date, alone, later.

Asking and being asked

There is no reason why girls can't ask someone out on a date. Guys, in fact, are usually pretty awkward and shy, and if you sit around waiting for them it may never happen.

I think it is important for girls to know that they don't have to do everything a guy says and that they shouldn't spend their whole lives wondering what they can do to make them happy etc.
Robyn, 17

Asking someone out

- Ⓖ Best to ask face to face if you can. Find the person when they're alone and say something along the lines of "Would you like to go out some time?" That way they can let you know if they're interested or not. Always have something in mind in case they say, "Sure. What and when?"

- Ⓖ If you don't know them very well, see if you can get their phone number and ring. But don't send an email or other message unless you're sure it would be kept private.

- Ⓖ Don't ask them in front of his/her or your friends – this could be embarrassing for both of you.

- Ⓖ If the other person says no in a rude or mean way, be assured they're a first-class arse and it's lucky you found out now. If they say no nicely, smile and move on.

When someone asks you out

- Ⓖ Only say yes if you really want to. Otherwise you're just giving them false hope.
- Ⓖ Don't rush off giggling to tell your friends in front of the person.
- Ⓖ If you're sent a message or email keep it private.
- Ⓖ Only ever say no in a genuinely nice way (see "Rejection" below).
- Ⓖ If you can't go to a specific event but you're interested in the person, make that clear: "I can't go because I have hockey practice every Saturday, but if something else comes up ask me again", or "I can't because I have to go to this family thing. But maybe another time?"

Rejection

Nearly everybody gets rejected at some point in their life, no matter how smart, gorgeous or popular they are. Sometimes rejection, like attraction, doesn't really make sense – it's not about how likeable we are, or how attractive, funny or adorable.

How to handle rejection

- Ⓖ Keep your dignity. Try not to make a scene, throw yourself on the ground, burst into tears, abuse them, sneer or say something rude. You can do all those things alone in your bedroom later.

⑥ Don't try to figure out why – it's not because you're fat, ugly or stupid, its just because they can't feel any "chemistry" or they have their own quirky reason. It means it wouldn't have worked out – so move on.

⑥ Don't wallow in self-pity, and make sure you're not obsessing about them just because you can't have them. Hold out for someone who'll really like YOU.

⑥ Get on with something else to take your mind off it.

⑥ Give it time: I guarantee you that after a while you'll notice things that will make you glad you didn't go out with that person.

HOW NOT to 'HANDLE' Rejection

HINT

The best dating advice ever   If the other person isn't interested, GIVE UP NOW. Anything else is a waste of time and liable to end with you feeling humiliated or dissatisfied.

If you do the rejecting

⑥ Tell them simply and make it short: "That's really nice of you but, I'm sorry, I don't feel the same", or "That's really nice of you but, I'm sorry, I'm kind of interested in someone else at the moment". Honesty and kindness are always best.

⑥ Don't try to make them feel better about the rejection by sending confusing signals such as flirting with them or saying, "Maybe next week".

⑥ Don't babble on, explaining why or giving excuses.

⑥ End the conversation nicely: "I'm sorry that I'm not up for that, but it's good to be friends, and I hope I'll see you around". Then leave them so they can have a moment to get over the rejection without you watching them.

⑥ From then on, when you run into them, say hi and don't ignore them.

On a date

First dates can be a bit nerve-racking, but here are some hints to help things go smoothly.

⑥ If it's just to the movies don't dress like you're going to your leavers' ball. Choose a favourite outfit that you feel good in (and use deodorant).

- Work out beforehand if one of you is paying or you're going halves. If the other person's paying for what you eat, or you're splitting the bill, don't order the most expensive things.

- Be safe: tell an adult where you're going and when you'll be back, and carry enough money for a taxi. Don't go anywhere that feels dodgy or dangerous. And if you begin to get a bad feeling about the person, or don't know them well, stay in crowded places (see the Savvy chapter).

> Don't rush into anything. Boys are not the world. I am 17 and I have never had a boyfriend and I don't feel less of a person because of it.
> Maddy, 17

- Don't do stuff you wouldn't normally do, such as drinking something unfamiliar.

- Think of some things you could talk about if the conversation dies. Have a few conversation starters, such as a mutual friend's latest news, or a favourite TV show, movie or album. Ask them about something you know they're into.

- When you ask them questions about themselves, listen to the answers. Seems obvious, but you can get caught up with nerves and end up not listening to what the other person has said.

- It's sometimes a good idea to admit that you are nervous, because they will be too. Always make light of it if things go wrong (say, if someone spills something).

- Don't agree with everything they say, but be polite. Better to say, "I've never thought about it like that", or "That's interesting, but I have a pretty different opinion…", than "You great hulking moron, that's the stupidest thing I ever heard".

- Turn off your phone while you're together, or at least put it on "silent" mode and be aware that every time you answer the phone on a date you're kind of saying "this call is more important than you right now".

- Don't talk about your ex, don't bitch, don't put yourself down and don't pretend you're not hungry.

- Try to have a good time instead of looking for faults or becoming negative.

- Never dump the person you came with and go off with someone else.

- If you've had a good time, say so at the end of the date. If you haven't, just say thank you. Have a few casual back-up lines ready in case they try to kiss you and you don't feel like it: "I never kiss on the first date", or "I think I'm coming down with a cold and I'd hate to give it to you".

> Younger girls need to know that boys don't only care about your looks. The good ones actually care about what is on the inside.
> Tamara, 18

Kissing

No matter how old you are, you're usually going to be a bit nervous about the first kiss with someone. Don't expect your first kiss to be that spectacular: like most things it takes a bit of practice. And it's not all about you – the other person could be a shocking kisser, or be even more nervous than you. Some things that will help you:

- ⚙ fresh breath – just so you won't have to worry about it, brush your teeth regularly, and if you think there's going to be a smooch, don't eat garlic or raw onions

Kissing takes practice

A second date

If you want to date someone again

✻ Tell them at the end of the first date that you'll be in touch or that you'd love to hear from them, but don't push to make firm plans.

✻ If you haven't heard from them within three days send them a message or ring and say, "Hey, I had a great time the other night", without actually asking them out.

✻ If they don't respond, or if they sound uncomfortable or not very interested, back off and move on.

If you don't want to date someone again

✻ It's important to try to avoid hurting their feelings.

✻ Don't give false hope. Say, "Thanks, that's really nice of you, but I don't think I really want to get into dating right now", or "I'm going to be pretty busy for a while, but maybe we'll bump into each other some time".

HINT

Date blabbing   Don't tell everyone you're going on a date, and don't tell everyone everything that happened. Respect the other person's privacy, and your own.

- moist lips – use a fairly standard lip protector, as too much gloss can make them sticky and lipstick might get smudged all over both of you
- the right position – stand or sit close to the person, lean in and tilt your head slightly to one side (if you see the other person tilting their head one way, go for the other side so you don't bump heads)
- closed eyes – not compulsory but can help you focus on the feeling (open them as soon as the kiss is over)
- breathing – remember to (through your nose when your lips are busy)
- the Tongue Thing – you can keep your lips closed, or open them slightly for a deeper, more sexy kind of kiss. The tongue gently licks the other person's lips or tongue. This is what's known as "French kissing" or "snogging". It can be awkward at first, but after a time it will feel natural.

Kissing problems

- Sucking at the other person's lips or face – most people don't like it.
- Lovebites, "hickeys" or bruises, created by suction or biting – they look tacky.
- Stubble rash or "pash rash" around your mouth, which can happen if you kiss your partner for so long that your skin is rubbed red – not a good look, and especially painful and long-lasting if he has shaving stubble.
- If your partner does any of the above, or otherwise kisses like a demented washing machine – all thrusting wet tongue – or does scared little nibbles that you don't like, stop and say, "Let's try kissing like this", and do something a bit more slow and sweet.

> Always be in a relationship with someone who makes you feel good about yourself and understands when you want to do girly stuff with friends.
> Sally, 18

It sucks when the feeling's not mutual!!!   Holly, 16

I went out with a guy who was 16 when I was 17 and he was only interested in what he could get out of me, and motor bikes.   Madeleine, 18

I've realized that I have never dated a guy my own age, they have always been a couple of years older. The maturity level is much greater.   Pippa, 18

Liking girls: same-sex relationships

In every society throughout history there have been homosexual women (lesbians) and homosexual men (gays), who are attracted to same-sex partners, and bisexual men and women who are attracted to both sexes.

There are other words for gay such as "queer" and "poof" for men, and "dyke" and "lezzie" for women. These were originally derogatory words, but have been "reclaimed" by some gay people, who can be happy to describe themselves that way – but not happy when a heterosexual (straight) person uses the terms as insults.

Working out your sexual identity is a part of growing up, and questioning your sexuality is totally normal. But you don't have to decide now. It's not as if you become a teenager and suddenly have to choose which door to walk through.

Your sexuality is up to you to decide, not for other people to "diagnose". Despite what some extreme religions believe, or even what people you know and love might say, being gay or bisexual is not wrong or bad, and it's not a disease or illness that needs to be "cured". It's just how some people are. Sexual orientation is in-built and not something that can, or should, be changed.

You probably already know or have met some lesbian people. You can't tell they're lesbians by looking – they don't all dress the same, have the same haircut, like the same music or use a secret handshake.

It's entirely legal to be homosexual in the UK, and gay people have most of the same rights and responsibilities as other people, although weirdly same-sex marriages (which became law in 2004) are called "civil partnerships".

Some people are gay: that's their business

FACT

Transgender   This is the word people use to explain that their bodies don't match the way they feel. A person may have female parts but feel male, or the other way around. Being transgender is not a choice; it's a rare but recognized condition.

How do you know if you're gay?

The physical and emotional changes of puberty can be pretty confusing. A lot of girls experiment with their sexuality while they work out how they feel and what their preferences are. (Having bisexual feelings can be particularly confusing and put you under pressure because some people want you to "make a decision – straight or gay", but you don't have to.)

Having a crush on someone of the same sex, such as a schoolteacher or a friend's older sister, doesn't necessarily mean you are a lesbian. Touching or experimenting or having sex with a girl doesn't "make" you gay, even if the other girl considers herself a lesbian. And having sex with a girl or a guy isn't a "test" that tells you whether you're gay or straight, because there is no test.

Some girls "just know" from an early age, or it kind of dawns on them that they only ever have crushes on, or are romantically interested in, other girls. Others try to suppress their real feelings and then finally accept them when they're adults.

If you think you might be a lesbian, take it slow and don't worry – even if you don't know any others now, you will. There are lots of places, festivals and clubs where people won't be shocked or tease you about your sexuality, and you'll find lesbian and straight friends you can be yourself with.

The important thing as you're discovering your sexuality is to find a non-judgemental person, or people, you can talk to without them betraying your confidence.

Being a lesbian

It can be hard as a teenager to find other girls who feel the same as you because they're often still working it all out or too scared to say anything about their sexuality. Lesbian relationships can also be difficult because of the ignorance and prejudice experienced: can you hold a girl's hand without being shouted at in the street? And it can be difficult to tell parents because they may have trouble sorting out their feelings and their fears that a lesbian daughter will face a lot of prejudice and may not have children later.

You may have to reassure some girl friends that you don't want to be their "girlfriend", and give them a little time to realize it's still the same old you. But they need to get used to this new aspect of your life.

I have lots of friends who are lesbians and they're as happy as Larry. (Larry's happy.)

Lesbians do not have to act like men or pretend they're men, and I don't know any who do. You don't have to dress outlandishly as a lesbian or have really short hair. You can be any sort of lesbian you like: you can wear

> I lean towards girls more. I only recently admitted who I am to myself ... I'm not quite ready to flaunt it yet (although the kids at my primary school and high schools seemed to know before I did ... funny how that happens).
>
> Emily, 17

lipstick and dresses and be interested in cooking and flower arranging, or be into motorcycles or rainfall averages. Don't be frightened by some of the images of lesbian life you might see on the web, in magazines or in porn – none of it's compulsory, and there's no one way to be a lesbian, or to be bisexual.

Coming out Coming out usually means to declare your sexuality. Don't feel you have to make a big announcement. (Quite a few people have done this and then changed their mind about their sexuality.) You may just want to tell family and one or two close friends.

Many organizations offer support to young people who are thinking about coming out, and most areas have gay and lesbian counselling services where you can talk to people who have been through it and get useful hints (see "More info" opposite).

Gay girl movies

Here are some movies available on DVD rental for teen girls featuring same-sex relationships (most are rated 15).

But I'm a Cheerleader
Coming-of-age comedy about a teenage girl sent to "straight camp".

D.E.B.S.
Schoolgirl secret agents in *Charlie's Angels* style parody.

Imagine Me and You
Typical British romantic comedy given a lesbian twist.

The Incredibly True Adventure of Two Girls in Love
Girls from different backgrounds fall for each other.

My Summer of Love
About friendship, love and mistrust.

Ten percent of young people identify as lesbian, bisexual, gay or transgender and we're sick of being ignored.   Donna, 16

I kissed a few girls and the word got around. I spent a lot of time denying the rumours, but got sick of it. That's who I am for now. Who knows? Who cares?   Elaine, 16

More info **on liking girls, and same-sex relationships**

www.llgs.org.uk
The London Lesbian & Gay Switchboard
runs a national helpline: **020 7837 7324**.

www.bbc.co.uk/switch/surgery/advice
On the BBC's teen site, The Surgery, click
on "Sex & Relationships" for articles about
exploring your sexuality, coming out and
finding a girlfriend.

www.lgbtyouth.org
The Queer Youth Network supports lesbian,
gay, bisexual and transgender young people
in the UK and has local youth groups.

www.scarleteen.com/article/gaydar
US site with articles and FAQs about coming
out, having same-sex crushes, gay parents,
sexual orientation and identity.

www.avert.org
This AIDS charity has lots of info about
exploring your sexuality and coming out,
plus real-life stories from young lesbians.
Choose "Teens" or "Gay & Lesbian" from the
menu bar.

www.divamag.co.uk
The UK's leading lesbian magazine includes
news, links, short articles and chat pages.

www.eachaction.org.uk
EACH is a charity that supports young
people affected by homophobia (anti-gay
attitudes and fear), and offers training and
guidance in schools.

www.fflag.org.uk
Site of the group Families and Friends of
Lesbians and Gays. Click on "Resources"
for a booklet on coming out to your parents.

www.opendoors.net.au
This Australian site has a booklet to
download called "The Only Way Out Is In",
for young people exploring their sexuality.

www.pinkpaper.com
The UK's gay, lesbian and bisexual
newspaper has news, entertainment and
events listings.

www.queery.org.uk
Choose "Advice & Support" to find gay and
lesbian helplines and local support groups
around the UK.

Relationships

After you've been dating for a bit, the two of you may decide you're a couple. Being in a couple involves both of you working out what it means and what the ground rules are.

Good relationships

When you're in a healthy relationship you:

- ♂ really like and enjoy each other
- ♂ trust and respect each other
- ♂ are honest with each other
- ♂ can be "yourself" and don't have to put on an act
- ♂ keep communicating and listening to each other
- ♂ can argue or disagree without fighting all the time
- ♂ can both say sorry
- ♂ don't have to spend all your time together
- ♂ have some, not all, things in common
- ♂ agree about whether you can both still date other people or only each other
- ♂ agree also that each partner would "call it off" before starting something with someone else or telling other people you're available
- ♂ don't really care if the other person doesn't look like a movie star or wears awful shoes.

FACT

If you think you'll have sex   Just because you're madly in love and trust each other that doesn't mean you should have a baby, or that you can't get a sexually transmitted disease. Always use a condom (see the Sex chapter).

Wrangling partners and friends

- Don't drop your friends when you get a partner. Try to spend some time with both.

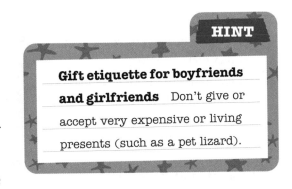

- Keep the full-on snogging and baby talk for private moments. Nobody else ever wants to see you all over each other or hear you call each other "iddle wookums".

- Be sensitive – don't go on about your partner to your friends all the time as if they should have one too.

- Make sure you don't betray your friends' confidences to your partner, or your partner's to your friends.

- If your friends don't like your partner, or your partner doesn't like your friends, see them separately but ask yourself, "Do they see something that I need to be concerned about?"

- Don't expect a girlfriend to tag along with just you and your partner – go out together in a group rather than a threesome.

- Try not to be jealous of a friend and your partner, unless you think either of them is flirting with the other or you come across them behaving in a way they wouldn't if they knew you were there: kissing on the lips, being madly passionate or… I don't know, wearing each other's underpants on their heads. Somewhat suspicious, I'd call it.

Problem relationships

Sometimes a relationship just isn't quite right. Some common aspects of an unhealthy relationship include:

- your partner is way older – it's generally not good when a young or mid-teenager goes out with anybody more than two years older, and it's definitely not good for them to go out with someone older than 20 (sure, it can be flattering, but he also might be unable to get a girlfriend his own age, or be too controlling)

- friends and family say they are worried about the relationship in some way

- your partner is often critical of you or doesn't seem to really like or respect you

- your partner is over the top about love – says they can't live without you, is too possessive and wants to be with you *all* the time

- one or both of you are very jealous, which leads to accusations and lack of trust

ⓖ one or both of you make the other "prove" their love by doing things they don't want to

ⓖ you bring out bad rather than good things in each other

ⓖ you fight a lot, disagreeing on nearly everything.

Abusive relationships

Even though you may love your partner, if they treat you badly they need to change or you need to leave the relationship. You must escape from a partner who constantly puts you down, frightens you, or threatens, hits or otherwise hurts you, mentally or physically.

Emotional, physical or sexual abuse is never right – in any kind of relationship – and must never be accepted. The Savvy chapter has info on the different kinds of abusive relationships and how to recognize when you're in one (and gives you the practical info you'll need to get out of one).

Break-ups

Some relationships are only good for a little while; others break up because one of the partners wants to move on. Sometimes it takes time to recover, even if you made the decision yourself or you made the decision together.

If you are the dumper

ⓖ Do it face to face. Never send a text message, email or letter: it's disrespectful, and could be made

A guy tried to force me once but then I dumped him. It didn't feel right.   Ruby, 14

Being single is okay

Many girls don't have a partner until they leave school. Others start panicking if they're single at 13. (Sit down and put your head between your knees and breathe slowly. For a few years.)

Being single is heaps better than being in a bad relationship. You're not automatically lonely just because you're not part of a couple.

Good things about being single include:

✳ you can do what you want when you want

✳ you can flirt with who you want when you want, and go on as many dates as you want

✳ you can focus on other things – friends, hobbies, sports, school

✳ you can plan great girls'-nights-in (or out!).

The best way to find someone, or to not mind about being single for now, is to be happy with yourself. So enjoy being single and get to know what you want and what makes you happy. One day it'll be as if your porch light has suddenly come on and all the moths are zeroing in. One day your moth will come. Until then don't settle for a cockroach.

public. If you absolutely can't face them, call. But make sure they're alone and can talk.

💬 Explain why you are breaking up with them.

💬 Talk about how you feel, rather than blaming the other person: say something like "I want to be single for a while", not "You turned out to be pretty boring".

I feel quite happy with my life at the moment being single. Maybe in a few years time I will feel the need to have a serious relationship.
Kelly, 18

💬 Make it a clean break, no matter how upset your partner is. If you're sure you have made the right decision don't get back together. This just prolongs everyone's agony.

💬 Don't gossip, spread rumours or talk about private moments you had with your ex.

💬 If you "cheated", think about how not to get into that situation again. (Note to self: break up first, then get together with somebody else.)

💬 Don't expect the two of you to be best friends straight away. That's unrealistic. It might take weeks for your ex to get over you, and they might never want to be friends.

If you are the dumpee

💬 Don't argue, don't beg, don't disagree with their decision, but feel free to say, "Of course I accept your decision that it's over, but I don't agree with those things you say".

💬 Don't see your ex at all for a few weeks, if that's possible. If they're at your school or work just avoid them as much as you can.

💬 After that see if you want to be friends. Not being "friends" is okay too. It doesn't mean you have to be enemies.

💬 Don't assume there's something wrong with you. You just weren't right for each other.

💬 It's all right to cry, get mad and feel humiliated – these are normal feelings. But try to do it in private with family and friends instead of with your ex.

- Give yourself a few weeks to get over it. Take it one day at a time, and don't feel bad if you have an overly emotional day (especially before a period).
- Prepare yourself for seeing your ex with somebody else.
- Even if they've behaved badly, don't gossip too much about it, or badmouth them, or tell their secrets. That just makes you look bitter.
- If your ex says nasty things or spreads rumours about you, be dignified and don't get into public or private fights. Tell a few close friends the truth and send them out to counterbalance the gossip.
- Don't rush into a new relationship just so that you can feel that "somebody" wants you.

> If you know the relationship you're in isn't working then, trust me, stopping it is better than dragging it out. It hurts when you break up with people but the longer the relationship the more it hurts.
> Ayesha, 18

Heartbreak Breaking up happens to EVERY-BODY – even the rich and famous – which is why so many songs are written about broken hearts. And while you're going through it, every heartbreak song seems to be about you. If you feel it's really making you depressed and your family and friends can't help, talk to a counsellor – your GP can help you find one (or see "More info" below).

Otherwise listen to the songs, watch some sad movies, have a bit of a wallow and talk it out with friends. Then, when you're ready, switch to up, optimistic, girls-are-strong, kick-arse songs and movies (see the lists coming up and the ones at the end of the F Word chapter) and get back into life. It takes time to recover from a broken heart, but you absolutely will.

More info **on relationships**

ChildLine: 0800 1111
Counsellors are available 24 hours a day, 7 days a week, if you need to talk.

www.abc.net.au/talkitup/talkitout/relationships.htm
Australian site on relationships and how to talk about them.

www.bbc.co.uk/teens/slink
BBC site for girls. The Games page has a "love calculator" and loads of other love quizzes, or you can confess to a crush on the "Crushwall".

www.connexions-direct.com
Choose "Relationships", then "Partners" for more info on love, dating, sex and break-ups, or call 0808 001 3219.

www.thesite.org/sexandrelationships
Choose "Singles" or "Couples" for advice on everything from crushes, unrequited love and first dates to long-distance relationships, jealousy and breaking-up.

I have doubts about my boyfriend. Like he's really sweet and there for me but I get bored with relationships. When I'm not with him I think about dumping him, but when I am with him I couldn't coz it's fun being with him. If that makes sense.   Kathryn, 16

At home I'm told you don't have to love a man to get married to them. As long as he respects you and he is Turkish, I should do it.
Yildiz, 16

I had a boyfriend for 3 years. The break up was inevitably difficult, but I'm glad it happened cos I need to develop on my own, without a boyfriend's influence.
Kylie, 17

I know this may sound stupid because I'm only 18 years old, but I seriously believe that if I let this one go I may not find another person to be my companion, that I may never find true happiness.   Rose, 18

Lists for every stage of love

Here are some lists of songs and movies to celebrate romance and help you through heartbreak and other bad times. Many of them are classics – oldies but goodies. Add your own favourites to the list, and don't forget to check the movie ratings to see what's appropriate for your age group.

Romance movies

An Affair to Remember Oldie but goldie, the inspiration for *Sleepless in Seattle*.

Bridget Jones's Diary Jane Austen, big undies and stupid jumpers.

Casablanca The black-and-white classic.

Eternal Sunshine of the Spotless Mind Forgetting and wondering.

50 First Dates Forgetting and believing.

Four Weddings and a Funeral True love, Brit-style.

Love, Actually Love, everywhere.

Much Ado about Nothing Shakespeare rides again.

The Princess Bride Silly and romantic.

Sleepless in Seattle Finding The One.

_____

_____

_____

Break-up wallowing songs

Always Something There to Remind Me Sandie Shaw

Cry Me a River Julie London

Crying Roy Orbison or kd lang

Don't Speak No Doubt

Go Your Own Way Fleetwood Mac

I Don't Feel Like Dancin' Scissor Sisters

I Will Always Love You Dolly Parton or Whitney Houston

Poor Me Coldplay

Poor Poor Pitiful Me Linda Ronstadt

Somebody's Crying Chris Isaak

_____

_____

_____

Movies for a good cry

Bambi Deer, dear.

Beaches Lifelong friendship, terminal illness.

Breakfast at Tiffany's Iconic Audrey Hepburn, sunglasses, cat.

Edward Scissorhands Trying to fit in and find love.

E.T. Phone home, for god's sake.

Ghost Nice boyfriend, but dead.

Little Women Sisterly love during the American Civil War.

Moulin Rouge! Boy sings, villain twirls moustache, girl dies.

Rabbit-Proof Fence Two little girls try to get back to their mum.

Romeo and Juliet Classic Shakespeare in modern gangster setting.

Steel Magnolias Great cast, terminal illness.

Titanic Love floats, ship sinks.

Get-over-it songs

Don't Need You to (Tell Me I'm Pretty) Samantha Mumba

Don't Tell Me Avril Lavigne

I Will Survive Gloria Gaynor

It's Raining Men The Weather Girls

Let Him Fly Dixie Chicks

No Man's Woman Sinead O'Connor

R.E.S.P.E.C.T. Aretha Franklin

Since You've Been Gone Kelly Clarkson

Strong Enough Cher

These Boots Were Made for Walking Nancy Sinatra

You Don't Own Me The Blow Monkeys or Leslie Gore (the girly original)

You're So Vain Carly Simon

→

Songs to get you in a good mood

Ain't No Mountain High Enough The Temptations

Bad Reputation Joan Jett

Beautiful Day U2

Blame It on the Boogie The Jackson 5

Born to Fight Tracy Chapman

Brown Eyed Girl Van Morrison

Can't Get You Out of My Head Kylie Minogue

Can't Hold Us Down Christina Aguilera

Celebration Kool and the Gang

Dancing in the Moonlight Toploader

Dancing Queen Abba

Dancing with Myself The Donnas

Do Your Thing Basement Jaxx

Don't Change INXS

Express Yourself Madonna

For Once in My Life Frank Sinatra or Michael Bublé

Free Your Mind En Vogue

From Head to Toe Elvis Costello

Get Happy Judy Garland

Girls Just Wanna Have Fun Cyndi Lauper

The Glamorous Life Sheila E

Good Vibrations The Beach Boys

Holiday Madonna

I Can See Clearly Now Johnny Nash

I Feel Love Donna Summer

I Got You (I Feel Good) James Brown

I Saw Her Standing There The Beatles

I'm a Believer The Monkees

I'm Coming Out Diana Ross

I'm Every Woman Chaka Khan

I'm Free Rolling Stones

I'm Too Sexy Right Said Fred

Independent Woman Destiny's Child

Just a Girl No Doubt

Keep on Livin' Le Tigre

Lovely Day Bill Withers

Man! I Feel Like a Woman Shania Twain

Move on Up Curtis Mayfield

Oh, What a Night Frankie Valli

One Love Bob Marley and the Wailers

Precious Things Tori Amos

Push the Button Sugababes

Respect Yourself The Staple Singers

Shakin' the Tree (Woman's Day) Peter Gabriel and Youssou N'Dour

Shine Take That

Sisters Are Doin' It Eurythmics with Aretha Franklin

Smells Like Teen Spirit Nirvana

Sound of the Underground Girls Aloud

Stupid Girls Pink

Take Me to the River Al Green

There's More to Life than This Björk

These Are Days 10,000 Maniacs

Tubthumping (I Get Knocked Down But I Get Up Again) Chumbawamba

Turn Off the Light Nelly Furtado

We Are Family Sister Sledge

Wild Wild Life Talking Heads

You Can Get It if You Really Want Jimmy Cliff

Young Hearts Run Free Candi Staton

Video India Arie

Walkin' on Sunshine Katrina and the Waves

What a Wonderful World Louis Armstrong

Woman Neneh Cherry

_____

_____

_____

_____

_____

* Now see the list of movies and books with feisty heroines in the **F Word** chapter!

15

SEX

You stand on your head, & I'll go into another room

totally safe sex...

You'll either look at that word sex and say, "Euww, yuck", or you'll be interested in reading on. If you think the idea of sex is gross then **don't read this chapter until you feel ready**. Or you can read it just to be informed. It's okay if you're not ready to actually do anything about it yet.

The main reason people have sex is because it feels good, especially with somebody they are attracted to or in love with. Nature has equipped us to enjoy having sex so that we do it a lot and that way have lots of children and keep populating the Earth – kind of like in those documentaries where fish lay about 67,000 eggs. **Luckily** we don't have to behave like mad fish. We get to wait until we're ready, decide on the right person, use contraception if we don't want to get pregnant, and **protect ourselves** against sexually transmitted diseases or infections.

Becoming a sexual person

You become a sexual person at puberty, when your hormone levels change and your girly bits start to mature – usually long before you're ready to have sex with somebody. (Scoot back to the section "Your girly bits" in Change, the first chapter in the book, so you know what sexual equipment you're working with, then come right back here.)

Sexual thoughts

As your body matures you start to have sexual thoughts and feelings, and to have crushes on and be physically attracted to other people. Everybody gets sexual thoughts or has sexual daydreams.

You don't have control over your sexual feelings in the way you do over your sexual actions. Sexy or curious thoughts can pop into your head at the most inconvenient times. Just as long as you know that thinking about something, or knowing about something, doesn't mean you have to do it, or that there's anything wrong with you.

Masturbation

Pretty much everyone starts to masturbate once they begin to have sexual feelings and become curious about their body. Masturbation means touching yourself for sexual pleasure. It's normal, healthy, shouldn't hurt, and everybody does it sooner or later (only not on the bus). Some girls do it once or twice a week; others have a craze of doing it every day for a while.

Girls usually touch and rub the area around the clitoris, the most sensitive part of their body, with their fingers or one finger. If they continue, the good feeling increases (they become "sexually aroused") and the clitoris enlarges slightly. But touching yourself there doesn't necessarily mean you have to keep on doing it if you don't want to. If you don't feel like going on that's fine: don't.

To help with lubrication so you're not dry, which can cause soreness, you can use your vaginal secretions, spit or a little bit of any oil that's safe for the body. Massage or body oil can be good, although some can include ingredients that sting.

Most girls masturbate while they are lying in bed or in the bathroom. (Lock the door first.) Some lie on their front and move their hips, others lie on their back and rub or gently flick their clitoris. There really aren't any rules – just whatever feels good.

Some girls put an object in their vagina. It should be well washed beforehand, and not

> Me and my boyfriend are getting ready to get into that kind of stuff.
> Pam, 14

> I want to know about the feelings and pleasure you get from it, but I guess that just comes with experience.
> Anonymous, 15

Stages

Usually the stages of becoming a sexual person go something like this:

✳ born with all girly bits present and correct

✳ go through the changes of puberty

✳ develop a regular period and ovulate once a month or so

✳ have some sexual thoughts now and again

✳ start being interested in guys (or girls)

✳ have more sexual thoughts

✳ learn how to masturbate to see what physical sexual feelings are like

✳ start relationships slowly, with kissing and cuddling and holding hands

✳ move on to sexual touching

✳ eventually decide to have sex with somebody who respects you.

sharp, breakable or something you can't keep a good grip on. You have to be over 18 to buy a vibrator (a battery-operated plastic object usually shaped like a penis).

Masturbation is very safe: you can't catch a disease or get pregnant. It helps you find out what you like and what's the best way to become sexually aroused – different things work for different people – so that eventually you can show a partner what you enjoy. And it's a good way to learn that sex is about what you feel, not what you look like.

Wait till you meet somebody nice. Sally, 14

One of my friends is going out with an older guy, and is thinking about having sex though she is far too young (12). I am really worried about her. All of my friends know too much about sex. We're still kids really so I don't like talking about masturbation and stuff. I still find it a bit gross. Bobbie, 13

In an episode of *Home and Away* they were going to have sex and then didn't really know what to do and I'm afraid that will happen to me. Clare, 13

Signs of sexual arousal

Signs of arousal include:

✱ wanting to keep being touched

✱ breathing faster

✱ feeling warm, tingly and sensitive (especially the nipples and the between-the-legs department)

✱ the vagina creating slippery "juices" (so that if sex happened it would be easier)

✱ getting hot and sweaty.

Feeling sexually aroused doesn't mean you have to have sex.

Orgasm

An orgasm is a big rush of sexual pleasure – the climax to sexual arousal. It's often known as "coming". It's followed by an intense feeling of release. Not everyone makes panting or breathy noises and then yelps, grunts, squeals or screams during orgasm like they do in the movies. But because it's such a great feeling many people do "let themselves go" and make a noise. It's okay either way. Afterwards you'll feel relaxed.

Usually masturbating, or being stroked or licked around or on the clitoris by a partner, is the easiest way for girls and women to orgasm. It is rarer for them to orgasm during penis-in-vagina sex because the clitoris isn't always stimulated while that's going on.

For guys, sexual stimulation, by masturbation or with a partner, leads to the penis becoming erect (hard). When a guy reaches orgasm he ejaculates (pronounced ee-jack-u-lates). This means the penis spurts out about a teaspoon of semen, a runny white fluid that contains sperm. The individual sperm in the semen are too tiny to be seen except under a microscope, but there are hundreds of millions of them in each ejaculation. (There's more on all this in "The penis" box later.)

Sexual touching

In the same way that enjoying masturbation and having an orgasm doesn't mean you're necessarily ready to have sex with someone, enjoying kissing and cuddling a guy doesn't mean you're ready to have sex with him either.

What do people mean by "sex" or "having sex"? Most people mean penis-in-vagina or "penetrative vaginal sex", otherwise known as "going all the way" or "doing it" (see "Going all the way" later in this chapter). But there are other forms of sex, such as oral sex (explained soon), and there can be many steps before – or instead of – "the final destination".

Taking your time

Becoming a sexual person is a big experience, and taking time to enjoy touching and exploring and being close to someone else is part of it. There are lots of pleasures to discover and finding out about them might follow this kind of order (or not):

- talking, going out, liking each other a lot
- holding hands
- kissing and cuddling
- open-mouth kissing
- stroking, kissing, licking or blowing on each other's neck and other places
- touching the breasts through clothes
- touching or kissing breasts
- hands down each other's pants, exploring.

> Going to a Christian school we don't get the real nitty gritty [information]. When the time comes it would be nice to know exactly what to do!!
> Karen, 13

> I don't like to talk about sex.
> Tara, 13

You might decide you want to go out with lots of guys over the next few years, having fun and a bit of a kiss and cuddle. You might find that doing intimate physical things with someone is so new and such a big deal that you want to go slowly for a while, enjoying, say, having your breasts touched but not yet feeling ready to have your clothes off. You might have gone further with somebody than you felt comfortable about and now want to go back to an earlier stage for the time being. Or you might decide that you're really enjoying all the things you're doing with the other person, including the physical stuff, and that if you keep liking each other and being together you'll probably become more intimate and perhaps end up having sex.

Because teenage guys are new to sex too, they often get to – or want to get to – orgasm quickly, but most girls like taking time to learn about and enjoy different stages of touching. Make sure you're not rushed.

Different strokes for different folks   Stroking can make us feel great. Having the private bits touched by a partner's hands can be part of "foreplay" leading to having sex. But it doesn't have to go all the way, and touching can be to any part of the body. Stroking hand motions are usually sexier than patting ones. It should always be done gently,

FACT

The "right" age for sex   There isn't one – instead there's just a huge range of who does what when. The most important thing is to know as much as you can before making your own decision.

especially at the start. If you're ready, it can also feel warm and wonderful for the body, including the private parts, to be licked or sucked.

When two people stroke each other's private parts it's sometimes called mutual masturbation; licking and sucking is known as oral sex. Often partners take turns.

As part of touching, the girl's partner might softly stroke or lick around the vulva and clitoris area. Often just around rather than right on the clitoris feels better. (A guy may think girls are more thrilled about the idea of a finger inside the vagina, so you might have to tell him about the magic clitoris.) If it's what the girl wants, the stroking or licking can continue until she has an orgasm.

Touching or oral sex needs to be "safe" (see "Safe sex" later in the chapter). Sexually transmitted infections can be passed on by hands, although the chance isn't as high as it is with oral sex. It's okay not to like giving oral sex or swallowing semen (which contains sperm). Oral sex is given as a favour; it's not compulsory.

> I've never even had a boyfriend and already heaps of people my age are having sex.
> Maya, 15

> I've heard of oral sex but I dunno what it is.
> Jordan, 14

Not such a good idea Some girls give oral sex, for instance after school, at parties or in school toilets, to one or more guys. Unfortunately it can mean a lot of problems for them. Although girls can't get pregnant by giving oral sex, there are at least ten sexually transmitted infections that can be passed on to them whether or not they swallow the semen. Also:

I'm scared of sex in general, and tampons. Bridie, 13

I've only kissed a guy once. Katrina, 16

We did sex-ed in year 7 (I'm in year 9), but that was just diagrams, but we need it now, and it needs to be explicit. My family don't really go there. I want to know everything there is to know really!! I want to know what to expect at my first time. Jacqui, 14

Friends of mine are starting to have sex in short relationships and on the spur of the moment, eg, in public toilets. It's a bit feral and unromantic. Tash, 15

I'm becoming a nun. Theresa, 15

- a guy who doesn't particularly care whose mouth he puts his penis into is likely to get oral sex from other girls as well – increasing his chances of getting and passing on a sexually transmitted disease

- the guy is probably unlikely to wear a condom, which would protect the girl against sexually transmitted infections

- if the girl gives oral sex to more than one guy who's not wearing a condom, she runs a much bigger risk of getting a sexually transmitted disease

- it can be hard for a girl to keep her self-respect, and the respect of others, if she's behaving like a sex servant, even a willing one.

Being the "go-to" girl for a guy to get quick sexual relief isn't cool, it's kind of sad. It doesn't mean "nothing": it means the girl is acting like a sex robot, instead of having a relationship where she is treated equally, fairly and kindly by someone who really cares about her.

Deciding whether or not to have sex

As you get older and know more people who have "gone all the way" or "had sex" (or *say* they have), and you see it in movies and on TV all the time, you could think that it's somehow compulsory. It isn't. (And don't forget that most people do it more than once in their life so we're not just talking about a one-off incident, but about beginning a lifelong sex life.)

A sexual relationship can be very intense, causing rushes of strong feelings about love and belonging. Even if you're not both in love, at the very least it should be fun and make you feel liked and respected.

The decision about when to have sex is not so much about how old you are or how developed your body is. It's about whether *you* feel really, really ready.

I'd rather stick a fork in my eye

Not feeling ready to have sex

If you're unsure, you're probably not ready yet. And if you're not comfortable with kissing, caressing with your clothes on, being touched on your breasts or between your legs, then you're definitely not ready to have sex.

You may not be interested in anything to do with sex

Deciding not to have sex

Not having sex is called abstinence, or celibacy (pronounced selly-bass-ee). If this is what you have decided on, nobody else's opinion should dissuade you.

Even though many girls are choosing to have sex at a younger age than in previous generations, you are not a statistic. And not all those girls were glad they did: many say they wish they'd waited. There's nothing wrong with not having sex until your late teens, early twenties or beyond. It's absolutely up to you.

But if you do decide to wait (say, until you're over 18, or married), make sure it's your own choice, not just what someone else expects of you. In some families, cultures and religions, having sex outside marriage is called a sin or a dishonour, even though it's natural to have sexual thoughts or to want to have sex.

> I like him, but do not want to have sex with him.
> Sash, 16

> I'd rather not have to think about sex.
> Hilary, 13

It's okay to "wait for the right person" – and it's okay to experiment, as long as you stay safe and are treated with respect and kindness. Sex isn't bad or wrong, and it doesn't make you bad or wrong.

Even if you don't have sex it's a good idea to make sure you know about contraception and sexually transmitted infections. Researchers say that about half the teenagers who sign "abstinence-until-marriage" pledges in the US have sex within the next year, and most don't keep the pledge until marriage. So it's best to be informed and to know how to use a condom if things do go further than expected and that's okay with you.

Virginity Technically you are a "virgin" if you have never had a guy's penis inside your vagina.

You may have heard that you're a virgin until your hymen is "broken". This is not true. (Your hymen is that bit of skin surrounding the entrance to the vagina described back in the Change chapter.)

Over the years most girls have probably done things, not related to penises, that have widened the opening of their hymen: played sport, used tampons or had a medical examination. So nobody

> I don't feel ready, personally. I have gone out with three guys in year 10 and every one of them have asked me for sex but I have always said no. One of them broke up with me because I wouldn't have sex with him.
> Emma 14

can tell (or claim) that a girl has had penetrative vaginal sex, or isn't a virgin, just because her hymen is stretched, torn or can't be seen.

Some girls will bleed a little the first time they have penetrative sex (from the hymen being stretched or pushed aside), but lots don't. If a girl doesn't bleed it doesn't mean she's had sex before.

Whether or not you're a virgin isn't important unless you want it to be. It isn't nearly as important as many other things, including whether you're healthy, respected, educated, happy or (on the negative side) exploited, worried, pregnant or doing something you really don't want to.

Since nobody can ever tell, even by looking at your vagina opening and hymen, whether you're a virgin or not, if you need to say you're one, say you're one. But don't fool yourself – if you and your partner do other sexual things then you're a sexual person.

Things to sort out before deciding to have sex

It's important that you choose somebody you get on really well with so that you can laugh about anything that happens during sex; you can keep asking if the sex is okay for the other person and what they'd like you to do; and you can feel comfortable telling them what they can do to make you feel good.

Bad reasons for having sex

✱ You're afraid that your partner will find someone else unless you do.

✱ The other person wants to.

✱ Other girls you know have done it.

✱ You've done it already.

✱ You want to make somebody like you more.

✱ You don't care whether you do or not.

✱ You want to rebel against, or get back at, strict or religious parents.

✱ You're too drunk or out of it to say no.

✱ You're too shy or too scared to say no.

✱ Your parents won't find out, so if you can "get away with it" you might as well.

✱ You're forced or pressured into it.

✱ You like the kissing and touching so you think that means you have to keep going.

I don't believe in sex before marriage and when I tell people I get weird looks.   Anna, 14

FACT

Older guys They're more likely to want sex before you're ready. The older they are, the more likely they are to be carrying a sexually transmitted infection: always use a condom.

Legally you're not considered old enough to say yes to sex until you're 16 in England, Scotland and Wales (or 17 in Northern Ireland), even if you feel ready. If you're under the "age of consent", as it's called, and you have sex with someone who is over that age, technically they're committing a crime, even if you agreed to sex.

It's completely wrong and usually illegal for anyone in a position of power or authority over you to have a romantic or sexual relationship with you. This includes teachers, coaches, social workers, relatives and friends' fathers. It doesn't matter what they say, or how confused or loyal you feel, this is not okay and

to avoid the 'Euwww' factor: don't go out with somebody heaps older than you

they are doing the wrong thing. Talk to a trusted adult about the situation.

Questions to ask yourself

- ⦿ Are you sure that *you* have chosen the person to have sex with and haven't been pressured? Don't just be grateful that someone has picked you.

- ⦿ Have you thought about why you want to have sex? Is it because the two of you have been with each other for a while, and you think this is the right person to share a caring time with, or because you're worried about not seeming cool or want to get the first time over with?

- ⦿ How will you protect yourself against pregnancy and sexually transmitted infections? What would you do if either of those things happened? (See "Safe sex" and "Contraception" later in this chapter, and see the Pregnancy chapter.)

Don't just be with someone for the sake of it or to show off. Don't be pressured into having sex.

Do what feels right for you and if your boyfriend doesn't like it he's not worth it! Missy, 18

eeny, meeny, miney...

CHOOSE YOUR PARTNER...
CAREFULLY!

Ways to say no to sex

"No."

"No, I really don't want to."

"I'm not ready for that yet."

"I don't want to go any further than this."

"I am happy to kiss you, but that's all."

"Let's just do this [*kissing or whatever*] for a while."

"I don't want to go any further than kissing, hugging and touching."

"I want to slow down."

"Slow down."

"Stop!"

🌀 Do you know the reasons why the other person wants to have sex?

🌀 Is the person kind? Do they usually listen to you? Do they want a real relationship or are they likely to "use" you? Are they discreet or a blabbermouth?

🌀 Can you talk to them about safe sex and contraception, and about what you need to get organized before you have sex?

🌀 Will you feel okay talking to them afterwards about the experience?

FACT

Sexual insults At some time in your life you'll probably be called a "slut" or "frigid", or both. Words that suggest you like sex but you shouldn't include "easy", "slag" and "whore", as well as "slut". (These insults are part of a stupid "double standard" that says men can have sex with lots of people but girls shouldn't.) Words like "frigid" or "cocktease" suggest you don't want sex but you should (or that a girl should be available to a guy who wants sex). None of these insults is true. They're just designed to humiliate or manipulate you.

⑥ Do you know what sort of relationship you want? Are you just having sex or going to be a couple? Is it a "one-night stand" or will you be having sex again soon? Every now and again or every week? Does your partner have the same understanding?

More info on deciding whether or not to have sex

www.likeitis.org
This youth site run by the Marie Stopes charity has info on sex, contraception and pregnancy.

www.ruthinking.co.uk
Site all about sex and relationships for young people. Choose "Lady lounge" for stuff on your first time, staying in control, peer pressure, love after sex and safe sex.

www.scarleteen.com
"Sex education for the real world": a US site designed for young people, with loads of articles and an email question service.

www.sexetc.org
US youth sex website run by teenagers.

A guy repeatedly asked and pressured me to "give him head" [*oral sex*]. When I kept saying no he started to manipulate and blackmail me saying that if I didn't do it he would spread rumours about me. Eventually he forced me to do it. For a long time I was very confused and felt shameful and dirty. I felt like no guy would ever accept me unless I had sex with them. I realize now that what he did was wrong and not my fault.   Heather, 16

I am a virgin, but I gave a guy a "handy" when I had a boyfriend and I felt so guilty. We all make mistakes, especially when we are drunk, and I am only young so it's not the end of the world.   Emily, 16

I'd like to advise against having sex before you're ready. Luckily, I didn't have a bad experience, but I lost my virginity when I was 14, and although it wasn't "bad", I wish now I hadn't done it. I haven't had sex again since, and hopefully next time it will be more enjoyable.   Annie, 16

If you feel like you're ready to have sex go for it, but don't do it when you are at school because it ruins your life.   Maeve, 13

Things guys can say to pressure you into sex (and handy replies)

"Everyone else is doing it."
"Well, you'd better go and have sex with everybody else then."

"It's okay because I love you."
"If you really love me you won't pressure me."

"If you don't, then you don't love me."
"That's just emotional blackmail. You wouldn't say that if you cared more about me than about having sex."

"I'll leave you if you don't."
"Okay then."

"I'll tell everyone you're frigid."
"I'll tell everyone I didn't want to, and you cried and said you'd tell everyone I was frigid."

"You made me think you wanted to."
"I like it when we kiss and touch, but I don't want to have sex."

"I have to have it."
"It's your choice to wait for me or to break up and do it with someone else."

"It's not fair. You just get me hot and then you don't want to. You're a cocktease."
"No, I'm not. I've told you that I like to kiss, hug and touch but don't want to have sex."

"It's medically bad for me to get aroused and then not have sex."
"Is not." (Guys are not harmed in any way by getting aroused and then not having sex.)

But if you don't have sex with me, my testicles will fall off...

You can start a juggling act

It's always OK to say 'NO'

Going all the way

If you've read this chapter, and thought about it, and talked about it, and sorted out all the questions you need to answer, and you still want to have sex, you are probably ready.

When you decide to have penis-in-vagina sex for the first time, the two of you should talk beforehand about how you want it to go. Here are some essentials.

> *I have done everything else except have sex. So I guess it seems like the next natural step.*
> Jan, 17

- ⑥ The sex should happen in a safe place. (Even though you obviously want privacy, it's a good idea to have some people you trust nearby.)
- ⑥ A condom will be used any and every time you have sex.
- ⑥ You'll organize the contraception, or he will. If it's not organized the sex won't happen.
- ⑥ The guy has practised putting a condom on, and will take it off straight after he's "come" (see the box "How to use a condom" later in the chapter).
- ⑥ You've talked about which things you'd like to do, and which ones you're not interested in. (Make sure your partner knows how you feel and respects your limits.)
- ⑥ If you or your partner says so, everything stops immediately, that second, no matter what stage you're at. Make sure your partner understands that "No" or "Stop" never means "Maybe" or "Go ahead anyway".
- ⑥ Nobody will take pictures of any kind.
- ⑥ Neither partner will be mean to the other one about anything that happens or is said.
- ⑥ The details of the sex will be kept private and won't be used as gossip.

What happens when you have sex?

Probably something like this.

- ⑥ As soon as the guy's penis is erect one of you gets a condom on it (for instructions, see the box "How to use a condom" coming up).
- ⑥ Holding the condom on at the base, the guy then gently starts to put his penis inside you, perhaps taking a little while to find the right place to slide it in and going slowly so that the vagina stretches to fit the penis.
- ⑥ Once the penis is inside your vagina you'll both usually start to move – the guy will pull his penis out slightly and then thrust forward all the way in again, creating an ongoing rhythm.
- ⑥ When the guy ejaculates you probably won't be able to actually feel it happen inside you, but you will most likely be able to tell from his actions and noises that he has had an orgasm (usually you can also tell because he stops doing the in-and-out business).

⑥ Even though it may feel nice for him to stay inside you, and he's feeling a temporary exhausted glow, you need to make sure that as soon as he has "come" he holds the bottom of the condom around the base of his penis and pulls out – you don't want to get any of that semen near your vagina or those pesky hundreds of millions of sperm may head up to try to get you pregnant. (It only takes one to do it.)

LEARN HOW TO USE a CONDOM PROPERLY

You should have the chance to have an orgasm as well as the guy – afterwards or before he has had an orgasm – through touching or oral sex. He should want you to feel good too. This means he may have to slow down (guys tend to go too fast).

Being new to sex

Don't expect the first time to be the most amazing experience of your life. Almost everybody says the first wasn't the best time (by far). It's not going to be like it is in the movies or, thankfully, on a porn site. It's you two, in real life, and you need to be prepared to smile when things aren't perfect, try again, and understand that if it's kind of romantic and sweet then that's a bonus. A lot of people's first-time reaction is "Huh? Is that all there is? After the big build-up?"

Don't expect to be "good at sex" for a while. It's an intimate act and "getting it together" can take time.

Like most things, it takes practice to know what you're doing and to be able to work out what you like. And it needs you to be able to talk about it comfortably with your partner.

Foreplay For sex to feel good, there generally needs to be more foreplay than in-and-out penetrative sex. Foreplay is all the stuff you do to get aroused beforehand: kissing, touching and perhaps licking and sucking (see "Sexual touching" earlier). It's for both partners

> I agreed when he asked, for him to penetrate my vagina, but when I told him to stop, after he first put it in, he didn't, and repeated it about four more times. It scared me that someone so close, whom I knew so well, would get so carried away so easily and would not listen when I said "stop".
>
> Jules, 16

FACT

How you look   Lots of girls worry about how they appear during sex: whether their body is the "right" size or shape. A good sex partner won't be concerned with possible (or imaginary) "flaws"; they and you can concentrate on the important thing – how you both feel. And anyway guys (and girls) are sexually aroused by all sorts of shapes and sizes.

to do to each other, to make them feel good on the way to having sex. It can feel great to avoid the private bits altogether and stroke the feet, fingers, arms – anywhere can be arousing if the right person is doing the touching and doing it well. You can experiment together to discover what you like.

How long will the sex take?   From the time the guy puts his penis in you until he comes could be only a few seconds or a few minutes. That's why just "doing it", without foreplay or the guy slowing down, can be boring and disappointing for you.

After orgasm the guy's penis goes limp again, and it may take a little while for him to get another erection. If he waits until his penis gets hard again, and you want to have sex a second time, he may last longer. (You'll need to use another condom.)

Dryness during sex   When you are sexually aroused, your vagina becomes slippery with a sexual lubrication your body makes so that it's easier for the penis to go inside you. If there is no natural lubricant it probably means you are too nervous or not aroused enough to have penetrative sex, and should have more foreplay before trying again.

If you are dry during sex there will be too much friction and you will be sore and get a rash, abrasion or even a bruise. Dryness can also cause a condom to break, so if you feel dry, stop. A water-based lubricant from a chemist or supermarket (they're sold near the condoms) is good to use around your vagina opening, and on the outside of a condom, to make things easier. (Don't use Vaseline, massage oil or any other oil-based lubricant because it can damage the condom.)

Does sex hurt?   It doesn't usually hurt, although the first time the penis may stretch your hymen (see the "Virginity" section earlier). There may be a small stab of pain, but this should only happen the first time or the first couple of times.

Sex can hurt if the guy puts his penis in too suddenly or roughly. Let him know what feels good, and if he has to change what he's doing. You're learning together. All sexual partners tell each other what's working, no matter how old they are or how many times they've done it before.

If sex is hurting, and it isn't because you're dry or the sex is rough, see a doctor.

The penis

A guy will be as sensitive and insecure about what his penis looks like, and how big it is, as you are about your body or girly bits. So don't laugh or point (not that you would, but you know what I'm saying).

The male genitals (boysie bits) are a package deal of one sausage-shaped penis and two testicles (nicknamed "balls"), which store the sperm. The testicles hang side by side behind the penis and are held away from the body by the scrotum, which looks more or less like a wrinkly, hairy sock with a pair of golf balls in it (one of the two usually hangs slightly lower than the other). Next time you're a little worried about your body image, think what it would be like to have a wrinkly, hairy sock hanging off you and calm down.

Most guys are uncircumcised. This means their penis head is naturally covered by a little polo neck called the foreskin, which is pulled back when the guy wants to wee. When the penis is erect, its head pokes out of the polo neck. When a penis is circumcised – a surgical procedure done for religious, cultural or occasionally medical reasons when the guy is a baby – the foreskin is cut away, so there is no polo neck for the penis head.

Both uncircumcised and circumcised penises can be properly cleaned. There is a higher risk of passing on sexually transmitted infections with an uncovered uncircumcised penis – but both kinds must be covered with a condom anyway, which makes the risk the same (much, much less).

Wee and sperm never come out of a penis at the same time, as the male body is programmed to do one or the other.

Don't forget that men and women are designed to fit together, so it's very, very rare for someone to have a penis too large for a vagina.

Don't get your idea of what a penis looks like from porn. Because, you know how there are those strange women with breasts bigger than their heads? Well, enormous penises are not exactly your everyday item either.

Erection

When a penis becomes erect, it gets bigger and harder, almost as if it had a bone in it, but it's just all the extra blood rushing to the area. An erect penis sticks out from a guy's body, angled upwards. Sometimes it bends a little to the left or the right.

Guys get an erection when they have sexual thoughts; while they're asleep; sometimes even from the vibrations in a train or bus; any time, really, if they're a teenager. They often have one when they wake up. Erections eventually go down again, whether or not a guy has come. A guy can't control when he gets an erection, and this can be really embarrassing for him.

Sexual positions   There are a number of possible sexual positions for penetrative sex. Here are some common ones.

- Both partners lie down, with the guy on top (the "straight" or "missionary" position).
- The girl sits on top of the guy, who's lying down – the penis should always go into the vagina slowly and gently, to make sure it doesn't hurt.
- The girl props on her hands and knees and her partner crouches over her, entering her vagina from behind.

It doesn't mean anal sex, which is when the penis is put into the anus. Most women don't have anal sex because it hurts them. Many gay men have anal sex (well, they don't have a vagina for penetrative sex). Anal sex, whether straight or gay, must involve a condom, with a lubricant, to protect against sexually transmitted infections (see the later "Safe sex" section). Anal sex is by far the most risky kind of sex for getting a sexually transmitted infection – up to ten times riskier than anything else.

Faking orgasm and not enjoying sex   Faking it: don't bother. Better to either say, "Oh well, I'm obviously not in the mood", or help the other person to do the things that arouse you. There's no rule that says you have to have an orgasm every time, you can still enjoy sex without one – but if you never have an orgasm, and your partner always does, that's not fair.

Many girls get worried and think there's something wrong with them because they don't enjoy sex. There isn't. It's not surprising girls don't enjoy it when so many of them are involved in a quick, fumbling meeting of bodies that ends as soon as the guy has come. In this case you have a couple of options: stop having sex with the guy; find another partner who will help you make sex something good for you too; or wait until you're a bit older, when it is often better.

Going back

What if you discover you weren't ready for your first experience, it was boring or it was horrible? Lots of girls have a first sexual experience that they didn't want to have,

FACT

What do lesbians do?   I'm reliably informed that lesbians just do all the stuff guys and girls do, like foreplay, but there's no penis involvement. A lot of the websites and magazines for gays and lesbians can be all about sex, even porn, but if you're a lesbian you don't have to have extreme sex. (See the Love chapter for more on working out if you're gay, dating, and groups to contact.)

If things turn scary

If you are not being listened to, or you feel you may be in an unsafe situation, here are some things you can say.

"I said STOP, and I mean it!" Raise your voice and shout it.

"My older brothers are picking me up and they'll kill you if they find you here with me." (Even if you don't have brothers.)

"I'm going to be sick." Put your hand over your mouth, pretend you're going to be sick, then get away from there.

"I need to go to the toilet." Then get away from there.

"I've got my period and there's blood everywhere." Then get away from there.

If necessary, you may have to fool the person by leaving your handbag or jacket behind, so that it's not obvious that you've gone. Try to sneak your keys, phone and money into your pockets or underwear, say, "Mind my bag for a minute. I'll be right back", then get as far away as you can. Find somewhere private and call your emergency number (see the Savvy chapter) to get picked up.

Rape or sexual assault

Sex without consent is a crime called rape or sexual assault, even if you were unable to say no because you were too drunk, or you said yes because you were forced or threatened (see the Savvy chapter for more info).

which made them feel used, or that they can't even remember because it happened when they were drunk or affected by drugs. It's a shame if that has happened to you, but you don't have to let it ruin your future experience of sex. Next time you have sex make sure you do it the way you'd like it to be.

And just because you had sex before you were ready that doesn't mean you have to keep doing it. You can stop and go back to waiting until you do feel ready.

If things went further than you wanted them to, think about whether somebody pressured you or somehow took advantage of you. If they did, don't be with that person any more: they don't respect you and can't be relied on as a friend. If you were both just "carried away", have a talk and explain that things went further than you meant them to, but that you don't want it to happen again and you need them to agree.

Wait until you've met someone you really really like and can see a future with before starting something up.
Michelle, 17

More info **on guy and girl bits**

Many pictures of penises available on the net are ridiculously large, porn-actor ones, or have symptoms of a sexually transmitted infection such as warts that will make you go euww.

en.wikipedia.org/wiki/Penis
Wikipedia has some pics of a pretty standard flaccid (pronounced flas-sid and meaning soft) penis and an erect one, and a diagram, as well as lots of penis facts.

www.sexualityandu.ca
Canadian site; click on "Teens", "What is sex?", then "Take a look at your body" for detailed diagrams of male and female bits.

I wish I had waited and I regret lots of things, but my theory is that if those experiences had not have happened I wouldn't be the person I am today. I respect myself so much more now, after everything that's happened.   Dee, 16

I once had a boyfriend and I was about 17. He called me about 2 days before Christmas and said we need to talk and blah blah. I thought he was going to break up with me. I went to his house and he started going on about when would we have sex? I wasn't embarrassed, I just told him I wasn't ready.   Caitlin, 18

I couldn't even remember his name or much else about him and kinda wish I waited now so that it was an experience that I could remember at least, and had a person to remember it with.   Carla, 18

One of my close guy friends keeps asking me to have sex with him and I keep saying "no", and he won't let up so I'm starting to think maybe I should just say "yes".   Vanessa

I lost my virginity at 13, and don't regret it. I was in a relationship with the boy for 9 months, and I am now 16. I have had 3 sexual partners and have been in long-term relationships with all of them and I don't believe in doing things with random people.   Salima, 16

I lost my virginity at 14 with my boyfriend at the moment. Most of my friends haven't even spoken to a guy let alone had sex (girls' school). It was good coz I wasn't pressured which I thought I might be coz he's 2 years older.   Kate, 14

Porn

There's so much pornography now on the net, in films, on DVDs and in magazines. And even music videos can look like a porn movie, with girls humping around, grinding their bottoms in a rhythmic circle as if they were having sex, and making orgasmic noises and pretending they're dying to "do it" with the star of the video – hey, the singer pays them to act like that so he can pretend he's a magnet for sex-crazed women.

Porn can give people some false and twisted ideas about sex, such as:

- women and girls always want it
- guys always want it
- all penises are huge
- all breasts are enormous
- women and girls are there for men to look at
- women and girls should dress to look like they want sex
- sex is always grunty and loud and fast
- it's okay to be mean or rough when you're having sex
- it's okay to force a woman or girl into it
- women and girls like being forced
- it's okay to make a woman or girl do anything you want
- all women and girls have to give oral sex and swallow the semen
- women and girls like it no matter what a guy does to them during sex.

Porn isn't a true picture of what sex should be like ...

Safe sex

If you have sex of any kind – vaginal, oral or anal – with a guy, even once, then it needs to be "safe sex". This means finding ways to cut the risk of getting a sexually transmitted infection (also called a sexually transmitted disease – STD).

Sexually transmitted infections (STIs)

STIs are diseases passed from one person to another during sexual contact: they are caused by a variety of bacteria, viruses and parasites and can infect many parts of the body after being "caught". They can be passed on in blood, semen and vaginal fluids, and by skin contact. (Some girls have been told that they can't get an STI from doing oral sex on a guy – this is a lie.)

The long-term effects of some STIs can severely affect your life, or even end it (see the "Sexually transmitted infections (STIs)" chart coming up). But most people with an STI don't know they have one.

In most cases using a condom during sex will hugely reduce your risk of catching an STI (see the box "How to use a condom", which follows). Condoms are most effective if they are used with a water-based personal lubricant, bought from a chemist or supermarket.

FACT

Contraception plus condom   The contraceptive pill doesn't prevent STIs. Even if you are on the Pill, your partner will still need to use a condom every time you have sex, with a lubricant, so that you enormously reduce the risk of getting an STI.

Symptoms of STIs   Many of the common STIs are "invisible": they don't have any symptoms, such as pain or outside body changes. So you can't tell who has one – or more than one – by looking.

Not all infections of the girly bits are STIs, but all symptoms need to be investigated by a doctor because the longer any infection goes on the more damage it can do (see the "Common infections of the girly bits" chart in the Body Maintenance chapter, as well as the "Sexually transmitted infections (STIs)" chart coming up, for details of symptoms and effects on the body).

Most sexually transmitted diseases have worse, or more complicated, problems for girls than guys (including not being able to have a baby later on), so please be careful and don't be afraid or too embarrassed to see a doctor. They see this stuff every day. Having an STI doesn't mean you are a "slut".

How to use a condom

✱ Buy a condom with a BSI or CE "Kitemark" on the packet; this means it's from a company that does proper safety testing.

✱ Use the condom within its use-by date.

✱ Don't use one that's been left in extreme heat (for example, in a car glove box on a warm day).

✱ Use a fresh one out of the packet.

✱ Make sure the packet and the condom are not damaged in any way.

✱ Don't damage the packet or the condom with fingernails or teeth when opening the packet (this is a common way to create holes or cuts in a condom).

✱ Never put one condom over another one. This is not safer – in fact it makes them both more likely to break.

✱ Put the condom on before the penis gets anywhere near the vagina.

✱ The condom should be held in one hand while the other hand squeezes the condom's tip. The space left by the air being squeezed out will be taken up by semen when the guy ejaculates.

✱ While the tip is still squeezed, the condom should be rolled down onto the erect penis – before any little drops of semen leak out of it, which can happen long before the guy ejaculates.

✱ Throw the condom away if it is accidentally put on inside out – use a fresh one.

✱ Put some water-based personal lubricant (from a chemist or supermarket) over it. Oil-based lubricants such as moisturisers and Vaseline can damage the surface of the condom, making it not as safe.

✱ Make sure that as soon as the guy has come, and while the penis is still hard, he holds the condom around the base of the penis and pulls out carefully (otherwise the condom could get left behind in there). He then needs to move away so that it doesn't accidentally spill near the vagina.

✱ The guy should tie a knot in the used condom so the semen doesn't come out, wrap it in tissue and then dispose of it in the bin, not the toilet.

✱ Use that condom (and all others) only once.

See also "More info" coming up soon.

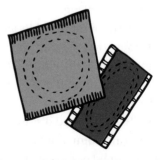

FACT

Condoms and trust Carrying and using condoms doesn't mean you don't trust a guy to be faithful. He, or you, could have caught an STI before you met, and could now pass it on without knowing.

If you've had sex without a condom or if the condom broke or split, or if you show any of the following symptoms in the next days, weeks or months after sex, off you pop to your doctor, local health centre, family planning clinic, young people's clinic or GUM (sexual health) clinic (see the "More info" section for this chapter, coming up):

- pain during sex
- pain when weeing
- redness, soreness, warts, bumps, swelling, blisters, scabby bits, itchy bits or sores on or near the vagina or anal area
- any abnormal discharge from the vagina such as pus (yellowy or stinky) or a "weeping" fluid (the usual, clear, egg-white sort of discharge, talked about in the Change chapter, is fine)
- lower "tummy" pain, with or without a fever, which comes and goes or doesn't go away
- swelling or lumps under the skin in the groin area.

If one partner is diagnosed with an STI, the other partner also needs to be checked.

Common symptoms for a guy include lumps, bumps, warts, red spots, sores, blisters, scabby bits or rashes on his penis (or around the area). If you see any of these don't have sex with him, don't touch his penis and tell him to get it checked by a doctor. The same applies if you notice any fluid coming from his penis when it's not erect, or if he says he has a pain in the testicles area.

> I discovered to my horror that I had contracted an STI and I had no idea I had it. (AND I don't sleep around at all. I got it from my boyfriend.)
> Ange, 18

Sexually transmitted infections (STIs)

Teenagers who have sex without a condom run a really high risk of getting, or passing on, an STI. You can get an STI on your first or any other experience of sex. If you've ever had vaginal, oral or anal sex, you should get tested for STIs. Doctors treat thousands of cases a year – most STIs are common, not rare. (Make sure you read the whole "Safe sex" section, especially the stuff about condoms, as well as this chart.)

Chlamydia

What is it? Chlamydia (pronounced cla-mid-ee-yar) is caused by a bacterium and is the most common sexually transmitted infection in the UK, especially among young people.

How you get it Having vaginal, oral or anal sex with someone who has it.

Signs and symptoms Usually none, but some girls have an unusual vaginal discharge, a burning sensation when weeing, pain during sex or bleeding after sex. Some guys notice a discharge from the penis or a burning sensation when weeing, but it's more likely that neither you nor the guy can tell he has it.

How you know you have it A lab analysis of a wee sample or a swab of the cervix (like a smear test – see "Smear tests" in the Body Maintenance chapter) taken by a doctor.

Effects If not treated, it can cause pelvic inflammatory disease (PID), which can mean that you'll never be able to have a baby. PID symptoms include tummy pain, pain during sex, heavy periods and fever.

Treatment Usually antibiotics, either as a single dose or a longer course or tablets taken for up to two weeks.

How to prevent it Always use a condom during vaginal, oral or anal sex.

Human papilloma virus (HPV), or genital warts

What is it?   A virus that causes visible or invisible warts on your girly bits. There are about sixty kinds of sexually transmitted wart virus. It's *very* common.

How you get it   Spread by skin contact during vaginal, oral or anal sex, whether or not warts are visible. Most people carry the virus without knowing they have it, and pass it on. About fifty percent of people have contracted at least one kind of sexually transmitted wart virus within only three years of first having sex.

Signs and symptoms   Many people have no visible signs at all, or there may be painless small pink or white bumps or larger cauliflower-shaped lumps around the vulva, vagina and anus (or guy's penis and anus). They can be different shapes and sizes, and are sometimes so tiny or difficult to see that you don't even know you have them. Some kinds of HPV cause changes to cells on the cervix.

How you know you have it   A doctor can often tell by looking. If there are no visible warts, a lab can analyze a swab of the cervix taken by the doctor.

Effects   After treatment warts may reappear but will eventually disappear. Some kinds of HPV don't cause visible warts but can turn into cancer of the cervix: that's why it's important to have a regular smear test – every girl or woman who's had sex, even if she's vaccinated against HPV, still needs to have one every three years (see "Smear tests" in the Body Maintenance chapter).

Treatment   An anti-wart liquid or cream usually removes any visible warts, or a doctor or nurse can freeze them. Severe cases will need heat therapy under general anaesthetic. If you're diagnosed with HPV, you'll probably have follow-up tests to make sure nothing nasty develops.

How to prevent it   Use a condom during sex. The HPV, or cervical cancer, vaccination will protect against several common and dangerous kinds of HPV (see "Immunization" in the Body Maintenance chapter). Most girls are now offered the vaccine when they are about 12 or 13, either at school or by their GP, but if you didn't have it then, you should still be able to have it up until the age of 18: ask your doctor, school nurse or a doctor at a sexual health (GUM) clinic about it.

$\rightarrow$

Genital herpes

What is it?   A virus called herpes simplex type 1 or 2, which causes sores on and in your girly bits. Once you've caught it, you always carry the virus and will almost certainly have recurring outbreaks of the sores. Herpes is *very* common, especially in females.

How you get it   Spread by skin contact during vaginal, oral or anal sex, even when there are no visible sores. Cold sores around the mouth are not all caused by an STI, but they can still be transferred to sexual areas. People may not even notice they're having an outbreak of genital herpes, but they still have it and can pass it on. If you're pregnant and have herpes tell your doctor, to avoid passing it on to the baby.

Signs and symptoms   Sometimes none; the first outbreak may cause flu-like symptoms, itching or tingling around the vaginal or anal area, and small blisters which break open as painful sores, taking one or two weeks to heal.

How you know you have it   A lab analysis of a swab taken from a sore by a doctor, or a blood test.

Effects   The first episode of herpes can cause pain and itching. Each outbreak can be less severe than the last and the symptoms can be less obvious, but you still have the virus.

Treatment   You can't get rid of the herpes virus: there's no vaccine or cure, but anti-viral drugs and ointments can relieve the symptoms of pain and itching. (Scientists are trying to develop a vaccine.)

How to prevent it   Always use a condom during sex. Don't have vaginal, oral or anal sex if a partner has sores anywhere.

Human immunodeficiency virus (HIV) and acquired immune deficiency syndrome (AIDS)

What are they? The virus known as HIV causes AIDS: the body's immune system is weakened until it can no longer protect you against infection and disease.

How you get HIV It is transmitted through bodily fluids: semen, blood, vaginal fluid and breast milk. There is no known case of HIV being transmitted through saliva. It can be passed on during vaginal, oral or anal sex or by sharing drug needles. New HIV cases are happening in the UK all the time. Many women have caught it during sex: it is *not* a disease that affects only gay men. In the UK, it is now more commonly diagnosed in straight people than gay people. If a person has HIV they can pass it on to someone else even if they are having treatment.

Signs and symptoms of HIV Sometimes none for a long time, or very common ones a few weeks after infection such as those of flu, tiredness and fever.

How you know you have HIV Blood tests.

Effects Someone who has HIV may not have AIDS: the progression to AIDS may take years. Because AIDS ruins the immune system, an infection eventually causes death.

Treatment Although drugs can slow the progression, there is no vaccine or cure.

How to prevent HIV Always use a condom during sex and don't share drug needles.

Gonorrhoea

Also known as the clap.

What is it? Gonorrhoea (pronounced gon-ar-rear) is a bacterium that gets into the throat, vagina or anus.

How you get it Can be caught during vaginal, oral or anal sex.

Signs and symptoms None, or an unusual (or heavier than usual) discharge from the vagina, and pain or burning when weeing. Guys might get a yellow or white discharge from the penis, and pain or burning when weeing too.

How you know you have it A lab analysis of a swab from the cervix taken by a doctor.

Effects Untreated it can lead to pelvic inflammatory disease (see "Chlamydia" earlier).

Treatment Usually an antibiotic pill, or sometimes an antibiotic injection.

How to prevent it Always use a condom during sex.

→

Hepatitis B

Also known as hep B.

What is it?   One of the hepatitis viruses, which damages the liver.

How you get it   Passed on in bodily fluids (see "HIV and AIDS" earlier). There is no known case of hepatitis B transmission through saliva. Most people who catch it don't realize they have it, but can still pass it on.

Signs and symptoms   Can include mild flu-like symptoms, lack of energy, loss of appetite, nausea and vomiting, jaundice (yellow skin and eyes), and a sore, enlarged liver.

How you know you have it   Blood test.

Effects   Untreated it can become chronic hepatitis, which can lead to liver cancer later in life.

Treatment   There is no treatment for hepatitis B. Extreme cases may need hospitalization.

How to prevent it   Get vaccinated against it, ask your GP or sexual health clinic. Always use a condom during sex and don't share drug needles.

Syphilis

What is it?   Syphilis (pronounced sif-il-is) is an infection caused by a bacterium.

How you get it   Caught through skin contact during vaginal, oral or anal sex. It's very easy to catch. Untreated you stay contagious and will develop worse symptoms later in life.

Signs and symptoms   Stage 1: often unnoticed, or briefly visible, sores in or around girly bits (or on the penis in guys). Stage 2: a red rash anywhere on the body and possibly lumps in the groin and under the arms, patchy hair loss, tiredness and flu-like symptoms.

How you know you have it   A lab analysis of a swab from a sore taken by a doctor, or a blood test.

Effects   It can progress to Stage 3, causing heart problems and brain damage.

Treatment   Usually one injection of an antibiotic, often penicillin (so tell the doctor if you are allergic to it), or sometimes a course of antibiotic tablets.

How to prevent it   Always use a condom during sex.

Trichomoniasis

Also known as trick or trike.

What is it? Trichomoniasis (pronounced trick-oh forget it) is a common vaginal infection caused by a microscopic parasite.

How you get it Mainly from sexual contact, especially vaginal sex. In rare cases it can be caught by sharing wet towels or swimwear.

Signs and symptoms None (especially in guys), or itching and a stinky, yellowy green, frothy, irritating discharge from the vagina. Can cause stinging when you wee.

How you know you have it A doctor can often tell by looking, or a lab analyses a discharge sample taken by the doctor.

Effects Untreated it can progress to pelvic inflammatory disease (see "Chlamydia" earlier).

Treatment Antibiotic pills.

How to prevent it Always use a condom during sex.

Pubic lice, crabs or pubic pediculosis

What are they? An infestation of tiny creatures called crab lice. They live in your pubic or underarm hair and, like hair lice, lay eggs (nits).

How you get them Sexual or close body contact, or sometimes by sharing sheets, towels or clothes. Unlike head lice, these critters can live for many hours away from a body.

Signs and symptoms Itching, or you might notice the tiny lice or their eggs.

How you know you have it A doctor can tell by looking.

Effects If not treated, itching becomes unbearable and scratching can cause infection.

Treatment Killed with a special lice shampoo or lotion. Dead lice and nits need to be combed out. All clothes and bedding must be washed in hot water to kill the lice. Repeat the treatment in a week.

How to prevent it Condoms won't help much to prevent the spread of pubic lice. Make sure whoever you have sex with isn't itchy down there.

Safe sex for lesbians   This can include avoiding oral sex if you have a cold sore; using a "dental dam" – a square of plastic to lick through, which will give you more protection from warts or herpes in the vulva area and stop vaginal fluid getting into your mouth (to make one you can cut a condom and flatten it out into a square); and wearing latex gloves.

More info on using condoms and on sexually transmitted infections

School nurses, practice nurses at your GP's surgery, family planning clinics, young people's clinics and GUM (genito-urinary medicine, or sexual health) clinics can help with info on condoms, which they often give away for free, and with info on STIs.

www.nhsdirect.nhs.uk and
www.nhsdirect.wales.nhs.uk
Find your local GP or sexual health clinic
(or get info) using the NHS Direct websites,
or call **0845 46 47**. In Scotland, use **www.
nhs24.com** or call **08454 24 24 24**. In
Northern Ireland, use **www
.healthandcareni.co.uk**.

www.brook.org.uk
Confidential sexual health advice for teens.
Choose "The facts" or "Your questions" for
info on STIs and condoms, or call their free
helpline: **0808 802 1234**.

www.avert.org
The international AIDS charity Avert has all
sorts of info on safe sex, condoms and STIs.
Choose "Teens" or "STDs".

www.fpa.org.uk
The Family Planning Association site has
loads on STIs, sexual health and condoms
(including a step-by-step guide). Click on
"Information" or search for anything you
have questions about. Click on "Find a
clinic" to get help in your area, or call the
FPA sexual health helpline: **0845 122 8690**
(or **0845 122 8687** in N. Ireland).

www.ruthinking.co.uk
Sex info site for young people. Search for
chlamydia, herpes or any other STI.

www.sexualityandu.ca
This Canadian site shows you how to put on a
condom. From the main page choose "Teens",
then search for "Condom demo". Condom
packets also have instructions in them.

I don't need to get info. I am the sexual encyclopedia. I'm not an idiot. I know what relationships and emotions are, I don't need to be directly told. I learn through experience. If you have sex and are stupid enough to not use a condom, chances are you'll get pregnant. What else is there to know?   Sophie, 13

Contraception

Contraception is a device, medical drug, procedure or practice used to try to stop pregnancy happening. It's also called birth control. And a damned good idea. Most forms of contraception are available for free on the NHS.

Condom

A condom protects against pregnancy as well as STIs – but is only very reliable when used properly. See the previous section, "Safe sex", for all the palaver about how to use condoms.

The Pill

The contraceptive pill is the most common reliable form of contraception that women use. The Pill uses a combination of girly hormones (oestrogen and progesterone) in certain doses to tell the body not to ovulate (release an egg) so that even if a hopeful sperm arrives in a fallopian tube there's no egg waiting to be fertilized by it.

> If you're not ready to be a parent don't have sex without a condom!
> Patti, 13

> Mum said if I did have sex, to tell her straight away, to use protection and to go straight on the Pill!
> Gabby, 14

The Pill is prescribed by your GP or a doctor at a family planning clinic. Occasionally doctors won't prescribe the Pill to anyone, or to girls under a certain age. If you have this problem go to a family planning clinic or special contraception clinic for young people.

Good points about the Pill

- ♂ It's the most reliable method of contraception if taken properly.
- ♂ It can help reduce period pain, heavy periods and other problems because the Pill causes periods to be shorter and lighter, as well as more regular. Many girls are on the Pill to deal with problem periods or severe pimples, not for any contraceptive reason.

Other points about the Pill

- ♂ It doesn't protect against STIs, so you always need to use condoms as well.
- ♂ The side effects can include "retaining fluid", breast tenderness, headaches, nausea, feeling bloated, mood changes and feeling "down". Some may go after the first few weeks; if not, another brand of the Pill can sometimes stop them.

> At school we were shown how to put condoms on bananas. I went home and told my mother who was thrilled to know I wouldn't be impregnated by a piece of fruit. Madeleine, 17

How to take the Pill

typical pill blister sheet

* There are several brands of Pill and they all work in slightly different ways, so get the doctor who prescribes them to show you a box and explain how to take them. Read the instruction leaflet carefully too.

* Most pills come in "blister packs", each containing 28 days' worth (21 pills). There are usually three packs, meaning three months' worth, in a box.

* Each blister pack usually has 21 pills containing the hormones oestrogen and progesterone (see "Your girly bits" in the Change chapter). You must take one pill a day every day for 21 consecutive days, whether or not you have sex.

* The very first time you take them, start the pills on the first day of a period. You'll see that the blister pack has the days of the week marked on it, so if the first day of your period is a Wednesday, for example, take one of the Wednesday (Wed) pills. The following day, take the Thursday pill next to it, following the direction of the arrows marked on

the pack. After 21 days of following the arrows, you should have taken all the pills in the pack.

* When you have taken all 21 pills, you have a break for a week, with no pills, or in some brands you keep taking a pill every day but there are 7 days of pills with no hormones in them (usually they're a different colour in the pack). The lack of hormones will trigger your body to have a period, usually two or three days later. After you have had seven "pill-free" days, start on the next pack of pills right away (on the same day of the week you took your first pill), whether or not you're still having your period.

* If you occasionally want to miss your period all together (maybe if you are going on holiday) start taking the new pack of pills straight away.

* Take each pill at about the same time every day – say, just before bed or at

☻ Combined with smoking the Pill raises the chance of serious side effects such as blood clots. If you are on the Pill don't smoke, and tell the doctor if you have a family history of strokes or blood clots.

☻ It can make you put on a bit of weight, but usually only a little.

☻ If you forget to take it or don't follow the instructions properly, it doesn't work.

breakfast time. (To remember, you could put your pills with your toothbrush or set a daily message or alarm on your phone.) You will not be protected against pregnancy until you've taken a pill each day for seven days in a row.

✱ Keep using condoms whenever you have sex, to protect against STIs.

✱ If you forget to take a pill and it's still within twelve hours of your regular time, take it as soon as you remember, and then take another one at the usual time the next day and continue as normal.

✱ If you don't remember until twelve or more hours after your usual time it's called a "missed pill", and you need to take the next one at the usual time PLUS the one you missed: that means you take two at the same time. Use condoms or don't have sex for a week – "the seven-day rule" – because you might not be protected against pregnancy. Keep taking the rest of the pills each day at the right time.

✱ If you are near the end of a pack when you miss a pill and there are less than seven pills left, start a new pack straight away, without taking a break. This usually means you skip a period, which won't harm you.

✱ If you vomit or have diarrhoea, a pill may not be properly absorbed into your system. Keep taking one each day, but follow the seven-day rule and use condoms or don't have sex until you have taken the pill for seven consecutive days without being sick.

✱ If a doctor prescribes you antibiotics or other medicines, tell them you're "on the Pill" because some drugs interfere with it doing its work properly.

✱ Make sure when you're getting near the end of a box that you go back to the doctor or clinic for a new prescription so you don't have a break in taking the Pill, leaving you unprotected against pregnancy.

✱ If you don't get a period during your pill-free week, or if there is something unusual about it, take a pregnancy test (see the Pregnancy chapter) or see your doctor, but remember that periods often get shorter and "lighter" when you're on the Pill. Also tell your doctor if you suffer from any of the side effects described in the pills' instruction leaflet.

Implant

This is a flexible white plastic rod, slightly smaller than a matchstick, which contains progesterone and provides protection against pregnancy for three years. (Progesterone causes thick mucus to form at the cervix, blocking sperm from getting through.) The rod is inserted by a doctor just under the skin of the upper arm, after a local anaesthetic. It can't be seen in the arm, but you can feel it under the skin with your fingers. It can be taken out by a doctor at any time if there's a problem.

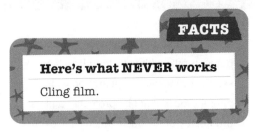

FACTS

Here's what NEVER works

Cling film.

Ask your local doctor if they are experienced in placing an implant, or go to a Family Planning clinic.

Good points about an implant

⊙ It's free, effective, lasts for three years and can make periods less heavy and painful.
⊙ There are not many known side effects.

Other points about an implant

⊙ It doesn't protect against STIs: condoms must also be used.
⊙ It often causes irregular period behaviour, such as spotting – light bleeding showing up as spots on your pants (sometimes every day), which is so annoying that up to a third of users get the implant removed after three months or so, if the spotting doesn't go away.
⊙ Some people find their period comes more often, or less often.

> I go to a Catholic school. Contraception is kind of frowned upon.
> Jane, 15

> They seriously need to give out condoms free. Most girls are too scared to buy them. [You can get them for free at young people's clinics.]
> Mia, 16

Injection

A doctor injects a slow-release progesterone called Depo-Provera into the upper arm or a buttock or thigh. Protection lasts for about three months, after which a user can get another injection. Depo-Provera can stop periods, and often stops ovulation. The body can take quite a while to start ovulating and having periods normally again, once protection from an injection has stopped.

Good points about the injection

⊙ It's "set and forget" for three months.
⊙ It's very reliable as contraception.

> Don't risk having sex.   Emma, 14

> Don't get pregnant to a dude.   Amy, 15

Other points about the injection

- ⊙ It doesn't protect against STIs: condoms must also be used.
- ⊙ Side effects include retained fluid, moodiness and spotting. It can also cause thinning of the bones, which usually stops after the injection wears off.
- ⊙ It can't be stopped if there are nasty side effects.
- ⊙ Another injection needs to be remembered every three months.

The info I've been given about not getting pregnant is to not have sex when you are at this age.
Emily, 15

IUD

An IUD or IUS (intra-uterine device or system) is put into the uterus, under general anaesthetic, by a surgeon and can stop an egg implanting for at least five years. It's not generally recommended for teens, and gives no protection against STIs.

Diaphragm (or cap), and ring

A diaphragm (pronounced dire-fram) is a little plastic doofer that looks like a tiny, flexible bowl. It goes into the vagina before sex to fit over the cervix, stopping sperm from getting into the uterus. The newer ring, which fits around the cervix and releases progesterone, can be left in for three weeks, but is expensive and has to be replaced each month. Diaphragms and rings are fiddly to insert and remove, not highly reliable and don't protect against STIs. Give 'em a miss.

Spermicide

This is a chemical designed to be put into the vagina before sex to kill sperm. It can be in the form of a jelly or ointment, a foam or a dissolving pill. It's messy, unreliable and useless against STIs.

Douching

"Washing" or squirting anything into the vagina after sex will not kill sperm and doesn't protect against pregnancy or STIs. Useless.

"Natural" methods

Grouped under the description "natural" are a variety of methods not involving a device or a medical drug or procedure. Generally they don't work.

Trying to avoid fertile days   The term "natural" contraception usually refers to women avoiding sex at a time when they think there's an egg waiting to be fertilized. (Various forms are known as "fertility awareness", the "rhythm method", "Vatican roulette" and the "Billings method".) Girls and women are most likely to get pregnant (are at their most fertile) when they ovulate – usually about halfway between two periods. But, especially during the teenage years, a menstrual cycle can be irregular so girls can never really know if or when they have ovulated. Even women with established cycles who carefully measure vaginal secretions and vaginal temperatures, so they can choose the "safe" days for sex, are sometimes caught out. This is a totally unreliable form of contraception, and doesn't protect against STIs.

Withdrawal   The guy tries to pull out before he ejaculates inside the vagina. This doesn't work because a guy always has a leak of semen before he ejaculates, and even if he doesn't ejaculate; and sometimes he may not withdraw in time or may "get carried away" and forget. It's not a form of contraception at all, and doesn't protect against STIs. Don't go there!

Sex during a period   Although getting pregnant is far less likely during a period than halfway between periods, it has happened, especially to young girls whose cycle hasn't sorted itself out yet. And sperm, the sneaky stuff, can stay alive for up to seven days inside the body, so having sex at a "safe" time might end up as a pregnancy anyway.

Sex without penetration   This includes oral sex; hands-only sex; and "dry sex", a term used to describe a guy with his clothes on having an orgasm against a clothed girl. Pregnancy is unlikely – as long as leaked or ejaculated semen doesn't accidentally go anywhere near the vagina.

Abstinence   The problem with abstinence (deciding not to have sex at all) is that, for almost every person who chooses it, a situation will come up in which they find themselves going ahead anyway. Often they have no condoms because they weren't expecting to have sex, and can end up pregnant or dealing with an STI.

Anal sex   Some people use it as contraception because sperm doesn't go into the vagina. It does not protect against STIs – and in fact is an easy way to get diseases and infections because the skin inside the anus is delicate and easily torn. A condom absolutely must be used. Not a good solution. Girls usually don't like it. (It hurts.)

I HOPE I'm not pregnant

'Natural' contraception

Operation

There are operations to make a guy or a woman infertile – unable to have a baby – but doctors will usually not perform these on somebody as young as a teenager, even if they want it.

Emergency contraception: the morning-after pill

This is a special dose of the hormone progesterone taken in pill form to prevent pregnancy after unprotected sex. It works by preventing that month's ovulation or, if fertilization has already happened, by stopping the microscopic egg from implanting itself in the uterus. The fertilized egg, so tiny you can't see it, comes out in your next period or is just absorbed back into the body. (This sometimes happens to fertilized eggs naturally.)

Although it's sometimes called the morning-after pill, the emergency contraceptive pill is best taken straight away, or as soon as possible after unprotected sex, and within 24 hours if possible – but definitely within three days. There can be a bit of bleeding a couple of days afterwards, as the body decides to clean house with a period.

The morning-after pill is not one hundred percent guaranteed but the earlier it's taken after unprotected sex, the more effective it is. If you need to use the morning-after pill take a pregnancy test about three weeks later, in case it didn't work. If the test is positive go straight to a doctor. Don't delay for any reason.

The morning-after pill is available for free from most GP's surgeries, family planning clinics, contraception and sexual health clinics, young people's clinics and some chemists. Women and girls over 16 can also buy it, without a prescription, at the chemist for about £25. Just ask for it at the desk where the prescriptions are taken.

I had unprotected sex once with my ex boyfriend and I was scared about getting pregnant so I went to the chemist and bought the morning-after pill.
Lydia, 16

FACT

Emergency only   Don't have unprotected sex because you think you can just get the morning-after pill the next day. It's much better for your body if you make sure you have safer sex using condoms properly, which protects you against pregnancy *and* STIs.

Although it should only be used in emergencies and not as regular contraception, if you live in a remote area, are going travelling or are using condoms for contraception, you could think about getting a morning-after pill in advance, in case a condom breaks. (Keep the tablet in a cool, dry place.)

The morning-after pill is not the "abortion pill" (that's explained in the Pregnancy chapter), and it does not cause an abortion. It prevents a pregnancy from beginning.

More info on contraception

See the earlier sections on "More info on deciding whether or not to have sex" and "More info on using condoms and on sexually transmitted infections" for sites that also give advice on contraception, and for details of the Brook and the Family Planning Association's helplines.

NHS Direct health line: 0845 46 47 (or NHS 24 in Scotland: 08454 24 24 24) Phone your local GP or this 24-hour helpline for free emergency contraception or info on missed pills or split condoms. You can also visit the "Emergency contraception zone" on the NHS Direct site for more details or to chat to an advisor online about emergency contraception: **www.nhsdirect.nhs.uk.**

www.brook.org.uk Choose "The facts" for info on all the different kinds of contraception available.

www.fpa.org.uk Search for "contraception" or "the Pill" for advice on how to take the contraceptive pill, emergency contraception and more.

www.thesite.org YouthNet website; search for "contraception" for info on what to do if you miss a pill.

My mum thinks I'm a sex-crazed teenager who has no control over my emotions... when actually I'm more interested in love than sex.   Jessie, 15

It is better if they love you. As time passed, my boyfriend lost his love for me, and it became just sex.   Poonam, 16

I wish I'd known that letting a guy have sex with you does not mean he'll love you.   Jessica, 17

Sex and love

A lot of people believe you should only have sex with people you love. Others think you should only have sex with somebody who respects you and is kind and considerate, whether or not you're in love.

One of the hardest things for girls to learn is that sex does not equal love for everybody. You may be in love, and feel that the sex makes it even more romantic, but for the guy it can be all about sex, not about love. Some girls feel that way too.

> My good friend and her boyfriend have sex then he ignores her then comes back to her when he wants more but he tells her he loves her but then ignores her again and she loves him to death and thinks he is the best thing in the world. Em, 16

Getting swept away

Because having sex does not necessarily equal love, it is a good idea to be cautious about your feelings at first. Having sex with someone is such an intimate experience that it can make you feel very close to that person emotionally, can be overwhelming, and can give you some kooky, if temporary, thoughts:

- We're going to be together forever.
- I could never love anybody else.
- We belong together.
- It doesn't matter if I get pregnant because we love each other.
- I'd do anything for him.
- We're in a long-term relationship. (Even though you've only known each other for six days.)

No matter what you're feeling, keep using condoms and sticking to the "essentials" of sex explained in the "Going all the way" section earlier. Planned sex, where you have everything ready, is just as romantic as unplanned sex – and in fact is usually better because you're not terrified about getting pregnant or getting an STI (which is really unromantic). Having condoms at home or in your bag doesn't mean that you're expecting to have sex. It means they're just there if you need them. You don't have to use them. (Unless you have sex. Then you really do have to use them!)

> My mum always tells me to wait until I'm married to have sex, and wait until I'm ready and I'm in love with the person. She reminds me a lot. Danielle, 15

CARING

Can I help you?

16

the environment

When you're a teenager you sometimes ask yourself the **big** philosophical questions such as "Why am I here?", "What's the meaning of life?", "What should I believe in?", "What's the **right way** to live?", "Why should I do the right thing when so many people seem to get away with doing the wrong thing?" and "How can I help to fix things in the world so it could be better?"

Discoveries in science and increased knowledge have disproved many previously accepted religious ideas, but we all still need to have a personal set of beliefs and to decide what's **important** and what's the right way to live.

What people believe in

Most people have been taught a certain religious faith or set of values from birth because it's the religion or philosophy of their family. There isn't a day when you turn 18 that you suddenly get to tick the box for "Zoroastrian", "Greek Orthodox Christian" or "Huh. Still Confused". Which god or belief system you have is usually an accident of where you were born, and into which family.

Religious beliefs

Most religions attempt to answer big questions about how people got here, what our purpose is on Earth, how we should live, and what happens when we die.

All cultures in the world have creation stories that try to explain how we got here. Most religions revere a specific god, several gods or a force of nature that is said to have created the world and to control it; recognize key prophets (interpreters of a god's will), teachers or elders; and follow a set of morals or a book based on an interpretation of the wishes of gods or prophets.

Depending on your family's religious tradition, you could be brought up to believe in the teachings of the Prophet Mohammed, an earth goddess, the Jewish or Christian God, Buddha, a giant crow who made the world or aliens who came to Earth and gave a set of rules to somebody who was standing in a paddock.

Religion also fulfils a basic human need for a sense of belonging and community: for a support group, a meeting place, celebrations to mark important occasions and a ready-made set of rules to follow. Most religions have observances and religious holidays; examples include Christmas and Easter for Christians, and the holy month of Ramadan for Muslims.

Common forms of observance include gatherings (often in a special place), prayer, song, and food, incense or other offerings made to the shrines of a god or several gods or ancestors. There are often rules about what you can eat, or how the food is to be prepared and stored, and which days or times must be set aside for worship or prayer.

Most believers think their religion requires them to live a moral life and to do good in the world. Many religious organizations are involved in charitable works such as helping the poor and disadvantaged.

Some religions want the children within their organization to be educated at a religious school, where they'll probably only mix with other people of the same beliefs. And some religious schools teach their own version of history, morals and even science (for example, "intelligent design" or "creationism" instead of evolutionary science). This can mean that students miss out on essential scientific information, sex and contraception education and learning about other views of life.

Many of the basic principles of old religions remain in place today – it is wrong to kill, you must treat others with kindness, do not steal – but often religions struggle to remain relevant, given the ever-increasing scientific explanations of the world, the pace of technology and the vast difference between life now and life hundreds or thousands of years ago when the holy books were written (for instance, many religions still teach that women are inferior to men).

New Age beliefs

Although the major religions of the world offer supernatural answers to questions about the "meaning of life", many accept that in the everyday world other factors – economics, science, politics, psychology – also influence people's lives. But there are still some ancient or traditional ideas around that have been recycled as what's often called New Age beliefs. These include astrology, clairvoyancy, "healing" and other crystals, witchcraft and spells.

Astrology   Astrologers continue to say, as they have done for thousands of years, that the stars determine a person's personality and their future. Constellations (combinations) of stars are said to resemble, say, a bull (Taurus) or an archer (Sagittarius), and people are sorted into one of twelve "star signs", which are believed to have certain characteristics. Astrologers draw up individual "horoscopes", using charts "connecting the dots" of the stars visible in the sky when a particular person was born, to decide the person's star sign and predict what they'll feel and do.

Indigenous people looked at the same stars in the same sky and imagined different pictures, and scientific advances in astronomy since then have proved that stars are really giant gaseous balls in space. So think of your horoscope as one-size-fits-all advice that could apply to just about anybody, and just read the astrology columns for fun.

"Types"   Some books and articles divide people up according to ancient ideas such as the earth, fire, air and water "signs", or types. Newer versions similarly sort people according to their birth date, their numerology, their body shape or their blood type.

People who see the world in this way often say that your personality, your future, your job, who you choose as a partner, how you relate to your parents and even what you eat should be dictated by which type you are. This is harmless fun – unless you take it too seriously and follow it.

Now that we understand so much more about science and psychology, we know that people are individual and complex, and it's not helpful to label them in this way or to tell them to run their life solely according to old superstitions.

I was a Pisces. Then the stars moved. Now I'm a small asteroid

Clairvoyants, psychics, fortune tellers and mediums   Clairvoyants and psychics are people who claim to be able to see hidden things – sometimes in the "spirit world". They can have good intuition and can be surprisingly accurate at guessing, or knowing, what's important to somebody; others have lots of stage tricks to make them seem as if they know stuff.

There's no harm in occasionally having a fortune teller or psychic read your palm or tell your fortune – unless you run your life by it, or take everything they say as a definite. Mediums, who claim they can recognize "messages" from the dead, are best left where they belong – in movies and TV shows.

Humanist (non-religious) ethics

Lots of people are atheists: they don't believe in a god. Others are agnostics: they're not convinced either way.

Many atheists are humanists: people who try to live morally, although not for religious reasons. Humanists reject religious answers that are not based on logic or evidence. They disagree with the way that some Churches resist change and discourage or even punish questioning. They place their faith in the laws of science, reasonable behaviour, social rules and independence of mind.

Humanists believe that you don't have to be religious to live by rules about kindness and not hurting others, or to do good in the world. They (like many religious people) oppose wars and terrorism carried out in the name of religion.

Tolerance

It's not possible to accept or agree with somebody's religion or value system if you are not convinced by it – every religion and culture has rituals or beliefs that are inexplicable to others – but one of the principles of a democratic society is that people agree to tolerate each other's beliefs: in other words, to respect another person's right to believe. While there are laws against trying to create hatred or violence based on religious (or racial or other discriminatory) grounds, everyone is allowed to discuss and question

FACT

"Karma"   Karma is the Buddhist, Hindu and Jain religious belief that being a good person will be rewarded with a better status when you are reincarnated (take on a new form after death), while bad behaviour will be punished by you being reborn as, say, an insect. It's often used by non-members of these religions as a warning: "Don't do that, you'll have bad karma". Don't interpret this to mean that if you have bad luck, or get sick, it's your fault. It isn't.

religious beliefs. It's part of the democratic concept of freedom of speech.

It's also each person's right not to have to live by someone else's religious rules. In secular democracies, like France and Australia, religion and government are separate: religion is a matter of private choice, whereas governments are elected to protect and promote the social well-being of everyone. Theoretically, the UK is a Christian country, the Queen is the head of the Church of England and there are still links between the Church and state. But, in reality, the Church isn't really involved in government and the UK is pretty much a multi-cultural secular society where religion is a private choice and all beliefs are tolerated and protected by law from discrimination.

People of strong religious (or minority) beliefs are expected not to interfere in the lives of the rest of the community, although some try to make the country's laws follow their views – say, by trying to make pregnancy termination illegal, or trying to stop gay people getting married.

Take some time

Most religious and many non-religious people set aside a time each day for something they might call prayer, meditation, reflection, "having some space", "communing with nature" or thinking.

Taking twenty (or even just a few) minutes in the day to walk or sit in a peaceful way and think, without your phone, music, TV or another distraction, can help you:

✳ become a calmer person

✳ come up with useful ideas and solutions

✳ work out what you hope for and how you could make things happen.

Religious discrimination It's illegal to discriminate against somebody at work, at school or any other place because of religious differences. Some people look different because of their religion. For example, some Muslim girls wear a headscarf or veil, some Jewish guys wear special kinds of caps and men of the Sikh religion wear turbans.

It's a sign of maturity not to make fun of somebody just because they look or dress differently. There's no reason why you can't quietly and politely ask someone why they wear or do certain things because of their religion, if you are genuinely interested, but it's wrong to do it in a way that might embarrass the person.

And if you're the person being asked, even though it may be the fifty-sixth time that week, try to be patient. The more people learn about each other, the easier it is for everyone to understand each other and to make friends, instead of feeling alienated from each other.

Fanaticism and extremism   Fanaticism is the term given to people who hold to their set of beliefs – religious or non-religious – so passionately that they try to make everybody else live by what they believe.

All the major religions have minority offshoots, including smaller, stricter and often weirder versions (there are some US Christians who interpret the Bible to suggest they should cavort with poisonous rattlesnakes). And most religions have some members who are fanatical.

Many fanatics want the religion to be the same as it was thousands or hundreds of years ago, and demand that strict rules or the words of a holy book be followed exactly – as interpreted by them. Because old holy books have nothing to say about recent inventions such as mobile phones or popular music or a million other things, extremists tend to think most aspects of modern life are evil, but tend to ignore obvious evils that weren't mentioned back then, such as child abuse and racism.

Most extremists hold that they must convert others to their views and insist that their beliefs alone should be legally enforced. Some use violence or threats to try to impose their ideas. Some animal rights fanatics in England dug up the dead body of a man's mother-in-law, and threatened the grandchildren of his cleaner, because he worked for a place that sold guinea pigs to scientific researchers. Some Christian anti-abortion fanatics bomb clinics that offer pregnancy termination. Some Muslim fanatics kill innocent people at random.

Obviously it's best not to engage with fanatics, and to try not to have anything to do with them personally. You can express your concern publicly and use the political system to oppose fanatics who want to destroy the democratic, tolerant way of life our society has chosen (see the "How to change the world" section coming up).

Cults   A cult is the name given to a secretive organization that tends to recruit members; to use psychological tricks to try to control the way members think, including sleep deprivation, the granting and withdrawal of affection and approval, and isolation from friends and family; and to teach that those outside the cult are bad people and the only world needed is the Church or organization.

Many cults are based on interpretations of the Christian Bible; others are presented as New Age studies or as "personal devel-

A frank exchange of views

opment" style courses about how to be more "successful"; and some are commercial ventures teaching you how to sell or market products. Examples of cults include the Exclusive Brethren, the Jehovah's Witnesses, Scientology (one of the many based on ideas about aliens) and Landmark Forum. Most cults somehow involve asking you to donate lots of money.

FACT

"Gurus" These are "teachers" who pass on their "wisdom". It can be dangerous to put all your faith in only one teacher (or friend or coach). Nobody, no matter how much older and more experienced than you, has all the answers for you or should isolate you from family and friends.

More info on religion, philosophy and ideas

www.askphilosophers.org
You can email questions on moral issues to a panel of philosophers at this US site and have them answered, or see what's already been discussed in the archives.

www.bbc.co.uk/religion
The BBC's religion and ethics pages give a round-up of the main UK religions, plus related news, message boards, faith in your area, and info on TV and radio programmes.

www.caic.org.au
The Australian Cult Awareness and Info Centre has info, support and personal stories.

www.humanism.org.uk
British Humanist Association, for people who want to live good lives without religious beliefs.

www.inform.ac
Based at the London School of Economics, INFORM provides balanced info about new religous movements and "cults".

www.interfaith.org.uk
The Inter Faith Network tries to build good relationships between people of different faiths in the UK; includes local groups, activities and resources for students and young people.

www.islamispeace.org.uk
Site challenging negative stereotypes of British Muslims, rejecting extremism and promoting understanding; includes a guide to Islamic history, beliefs, arts and lifestyle.

www.liberty-human-rights.org.uk
Liberty is a UK organization that tries to protect civil liberties and promote human rights; issues include free speech, equality, privacy, asylum and young people's rights.

www.religioustolerance.org
Canadian site that explains the beliefs of different religions without making judgements.

Eyewitness: Religion by Myrtle Langley, **Dorling Kindersley**
Brief explanations of most of the world's major religions.

Ideas That Changed the World by Felipe Fernandez Armesto, **Dorling Kindersley**
Brilliant overview of old and new spiritual ideas, political movements, and different ethical and philosophical ways of thinking.

God Is Not Great: How Religion Poisons Everything by Christopher Hitchens, **Atlantic Books**
Expresses the view that religion is holding the world back from progress and peace.

Beliefs round-up

Some religions with one god

- Christianity
- Islam (Muslim)
- Judaism (Jewish)
- Sikh
- Mormon (Church of Jesus Christ of Latter Day Saints)

Some religions with several gods

- Hinduism
- Hare Krishna (Krishna as the supreme god)
- Jain
- Yoruba
- Shintoism

Some religions with teachers, prophets or gurus

- Christianity, Islam, Sikh, Mormon
- Confucianism
- Buddhism
- Baha'i
- Zoroastrianism

Some indigenous belief systems

- Various Aboriginal
- Traditional Mayan
- Traditional Inuit
- Maori
- Native American
- Various Pacific Islander
- Various African

Some New Age religions

- Nature worship
- Wicca (modern witchcraft)
- Goddess and earth worship
- Neo-druidism
- Paganism

Some spiritual movements

- Taoism
- Yoga and meditation
- Falun Gong
- Animism
- Zen

Some other belief systems and philosophies

- Capitalism
- Communism
- Fascism
- Social Darwinism (dominance by the rich and strong, survival of the fittest)
- Nihilism (nothing matters)
- Humanism
- Unitarianism
- Scientific approach – acceptance of explanations based solely on verifiable data and research (such as evolution) to explain life
- Green living
- Plus too many other non-religious beliefs to list here!

How to change the world

Your religion or philosophy can make you think not just about yourself, but about the bigger world and what you can do to make a difference (apart from having green hair). Heaps of young people are trying to change things for the better. Others would like to but don't know how they can help.

Being active in politics, protests, social justice causes and charitable causes can make you feel you're involved in something important, that you're doing a good thing. And getting involved is just a phone call or a mouse click away.

Voting

In a democracy everyone has the right and responsibility to vote for the people they want to represent them in government. In the UK, you can't vote until you've turned 18 but you can register (enrol) to vote when you turn 16 – that way you'll be ready to vote if the government calls a snap election just as you turn 18.

The process differs slightly throughout the UK, so contact your local council to find out how to get your name on the electoral register, or see "More info" at the end of this chapter. In most areas, a form is automatically sent to every house once a year so that the register can be updated and you need to fill in all the information requested.

Activism

Activism is about having a say in the issues that affect your life and the lives of others – even if you're not old enough to vote. An activist is someone who seeks to create positive change, often by influencing decision makers or taking action in a social or political way.

Some ways to be an activist

- ❻ Join a charity, a political party, a church, or a protest or issue-focused group.
- ❻ Write letters, make phone calls and send emails to your local member of parliament (MP) or a minister heading a department to ask the government to change or make a law.

๑ Create or sign a petition asking the government to change or make a law.

๑ Use blogs or social networking sites to get your voice heard online.

๑ Contact the media, from local papers to radio and TV shows, to express your view.

๑ Protest peacefully by going to meetings, rallies and marches about an issue that matters to you.

๑ Help organize or go to fundraising events and concerts.

๑ Raise money for special projects (such as building a school in another country).

๑ Participate in a boycott (a campaign convincing people not to buy a product such as animal fur, or products made by a company that you feel exploits workers or the environment).

๑ Invent publicity stunts (legal ones that don't harm yourself or other people).

๑ Get involved in global campaigns (for instance, against climate change) – or join a small, local volunteer programme such as visiting old people to cheer them up.

What activism has won   Young people have almost always been a major part, if not the leaders, of social movements and social change, and not always just ones concerned with youth issues.

Successful activism has led in many places to the vote for women; equal rights for people with dark skin; workers having the weekend or a day off each week; children not being forced to work for no or little pay; democratic governments in countries where there were dictators; large fines for polluters; agreements on debt relief for developing countries; laws banning things as diverse as landmines, the ivory trade and fox hunting; and governments signing global agreements on human rights and environmental issues.

The cynical may say the world is in bad shape – but it would be in much worse shape, or no shape at all, if it were not for activists and young people who care.

"Think global, act local"   This means that because we care about the effects our actions have on the wider world we will make small changes in our own lives – and if that encourages everyone else to do the same, all the little changes will add up to a great big change. For example, actions that are good for the environment include walking or cycling short distances rather than going by car, switching to energy-saving light bulbs, taking a reusable shopping bag instead of getting plastic bags, conserving water and recycling your rubbish.

Pick a cause   Don't be bamboozled by the range of possibilities. The important thing is to pick just one cause you feel passionate about, and start doing something about it.

This could range from becoming a member of a group that tries to save animals and their habitats (such as the World Wildlife Fund), or boycotting shops that exploit foreign workers, to finding out about each political party in the UK and joining a youth organization affiliated to the one you think most reflects your own beliefs and values.

Fundraising

Teenagers tend to have lots of enthusiasm and energy, and they like to help others, so it's often young people shaking collection tins and knocking on doors to raise money for charities. But it's really only the right thing to do if most or all of the money is going directly to a charity. Many charities have their own shops and websites, and they give all their profits to the good cause, not a tiny percentage.

Although "philanthropist" (pronounced fill-an-thro-pist) is a word often used to describe rich people or organizations that donate lots of money, you're still being a philanthropist every time you drop a coin in a collection bucket; buy a raffle ticket when the money raised goes to a good cause; buy a copy of *The Big Issue* magazine from a homeless person; or give your old (but still good) clothes to the local charity shop. (You may want to ask an adult to help you check out for a charity's registration number or fundraiser's official ID badge, so you know that they're legit.)

There are lots of ways you can be involved in fundraising.

- Talk to your family about making an automatic small monthly contribution from a bank account to a major charity on behalf of the whole family.

- Ask your parents what you can donate (in addition to old clothes) if you can't give money. Perhaps old books, CDs or games you don't use anymore.

- Try to use services or buy products that give a percentage of their proceeds to charities, but don't be sucked in: ask for the details. It may be better to buy something cheaper elsewhere and donate the money you've saved directly to the charity.

- At Christmas and birthday times remember the charities that sell cards and donation presents (such as a gift certificate saying a goat has been bought for a village in Africa in the name of the person receiving the gift).

- Shake a collection tin for your local children's hospital.

- Join in readathons, sponsored walks and other fundraising campaigns (except ones that mean you can't eat for a period of time – donate money instead and keep eating to have energy for the cause).

Volunteering

If you don't have lots of money (and let's face it, if you do you're probably off playing polo in a tiara, not reading this), you can volunteer your time. Volunteering means you're performing a service, but not getting paid in money. In the UK, around twenty million people do some sort of volunteer work, just using the time they can spare, even if they're busy. It can also be a fun way of regularly meeting up with friends.

Some common volunteering ideas include:

- dog-walking or doing odd jobs for elderly or disabled people
- tree planting for conservation projects or collecting litter from local woodlands

- activities to raise money and awareness
- being a mentor for other young people
- teaching computer skills to older people
- helping children improve their reading and writing skills
- helping refugees and immigrants to learn English
- working in a charity shop or an organization's office
- delivering "flyers" (info sheets) through letterboxes
- doing voluntary first aid with St John's Ambulance
- volunteering abroad during school holidays or a gap year.

It's best to do your volunteer work through an accredited organization, and to make sure your parents are on hand to help with any problem. Make sure that the type of work you're doing is suitable for your age group, and that you know exactly what your duties and responsibilities are going to be before you start. Always let people know where you are going when you do your volunteer work.

Although you don't get paid for volunteering, there are other benefits:

- the good feeling you get from helping others
- gaining work experience and other skills (it looks great on your CV too)
- learning useful social and organizational skills
- your parents see you can be more responsible and give you more freedoms
- you're not so bored
- it increases your confidence
- you can make new friends.

Being active in the world gives you a new perspective on life and makes you realize you can get things done.

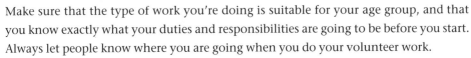

Many times my parents do not take my ideas on society seriously. I am consistently labelled as going through "a stage" when I question what we are told through the media, and present my views on such things as religion, abortion, pollution and world conflict. I have very different views to my parents but I don't think that a difference in opinion should equate to being categorized as going through "a stage". Eloise, 17

More info on getting involved and being informed

UK

www.aboutmyvote.co.uk
The Electoral Commission site explains how to register and how to vote. Also has details of local elections and a polling station demo.

www.eoni.org.uk
The Electoral Office for Northern Ireland has registration forms, voting info and FAQs.

www.direct.gov.uk/en/YoungPeople
UK government site for young people, with info on everything from politics, crime and justice to careers, learning and leisure.

www.headsup.org.uk
Site for teens to discuss politics and current affairs, and tell politicians what they think.

www.peopleandplanet.org
Student activist site that campaigns on world poverty, human rights and the environment.

petitions.number10.gov.uk
Sign or create petitions on any issue, and send them to the Prime Minister online.

www.theyworkforyou.com
Find out who your MP is, how to contact them and which issues they feel strongly about.

www.thesite.org/homelawandmoney
Choose "Activism" for stuff on politics, campaigning, fundraising and the big issues.

www.ukyouthparliament.org.uk
The UK Youth Parliament is for 11–18 year olds who want to help change the world.

www.funkydragon.org
Site for young people wanting to get their voices heard at the Welsh Assembly.

www.niyf.org
Northern Ireland Youth Forum.

www.scottishyouthparliament.org.uk
Scottish Youth Parliament.

www.labourparty.co.uk and **www.conservatives.com** and **www.libdems.org.uk** and **www.greenparty.org.uk**
Sites of the major UK political parties.

www.snp.org (Scotland); **www.plaidcymru.org** (Wales); **www.dup.org.uk**, **www.sinnfein.ie**, **www.uup.org** and **www.sdlp.ie** (N. Ireland)
Sites of the major regional political parties.

The world

www.amnesty.org.uk
Amnesty International campaigns for human rights in every country.

news.bbc.co.uk
The BBC news site will keep you informed about what's happening around the world, and has country profiles and in-depth articles.

www.theinsite.org
US site "for teens and young adults to turn their world around".

www.una-uk.org/youth
The United Nations Youth Association of the UK; its members campaign on global issues.

Young people

www.byc.org.uk
The British Youth Council is run by under-26s to promote young people's rights and campaign on issues like the voting age.

www.envision.org.uk
Envision helps young people to start up their own local social and environmental projects.

www.girlguiding.org.uk
As well as doing community service and learning new skills, Guides do lots of outdoorsy stuff, travel and make new friends.

www.theaward.org
The Duke of Edinburgh's Award gets young people to do a "service" in their community, learn new skills and go on expeditions.

www.wearewhatwedo.org
International movement encouraging people to change the world with everyday actions.

www.youthnoise.com
International social networking site for young people to talk about big issues, raise money and get involved in various causes.

www.ywca.org.uk
Campaigning charity that works to improve the lives of young women in the UK.

Environmental groups and campaigns

www.campaigncc.org
The Campaign against Climate Change site has details about marches and events all over the UK run by lots of different charities.

www.foe.co.uk
Friends of the Earth.

www.greenpeace.org.uk
Greenpeace.

www.rspb.org.uk
Royal Society for the Protection of Birds.

www.wwf.org.uk
World Wildlife Fund.

www.ypte.org.uk
The Young People's Trust for the Environment encourages teens' understanding of the environment and the need for sustainability.

Charities and organizations

www.charity-commission.gov.uk
The Charity Commission has info about every registered charity in the UK.

www.careinternational.org.uk
Care International is an aid agency that fights poverty and injustice around the world.

www.helptheaged.org.uk
Charity focusing on the needs of older people.

www.oxfam.org.uk
An aid organization that works to end poverty and suffering around the world.

www.redcross.org.uk
The Red Cross is a humanitarian organization that helps in disaster and war time.

www.rnib.org.uk
The Royal National Institute of Blind People supports people with sight loss in the UK.

www.savethechildren.org.uk
Save the Children fights for children's rights in the UK and around the world.

www.sja.org.uk
St John Ambulance provide first aid at public events, emergency response and training. Young volunteers can join Cadets units.

www.unicef.org.uk
The United Nations International Children's Emergency Fund.

www.worldvision.org.uk
Sponsor a child, or donate to campaigns against child poverty and exploitation.

Volunteering

www.do-it.org.uk
A national database of volunteering opportunities. You can search by town, availability, activities and areas of interest.

www.earthwatch.org
Earthwatch runs conservation projects around the world – great for gap year adventures.

www.youngtimebank.org.uk
Helps young volunteers set up projects that make a difference in their communities.

www.volunteering.org.uk (England);
www.volunteerscotland.org.uk (Scotland);
www.volunteering-wales.net (Wales) and
www.volunteernow.co.uk (N. Ireland)
Sites with info, resources and volunteer opportunities for each region of the UK.

www.youthactionnetwork.org.uk
National organization for youth volunteering.

Books

Change the World for a Fiver by We Are What We Do, Short Books
Lists fifty simple actions to improve your life and the world.

The Rough Guide to Ethical Living by Duncan Clarke, Rough Guides
Covers ethical and environmental issues, and has tips on reducing your carbon footprint.

365 Ways to Change the World by Michael Norton, Penguin Books
Lots of ideas on how to help others and make a difference locally and globally.

I like learning about things. I wish there wasn't so much pressure placed on it, it should be done for the love of it.   Cecily, 17

I don't copy what everyone wears, I like having my own individual image. I think a lot before I buy clothes, and I try and find things for reasonable prices.
Laura, 15

I love make-up. I always wear lots of it – even to bed.   Chloe, 14

INFO TO GO →

PART 4

17

SCHOOLWORK

You're supposed to think your school years are the best time
of your life – as if you didn't have to deal with hormones, and
negotiating every last molecule of life at home, and parents
and teachers throwing hours of **homework** at you and telling
you that if you don't pass your exams you'll be stuck in a dead-
end job, packing toenail clippings into tiny boxes for the herbal
cure market.

   It's a colossal pain in the buttockular region, but whether
you're in **school, college, university, a training scheme or an
apprenticeship,** you'll have to get the studying done so that one
day you'll be freeeeee. And also not have to pack toenail clippings.

Homework and study

When to study and do homework? Every waking minute of your life that you're not at school, according to some parents – but that's just going to drive you nuts and won't work anyway. There's really only so much homework and study time you can take.

It's dull but true that if you get the work done earlier in the night it will be easier and you'll remember more. Anything after midnight and you're wilted and not taking it in (see the Brain chapter).

Sadly you'll need to be organized.

A homework or study plan

Keep a schedule for your homework and study so you know how much time you can spend on each subject or project. It means you won't end up writing 67,000 words for an essay on frog spawn that isn't due until the end of the week, then suddenly realize you've not done the maths questions that have to be in tomorrow.

> I can't concentrate easily, so I find if I work for slots of say 45 mins and then have a 10 min break it's easier. Because your brain absorbs only in the first 30–45 mins.
> Amelia, 17

Work out what homework or studying you need to get through in the next few days or weeks, and how much free time you have available, then divide that time between school tasks and other things you want or have to do. It's probably something you can draw up on a Sunday night.

Put your plan in writing (pencil might be good so you can rub something out if your schedule has to change), then pin it up above your desk or near wherever you study, or keep it in your diary. There's a schedule on the next page which you can photocopy and fill in.

You'll probably need to spend more time on the subjects you find the hardest, which is annoying. Pencil in a fun thing for the end of each session so you have a reward.

If your schedule is so chock-a-block that it's stressful and scary, talk to a teacher or parent about what you can do to ease the pressure.

HINT

Back-up Make sure, if you use a computer, that every hour or so you save your work somewhere else (for instance, on a memory stick or disk), especially if you share the computer with somebody else.

Homework and study schedule*

Monday		dinner	

Tuesday		dinner	

Wednesday		dinner	

Thursday		dinner	

Friday		dinner	

Saturday		lunch	

Sunday		lunch	

* Remember to write in sport or other exercise time.

When homework is too hard

Your homework might be too hard because:

✳ your school is insisting on too much (check your school's homework policy if you think you're being given too much)

✳ your school has misjudged what you can handle

✳ you're experiencing a temporary difficulty or personal stress

✳ you just reeeeally hate doing homework so can't get it organized

✳ you have a learning disability (many people do).

Talk with teachers and parents to see if you can work out your situation. Maybe it would help if they showed you another way of learning or studying the subject. Schools have to provide students with an education suited to their individual needs, including help with learning difficulties. (Specialized help is available for learning difficulties: see "More info on schoolwork and reading" further on.)

Your homework and study spot

Some people can work in the kitchen while six brothers and sisters are having a fight over the last scoop of ice cream, but most people need a bit of quiet space somewhere. Your own bedroom is probably best, although there are usually lots of distractions (not to mention that bed just tempting you to have a nap or maybe a pillow fight). Sometimes a suitable study space can be in a quiet corner of another room, a parent's home office, at school or the local library, or at granny's house.

Here are the general requirements:

- ⊚ a work space that's big enough for all your stuff (and for you to be able to leave it there if possible)

- ⊚ peace and quiet – some people suggest total silence, while others think a little bit of low background noise, such as the radio or a CD, is probably okay if you don't find it distracting

- ⊚ a chair and desk or table at a good work height – as a general rule you should be able to sit up straight with your feet on the floor and your hands no higher than your elbows when you're typing or writing (if your desk is too high you need to make the chair higher and use a footrest, such as a couple of old phone books taped together)

- ⊚ good desk lighting and a comfortable room temperature (not too hot or too cold)

- ⊚ a study area that doesn't start looking like a compost heap. Keeping it tidy will create the comforting illusion that everything is always under control (ha!).

> Make lists of homework you have to do and then stick to them. Focus on your goal. If you haven't studied and you should have and the test is happening… don't panic: it's too late to panic.
> Mallika, 18

You Need good Lighting to Study

Learning stuff

What kind of learner are you? Some people remember facts better if they write them down or do, say, a science experiment for themselves rather than just reading about it. Others need to talk things out. Some people like to take in a whole lot of information by reading and re-reading. Others remember it in important points or by making notes. And some people have to do something new, such as essay writing, over and over again until they're used to it.

Find out which way you learn best by talking to your parents and teachers. Then incorporate that style into your studying whenever you can.

Developing your reading skills

It's really important to be able to read pretty easily, not just because school-work is too hard otherwise but because, no matter what job you end up doing, it'll be more difficult if you can't read quite quickly. And unless you can also write reason-ably well you won't be able to go for as many jobs or feel as confident about all sorts of things.

find a quiet spot to study: try JupiteR

If you don't like reading, try to find written stuff in books, magazines and online about things you're interested in, whether that's tennis, hip-hop or the life-cycle of the mayfly. The more you read writing that grabs your attention, the more you'll absorb how to spell things and put sentences together. It magically makes you a better writer as well as a better reader.

If you're having ongoing trouble with reading (and lots of people do) it's your school's responsibility to get you extra help. And if your parents can afford it, maybe you can have extra tutoring too.

You have a right to be able to read, write and spell by the time you leave school. If that hasn't happened and you've done your best, try not to feel ashamed. It isn't your fault; you've been let down. Bluffing your way through will be a strain, it won't work forever and it'll restrict your life choices. You can get free lessons to boost your literacy and other key skills through training and employment schemes after you've left school (see "More info" at the end of this section).

Smart note-taking in class

You don't have to write down everything your teacher or lecturer says: just note the important bits.

Try to make your notes in brief but clear point form – they'll need to make sense to you later. Writing "remember the thing" just isn't going to help. Jot down any questions you want to ask as they come up during the session and raise them as soon as you

Pay attention during the year and it's much easier at the end.
Kirsty, 18

Make sure that you ask if you do not understand and keep asking until you do. Don't leave things to the last minute.
Kate, 16

can (making a note of the answer). After a class go back over the notes, and ask for help if something doesn't make sense or you can't remember what it means.

Here's a big tip: the crucial time to take stuff down in class is usually the first ten minutes, when most teachers or lecturers summarize what they're going to be talking about; and the last ten minutes, when you're given important info such as recommended references or extra material, what you need to do for homework or when an assignment is due, and any change in class schedule, venue, or somewhere you need to be at a certain time, and anything you need to bring. So if you must zone out or have a chat about a blonde starlet's latest wardrobe malfunction, try to do it in the middle of the lesson, not right at the start or the end. Of course some teachers may spring important stuff on you in the middle. Mwa ha ha! (Evil teacher laugh.)

> When you get homework do it ASAP, at the end of each class go over material learned, ensure u understand it as u go (especially at yr 11 & 12 level), prepare 4 exams slowly, don't cram study for it, ask teachers for help.
>
> Rachel, 17

Smart note-taking as you read

You know that feeling when you get to the bottom of a page and have no idea what you've just read because you've been kind of thinking about something else? It doesn't really matter when you're reading the book for fun, but it's a bad way to study.

Before you start to read, think about what you need to get out of the piece of writing.

- Do you need to remember a whole bunch of facts, or just have a general idea of what the writer is going on about?
- Will you need to remember which order things happened in?

Then, as you read:

- keep in mind questions set by your teacher
- underline stuff, and pencil comments and questions in the margin
- make separate notes that sum up what you've read
- jot key words on sticky notes and attach them to your forehead. (Or maybe not.)

Exams

Here are some revision strategies.

- Get hold of previous exam papers if possible, and do some "under exam conditions" (such as in a set time and without notes) to see how you go.
- Find out from your teachers whether questions will be multiple choice, short answers, essays or some wacky thing such as drawing a diagram of your feelings.
- Listen to your teachers' hints. They've seen lots of people go through this. Ask

General study tips

✱ Don't wait until the week before an assignment or an exam, or the end of term, to get help on a tricky subject. If you don't understand something, ask.

✱ Don't keep putting stuff off or it will pile up – in your bag, on your desk and in your head. Aim to do a little bit every night instead of seven hours on the weekend.

✱ Plan quick breaks (every half hour or so) in your schedule. Get a glass of water (not having enough water, like looking at computer screens, is a big cause of headaches). Stretch your arms, legs and back. Go to the toilet.

✱ Don't get sucked into the whirling vortex of a TV show or a phone call so that breaks become too long: make rules for yourself about recording the show or saving the call for a reward later.

✱ Don't try to boost yourself with a sugary snack or a coffee when you're flagging, even though it's really tempting: this is likely just to make it harder to sleep afterwards. Good energy snacks include almonds, fruit or fried rice with some veggies as well as protein.

✱ Try relaxation techniques before studying or to wind down afterwards. Do a few stretches – this can help to settle the info in your brain as you go back over it in your head. Or you might like to drive everything out of your head for a while with a crazy dance.

What can help is a fast walk for half an hour or an hour – obviously this is fine during the day, but not such a helpful tip for a winter night when your parents would be more likely to let you go out with a gang of marauding tattooed bikers than go for a walk alone in the dark (if your family is a lovely gang of tattooed marauding bikers please change this reference to pale, blank-eyed strangers wearing floral duvet covers).

them for sneaky study tips and ideas, and about tricky exam questions or wordings that have bamboozled students in the past.

ᕕ Before an exam ask your teacher if you should read *all* the questions before you start. It's usually a must.

ᕕ Tell yourself that you've studied hard and you're prepared (unless it's a preposterous LIE, in which case just do your best and keep everything crossed except your eyes). Tell yourself you are going to do well – and that if you don't it's not your fault, because you've done everything you could.

> Remember that the world doesn't end if you don't get an A. You can only try your best. If you know deep down that you didn't try your best then try harder next time. If you did do your best, then be content with the grade you get.
> Melissa, 18

ᕕ Don't aim for perfection, aim to do the best you can. If you think that anything less than an A* or 99.9 percent is a failure, then you're setting yourself up for disappointment. Exams are a small part of a long life and you'll get through this time. Failing or not getting the mark you want is NOT the end of the world.

ᕕ Don't panic cram. If you haven't given yourself enough time to study, staying up studying all night before the exam won't help: you'll be too tired to make sense.

ᕕ Don't use drugs to stay awake to study or before an exam. All the drugs that make you more alert make it harder to take in and remember information. Even too much caffeine can mess you up before an exam. And any drugs, including alcohol, that you take to relax could affect your memory and your ability to coordinate thinking and writing, completely stuffing up your chances of passing the exam.

ᕕ At the start of an exam check out which questions are worth the most. Question One may be worth ten percent of the total mark and Question Two fifty percent. Jot down how much time you'll give to each question on the basis of their importance and stick to it.

ᕕ You may need to quickly plan your answer before you start each essay-style question.

ᕕ Read exam paper instructions carefully and make like a robot, always obeying the key words in the questions, such as "List…" (meaning points, not complete sentences, will do); "Imagine you are…" (write in the "first person" – "I am Prince Horatio, ruler of everything I see and also the stuff in the laundry"); "Compare and contrast…" (point out the similarities and differences); "Outline" (be brief, but not too brief); "Describe…" or "Explore…" (you have permission to go on a bit); "Show how you reached the answer" (make it clear how you worked out your solution – you could get extra marks even if your final answer is not quite right); and "Write a sentence on…" (jabbering on for a page won't get you extra marks).

◎ Answer the questions you find easiest first, to get you started, if it's all a bit daunting, but keep to the time plan you've made – if you're still wrestling with Question One by the end of the exam you won't have racked up enough marks.

◎ If you look at a question and go blank put both feet flat on the floor, close your eyes and breathe deeply a few times to calm down. Move on to the next question and come back to the hairy one later.

◎ If the exam is not what you expected don't freak out and write nothing – trying always counts for something, especially if you have to make a complaint or appeal afterwards.

◎ Resist any temptation to cheat. There is no possible good outcome: you either get caught or, if you don't, you always know you cheated.

◎ When the exam finishes, join in a bit of screeching and pretend fainting with friends about how hard or easy it was, and then move on. Try not to stress too much about something that you now have no control over.

Exam results   And then the horrible wait… Sometimes it's just you but sometimes, especially in your final year at school or college, it can seem as if half the known universe wants to find out how you did and what results you got.

Talk to your parents about how you think you did, and also about what to do if you don't get the marks you want.

Often your marks are not just about how well you did, they're about what other students did. A score of ninety on an exam one year could end up being a seventy-eight in another year. If the results are not what you hoped for, talk to your parents and teachers (or a school careers counsellor if your school has one) about how you might improve for the next year at school or what your options are after leaving school (and see also "More info" below).

More info on schoolwork and reading

www.bbc.co.uk/schools
The BBC's school site has info, games and learning resources for 5–16 year olds. Click on "Study skills" for revision and study tips; "Bitesize" for interactive learning, revision guides and tests; or choose from the subject lists for your age group. Also has info for parents and teachers.

www.ltscotland.org.uk/studyskills
This site by Learning and Teaching Scotland has loads of interactive activities to help you become a better learner; just click on your age group to get started.

www.thesite.org/workandstudy/studying
YouthNet's study and exam tips are aimed at 16–21 year olds, but can be useful for

younger teens. As well as info on revision, writing essays, research and motivation, there's loads of stuff on student life.

Mind Maps for Kids: An Introduction
by Tony Buzan, Thorsons
Different, fun ways to organize and display all sorts of info so you remember it and understand it better.

Reading help: there's a mish-mash of local and national literacy and "skills for life" programmes on offer, but contacting your local council, adult education college or library is usually the best place to start.

www.learndirect-skills.co.uk
Backed by the UK government, Learn Direct offers English and maths courses and other "skills for life" programmes. Call them for free on **0800 015 0450**. If you live in Scotland, visit www.learndirectscotland.com or call **0808 100 9000**.

www.bbc.co.uk/raw
Call the BBC's reading and writing helpline on **0800 015 0950** from anywhere in the UK for confidential help and support.

www.connexions-direct.com
Connexions is a government-run info and advice service for young people in England. Call their helpline on **0808 001 3219** to speak to a personal advisor about education, training or anything else that's worrying you, or to get help in your area.

www.direct.gov.uk/en/EducationAndLearning
Government site with all sorts of info and links to help you learn. Choose "14 to 19" or "Adult learning" for stuff on training, further education and "skills for life" schemes to help you improve your reading and get into work.

www.dyslexiaaction.org.uk
A national charity that supports people with dyslexia and other literacy difficulties.

GAAH! I am going to finish school and spend the rest of my life living in a cardboard box deliberately not thinking academic things.   Emily, 16

I find studying with my best friend useful because she is really motivated and if I am at her house then I am not as easily distracted!   Zoe, 17

It's so easy to get bogged down by pressure at school. I based my entire self-worth on how well I did at school, and when I got too sick to keep going, I lost sight of who I was and why I was even alive because I didn't have academic achievements to base that on. I have to fight to keep the obsession at bay.

Amelia, 17

You live two lives, one being yours with your family, friends, sport and spare time and the other your schooling life with homework, exams and assignments.
Nita, 16

Education and careers

Even though it can seem like a good idea to leave school at 16 to get a full-time job so you have some money and don't have to go to school any more, here's the thing: a boring, dead-end, low-wage job is worse than school because you can be stuck in it forever. If you leave school young for an unskilled job it probably won't offer you very much opportunity to either get out of the low-pay area or learn more stuff to get into a better job.

> It seems like everyone else has a plan and knows what uni they want to go to and what courses to do so they can have the type of career they want. I have no idea about any of those things.
> Marianne, 15

Finishing school, getting skills training or doing further education may take some more years, but will usually get you a better job, with more pay. Very few well-paying jobs involve no training or education. In fact I can't think of one. Except princess. So unless you were born with your own tiara, read on.

Choosing a career

A few people are sure from an early age about what they want to do, but most have a sorta, kinda general idea of what area they'd like to work in, or they can't make up their mind. It's always good to have a few ideas so that if you don't get into the course or career you want you have a couple of back-up plans. Make sure, though, that all your back-up plans have some attraction for you, or you'll probably end up dropping out of courses halfway through.

There is no one right answer to "What am I going to do?", just a range of possibilities. Sometimes not getting into your first course choice opens up a whole lot of new opportunities that end up suiting you better. Sometimes you get your first choice but change careers later anyway. (Many people now swap between careers throughout their life, so don't feel you have to choose something and stick with it forever.) And sometimes the original idea for a career becomes a hobby, while you find a different area to earn money in.

You're not locked in. If you do something only because it's in the family business, or it's what your parents want you to do, you may be setting yourself up for always wishing you'd done something else.

What would suit you? Talk to your friends, parents and teachers about what jobs they see you as being suited to. Think about the talents and abilities people have complimented you on, and the hobbies and activities you like doing. Work out what sort of job would suit your personality.

> I'm at university. It's wonderful – a true paradise for the likes of me. Jade, 18

- Would you prefer to work in a laboratory with unknown elements?
- Would you rather have a job where you chat to people a lot?
- Would you be happy to work a night shift for more money?
- Would you like a stable job in which you do the same thing every day, or one that throws up challenges you have to figure out?
- Do you want to travel?
- Did you spend your entire childhood doing hairstyles for your dolls, or wanting to weld their naked, headless bodies into modernistic sculptures?

Your school may have a teacher or careers counsellor who can help you try to match your interests and talents to a potential career. Try some work experience, community involvement or volunteer work. Go to the employment section of the newspapers or one of the major job websites, make a list of all the occupations that look interesting and find out about the skills needed to do them. Wages can also be good in areas where there is a skills shortage: if, for instance, there are not enough metallurgists, being one will mean you are in demand and can choose where you'd like to work – and you'll probably be paid extra. Use the contacts given in "More info" further on to research the areas you're interested in, and to find out whether there are certain subjects or qualifications you need to get into a particular course or career.

No matter what job you'd like, you'll need the best skills you can manage in English – both spoken and written – and some maths, for running your own finances for the rest of your life and making sure you don't get ripped off.

Education options

After the age of 16, you might feel like the world's yours for the taking – school is no longer compulsory and you're free to do what you want. But making big decisions about your future can be scary. Staying on at school isn't for everybody, but carrying on with "further education" or some kind of training gives you loads more choices in the future. Options include studying at a sixth-form college, where there are usually more choices on offer, or doing specific vocational training or an apprenticeship ("vocational" means relevant to a job).

The government seem to like confusing everyone by introducing new qualifications and regularly re-naming or re-organizing things, so use the list coming up as a guide, but check with your school or college or your local careers advisor, or on the websites coming up in "More info", to get the latest info on exactly what's available in your area.

FACT

Studying abroad   Exchange programmes are schemes that place students for anything up to twelve months in a "host family" overseas – usually one that has a kid about your age so you can go to school together. You need to go through a recognized scheme and be sure you'll enjoy a different life (ask at your school or see "More info" later). Over-18s are also often able to study at an overseas university (your uni should be able to give you the info).

The main qualifications possible after age 16

⊙ **AS-levels and A-levels**   If you've done well in your GCSEs, you could take between two and five of these academic qualifications, which are available in loads of subjects. They're a good route into "higher education", like a university degree, which then offers the possibility of a professional career as, for instance, a doctor, lawyer, engineer, teacher, veterinarian or chemist (but going to university is not a guarantee of getting a job). Highers and Advanced Highers are the Scottish equivalent.

⊙ **NVQs (National Vocational Qualifications)**   These practical, work-based qualifications help you learn the skills you need to do a particular job, from plumbing or IT to hairdressing or childcare. You take them while working in your chosen job or by combining a work placement and part-time study at college. The Scottish equivalent is an SVQ.

⊙ **Edexcel BTECs, OCR Nationals and City and Guilds qualifications**   Similar to NVQs, these are all work-related qualifications run by different organizations. They train you to work in a particular industry or vocational area, like travel and tourism, engineering and transport, or health and social care.

⊙ **Diplomas**   Intended to bridge the gap between academic and vocational learning, Diplomas were introduced to some schools and colleges in September 2008 in a handful of broad subject areas. They include some work experience, as well as more traditional studying in class.

⊙ **Skills for Life**   These are qualifications in literacy, numeracy and Information and Communication Technology (ICT) for people who don't already have English or maths qualifications. They can help you get onto other courses or prepare you for work.

I don't know what I want to do with my life and I don't want pressure from family to go down a path I might not want to take.   Carla, 18

Higher education costs

Costs you should be aware of
can include:

�֍ fees

✷ student loans, with interest

✷ living expenses (rent, food,
   transport, fun).

When the current lot of politicians
were in post-school education it was
free, but they've now made higher
education an expensive business,
with many students forced to build
up huge amounts of debt.

You can find out what you'll be
in for, and whether you're entitled
to a government grant, university
bursary or studen loan, by talking to
the college or uni you want to attend
(and see also the websites listed in
"More info").

⊚ **Entry to Employment (e2e)**
This scheme is for 16–18 year olds
in England who don't feel ready for
further learning, employment or
an apprenticeship. It will help you
develop the key skills you need after
leaving school, and you'll be given
an allowance while you train.

⊚ **Specific job training**   The armed
forces and emergency services
usually train their own cadets, and
you get recognized qualifications as
well as a job. You have to be at least
16 to join the armed forces and 18
to join the police or fire brigade.

Apprenticeships   Apprentices learn new
skills, gain qualifications and earn money at
the same time. Apprenticeships tend to last
for one to two years, or longer, and wages
are usually low, but your employer should
teach you everything you need to know
about your chosen career and you should
get an NVQ or another vocational qualification at the end. After you're qualified,
the wages can become much higher – especially in areas where there's a skills shortage
and in some traditionally guy-dominated industries such as plumbing, electrical work,
mechanics and building. There are programmes that encourage girls to enter these areas
(see the WISE campaign in "More info on careers and education" coming up).

College, university and part-time courses   All big colleges, unis and other institu-
tions have open days so that you can wander around and get a feel for the places and
what they have to offer. Most have careers counsellors or departments to help with
course information and career planning (and to help students decide what to choose if
they change their mind in the middle of a course).

If you're not sure what you want to do, or think you'd like to be able to change your
mind easily, a general qualification focusing on business skills, science or humanities,
for example, might be better than choosing a very narrow specialty such as tulip breeding. (Although, if tulip breeding is the only thing you've ever wanted to do, I reckon

you could find a course at a horticultural institution, or in Holland, if you're single-minded and determined enough.)

You can finish your last year of school and go straight on to further study, or take a "gap year" to work or travel before enrolling for more training or education.

Sometimes people who've been working for several years (either following school or after taking a further education course) decide they want to get into a different type of job. Having a long-term goal like this often means working in one job during the day and learning or training for the other job when they can, by studying part-time or at night.

Many courses can be done part-time in colleges or adult education centres – or even online or through distance learning programmes (for people living away from major cities), using printed notes, audio downloads, videos and DVDs, lessons on disk and email. It can be hard work, and you need to be focused, and know that for you the achievements will be worth the effort and sacrifice.

School got too much for me. I'm in year 12 but because of my situation I've had to stop. I'm getting a job. It has been the best thing for me. Lara, 17

I have many interests and it's too hard to choose which one I should follow professionally. I know that whatever I choose I have to put my heart and soul into achieving a great outcome and I just don't think I am ready for that yet. Becky, 18

I don't feel confident about leaving school ... school is a comfort zone and uni is out of that zone, but I'll be fine ... I'm sure I'll work myself into it. Monica, 16

I got an apprenticeship and if I want to go to uni later I still can. Eva, 18

A-level exams are over-rated. I didn't do very well but I'm making money and enjoying life. Beth, 18

I feel confident that I will get into a hairdressing school when I finish secondary school. Priya, 16

I wish I could focus more. I took a year off to work (last year) and it was hard work, but it really screwed my head on. I used to muck around in school and hate it so much but I love it now and am doing really well. Fran, 18

More info on careers and education

Career options

Most schools, colleges and unis offer advice on careers and further education, or can put you in touch with a local careers advisor.

www.connexions-direct.com
Connexions (the government support service for 13–19 year olds) has loads of careers info – but it can be hard to find. Browse the "Careers" section, or choose "Careers resources", "Download publications", then "Working in" for booklets about different jobs. Choose "Local services" to find an advice centre, or speak to a personal advisor on 0808 0013219.

www.careers-scotland.org.uk
This Scottish careers site is useful even if you don't live or work in Scotland; it's got detailed job profiles, careers advice, education options and a CareersMatch service.

www.careerswales.com
Government site offering free info, advice and guidance on careers, education and training in Wales. Choose the area for your age group.

www.careersserviceni.com
Careers, education and training advice from the Department of Employment and Learning in Northern Ireland. Choose "Careers Service NI" to find a careers office in your area.

www.direct.gov.uk/en/YoungPeople
Government site; choose "Work and Careers" for info on planning your future, work experience, your rights and responsibilities, and getting your first job. Lots of useful links.

www.insidecareers.co.uk
Has careers advice, company profiles, job vacancies and more, but you need to register to see most of the info.

www.jobcentreplus.gov.uk
Government agency that helps people get into work. Choose "Contact" to find your nearest Jobcentre, or call 0845 606 0234.

www.prospects.ac.uk
The UK's official graduate careers site. Choose "Jobs & work" for descriptions of different jobs, to find out what jobs suit your interests, and to get tips on job hunting, writing CVs and interview techniques. Choose "Communities" to search for work experience placements.

www.wisecampaign.org.uk
A campaign trying to get more girls and women into careers in science, engineering, technology and construction.

Further education

See also the careers sites and organizations listed above, or ask your school for more info.

www.direct.gov.uk/en/EducationAndLearning
Official info on all your post-school education options, including A-levels, NVQs, Skills for Life, e2e and apprenticeships; choose "14 to 19: your life, your options". To find out about colleges, courses and training schemes in your area, choose "Find your local 14–19 prospectus".

yp.direct.gov.uk/diplomas
Government info on "Diplomas", the new qualification introduced to the UK in 2008.

www.thesite.org/workandstudy
The YouthNet site has loads on post-school education, training and careers. Choose "Post-GCSE options" to find out about all the qualifications and training options open to you. Also has stuff on apprenticeships, going to uni, getting a job, and loads of helpful links.

www.open.ac.uk
The Open University is the biggest provider of distance learning in the UK (over-18s only). Choose "New to the OU" to find out more.

www.qca.org.uk/14-19/qualifications
Info from the Qualifications and Curriculum Authority explaining the main qualifications open to you from the age of 14.

Apprenticeships

Many career sites (including those listed above) have stuff on apprenticeship, or you can use your search engine to look for apprenticeships in specific companies.

www.apprenticeships.org.uk
Official website, run by the Learning and Skills Council, about all the apprenticeships on offer in England and how to apply. You can also call their apprenticeship helpline on: **08000 150 600.**

www.scottish-enterprise.com/modern-apprenticeships (Scotland)
www.careerswales.com/youngpeople/choices16/apprenticeships_training.asp (Wales)
www.delni.gov.uk/apprenticeshipsni (Northern Ireland)
Official info on apprenticeships available in each different region of the UK.

Student exchanges and gap year options

Ask your school, college or uni about any exchange programmes they're involved in. See also "More info on getting involved and being informed" in the Caring chapter for volunteering opportunities abroad.

www.britishcouncil.org/erasmus
Erasmus is a European exchange programme for students who want to study part of their degree in another country; it's particularly popular with students on language courses.

www.gapyear.com
Has plenty of stuff to get you dreaming about student exchanges, work placements and volunteer projects overseas, and other things you might do in a gap year.

www.gogapyear.com
Gap year advice from the British Foreign and Commonwealth Office (FCO).

www.statravel.co.uk
This youth-oriented travel agency site has a whole section on gap-year travel.

Rough Guide First-Time Around the World by Doug Lansky, Rough Guides
OK, we might be a bit biased, but this great book really does cover everything you need to know if you're planning a gap year working, volunteering, studying or just travelling abroad.

Financial help for students

Your Local Education Authority (LEA), school or college should also be able to tell you how to get financial help while you study.

ema.gov.uk
If you're 16–18, from a lower-income family and want to stay in education or training, you can apply for EMA – an Education Maintenance Allowance. Use this site to find out if you're elegible and how to apply, or call the EMA helpline on **0800 121 8989.**

www.studentfinancedirect.co.uk
To find out if you're entitled to government grants or student loans at uni, and to apply online, choose "I am planning to go into higher education". Click on "Find my local authority" if you'd rather not apply online, and on "My home is not in England" for contact details in Wales, Scotland and Northern Ireland.

WORK

today the sink,
tomorrow a head chef!

No doubt you've worked out that money can't buy you love or happiness or health. But you're going to need some other stuff that money *can* buy, such as **lunches and shoes**. So unless you have a pirate treasure chest full of gold doubloons, getting money for things you want means finding work.

Lots of young people need a part-time job to get them through the last years of school, college or uni, but have to balance things carefully to make sure their studies don't suffer. (See the Schoolwork chapter for info about careers, and the Money chapter on how to manage your cash.)

But how do you find a job? And how do you apply for it? What should you wear to the interview and to work? What can you do if the boss tries to **rip you off**? How should you behave at your job? (Out in the real world if you sulk, roll your eyes or mutter, you don't get sent to your room – you end up getting the sack.)

Looking for a job

There are some things you need to consider when you're deciding which jobs (part-time or full-time) to apply for.

- What kinds of jobs are you suited to (for instance, working in the kitchen or working "front of house" as a waitress)?
- What are you qualified for, or most likely to get?
- How many hours can you work, and on which days?
- How far can you safely travel, and at what times of the day or night?
- Will it cost too much to get there and back?
- How much will you accept as an hourly rate of pay?
- Is there a low training wage that automatically becomes a better wage later?
- When you turn a certain age, and should be paid more, will you be replaced with a new junior on a lower wage?
- Do you get a free meal?
- Is a uniform provided or do you have to buy your own work clothes?
- Is there a discount on the company's goods (and are the products the sort of stuff you'd want anyway)?

> I don't really like taking money from my parents all the time, I feel guilty. I'd like to have more independence which is why I think I'd like to get a job.
> Elyse, 17

Job advertisements

Here are some good places to look for a job:

- employment websites, many of which will keep track of job ads in your local area and chosen fields (search for "career" or "job" in a UK search engine)
- employment ads in local and national newspapers
- Jobcentre Plus – the government's one-stop shop for people looking for work, wanting career advice or claiming benefits
- local recruitment agencies – they're often good places to find temporary work during the holidays, as well as part-time and full-time jobs, and they do some of the hard work for you, like tidying up your CV, arranging interviews and giving advice

If I can't be a mechanic, I'll be a florist!

⑥ community noticeboards in local shops, supermarkets, libraries, post offices and colleges

⑥ restaurant and shop windows (these often have notices saying they're looking for staff).

"Word of mouth" is also a good way to learn of positions coming up. Friends with jobs may hear of vacancies, and bosses are often pleased to interview or try someone out on a recommendation.

> It is so hard to have enough money to move out, especially if you are a full-time student.
> Erica, 18
>
> Juniors don't earn enough.
> Melissa, 17

"Advertising" yourself   Places that tend to have a high staff turnover, such as shops, fast-food restaurants, cinemas and supermarkets, will usually accept a brief, one-page CV from people looking for work, or allow you to fill in an application form in case a job comes up. The bosses keep a folder of CVs and forms and may phone you when they need somebody (see "Your CV", coming up).

When you leave a CV choose a quiet time in the day's trade, and never interrupt when someone is talking to a customer or client. Come back later if it looks frantic.

Ask to speak to the manager. Smile when the manager sees you and say you'd like to leave your CV in case there's a job in the future, adding, "I don't want to hold you up, but please call me if you need any more details". Thank them, smile again and leave.

You can practise your "spiel" with friends and family beforehand. It will get less scary, and you'll get better at it, every time you approach someone.

More info on looking for a job

www.jobcentreplus.gov.uk
Jobcentre Plus is a government agency that supports people trying to find work. You can look for jobs on their website (Choose "Jobsearch"), in your local Jobcentre office or by calling **0845 606 0234**. Choose "Contact" to find your local Jobcentre, where you can also arrange to see an advisor.

www.direct.gov.uk/en/YoungPeople/ Workandcareers
Government site with all sorts of info, tips and links for young people looking for work, including advice on holiday jobs, starting your first job and creating your first CV. Choose "Find a job now" to search for job vacancies in your area.

Applying for a job

Sometimes you're just expected to call a number given in a job advertisement to have a chat, perhaps followed by an interview; but often you're required to apply for the job in writing, by supplying a CV or filling in an application form. This doesn't mean you can't ring if you have queries about the job: companies and organizations often expect that people will phone them for more information before applying.

Your CV, or résumé

A CV (short for the Latin name *curriculum vitae*), or résumé (pronounced ray-zoo-may because it's French, but usually as rez-you-may in the UK), is a summary of who you are, your relevant qualifications, any previous work experience and your contact details. It should always be sent, with a covering letter (see below), when you apply for a job (unless the ad asks you to fill in a specific application form instead, which usually asks for all the same info anyway).

Obviously as a teenager you are not going to have a huge CV, and it probably won't include the Nobel Peace Prize, but even a brief one-pager helps a potential boss to remember who you are and what you might be good at.

A CV needs to be:

- ⊙ brief – employers may look at hundreds
- ⊙ adaptable – so that you can make small changes to it to fit a specific job application
- ⊙ typed (not hand-written)
- ⊙ well laid out so the reader can find relevant information quickly and you look like an organized person
- ⊙ checked by someone else before you send it as it's hard to pick up your own errors. Avoid spelling or typographical slips such as "Ive always Wanted to wrok hear" (there are four mistakes in that sentence).

> Getting a job and making your own money gives you great independence.
> Emma, 17

Teachers, job centres, careers advisors and many websites can help you to put together a CV.

Setting the information out in bullet points helps make a CV easy to read. Use the following headings to write your own.

Personal details   You can give your age or date of birth if that's relevant or you want to, but should always include your:

> I wish I had a part-time job to pay my own way through life,
> but I just don't have the time.   Becky, 18

- ⑥ first and last name
- ⑥ address (the full address is optional – you can just put your town if they can contact you by phone and email)
- ⑥ email address
- ⑥ contact phone numbers.

> I think having a part-time job is great. I have a bank account and a debit card set up and it helps me learn how to manage my money.
> Laura, 15

Make sure you have a sensible message on your home and mobile answering machines. "Hello, you've called Kelly. Please leave a message and I'll get back to you as soon as I can" is good. "Heeyyyy, wassup? It's Kel Kel, dudes. Wanna PARRRRTY?" is really not.

Likewise lose the cutesy email address. Get a simple email address that uses your first and last name, adding a middle initial or extra number if you need to. Trust me, bosses are less likely to hire someone with an email address such as horny-pantz@googlemail.com, slapme@yahoo.co.uk or nutbag@hotmail.com. Seriously, what kind of boss wants to give the keys to their building to someone who has voluntarily called themselves Dumchik?

Be aware that many potential employers will search your name on social networking websites such as Facebook, MySpace and Bebo, so make sure your public pages make a good impression.

Education and qualifications List your main educational achievements, with their dates, working down from the highest or most recent one: for example, put your A-level results or NVQ qualification first, then your GCSE results. Also give details of any extra training you've done, even a two-day computer course.

Add any other specifics that could be useful, such as relevant subjects you've studied (business studies, IT, first aid, and so on). As well as adding to your skills and qualifications, these show you're practical, versatile and someone who likes to keep busy.

Work experience List any previous jobs, starting with your most recent one and working backwards in time if you have had a few. Give details of the employers or companies, their location, the period of time you worked with them, the hours worked each week and your job titles. If a job title was vague, such as "assistant" or "office duties", add a couple of sentences to explain what you did. You can also include any voluntary work or unpaid work experience.

Skills and interests Employment people often talk about "hard skills" and "soft skills" – you don't need to use these terms in your CV, but it's valuable to give examples of both.

"Hard skills" are things such as being familiar with various computer programs, an ability to use particular office equipment, cash register expertise, typing skills, knowledge of another language, and experience answering the phone and handling customer queries at the front desk of your mum's office during holidays.

"Soft skills" are things such as hobbies and interests, which give employers hints about your personality. But only list those relevant to the job. You're not posting a profile on a social networking website, so you need to say more than "I like reading, ponies and making up funny stories".

This is where you could put the things that show you're "good at talking through a problem and thinking of possible solutions", "good at talking with people", or a "team player" (good at working with other people). These might include being a mediator at school, helping with bullying problems; being the coach or manager of your netball team, who has to choose positions in the team and deal with personality clashes; or working on a community service project that involves you sitting and talking with older people.

Try to include anything that will make you stand out from fifty other applicants. What makes you different? "Member of the school debating team, years 10 and 11" can tell a potential boss you're persuasive, confident and can express an opinion; "Co-organizer of field trips to an animal sanctuary, fossil reserve and other sites, involving making bookings and itineraries" shows wide interests and organizing ability; "Member of the school fundraising committee" suggests a joiner who is not narrowly focused on schoolwork. Don't put "I like tennis", but you could put "Penzance Tennis Club member since 12 years old, in charge of court maintenance for the last two years and member of the social committee". That says you're fit and outgoing, and that you take on responsibility and make time for hobbies and interests.

References   Provide the names of two or three people who can give you a reference – speak on your behalf about your work and personal abilities. This makes them a "referee", but not the sort with a whistle around their neck. A referee could be a teacher, a neighbour you've done chores for, a sports coach or a previous boss.

Sorry to be blindingly obvious, but if you don't know what someone thinks of you, or you know they dislike you, don't put their name down. Always ask a referee beforehand if you can add their name, and ask them what they would say about you. (This is crucial: if you don't like what they'd say don't include them as a referee.)

Let your referees know that they may get a phone call from a possible employer, and perhaps let them know about jobs you've applied for as these come up. Give them a copy of your CV, and make sure you keep their contact details (as well as your own) updated.

The covering letter

A "covering" or application letter, included with your CV, is essential because it lets an employer know that you have really thought about the advertised job and why you would be suitable for it. Job centres, parents, teachers and career websites can help you with this covering letter.

The letter should:

- ⑤ be no longer than a page or a bit over
- ⑤ be set out as a business letter and include at the top, in separate blocks, the employer's name and address, your own address and the date (have a look at one to see how this is done)
- ⑤ be businesslike and to the point, not rambling
- ⑤ include details that relate specifically to the particular job, such as why you think you would be good at it
- ⑤ show that you know something about the company you're applying to and are enthusiastic about the kind of job you'll be doing
- ⑤ answer any specific questions or supply any information requested in the ad itself – an easy way to do this is to repeat back the question in your answer (for example, if the ad asks for "details of any relevant skills" start your sentence with "Relevant skills that I have for this position include…")
- ⑤ be triple-checked by somebody else for errors and sentences that don't read well.

> It's very hard to find a part-time job when you study full time at uni and don't have a car (or transport late at night).
>
> Katherine, 18

More info on your CV

See also "More info on looking for a job" a few pages earlier, and the careers websites in "More info on careers and education" in the Schoolwork chapter.

www.cvbuilder-advice-resources.co.uk
Really useful step-by-step "CV Builder" courtesy of the government's Learning and Skills Council. As well as helping you create your CV from a choice of templates, it has example CVs, real-life stories and tips for interviews, covering letters, application forms and tips for building your confidence.

www.connexions-direct.com
On the Connexions site for 13–19 year olds, choose "Work", then "Before getting a job" for help with CVs, interviews and job hunting.

www.thesite.org/workandstudy/
gettingajob
Info for young people on part-time and temp jobs, applying for a job, CVs, covering letters, application forms and interviews.

The job interview

Yay for you – getting a job interview is an achievement in itself, even if you don't get the job. It means that your CV and application letter were good.

> Job interviews – very daunting. When you have too many turn-downs, it can get you thinking, "what's so wrong with me?"
> Layla, 18

Some hints for job interviews

You'll need to start preparing a few days before an interview.

ⓖ Do your research so you can seem clued up at the interview. Find out a bit about the place where you've applied to work: check out its website; maybe, if it's a shop, spend some time looking at the layout and how the staff behave (but try not to look like a lurking shoplifter); and perhaps even talk to someone who already works there.

ⓖ Practise! Do fake interviews with family, friends or teachers. Politeness (see below) is something to practise as well as answers to possible questions. Doing drama or public speaking at school is fantastic preparation.

ⓖ Check out the hints given later in this chapter on dressing for work, then organize what you're going to wear. Your potential boss doesn't want to see your belly button ring (and if they do, then you don't want that job).

Just before the interview make sure you do the following things.

ⓖ Be on time. (In fact, planning to be a little early is good in case you get lost.) If you're running late call and explain why, with a sincere apology.

Possible job interview scenarios

Interviewer's questions

"Tell us a bit about yourself."

"Why do you think you'd be suitable for this job?"

"Why do you want this job?"

"What experience do you have?"

"What would you do if a customer pushed in ahead of others in the queue and was very rude about the service?"

"Do you think you can handle the responsibility? Why?"

"What are your strengths?"

"What are your weaknesses?"

"What do you want to get out of the job?"

"Where do you see yourself as being in five years' time?"

Your questions

"What would my duties be on a typical day?"

"Are there any other duties that could come up?"

"Why is the position vacant?"

"Will I know my hours a week in advance or a day?"

"Are there opportunities for training and advancement?"

"When will I hear back from you?"

Questions NOT to ask

"Will I get a discount on your stuff?"

"Do I have to wear that dumb uniform?" (Ask instead, "What are the uniform requirements?", "Would I need to supply my own uniform?", or "What is the dress code here?")

"What will the pay be?" (Wait for the interviewer to tell you what the rates of pay are, although they are more likely to do this later when they offer you the job.)

Contracts

Never sign a contract at a job interview. Take it away and ask a parent or another adult to check it first (see "Your Rights as a Worker" coming up).

⊙ Take some deep breaths while you wait. Remind yourself in your head a couple of times to speak slowly (we often babble when we're nervous).

⊙ Read through your application letter and CV in case an interviewer asks you something about them – always take copies with you.

Finally, in the interview itself, make sure you "do yourself justice".

⊙ Greet your interviewers (and any office staff) with a smile, make eye contact and say "Hello". Try not to swear. (I know you probably won't, but it's surprising what nerves will cause people to do!)

⊙ Be aware of your body language: don't, for instance, slide down or slouch in the chair. The worst thing you can do is chew gum.

> Since I got a job my self confidence has improved, because in my industry I'm forced to talk to all kinds of people and this helped me come out of my shell.
> Ash, 18

⊙ Present a cheery, positive attitude and look interested.

⊙ Be confident. Take your time to answer questions, and think about what you're going to say before it comes out of your mouth. If you don't understand a question ask them to repeat it. If you don't know the answer say, "I don't know, but I'd hope that either your training would prepare me or that I could ask a supervisor, to make sure I was representing company policy".

⊙ If it seems natural, say something that shows off your knowledge of the company. Asking a few questions will also show that you're smart and keen: "Why do you have four people in every store?", or "What's the most popular item with local customers?"

⊙ Don't freak out. Some employers might deliberately ask you difficult or frustrating questions to see how you handle pressure. Sometimes at an interview one person will be nice and another one a bit stern or rude, to see how you react. Always stay calm and polite.

⊙ Use your common sense if you're asked a "hypothetical", or "What if", question. This could be something like "What if the office catches on fire?", "What if a

HINT

Look for opportunities to be different   If the chair breaks underneath you during the interview say something like "Is this a test?", or "And I can fix chairs with sticky tape!"

customer starts shouting at you?", or "What if somebody demands a refund?". You're not expected to know the rules and procedures of the workplace but to think up a reasonable response. You might say you'd be guided by whatever the company policy was, or that you'd inform the appropriate manager. Talk about how you'd try to keep a customer happy by, say, promising a follow-up phone call to check they were satisfied.

After the interview

If the boss rings to say you've got the job, be ready to discuss the wage they offer. Try to find out what rate of pay is standard for that kind of job. Sometimes the ad will have said what the pay range is, or a friend who works for the same company may have told you already. You can also ask friends and family who do similar jobs if the rate of pay seems fair, or you can compare it to what other companies pay by looking at ads online, in newspapers or in Jobcentres. Check that you're being paid at least the National Minimum Wage for your age group (see "Youth wages and rules" a bit further on and "More info on workers' rights and responsibilities" at the end of the chapter).

If you don't get the job, ring and politely ask:

- ○ "Is there anything I could have done to be a better candidate?"
- ○ "Could you please keep my details on file in case something else comes up?"
- ○ "What's the best way to know when another job comes up there?"

Getting knock-backs can make you feel lousy until you realize it happens to everyone. It's hard, but stay positive and don't give up. Keep reminding yourself about your good points and why you're outrageously employable – and that every "failed" job interview is good training for that great interview you're going to do in the future for the job you really want.

Being a good employee

Getting the job may seem like the biggest hurdle, but once you're in you have to show you're serious about it and deserve to be kept on past the "probationary period", or to have your contract renewed if the job is short-term or temporary. There are a bunch of skills that all bosses like and want to see displayed on the job.

Character "attributes"

Bosses usually look for what the employment industry calls "attributes", or "employability skills", in workers – good characteristics such as being likeable, honest, loyal and a trier.

Good attitude   Be positive and enthusiastic. Smile genuinely at clients and customers. Instead of saying, "I don't know how to do that, so I can't", try "Can you show me how to do that so I know how to do it properly myself next time?"

Demonstrate that you're efficient and hard-working. When you're given a whole lot of instructions about things to do during the day, write them down and tick them off as you complete them.

Communication skills   Try to listen, and let people know when you understand. Speak and write clearly.

Negotiate instead of reacting against something. If someone complains, you should say, "Thanks for letting us know. Let me write down the details and your phone number, so someone can get back to you", or "I don't know the answer to that, but let me find someone who does".

Practise some useful phrases so you don't end up standing there with your mouth open. If you work with the public you'll have to deal with rude and slightly nutty people at some point. Ask in advance about the company's policy on what to do.

> *I go to work even when I'm really sick just so I know I'll have enough money to get through the next week.*
> Rach, 17

Teamwork   You'll need to get on with other people and try to reach solutions together. You also need to have enough sensitivity and brains to understand that you can't make sexist or racist comments that will upset your co-workers.

Independence   Try to handle situations and solve problems yourself, but ask for help when you need it – especially when you've just started a new job – so that time isn't wasted.

Flexibility   Whether it's a part-time or a full-time job, employers are looking for young people who will stay five minutes or half an hour later to get a job finished, rather than leaving five minutes early each day. Bosses are more likely to cut you some slack (say, let you go early one day) if you've been flexible.

Basic business skills

All your jobs are going to involve you using some business skills. You'll feel more confident at work if there's stuff you're already able to handle.

✶ You'll need some basic maths, whether you're giving change, measuring something or working out a budget or estimate.

✶ You'll also usually need to work with some kind of technology, from a cash register to a computer. (And oh how they love giving the young folk all the grunt work.) Make sure someone explains to you how all the equipment works.

But if your half an hour overtime starts happening regularly you should probably be getting paid for it. And be wary of bosses who get you to do hours of work for free before they'll consider employing you. Unless you're doing a formal work experience placement, an official apprenticeship or vocational training programme, or voluntary work, you have a right to be paid a minimum wage for the work that you do. (See "Youth wages and rules" a bit further on.)

Dedication and focus Turn your mobile off at work and tell friends not to call at all, and family to call only in an emergency. Don't use a company phone to call friends or family unless it's a quick local call that you can't avoid, it's in your break time and you've asked permission. All companies keep track of their phone calls, so you will be caught.

They can also keep track of what a work computer has been used for, so make sure you're allowed to use it for browsing the Web or sending personal emails (in your own time, not work's). Looking at porn is usually grounds for instant dismissal (the sack), so if you're working on your computer and a porn site pops up, through no fault of your own, always let the boss know.

Honesty Some people steal from work – little things such as pens and paper, or big things such as money from the till. Always ask permission before you take something. Don't think you won't be caught stealing. Not only do all companies have ways of tracking their stock and money (and maybe hidden cameras), but there is usually a policy to report larger thefts to the police.

Suitability The key to doing your job well is enjoying what you do. Demonstrating all the above attributes is a tough call if you hate your work. But when you want to get a new job you'll need a good reference from your present boss, so think of developing a positive attitude as an investment.

If it gets really hard, scream into a pillow when you get home, grumble to friends and family, not your co-workers, write a film script about it, or make notes on How Not to Run a Business for when you have your own. Treat every situation as one you can get something out of, even if it's "only" experience. Or a great story.

If you aren't happy in your current job start thinking about what you'd like to do instead (the "Choosing a career" section in the Schoolwork chapter has lots of ideas about how to begin deciding).

Clothes for work

Some jobs come with a complete uniform. Others have bits: you may have to wear their shirt and baseball cap, but supply your own trousers. Being a waitress often involves wearing a white shirt and black skirt or trousers. Some jobs require protective clothing, like goggles or steel-toecap boots, because of health and safety rules, but the company should provide these for free. Before your first day, ask the boss or a co-worker what's expected of you, and if the company has some kind of "dress code".

It's illegal for a boss to try to force you to wear clothes that make you feel uncomfortable or exposed, such as a low-cut top or something see-through (see the section "Your rights as a worker" coming up to find out what you can do about it).

If it's up to you to decide what to wear you can put together your own "uniform" so you know it's always clean and ready for work. Something that doesn't show the dirt and looks professional may be appropriate, depending on the job. Trainers are not acceptable at most jobs, but required for others. One knee-length dark skirt or dark trousers (not jeans) with two shirts might get you through, if you've got time to wash them regularly.

A Bad Look for Work

Bad looks (in most cases) for work – and job interviews – include:

- ☻ grubby hair, fingernails or clothes
- ☻ pigtails (too little-girl)
- ☻ heavy obvious make-up and very dark lipstick
- ☻ arms full of bracelets, huge dangly earrings and loads of bling
- ☻ visible underwear of any description – this means bra, bra straps, the back of a thong or g-string, etc
- ☻ mini-skirt, very short dress or hotpants

ⓖ exposed cleavage (between-the-breasts area) or part of your breasts

ⓖ exposed tummy

ⓖ flip-flops

ⓖ very high heels.

Good looks (in most cases) for work – and job interviews – include:

ⓖ clean hair tucked out of the way behind the ears
or tiedback in a neat plait or ponytail

ⓖ clean, shortish fingernails

ⓖ natural make-up or none

ⓖ clothes that are obviously for daytime, not what you'd
wear to a party or out at night – no sequins, for example

ⓖ low to mid-heel shoes

ⓖ no visible tattoos – most jobs don't allow them

ⓖ no visible piercings (except small earrings) – again most
bosses will ask you to take any out while at work.
(On the other hand, if you're working in a shop
that sells rubber vampire bats, looking like a full-on
goth could be positively required.)

Your rights as a worker

In a part-time or full-time job you have some rights protected by law, and others that are negotiated when you take the job. These rights cover things such as how long a shift can be; the possibility of holiday and sick pay; whether you can be suddenly sacked; how much and how you are paid; what your boss can deduct from your wages, like government taxes and national insurance; the safety of the workplace and your tasks; and how a boss and your co-workers are allowed to treat you.

Depending on how your job is classified, you'll have different rights. "Permanent" part-time and full-time employees usually have more rights and benefits than a temp or agency worker employed on a casual hourly or daily basis, or as the work becomes available. But every worker has some basic legal rights (see "More info on workers' rights and responsibilities" at the end of this chapter).

Youth wages and rules

The government sets minimum wages and working conditions, so even if you sign an agreement with a boss or a company they must still make sure you get all the basic rights and benefits you're entitled to.

Most workers in the UK have the right to be paid the National Minimum Wage, which changes slightly every year. It's supposed to protect people from being underpaid or exploited by their bosses. But employers say they need an incentive to hire young people, so the government has set lower "young worker" or "development" wages for people under 21, which means you can be paid less than an adult to do the same job. There are three levels for the National Minimum Wage: the adult rate; the "development" rate for 18–21 year olds; and the "young worker" rate for 16–17 year olds.

If you are under the school leaving age of 16, it's illegal for you to have a full-time job and you're not entitled to the National Minimum Wage. There are also strict laws about where, when and how long you can work, and about what kind of job you can do. (For more details, see the government websites coming up in "More info".) If you want to get a part-time job after school or on the weekends before you're 16, your boss has to tell your Local Authority so they can check you're not in danger, get your parent's permission and issue an employment permit.

What you don't have to put up with

There are laws that protect you from being hurt or harassed, or being made to feel embarrassed or uncomfortable at work. They protect you against discrimination based on your religion or beliefs, race, skin colour, disability, age, sexual orientation and gender (whether you're male or female). Laws also protect you against workplace bullying and sexual harassment (including intimidating stares or comments and pornography in the workplace).

> My bosses at work are forever trying to change me into someone else.... This makes me doubt if who I am is a good person.
> Kate, 17

To fix a work problem you can try talking to:

- ⚅ your boss (unless the boss is the problem)
- ⚅ your boss's boss, or the HR (human resources) or personnel manager, or equal opportunities officer, if your workplace has one
- ⚅ your trade union or a union helpline
- ⚅ your local Citizens Advice Bureau
- ⚅ the Advisory, Conciliation and Arbitration Service (Acas) or the Equality and Human Rights Commission (see "More info" a bit further on).

HINT

Out of there   Don't stay in a job where the atmosphere is all about fear and intimidation. You only have one life and there's no point wasting it by being around people who miss being the school bully.

Exit strategies

Resigning from a job

Keeping a good employment reputation is important for future jobs. Stay professional, hard-working and polite right up to when you leave your present job: you'll have a better chance of getting a good reference.

✻ Usually it's best to resign after you've found another job so you're not left without an income. And it's always easier to get a job if you already have one: you seem more employable.

✻ Never resign when you're angry. Don't tell the boss what you think of them. Don't shout, slam doors, swear or behave as if they're your parent.

✻ Don't walk out in the middle of a bad scene (unless it involves a serious safety or harassment issue) or just leave one day, and never go back, without an explanation.

✻ Tell your immediate boss you're resigning before you inform the big boss or the HR (human resources) or personnel officer.

✻ Put your resignation in writing, with the date you're leaving, and keep it short. Don't give detailed reasons: just say it's time to move on, or another opportunity has come up that you feel you need to take. Many job search websites have sample resignation letters and advice on how to resign with dignity.

✻ If you agreed when you took the job that you'd stay for, say, two weeks after resigning, you'll need to do that (it's called "working out your notice"). Even if it's not part of your contract, it can create goodwill to stay on for at least a few days so that the company can try to fill your position.

✻ Talk to the accounts department or boss to make sure you're given a P45 form (a record of how much tax you've paid) and any other paperwork when you leave.

✻ Ask for a written reference to be ready when you leave.

✻ Return anything of the company's you still have, such as a uniform, key or mobile.

If you're fired or made redundant

✻ Check with an independent person, such as a government, citizens advice or trade union advisor, about whether your rights and entitlements have been met.

✻ If it's appropriate, ask for a reference. You may have been "let go" (made redundant) just because there's no more work for that season, or because the company can't afford to pay you anymore.

It can be hard not to take it personally, even when it's not your fault. Government and job search websites often have useful info about being sacked.

More info on workers' rights and responsibilities

www.direct.gov.uk/en/Employment
Government site with all the latest info on employment rights and contracts, pay and the National Minimum Wage, holidays and benefits, health and safety, redundancy and dismissal, discrimination and trade unions. Also has lots of "Where to get help" links.

www.direct.gov.uk/en/YoungPeople/ Workandcareers
All about young people's working rights. Choose "Employment rights for young people" for the rules on what work you can do, and when, where and how long you can do it. Choose "Get a statement of your employment rights and responsibilities" for a personal summary of your working rights.

www.worksmart.org.uk
Everything about your working rights from the TUC (Trade Union Congress). You can call their Know Your Rights helpline for advice on **0870 600 4882**.

www.hmrc.gov.uk
The site of HM Revenue & Customs (the tax office) has info on tax and national insurance, and a calculator to check you're paying the right amount; choose "Employees and individuals". You can call the National Minimum Wage helpline on **0845 600 0678**.

www.acas.org.uk
The Advisory, Conciliation and Arbitration Service gives free help and advice on employment rights issues. Call their helpline on 08457 47 47 47. In Northern Ireland, contact the Labour Relations Agency: **www. lra.org.uk** or **028 9032 1442**.

www.equalityhumanrights.com
The Equality and Human Rights Commission advises on discrimination and human rights; click on "Your rights" for more info. Call their helpline on **0845 604 6610** (England); **0845 604 8810** (Wales); **0845 604 5510** (Scotland). In Northern Ireland, see **www.nihrc.org**.

19
SAVVY

Call somebody to talk to

Part of growing up is learning how to be savvy (smart) enough to **look after yourself** and decide which situations and places are safe for you. Throughout this book there are lots of basic ideas to help you deal with situations confidently, including in the chapters on Drinking (not getting out of your freaking mind and putting yourself in danger), Drugs (ditto), Friends (how to handle personal and electronic bullying) and Money (avoiding scams). This chapter looks at smart web use; has info on being savvy when out and about, partying and at home; gives self-defence tips; explains how to get out of abusive relationships; and tells you what to do about assault and violence.

Smart surfing

How can you get savvy about using the web, email, chatrooms and blogs? Social networking, message and blog sites, like mobile phones (see the Friends chapter), can be used to spread mean, horrible gossip and lies – and they're where some creeps try to find victims.

Safety pointers

Here are the safety pointers to keep in mind when you're using computers.

- Never allow someone to take a video or picture of you (such as when you are drunk or topless) that you wouldn't want your parents to see online. Pics, including those taken on mobile phones and webcams, can be posted on the Internet and seen by millions of people.

- Be very careful about what you say and which photos you put on a blog, online community or social networking site. Your parents, teachers, bosses and everyone you know can get access to the stuff, and perhaps even copy or re-post it. Many sites remain active for years.

- Make sure the "privacy settings" on the social sites you use are set as high as possible. They help you control who can see what on your pages, and can stop strangers accessing your personal information, photos and messages. But remember your account is only as safe as you make it – your info won't stay private if you make friends with every Tom, Dick and Harry you meet online.

- Don't send any email that you wouldn't want re-posted around the world. One girl sent a message about sex to a guy and the next thing she knew he had sent it to a friend, who sent it to some other friends, and so on until it had made it to several hundred thousand people, including her parents and teachers, and newspapers and blogs in other countries – with her name still attached.

- Don't stand for anyone sending you porn pictures or info by email (or mobile phone), or putting it where you work or study. It's illegal.

- If you get a porn or harassing message, report it to your service provider or the person overseeing the site.

- If you're at work, school or home and porn sites keep popping up on your computer, tell a parent, teacher or boss – they may be able to adjust the computer's "security settings" to stop the sites coming up. Telling a teacher or boss will also stop them thinking you deliberately accessed the sites, which can be grounds for suspension or sacking.

- Never choose an email address or a message or a chatroom name that makes you sound like a young girl, somebody who wants sex or a person who's available to be exploited (or one that makes you look desperate for new friends). Chick, Sexygirl,

amazon.co.uk

Thank you for shopping at Amazon.co.uk!

Invoice for
Your order of 26 June 2013
Order ID 203-3645157-2054714
Invoice number DGsh6kHYR
Invoice date 26 June, 2013

	Billing Address **Kit Whitfield** 10 Cornflower Terrace London SE22 0Ht United Kingdom	**Kit Whitfield** 10 Cornflower Terrace London SE22 0Ht United Kingdom

Qty	Item		Our Price (excl VAT)	VAT Rate	Total Price
1	**The Rough Guide To Girl Stuff** Paperback, Cooke, Kaz. 1848360185 (** P-1-B256G1t2 **)		£9.65	0%	£9.65

Shipping charges

	£2.75	£2.75
Subtotal (excl VAT) 0%		£12.40
Total VAT		£0.00
Total		£12.40

Conversion rate - £1.00 EUR 1.18

Teenhottie and variations on the theme such as Candiibabe could be a magnet for creeps.

⑥ Don't ever put into an email, chatroom or blog your real last name; your neighbourhood or town; your phone number; your street address; the name of your school sports team; or anything that gives a clue to your whereabouts. And make sure you don't accidentally give away details in something you show or write, such as a pic of a nearby landmark or your house, or the local shopping centre's name (see "Online creeps" below). Just put something vague for where you live such as "the Scottish Highlands" or "London". That way nobody seriously weird can find you.

Hi, I'm Tex. Send me $9000 and call me, 'Big Boy'

you NeveR KNOW WHO you MigHt Meet ...

⑥ Don't give your email address or other details to a website you've accessed so that you can get "free" stuff or look at something. This is usually a trick to get your details so they can find you – either to send you boring ads or to try to get your banking details and steal from you. Be very careful about giving any details online, and if you're under 18 always ask a parent first.

⑥ Never send banking or other financial details over the net, even if you get an email asking for them. This is always a scam (see the "Email and phone scams" section in the Money chapter).

⑥ Be careful not to accidentally give away details of your name and location on emails you send – sometimes the info you filled out when you got your email account is included.

Online creeps

Creeps get onto sites and say revolting things or, worse, try to meet you. You may think you're talking to a cute young guy, but it could be a dirty old man typing with one hand and fiddling with his willy with the other. Euwwww!

FACT

Break the chain   Don't ever send on a "chain" email or text message, even if it says you need to send it to a list of friends or something bad will happen. It's just crap.

Criminals who want to have sex with girls regularly go online pretending to be your age, and even pretend to be a girl when they're a man. They research bands, TV shows, movies and other stuff teenagers like, so that they can sound younger. Their aim is to meet you or to find out where you live.

They could:

⊙ send you a photo or some webcam footage of somebody else – a young, hot-looking guy, for example – so that you are fooled into thinking you're talking to someone your own age

⊙ try to turn you against, or encourage resentful feelings towards, parents, teachers or anyone else, such as friends, who might be rightly protective of you

⊙ chat to you in a way that makes you think they are wise, kind and the only person who understands you

⊙ start asking you to keep things they say a secret

⊙ offer you presents or money to gain your confidence, or promise you things if you agree to meet them

⊙ try to trick you or talk you into telling them about your sexual feelings, or say sexual things to you in the chatroom

⊙ use a sexual thing or thought you've told them to try to blackmail you by saying, "I'll tell your parents/friends/ school you said that, unless you do what I want you to do".

Meeting someone from online

Never go on your own to meet someone you got to know online. Each year girls disappear all around the world after going to such meetings, and many more have been assaulted by men who arranged a meeting by pretending to be a girl, a young guy or someone nice.

If you set up a meeting with someone you met online:

✳ tell a parent and friends where you're going and let the person you're meeting know you've done this – any reason they wanted to keep it a secret would be a suspicious one

✳ meet at your house while a parent who knows about it is at home; or in a public place where there are lots of other people (such as a shopping centre or cafe) and take a parent, adult friend or more than one friend of your own age

✳ never, ever agree to go to another place with the person who meets you – they could be leading you somewhere dangerous – and never get into a car with them (see the box "Resisting force" later in this chapter).

Don't talk to a person online who does any of these things. And tell an adult you trust about them straight away: you could be saving another, younger kid later on who isn't as savvy as you.

More info **on smart surfing**

See also the "Cyberbullying" box and "More info on bullying" in the Friends chapter.

www.netsafe.smallmajority.co.uk
Tips on staying safe in chatrooms from the Scottish police and government; choose "Teen's guide" to see video clips.

www.safeteens.com
A US site with heaps of info about being smart online and knowing all the tricks of scammers and creeps.

www.thinkuknow.co.uk
A UK government site with stuff on having fun and staying in control online – just choose the section for your age group. Weird or worrying online behaviour can be reported by clicking "Report abuse".

The Rough Guide to MySpace and Online Communities
by Peter Buckley, Rough Guides
Tells you how to set up a profile, make friends online, chat and create a blog, and has lots of good advice on privacy settings and keeping your account secure. Reassure your parents by getting them to read the "Tips for parents", "Common concerns" and "Playing it safe" sections.

Personal savvy

Because you'll be going out more and more as you get older it's smart to be clued up on avoiding trouble, and on what to do if things turn nasty or scary (see also "Sexual assault" later in the chapter and the "If things turn scary" box in the Sex chapter). There are lots of tips coming up about different situations, but here are some general pointers:

- always keep your mobile phone charged, topped up with credit and in a safe place in your bag or a pocket
- have somebody you can always call on in an emergency – see the "Your emergency contacts" box a couple of pages further on
- call 999 if you believe that you're in real immediate danger (or you're in need of medical help and an ambulance)
- do some self-defence classes – local councils and schools should have details of classes.

Never let anyone say "You're being paranoid", or "You worry too much", and get you to go somewhere or do something that seems dangerous, such as into a dark, scary place where there are no people to be seen. Guys don't tend to worry about that stuff because they've been taught all their lives how to react to physical pain or aggression, especially on the sports field. And they're not targeted for sexual assault as often as girls. So do what's best for you.

Everyday security tips

A lot of security tips just become part of your routine and then you don't have to think about them any more. And there are some "stranger dangers" worth knowing (even though most people who are assaulted are attacked by someone they know, not a stranger).

Out and about walking

- ⓞ Try not to walk home (or be on public transport) when it's dark or there are few people around. When in doubt, head for the crowds and bright lights of open shops, restaurants and other public places.
- ⓞ Vary your routine – such as where you jog early in the mornings or when you leave work – and change the journeys.
- ⓞ Be aware that a surprising number of attacks happen in the early morning, not just when it's dark.
- ⓞ Try to take a dog or a friend if you walk or jog.
- ⓞ Always walk or run against the traffic so that you can see what's coming.
- ⓞ Think about not using earphones up loud – music or talk in your ears means you can get distracted and step onto a road without hearing traffic coming. You also can't hear someone coming up behind you.
- ⓞ If a strange adult takes a picture of you with their phone, take their photo too (if it's safe to) and keep it to show to a parent.
- ⓞ If someone is acting creepy or following you, make sure you get a good look at their face, and that they know you have. Try to avoid them, perhaps by crossing the road, and head towards other people or a busy public place. If you can do so safely, you could take a picture of them with your mobile phone and send it straight to a friend or family member. This way the person knows they can be identified.
- ⓞ Stay alert, be aware of your surroundings and look as fit as you can: attackers prefer women who are distracted (on the phone, reading, listening to music, looking in their bag, studying a map or timetable). They also prefer women who look vulnerable and timid, and wear high heels or tight skirts that prevent them from running properly. Always walk with confidence, looking around you (and if necessary take your shoes off and run).

TaKe a DoG

ⓖ Have a spare key hidden outside your house (but not somewhere obvious such as under the mat or a pot plant or rock) so that even if you haven't got your own key you can get inside quickly.

Out and about on public transport and in cars

ⓖ Wait for public transport in a busy and well-lit place, and try to get someone to meet you at the other end if you have to get off at a quiet stop or station.

ⓖ Sit near the driver if possible, or at least where the driver can see you, and on the lower deck of a double-decker bus. On other kinds of public transport, try to avoid empty carriages and quiet areas, but sit in a corner where you can see everyone who gets on or off, and nobody can get behind you.

ⓖ Don't get onto public transport if you're going to be alone with a creepy person. Sometimes you don't know why you think there's something odd. It doesn't matter. Trust your instincts: if someone seems dodgy they probably are (and likewise with a place).

ⓖ Always call and book a licensed cab instead of hailing one on the street, if you can. This means the cab company will have a record of who the driver is, and he's less likely to do anything rude or horrible. Try to share cabs with friends, especially at night.

ⓖ Keep some taxi money at home for emergencies.

ⓖ Don't enter a car park if it's empty except for someone you feel uneasy about. Get a security guard or a person you trust to walk you to your car.

ⓖ Never go over to a man in a deserted car park who says he needs help. Get in your car, lock the doors and use your phone to ring the emergency number for him.

ⓖ Don't faff about looking for your car or home keys: always have them ready when you get to the door.

ⓖ Lock all car doors, whether you're in or outside the car, so someone can't jump in. This goes for daytime as well as night-time journeys, and sitting in the car reading a magazine while eating takeaway. Make it a habit: if you're in the car, the doors are locked.

ⓖ If a car pulls up when you've broken down in a deserted place check all your doors are locked and the windows up. Call a roadside assistance company, family member or close friend to come and get you. If you don't have a phone, open the window a crack and ask the person to make the call for you. Don't get out of the car or let them in. You can wait.

ⓖ Never, ever hitchhike. It's dangerous, and you never know who's stopping to pick you up.

ⓖ Never get into a car when ordered to by a man, even if he has a weapon – resist (see the "Resisting force" box).

Your emergency contacts

Have at least one or two emergency contacts for late-night or other rescues – which you use if your only alternative is doing something dangerous, like walking home at night on your own or getting into a car with people who are drunk, or if there is some other situation you know you should get away from.

✱ Ideally an emergency person should be older and sensible, and either drive a car or be able to pay for a taxi for you. It could be a parent, an auntie or uncle, a grandparent, an older cousin, a sister or brother, a friend or the parent of one of your friends.

✱ Your emergency person needs to agree that you can ring them and they will come and get you at any time of the day or night (or call a taxi for you), no matter what.

✱ Memorize their phone numbers.

The deal is you try never to get yourself into a stupid or dangerous situation – and the emergency person never screams at you for waking them up in the middle of the night.

ICE

Put the initials ICE (short for "In case of emergency") in front of the phone number of anyone in your mobile's contacts list who you would want called in an emergency; for example, ICE Dad, ICE Mum or ICE [*big sister's name*].

Ⓖ Generally avoid getting into a car or going somewhere with a group of young men. Groups tend to be more dangerous than a guy on his own.

Out and about partying

Ⓖ Don't wander off outside at a party or go down the road or to a park – stay where there are friends or parents nearby who can help you if things get nasty. (See also the Drinking and Drugs chapters for good stuff on partying savvy.)

Ⓖ If something seems off or wrong about an older guy, and the way he looks at you or speaks to you (he seems extra intense in a weird way or too charming to be true), be extra careful.

ooh, no you don't...

If it feels weird it PROBABLY is... time to Back out

Resisting force

✤ Scream, fight and run away if a guy tries to corner you or stop you getting away – and keep screaming. He'll be looking for an easy target, and is more likely to give up on you.

✤ When someone has hold of you always fight back if it's possible – biting, kicking and punching – and make a lot of noise. Attackers want someone who is quiet and no trouble. If you hurt his testicles, you're trouble. Remember this is a guy who will definitely hurt or rape you if you don't fight. If you do fight, you may get away.

✤ "Weapons" you can use include keys, sharp edges of heavy books, even the heel of a shoe held in your hand.

✤ If struggling and screaming doesn't scare him off shout, 'Dad!' or 'Help! Fire!', to attract other people's attention.

✤ Break away and run into a shop or anywhere else that's crowded, and yell for help. Always choose crowds with women as well as men if you can.

✤ It's worth having some training in self-defence.

⊙ If you are at big end-of-school celebrations or Freshers' Week events at the start of uni watch out for older guys who hang around hoping to find girls drunk enough to assault.

And when the party's at your place:

⊙ Plan things in advance – warn the neighbours, make sure any valuables/priceless family heirlooms/pets are safely locked away, cover up the sofas in case of spills – and make sure you know what to do and who to call if there's a fire or other emergency.

⊙ If you don't want your parents there (and can convince them to go out) arrange for some other responsible, older person to be at the party, just in case something goes wrong. Big brothers, sensible older cousins and muscley uncles are ideal for keeping out scary gatecrashers or helping when drunk friends pass out on the bathroom floor.

⊙ If your parents are away for the night, don't tell lots of friends or word will get around and you'll suddenly have a house full of unwanted guests. Keep the guest list small, ask friends not to invite other people along, and absolutely, definitely don't announce your party on a social networking site, blog or anywhere else online – you don't know who might turn up wanting to cause trouble.

⊙ If scary people you don't know do arrive and there are no adults around to make them go, leave the house (taking friends with you). Go to a neighbour's and call the police on 999 straight away. Your parents will be pleased the uninvited guests got chucked out before any damage was done – to you or their house.

At home

⊙ Make sure people outside can't see inside.

⊙ Get a spy hole in the front door, and if you're home alone, don't answer the door to anybody who's not a close friend or relative.

⊙ Don't leave ground-floor or accessible windows open at night, even when it's hot, unless they have bars on them.

'There's a stranger called Bevan throwing up in your dad's underwear drawer'

⊙ Don't give your key to friends. Make sure you know exactly how many copies are out there and who has them. Change locks when you move to a new place.

More info on parties, personal safety and knowing your legal rights

See also the Drugs and Drinking chapters for stuff on staying safe at parties.

www.bbc.co.uk/parenting/family_matters/celeb_teenparties.shtml
Although this party advice is meant for parents, it's useful for you too – and it might help you convince your parents that you're responsible enough to throw a party.

www.thesite.org/travelandfreetime/goingout/houseparties
The YouthNet site has all sorts on info on parties, from tips on caring for a drunk friend and protecting your stuff from fire and thieves to cleaning up afterwards.

www.bbc.co.uk/switch/slink
On this BBC site for girls, click on "I love me", then "Be safe" for the basics on being savvy, whether you're out and about, at home or online. Also has info on personal alarms.

www.livelifesafe.org.uk
Advice on being clever when you're out and about from the Suzy Lamplugh Trust. Choose "Safety sense" for tips on everything from travelling by bus or taxi to being home alone, or do one of their games or quizzes to see how streetwise you are.

www.thesafetybox.org
Choose "School and youth programmes" to find out about courses to help you avoid and handle dangerous situations.

www.childrenslegalcentre.com
The Children's Legal Centre is an independent organization that gives free legal advice to children and young people.

www.adviceguide.org.uk
Citizens Advice Bureaux offer free, confidential advice on issues like your legal rights, discrimination, money, benefits, work, health, education and consumer affairs. Choose either England, Wales, Scotland or Northern Ireland from the menu at the top of the page, then "Find your local CAB" to talk to an advisor in your area.

www.rizer.co.uk
Designed by young people for young people, Rizer is an info and advice site about crime and the law. It's got personal stories, a guide to the youth justice system, facts and figures, and info on your rights.

www.yourrights.org.uk
Human rights info from the UK charity Liberty. Choose from the "Your rights" list, look under "FAQs" for common questions, or select "Get advice" to ask a specific question.

Abusive relationships

Abuse – which includes physical violence, sexual assault and emotional or psychological cruelty – can occur to rich or poor, and in any kind of relationship: within the family or from a boyfriend or girlfriend, and at school or work (see the Friends and Work chapters). Abuse is wrong and against the law. No matter what anyone says, nobody has the legal right to abuse their partner, child, sister or brother, or anyone else.

It's important to remember that if you're abused it's not about what you have done: it's about how the abuser is choosing to behave. If you are abused it is never your fault. No matter how bad your behaviour, no one, not even a parent, has the right to abuse you.

The different kinds of abuse

Abuse can be physical or mental; it can be obvious or subtle, out in the open or hidden and kept secret.

Emotional abuse Emotional abuse occurs when one person creates feelings of low confidence in someone else or an atmosphere of fear by scoffing at, being sarcastic or hurtful to, putting down, criticizing, demeaning, insulting or threatening someone with less power.

Emotional abusers often use these kinds of phrases:

- ⊙ "You're stupid."
- ⊙ "You can't get anything right."

G "You're an embarrassment."

G "Nobody else would want you."

G "Nobody wants to hear anything from you."

An emotional abuser often teases or humiliates the other person, either in private or in front of others, and then claims "It was a joke" instead of saying sorry.

Emotional abuse can also include what's known as "controlling" behaviour. The abuser might:

G constantly check up on the other person and follow them around, and then make accusations (often that they've been unfaithful or disloyal in some way)

G continually tell them what to say and how to behave

G insist on knowing where they've been, who with and exactly what they were doing, every time they go out (not the same as a parent wanting to know where a child is, to make sure they're safe)

G forbid them to have friends or contacts outside the relationship

G threaten violence if they are not obeyed

G tell the abused person they can't go out unless the abuser is with them

G not allow an adult to choose what to spend money on.

"Emotional blackmail" can also be used: the controlling person says that they'll be upset, get sick, hurt themselves or somebody else, or commit suicide, unless others do what they want.

Physical abuse   Physical abuse by one person against another includes:

G having an intimidating or frightening anger or rage

G throwing things

G destroying the abused person's belongings

G threatening punishment or violence against the abused person or their loved ones

G hitting, pushing, slapping, kicking or otherwise physically hurting the other person in some way

G keeping or showing weapons.

Sexual abuse   Sometimes a person uses emotional blackmail, intimidation, threats or violence to force another person to do sexual things (see also "Family abuse", below, and "Sexual assault" later in this chapter).

Family abuse

In a family the abuse might be against a partner, the kids or the whole family. Physical abuse is often called domestic violence and, because it involves physical threats or injury, often with shouting and loud noises, it is the abuse most easily spotted by outsiders. But emotional abuse can also be used in a family; for example, a mum might be

Legal rights of children and young people

All kids and young people have human rights. The UK signed the United Nations' Convention on the Rights of the Child (UNCRC) way back in 1990, agreeing to its contents. The convention sets out and protects the rights of children up to the age of 18. Under it you have the right, among other things, to:

✷ freedom from economic and sexual exploitation

✷ have your own opinion

✷ education

✷ health care

✷ a safe place to live

✷ economic opportunity.

controlled by the fear of her child being hurt, or a child controlled by the fear of their mum being hurt.

Sexual abuse of children and teenagers also occurs within some families. The abuser can be a parent, a parent's partner, a sibling or another relative (or a teacher, sports coach or some other adult trusted by the family), who might:

- ⚬ touch or do things to the child or teenager's private parts
- ⚬ make the child or teenager touch them sexually or have some kind of sex with them
- ⚬ look at the child or teenager's private parts in a sexual way
- ⚬ expose their own private parts to a child or teenager, or make them watch them do something sexual
- ⚬ insist the child or teenager looks at pictures or films (on a computer, TV or somewhere else) that seem wrong and make them feel uncomfortable
- ⚬ do or say something else that feels wrong or creepy.

The abuser might say things such as "It's normal", "Don't tell anyone", and "It's our secret". Often they might threaten to hurt the kid (or somebody else), or to shame them if they tell anyone what's going on. Or the abuser might say that nobody will believe the kid if they tell.

If you are being sexually abused you need to know that what they are doing is:

- ⚬ against the law
- ⚬ never normal or right

FACT

A form of child abuse　One parent abusing the other is also a form of child abuse because they are not making the child's home a safe or happy place to be.

ⓖ and, no matter what they say, not your fault – by doing this to you they have
 betrayed your trust in them and that is very wrong.

Sexual abuse can be confusing, especially when the person doing the abusing is someone you love or have been taught to trust or obey. It doesn't happen because a person
"can't control their sexual urges", or because the way you look or behave "makes" them
do it. You might feel guilty or ashamed, but you are not the person responsible for doing
the wrong thing. The abuser knows what they are doing and that it is wrong, and has
made a choice.

What to do about family abuse   It can be very hard to know what to do or who to
trust after emotional, physical or sexual abuse. But you can go one step at a time, without anyone in the family finding out at first. You need to tell a trusted adult or a doctor,
or call an anonymous helpline (see "More info" at the end of this section).

You can't fix this by yourself, but there are ways to make your life safe, and there are
people who will help you.

Abusive boyfriends and girlfriends

Even though you love your boyfriend or girlfriend, if they treat you badly – emotionally,
physically or sexually – they need to change or you need to leave the relationship.

Unacceptable behaviour includes doing some or all of the things described in "The
different kinds of abuse" section above. The other person may also:

ⓖ always put you down and be unkind to you

ⓖ make you wait on them and serve and fetch things, and enforce
 in other ways the notion that men are the boss of, or are superior to, women

ⓖ force or pressure you into doing sexual things (of any kind)

ⓖ accuse you of flirting or being "unfaithful", without evidence,
 or be excessively jealous

ⓖ be unfaithful (even though you are "not allowed" to be).

Many people in an abusive relationship start to think they deserve to be treated badly.
This is never true.

How to get out of an abusive relationship

ⓖ Tell a trusted adult what you're going through, and ask them for help – whether it's
 advice or just being there to support you and help protect you.

ⓖ If you want to give it another chance, tell your partner you don't like certain aspects
 of their behaviour – that it makes you feel upset and disrespected. Tell them that
 they need to change. If they agree or get counselling, that's a good sign. But put a
 time limit on the change, such as a couple of weeks (even if only you know about

Bad boyfriend or girlfriend material If someone tries to force you to do something you don't want to do, or makes you scared, drop them. Don't be with them again.

the limit), and if the change doesn't happen, then break up. Many people believe promises to change that never come true, or only a bit, so make sure you stick to your time limit. Don't keep giving them another chance. It's not enough that the person feels bad and says they love you – their behaviour must change.

⊙ Write down the abusive behaviour so you have a list to remind yourself of what's really happening.

⊙ Make a plan to end the relationship: work out where and when you will tell the person. Don't break up face to face and alone if you're scared the reaction will be violent or threatening. You can do it on the phone or have somebody with you.

⊙ If you are threatened, tell the person that you have told many people about their abusive behaviour, and that they will protect you. Get an adult, parent or teacher to talk to the person and explain that they can't threaten or harm you in any way, and that they will be watched.

⊙ Remember that it's a crime when someone stalks you – repeatedly harasses, follows, intimidates or calls you without permission. Contact the police if necessary.

Don't be ashamed of yourself, even if you feel you stayed with them too long. Get help to stand up for yourself, and have support around you. You are not alone.

> I started dating a guy at my school. We skipped school and he raped me. I never told anyone, but he did. He spread all sorts of shit around school about me. I went from an A student to barely passing. Sex is meant to be good and fun, but that goes for both of you. Don't feel pressured – you'll just regret it later.
>
> Georgie

More info on abusive relationships

There are ways of anonymously getting help for all the kinds of family abuse, such as these crisis lines:

ChildLine: 0800 1111

Samaritans: 08457 90 90 90

England Domestic violence helpline: 0808 2000 247
www.womensaid.org.uk

N. Ireland Domestic violence helpline: 0800 917 1414
www.niwaf.org

Scotland Domestic abuse helpline: 0800 027 1234
www.scottishwomensaid.org.uk

Wales Domestic abuse helpline: 0808 80 10 800
www.welshwomensaid.org

www.burstingthebubble.com
Australian site with info, advice and links on what to do about violence and abuse in your family, or how to help a friend.

www.thehideout.org.uk
Women's Aid site for kids and teens. Helps you understand what abuse is and what you can do about it. Has real-life stories and videos from other teenagers.

www.there4me.com
Interactive info and support service for teens. You can ask questions about violence, abuse or anything else that's bothering you by email or chat privately online to a trained NSPCC advisor.

Abusive boyfriends or girlfriends: if you're scared that you're in immediate danger call the police on 999. If you need to talk to someone about what's happening call the following helpline, or one of the other regional helplines on the left.

National Domestic Violence Helpline: 0808 2000 247
This free, confidential helpline is run by Women's Aid and Refuge to help women and children affected by any kind of abuse. Their websites, **www.womensaid.org.uk** and **www.refuge.org.uk**, also have info to help you recognize and avoid abusive and violent relationships, and contact details for women's organizations in your local area.

www.dvirc.org.au/whenlove
When Love Hurts is a great Australian site for young women about abusive or controlling relationships with boyfriends or girlfriends. Has good checklists, quizzes and real-life stories.

www.respect4us.org.uk
Interactive teen site from the UK charity Womankind that challenges ideas about violence in relationships, sexual harassment and bullying, and to help girls and boys learn to respect and understand each other.

www.uhavetheright.net
US site about teen dating violence and the difference between healthy and unhealthy relationships.

I've been raped by 3 different males; I would like to know the best way to deal with it without having to go to the police.   Anonymous, 17

Sexual assault

Any sex without consent is a crime called rape. These days the crime is often referred to as sexual assault to emphasise that, although it is sexual, it's also a physical assault on another person. The term sexual assault can also cover many different things, including groping someone's private parts.

A guy commits rape if, against your will, he has penetrative sex with you (the penetration can be with a penis, fingers or objects, and in the vagina, the anus or the mouth). Other words used are forced sex, non-consensual sex or sex with coercion.

Legally rape is about whether or not you consented – wanted it to happen. Rape is rape, whether physical force or violence was used, you were threatened, you were too drunk or out of it to give your consent, or you "gave in" because you were too scared or couldn't see a way of escaping.

> **FACT**
>
> **No joke** Rape is something that is joked about by ignorant people. Once you know what it involves, you understand why there is nothing funny about it. Don't let people make jokes about rape around you.

Rape is usually, but not always, a very brutal crime accompanied by threats, or violence and injuries. Gang rape means rape by more than one guy.

If the rape is by someone the raped person is going out with, some people call it "date rape" (see the box "Sex without consent" coming up). This is also the name some people use when a rapist gives a person drugs that make them partly or completely unconscious (also called drug-assisted rape). (Most rapes don't require a drug slipped into somebody's drink, as sadly many girls drink enough voluntarily or accidentally to put themselves into a state in which they can't fight against or try to avoid a sexual assault.)

See "Personal savvy" earlier in the chapter for tips on how to avoid dangerous situations and how to resist an attack.

Getting help after an assault

Just as consenting sex can give you intense feelings of being cared for and a sense of intimacy, rape and sexual assault can often

BEING assaulted is NEVER your fault

cause serious and long-lasting feelings of violation, terror and even shame because many groups in our society are ashamed of sex.

The possibility of pregnancy or a sexually transmitted infection adds to the distress. It can also be very worrying for somebody if they know they were raped but can't remember what happened (usually because they were drunk).

You *can* get help.

- ☾ Call the police on 999 if you are in immediate danger afterwards or to report an assault straight away, or go to your local police station (you can ask to speak to a woman police officer).

- ☾ Tell someone you trust about the assault so they can help you with the following steps.

- ☾ Get medical help and counselling: all large towns and many other areas have a sexual assault service staffed by women who can help you – whether you were assaulted by somebody you know or by a stranger, and whether or not you want to involve the police (see "More info" below). They can recommend kind doctors to help you.

Sex without consent

Sometimes sexual assault happens when a guy won't take "No" or "Stop" for an answer, and keeps trying to pressure you, push you, take your clothes off, stop you from getting up – things like that.

You need to know that:

✷ even if there is no physical violence, it is still sexual assault if you are forced into sex by verbal threats, name-calling, nastiness, emotional blackmail, threats that he'll tell people something mean or made up, or claims such as "I know you want it"

✷ someone who does this to you after understanding that "no means no" is NOT good boyfriend material, and you shouldn't be alone with him again

✷ it's okay to have agreed to do something and then have second thoughts and say no. A guy MUST stop when you say no, always, no matter what.

FACT

Nobody ever "asks for it"   Whether or not you have already had sex with them or they are your boyfriend, or you were wearing "revealing" clothes, nobody has the "right" to rape or assault you. Rape or assault is never acceptable, and never your fault.

⚈ As soon as possible after you have been raped, but definitely within 72 hours (three days), go to your GP, a family planning/contraception clinic or a young people's clinic and ask for the emergency contraceptive pill (morning-after pill), which should prevent pregnancy (see "Emergency contraception" in the Sex chapter). Do a pregnancy test three weeks later to make doubly sure. Also see a doctor to check you have not been given an infection that could cause health problems in the future. You can go to your GP, a sexual health clinic or a young people's clinic (see the contacts under "More info on sexually transmitted infections" in the Sex chapter).

⚈ Think about having ongoing counselling – many people find it helps them work through their feelings after an assault. Counselling can be free on the NHS or through various support services: ask your GP about it or see "More info" below.

If the assault is ongoing   If you continue to be assaulted by a person in your family, an adult in a position of trust, a boyfriend or someone else, there are many services that will help you choose how you want to handle the situation and help you through it.

You can also call the police or take out a court order, called a "restraining order", to make the person leave you alone and stay away from you and your home, school or work. If you are under 18 a parent or the police can take out the order for you.

More info on sexual assault

See also the sites and organizations in "More info on abusive relationships" a few pages back.

ChildLine: 0800 1111

Samaritans: 08457 90 90 90

www.rasasc.org.uk
The Rape and Sexual Abuse Support Centre is a charity that offers support and info to survivors of sexual assault, and can put you in touch with services where you live.
National helpline: 08451 221 331

www.rapecrisis.org.uk
On the Rape Crisis site, click on "Centres" to find rape crisis groups, services and local helplines in England and Wales.

www.rapecrisisscotland.org.uk
In Scotland, contact the Rape Crisis Scotland Helpline: 0808 801 0302.

www.rapecrisisni.com
In Northern Ireland, phone the Rape Crisis Centre's Crisis Line: 028 9032 9002.

www.victimsupport.org.uk
Victim Support is an independent charity that helps people who have experienced any kind of crime, including sexual assault. Call their UK-wide helpline for info or support, or choose "Contact us" to find help in your area.
UK supportline: 0845 30 30 900

www.aboutdaterape.nsw.gov.au
Australian site with info on rape that was committed by somebody you know.

www.homeoffice.gov.uk/crime-victims/
reducing-crime/sexual-offences
This government site has info about
reporting sexual assault and getting help.
Choose "Sexual assault referral centres" to
find specialist local places where you can
get medical help and counselling.

www.rightsofwomen.org.uk
A voluntary organization run by women
that offers free legal advice to women.
Their Sexual Violence Legal Advice Line is
available on Monday and Tuesday mornings:
020 7251 8887.

www.roofie.com
The Roofie Foundation deals with drink
spiking and drug-assisted sexual assault.
Includes tips on how to avoid drink spiking
and what to do if it happens to you.
Helpline: 0800 783 2980

www.thesurvivorstrust.org
On the Survivors Trust site, click on
your area on the map of the UK to find
support groups where you live or choose
"Information for survivors" to find out more.

www.youthinformation.com
On the National Youth Agency (NYA) site,
choose "Justice & equality", then "Crime" for
articles and links about rape, sexual assault
and personal safety.

My friend got drunk one night and her sister's boyfriend's friend raped her. She
hasn't told anyone 'cause even though she said no, she thinks that she must have
done something to make him think she wanted it.   Claire, 14

I have been sexually abused four times and mainly coz I didn't have the courage to
make them stop. Despite what people say it's not that easy to say "no". You freeze.
It sends you crazy inside your head and makes you wonder whether it's your fault.
Tell someone what has happened.   Lou, 16

20

BODY MAINTENANCE

Women tend to understand that their bodies need check-ups and regular maintenance, whereas most men will only go to the doctor if their leg has fallen off – and even then they'll forget to bring the leg. **Good health** is partly about luck and genes, but it's also partly about taking care of yourself.

Managing your health

Almost every health problem can be better managed and is less serious if you take it along to a doctor straight away.

Your NHS medical card

In the UK, most medical treatment is available for free on the NHS (National Health Service), whether it's a short consultation or check-up with your local doctor or GP (general practitioner) or an operation you might need in an emergency. The NHS is paid for by the government using money collected in taxes. Most adults have to pay a small set fee for prescriptions for medicines and for dental care, eye tests and some other treatments, but if you are under 16, or under 18 and still at school or college, you do not need to pay for any medical care.

All babies born in the UK are given an NHS number on an NHS medical card at birth, which proves who you are and that you're entitled to free treatment. You will be asked for your medical card when you register with a new doctor. If you don't have one or you have lost it, the doctor's surgery (the usual name for a doctor's office) will give you a form to fill in or tell you how to contact your local Primary Care Trust (PCT) to get a new one. (You could also ask a parent or your previous doctor to look at your old medical notes to find out your NHS number for you.)

Going to the doctor

Whether you want to go on your own or with a parent, you'll need a doctor you feel you can talk to. Most teens see the same local GP as the rest of their family, but you can try a new one at the same surgery or health centre, or at a different surgery if you prefer. Maybe a friend can recommend one. There are lots of great GPs: you just have to find one. Feel free to "shop around".

It's normal for a doctor to check your breasts for lumps and suggest you have a regular smear test (see "Girls' and women's health" coming up). If your usual doctor is a man, but you'd prefer to see a woman doctor – say, if you're having your girly bits checked out – ask when you're making an appoint-

ment. Most surgeries will arrange it if they can. It's also okay to ask if you can have somebody such as your mum, auntie or friend's mum, or a female nurse, in the room with you for the examination.

Always tell your doctor if you:

⑥ have sex, or have ever had sex, and if you use or have used any contraception

⑥ could possibly be pregnant

⑥ have taken or are taking any medications, including herbal ones (see the "Complementary medicines" box coming up)

⑥ are worried about anything, or have a question, no matter how silly it seems.

FACT

Health websites Medical info on websites can be old, irrelevant to your own country, biased (pushing a particular line) or utterly made up. If you have a diagnosed condition or illness, it's always a safer bet to find a support group near you, which can tell you what the most reliable, relevant and up-to-date sites are (to search, enter the name of the disorder or illness, then "support" and your area). When in doubt, and before ANY self-diagnosis or treatment, see a real doctor.

Privacy Doctors must keep all information about patients confidential, whether you ask them to or not. This means they're not allowed to discuss your condition with anyone (including a parent) unless you give them your permission. In very rare cases, if you are under 16, a doctor may have to tell somebody when they believe you are in danger from yourself or another person, or you may be a danger to someone else. But even in these rare cases it doesn't always have to be your parent who is told.

Immunization

You should have had all your childhood immunizations (also known as vaccinations) by now to protect you against various diseases. You will need some teenage boosters (additional doses of injections you had as a child), and to have extra vaccinations if you travel abroad to places where different lurgies lurk.

Check with a parent: you should already be protected against tetanus, diphtheria, whooping cough, polio, measles, mumps, rubella, Hib, meningitis C and pneumococcal infections (PCV). A lot of the vaccines are given in one injection, so you have a minimum number of jabs, not one per disease. Teenage boosters for some of these immunizations are given, usually at your school.

Some of the vaccines may not have been available when you were little, so you may have to have them now. Ask your doctor what you need. Any immunizations on the government's recommended list (called a "schedule") are free. You may have to pay for other vaccinations, such as extra ones you need for travel, but check with your GP first.

At about the age of 12 or 13, all girls should now be given the human papilloma virus vaccine as it protects them from most strains of HPV, which can cause cancer of the cervix (see "Girls' and women's health" coming up). This way the vaccine can be most effective. If you didn't have the HPV vaccine when you were 12 or 13 (school year 8), you will probably be offered it by your school or your GP sometime before you turn 18. If you are not offered the vaccine or if you have any questions, contact your doctor yourself. It's best to have the vaccine as soon as you can, whatever age you are, and whether or not you've had sex (HPV is sexually transmitted).

Complementary medicines

For some illnesses and conditions, "alternative", "complementary", "naturopathic" and herbal remedies can help or even deal with the problem. But for others, natural medicines alone will have no hope of helping (you wouldn't go to just a naturopath for a broken arm).

- Make sure your practitioner belongs to one of the professional organizations in "More info" at the end of this section. Many alternative and herbal remedies can be dangerous for young people (especially in pregnancy) if wrongly prescribed or even just used at all, so you need to go to a very experienced herbalist or naturopath.
- Tell your doctor about any complementary medicines or treatments you're taking, preferably before you take them.

Teeth

You just need to:

- clean your teeth really thoroughly with toothpaste and a toothbrush morning and night
- use dental floss between your teeth every couple of days, when you can feel stuff stuck between your teeth or, let's face it, when you remember
- see your dentist every six or twelve months
- always choose sugar-free chewing gum (but don't have too much – sugar-substitute chemicals, in large doses, can cause diarrhoea).

Hearing

You can do permanent damage to your ears (damage that can't be cured) by:

✱ listening to music at high volume using earphones

✱ going to live gigs and to clubs where there's loud music

✱ playing in a band, especially drums

✱ working in factories or computer rooms where there's enough noise to cause "industrial deafness".

What to do in noisy places

The experts say that if you're somewhere where it's hard to hear people speaking, then the noise is enough to start causing damage to your hearing. Here's what they suggest:

✱ throw some industrial or super-strength earplugs (from the chemist) into your handbag and keep them there ready

✱ use the earplugs as soon as you notice a place is too noisy and keep them in until you get out of there.

Personal music devices

Anything above about two-thirds of maximum volume on your headphones can cause hearing damage. To protect your hearing:

✱ don't listen to a personal music device for more than an hour a day

✱ keep the level at no more than ninety decibels – even one hour at maximum volume can cause some permanent damage

✱ don't turn it up louder if you can't hear the music over traffic or public transport noise – upping the volume, apart from being dangerous if you're walking, will cause hearing loss over time.

FACT

First aid   Courses in first aid can be a great way to find out more about how the body works and to learn how to save a life or deal with an injury in an emergency. They're also a bonus skill likely to impress people thinking of hiring you for a job.

Bad breath

For at least a hundred years the companies who make breath-freshening mints, mouthwashes, toothpastes and chewing gums have paid for ads designed to make us feel squirmy and scared about having bad breath, or halitosis (pronounced hally-toe-sis).

What causes bad breath?

- Bacteria in your mouth: the bad breath is basically the smell it gives off.
- Not brushing your teeth (and tongue) regularly: the stinky bacteria tends to grow on little bits of food left in your mouth.
- Some foods: garlic and onion, for instance, can make your breath smell of them for a little while.
- Not eating for long periods: your saliva isn't being stimulated to wash bacteria and plaque away.
- Smoking.
- Low-carb and other diets.

How to get rid of bad breath

If bad breath isn't kept away by cleaning your teeth regularly, your dentist can help.

Teeth whitening Despite all those grinning Hollywood starlets' faces flashing shiny sets, teeth aren't supposed to be toilet-bowl white. Most people only require a whitening product if they have badly stained teeth. Don't be sucked in by advertising telling you that you "need" one.

Most whitening toothpastes, chewing gums and other products sold over the counter take too long to work, or don't work at all. If your dentist agrees you need one, ask them about products that won't hurt and will whiten your teeth safely.

Intense teeth-whitening procedures, where a laser light is shone onto your teeth for a few minutes at a time, can be really painful. Even after paying for this hugely expensive treatment, many people bail out halfway through.

FACT

Holes The biggest causes of holes in teeth are believed to be sugary fizzy drinks and sports drinks. It's much better to drink water, which doesn't contain any sugar (and you can get it for free from the tap). Tooth decay causes really painful holes, which usually means an uncomfortable and expensive trip to the dentist for a filling.

More info on managing your health

www.childrenfirst.nhs.uk/teens
Health site for teens from Great Ormond
Street Hospital. Choose "Health" or "Girls
only", or search for a particular issue.

www.nhs.uk/LiveWell/TeenGirls
Tips for teenage girls about living a healthier
lifestyle; includes real-life stories and videos.

www.nhsdirect.nhs.uk
Get info and advice about health problems
or medical services, or search for doctors,
dentists and clinics where you live. Click
on "Common health questions", then "NHS
services", then "You and the NHS" to find out
how to get an NHS medical card and number.
NHS Direct health line: 0845 46 47

www.nhs.uk (England)
www.nhsdirect.wales.nhs.uk (Wales)
www.nhs24.com (Scotland)
www.healthandcareni.co.uk
(Northern Ireland)
Regional NHS sites to get health advice and
find doctors, dentists and other services.

Immunization

www.immunisation.nhs.uk
NHS site with up-to-date info on the UK
immunization schedule, so you can find out
which jabs you should have had when. It also
has stuff on all the diseases, why vaccines
are important and how they work, plus FAQs.

Hearing

www.dontlosethemusic.com
Site for teens about how loud music from
gigs, clubs and headphones can damage
your hearing. Has tips on protecting yourself,
real-life stories, FAQs and product reviews.

www.hearnet.com
US site with links to music videos and info
about how to protect your ears.

Teeth and bad breath

www.dentalhealth.org.uk
British Dental Health Foundation site: choose
"Public", then "Information leaflets" for info on
caring for your teeth, bad breath, decay, diet,
braces and everything else to do with teeth.
Dental helpline: 0845 063 1188

First aid courses

www.sja.org.uk
St John Ambulance: choose "Training
courses", then "Courses for young people".

Natural therapists

www.nimh.org.uk
The National Institute of Medical Herbalists;
click on "About medical herbalists" for more
info and to find a practitioner in your area.

Girls' and women's health

You don't have to have had sex, or be planning to have sex, to look after your sexual health and your girl parts designed for having a baby. Male and female doctors see patients' girly bits all day long and are very used to it – one of the reasons they're able to tell you whether everything is normal is because they see so many different people's bits.

People specializing in sexual stuff, such as contraception, sexually transmitted infections (STIs) and pregnancy tests, can be found at family planning clinics, young people's clinics and sexual health or GUM (genito-urinary medicine) clinics, and their advice, treatment and other services are all free (see also the Sex and Pregnancy chapters). You can also get help with all this sexual stuff from your local GP.

There are medical specialists (called gynaecologists, pronounced guy-no-colla-jists) who deal with everything to do with sex, contraception, breasts, pregnancy, ovaries, the vagina, the uterus and the cervix. But your first stop should be your GP (or a family planning clinic doctor), who can give you a check-up and refer you to a gynaecologist if necessary.

If you're ever worried about anything to do with your girly bits or breasts, or notice anything unusual about your period or vaginal secretions (see the Change chapter), or if you have any other questions about your body, ask your GP for a check-up.

Breast checks

All breasts have their quirks. A lot of girls and women just naturally have lumpy bosoms, and breasts may feel different around the time of a period.

Once you've developed breasts you should check them after each period for lumps, bumps or changes that don't seem to be just about them growing to their eventual adult size. Ask your GP to show you how to do this and what to watch out for. Doctors say girls in their teens should still look out for changes, even though their breasts are supposed to change.

Time to come out .... for inspection!

Be on the alert for:

- a lump, bumpiness or thickening in or on your breast that isn't normal for you
- puckering or dimpling of the skin
- unusual redness or other colour change to the breast
- nipple changes such as altered shape, sores or an ulcer, a different skin feeling (say, rough), more redness than usual, or an in-drawing of the nipple that wasn't there before
- liquid or anything else coming out of the nipple (little hairs are normal)
- unusual pain that's in only one breast and isn't your normal tenderness before a period.

Having any of the above symptoms does *not* automatically mean you have cancer or even a problem. Usually a lump is not cancerous, but any symptom must be checked out immediately by a doctor – in the next day or so after you find it – to make sure.

Breast cancer happens rarely in teenagers and young women, but, when it does, "catching it early" will give you a very good chance of getting rid of it before it can get worse.

Infections that aren't necessarily sexually transmitted

Many infections that affect your girly bits, give you a yukky discharge (see "Clear or white stuff" in the Change chapter) or make you itchy are not sexually transmitted at all: they're just things that girls and women get from time to time and need a bit of treatment for. For details see the "Common infections of the girly bits" chart coming up.

Tests for these infections (and for STIs) can be done at the same time as a smear test, using a separate swipe-stick, but your GP will sometimes diagnose them simply by hearing you talk about your symptoms and looking at your girly bits.

Common infections of the girly bits

You can get these infections of the vagina and vulva area without ever having sex, but sex can be one of the ways some of them are made worse or are passed on. They are all easily treated, and early treatment is always best. Vaginal infections are made worse by lack of air around your girly bits, so avoid thongs, g-strings, tight jeans and nylon or closely fitting undies. To help prevent infections and irritations, wash your girly bits with a mild soap substitute, and don't use perfumes or talc in the area. Always wipe toilet paper back towards the anus, not from there towards the vagina.

Candida, or thrush

What is it? An infection of the vagina caused by unusually high levels of a natural organism (yeast) in the vagina. It's very common.

How you get it The organism can get out of balance in the vagina if you're taking antibiotics, have a weak immune system, are pregnant or if yeast from the bowel enters the vaginal area.

Signs and symptoms Vaginal itching or soreness, a thick and clumpy discharge and a stinging sensation when you wee.

How you know you have it A doctor can often tell just from your symptoms, but might get a lab to analyse a swab from your vagina to make sure.

Effects No long-term health risks or side effects. It's just incredibly annoying.

Treatment Antifungal tablets, cream or pessaries (dissolving pills you pop inside your vagina). Sometimes it goes away without treatment.

Bacterial vaginosis (BV), or gardnerella infection

What is it? An inflammation of the vagina caused by natural bacteria in the vagina.

How you get it The bacteria get out of balance.

Signs and symptoms Sometimes none, or you might notice a fishy smell, white or grey and watery discharge, and mild irritation.

How you know you have it A doctor can often tell by looking, or a lab analyses a swab from high in the vagina taken by the doctor.

Effects No big deal usually, but must be treated before any uterus surgery.

Treatment Antibiotic tablets, but it sometimes goes away by itself.

Urinary infections, including cystitis

What are they?   Infections of the weeing system, including urethra, urine and kidneys.

How you get one   By micro-organisms (bacteria) getting into your body.

Signs and symptoms   Wanting to wee all the time (even if only a few drops come out), burning when weeing, blood in your wee and pain above the pubic bone.

How you know you have one   A lab or "dipstick" analysis of a wee sample, organized by a doctor or nurse, to find out which infection you have.

Effects   If an infection spreads to the bladder or kidneys, it can cause permanent damage.

Treatment   Usually antibiotic tablets as soon as possible. Early treatment can stop it spreading to the bladder or kidneys. Chemists also sell sachets of sodium citrate powders for cystitis which stop wee stinging, but don't cure the infection.

Vulva problems

What are they?   Inflamed or itchy skin around your girly bits.

How you get them   They can be due to many things, including dermatitis (or eczema), tinea, psoriasis and vulvodynia (a painful condition of the vulva). The most likely condition is a common skin rash, but it could be more serious so always ask a doctor to check.

Signs and symptoms   Can include itchiness, broken skin, stinging, swelling, redness, lumps, scaly bits, pain or an abnormal discharge.

How you know you have one   A doctor can often tell by looking, or a lab analyses a discharge sample or outer skin cells gently collected by a doctor or nurse.

Effects   Most skin conditions will have no long-term effects, but some can be symptoms of a more serious illness.

Treatment   Usually ointments or creams, either prescribed by a doctor or bought over the counter from a chemist.

Smear tests

The smear test checks for changes on your cervix (that spongy bit between the top of your vagina and the uterus opening – see the Change chapter) that can lead to cervical cancer without treatment. It's also called a pap smear or pap test. They're usually done by the practice nurse at your GP's surgery or health centre, or sometimes by the GP. They're also available at family planning clinics and sexual health (GUM) clinics.

Current NHS policy says you don't need to have smear tests in your teens. Cervical cancer is very rare in young women, so you probably won't have your first smear test until you're in your twenties, but this policy may change.

In England, women usually get a letter from their GP or Primary Care Trust (PCT) telling them to book an appointment for a smear test just before they turn 25; in the rest of the UK, it's usually 20. If you think you could have come into contact with somebody who could have come into contact with the HPV virus (there may be no symptoms, or there may be warts on the genitals), ask your GP for advice about a smear test, or go to a sexual health clinic.

Once you start having smear tests, the NHS will call you back for another one every three years. Most forms of cervical cancer are caused by variations of the human papilloma virus (HPV), a sexually transmitted infection. There is now a new injection that will prevent most forms of cervical cancer (see "Immunization" earlier), but to be safe women still need to have regular smear tests. A smear test will only guard against cervical cancer, not ovarian or other cancers.

What happens during a smear test   It's best to have a smear test in the middle of your menstrual cycle (between your periods) if possible, but it's better to have one at any time than not at all. The test only takes five minutes or less from beginning to end.

- ⊙ You take off everything on your lower half, including your undies, and hop onto the couch in the nurse's or doctor's office.
- ⊙ The nurse or doctor will ask you to lie with your knees bent and your legs spread apart, but your feet together.
- ⊙ The nurse or doctor will put a little lubricating jelly on a sterilized instrument called a speculum, which they will carefully push into the very start of your vagina, and then gently open it to hold the walls of the vagina apart a little. Because your vagina is very stretchy, this shouldn't hurt, but it may feel odd and uncomfortable.
- ⊙ Then they will push a long, thin plastic stick (with no sharp ends) inside you, use it to gently swipe off a couple of cervix cells, then pull it out carefully and transfer the cells to a slide to be analysed by a laboratory. Again it can feel odd, but shouldn't hurt. Very occasionally afterwards there is a tiny amount of spotting or bleeding.

Smear test result   If the result shows you need treatment or another check-up, the doctor or nurse will contact you to let you know. Sometimes people need to have the test again because the result was unclear, but usually there's nothing wrong. If the test shows everything's fine, you just need to come back for your next test three years later (your doctor or clinic will usually send you a reminder if you forget to book an appointment yourself).

More info on girls' and women's health

See also the teen and NHS sites in "More info on managing your health" earlier and the "More info" sections in the Change and Sex chapters.

www.bbc.co.uk/health
Choose "Women's health" for all sorts of info on women's bodies and health issues; also has an A–Z of common illnesses.

www.fpa.org.uk
The Family Planning Association has info on your body, vaginal infections, sexual health, pregnancy and contraception. Read their information leaflets, search for a particular issue, go to "Find a clinic" to get services in your area, or call their helpline: **0845 122 8690** (or **0845 122 8687** in N. Ireland).

www.breakthrough.org.uk
The Breakthough Breast Cancer charity site. Choose "About breast cancer" for info on breast awareness and what to look out for.

www.womens-health-concern.org
Women's Health Concern (WHC) is a charity that offers advice and support on women's health. Choose "Help and advice", then "Health information" for fact sheets on girly health issues like breast checks, common infections and endometriosis. You can also email their nurses for confidential medical advice.

www.womenshealthlondon.org.uk
Site with useful online booklets about smear tests, periods, HPV, thrush and other problems of the girly bits.

www.youngwomenshealth.org
US site of the Boston Children's Hospital Centre for Young Women's Health.

MIND HEALTH

Although "mental health" (the usual term for mind health) sounds a bit strange, **it's a good thing**. It means you're feeling optimistic, capable, confident and pretty happy about life, and that you can deal with most problems and **keep things in perspective** (not feeling utterly furious or bursting into tears because you broke a fingernail).

Good mental health allows you to cope pretty well with the stress that everyone experiences, have **fairly stable emotions** rather than wild mood swings, and react rationally to things, which helps keep relationships from turning into confusion and fighting.

Mental health problems

It's normal to feel down, overwhelmed or sad sometimes, especially as a teenager, and most people have
the skills to bounce back after a "low". The Feelings
chapter talked about how being moody is part of
growing up. Feeling angry, confused, powerless, worried about schoolwork or friends, stressed, anxious,
unhappy – most of us go through these emotions, sometimes without really knowing why. This
doesn't mean we're mentally ill.

> Self-harm and depression
> has become such a huge
> epidemic and a lot of girls
> who do it feel like freaks, or
> like they are the only person
> doing it, and don't know
> how to stop.
> Emma, 17

But these feelings can get out of control, seem like they're ruling our
life, and be a symptom of a mental health problem that we need to have assessed and
then get some help to fix.

Getting help for mental health problems

Mental health authorities estimate that about one in five people will experience a mental health problem in their lives. For most people it can be just a stage in their life that
they overcome with time and good support. There are lots of ways available now to
recover from or manage a mental health problem, and the earlier you get onto it the
better.

A good idea is to start by talking to your parents, a friend, a relative, a friend's parent,
your doctor, a teacher or school counsellor, or even a confidential helpline counsellor.
Some local councils also have youth officers who can refer you for help.

It's important to have a professional assessment so you know what you are dealing
with. A doctor can refer you to a counsellor (therapist) or a psychologist who is trained
in talking about mental health problems and helping people work out strategies to
overcome them.

Only a psychiatrist – a medical doctor who has specialized in problems of the brain
and mind – or a specialist psychologist can diagnose a mental illness (see "Mental Illness" coming up).

Don't be afraid to try another specialist if the first one doesn't work out for you. Go
back to your GP and ask for another recommendation.

FACT

Mental health websites   Websites can be useful places to get
information, but a lot of it may be wrong, simply ill-informed opinion
or out of date. So find a big, reputable, local mental health site that's
updated often, such as mind.org.uk (see "More Info" coming up soon).

There are a range of options for treating mind health problems, including:

- talking therapy (counselling)
- cognitive therapy – learning strategies to manage or change feelings and reactions
- possibly drugs (which can only be prescribed by a doctor or a psychiatrist)
- alternative treatments as part of a combined medical approach (these might include yoga, relaxation techniques, vitamins and herbal preparations) – but you need to tell your doctor which ones you are using or have used.

All treatments for mental health problems take time. There'll be good days and bad days and some steps backwards, but you'll know you're heading in the right direction.

Some facts about mental illness

- ✳ These days we know that having a mental illness is common and nothing to be ashamed of.

- ✳ Mental illness has happened throughout history, in all countries, to all sorts of people.

- ✳ Somebody with a mental illness can't just "pull themselves together". The illness is not their fault. Something is out of balance in their brain.

- ✳ With help, most people can find ways to control and live with, or recover from, a mental illness.

Mental illness

A mental illness is at the serious end of mind health problems and needs specialist medical help. Mental illnesses that teenagers can experience range from severe anxiety, major depression, bipolar disorder (huge ups and downs), obsessions (with eating, body image or other things), and self-harm, through to the rarer psychosis (not being able to tell what's real from what isn't).

Most mental illnesses cause a person to be unable to keep things in perspective. For example, a depressed person will think nothing is ever going to be fun or interesting again; a person with anorexia may think they're "fat" when they're dangerously thin; and a person suffering from psychosis may believe they can hear voices.

To the person with the mental illness, these things are absolutely real. They are not pretending, or just trying to be special or different.

What causes a mental illness?   Mental illness is frequently associated with an imbalance in brain chemicals. Often the trigger for the first episode of mental illness is some kind of stress: family trouble, severe illness or other worries, perhaps social or financial. It's now known that alcohol and illegal drugs can also trigger a mental illness in somebody

Who to tell about a mental illness

There is such a high level of ignorance in the world about mental health that you may want to keep a mental illness to yourself – not because it's shameful, but just because you don't want to be "labelled" or feel like answering questions about it. Your doctor and family will have to know so they can help and support you. You can make the decision together about who to tell, and who can help share your worries.

with a predisposition (see the Drinking and Drugs chapters). Some people may have the predisposition but it is never set off, perhaps because they avoid drugs, have a personality that minimizes stress or are just lucky.

Does mental illness "run in the family"? Some people have a family history of mental illness, and this can make them more predisposed to mental illness themselves. The predisposition may never become an illness, but is more likely to if there's a trigger such as severe stress or drug use. Most people with mentally ill relatives never develop the illness themselves.

Diagnosis of mental illness   Your doctor, and the psychiatrist you're referred to, will talk to you about:

○ what you are thinking and feeling
○ your medical or psychological symptoms
○ things such as your relationship with your family and how you're going at school or work.

Perhaps after two or three visits to the psychiatrist you'll be given a diagnosis – in other words a name for your problem – and some ideas about what treatment might be most useful. (Sometimes the diagnosis varies depending on the psychiatrist.)

At first for some people it is a little scary getting a diagnosis because it means you have a recognized problem. But it's also a huge relief: "I have recognized symptoms, and now I can get help to manage my problem."

Living with someone who has a mental illness

Living (or being friends) with someone who has a mental health problem can be hard, disruptive and even heartbreaking at times. When they're struggling it can be very difficult for you to know what to do or say.

Often it can seem as if the attention is on them all the time, and that no one is thinking about what you need. This can leave you feeling angry and frustrated, and maybe then guilty and upset. But it's normal to feel these things.

If it's a parent who is having trouble sometimes the kids are expected to take on all responsibility. If you have a single parent who is mentally ill it is a good idea to try to find another adult who you trust, to talk to and to help you out with day-to-day things when needed. *You* deserve support and help too (see "More Info" below).

More info on mental health problems

www.mind.org.uk
Mind are one of the better-known mental health charities (you might know them already thanks to their charity shops). There's loads of helpful info and advice on the site to download and also a handy postcode search that'll help you find more help local to you.

www.sane.org.uk
SANE is one of the UK's biggest mental health charities. Their site has lots of clear information about specific problems and conditions. SANE also offers confidential advice. You can email questions, which will be answered within five days. The helpline is open from 6am to 11pm, daily: 0845 767 8000.

www.childrenfirst.nhs.uk
Click through to "Teens" and then "Mental Health" to unearth a wealth of information. Within the "Real stories" section you can listen to podcast recordings from other teenagers who live with mental illness.

www.youngminds.org.uk
From the main page, click on "young people". There's lots of great advice, real life stories and quick facts for teenagers.

www.samaritans.org
Aside from offering the UK's most famous helpline, The Samaritans have some useful help filed away under "Your Emotional Health". **Helpline: 0845 7909 090**

www.mentalhealth.org.uk
This is a great site with loads of info on specifics, such as food, anger, alcohol, exercise, and how they affect your mental health.

My friend became anorexic on a diet. I hate them.   Mina, 15

My brother has got a brain injury and my mother has manic depression. I'm a young carer so that takes up my time.   Mary, 17

Depression

Diagnosed depression is different from the odd day of feeling "blue" and a bit down that everyone experiences, and which the Feelings chapter talked about. People who are seriously depressed often lose interest in everything and have no hope that things will ever get better. Being severely depressed is like having all the lows and none of the highs of life, as if someone pulled a plug at the bottom of your mind and let all the fun run out.

Almost everybody will know somebody who goes through periods of depression.

> I have depression, so often I struggle to stay positive and keep going. I am sad when I get bad marks for schoolwork, or when I fail at anything I give a decent shot at. Anything as small as a fight makes me really upset because I tend to worry about the worst that could happen.
> Isabel, 16

Warning signs of severe depression

People who are severely depressed may:

- ✪ feel "empty" or "numb" inside; be angry, irritable or sad all or most of the time; cry a lot; and lose their temper over what other people would think were small things

- ✪ believe they are ugly, wrong, useless and unlovable

- ✪ lose interest in everything they usually like (favourite foods, school, work, hobbies, sports, friends, family), have no energy, and feel really tired all the time and that they can't be bothered doing anything

- ✪ have trouble with sleep – usually wanting to sleep most of the time, or perhaps not getting much but instead lying awake worrying or feeling blank

- ✪ be unable to concentrate, remember things or finish tasks

- ✪ experience the bad feelings for days, weeks or even months

- ✪ have recurring or constant thoughts about dying or what it would be like to die, or think everyone would be better off if they were dead (see "Suicide" later in this chapter).

What causes depression?

There usually isn't one cause of depression but rather a combination of things beyond a person's control, which pushes them over the line. Sometimes it's not obvious what the cause might have been.

Contributing factors may include:

- ✪ an imbalance of brain chemicals – the mood-regulating chemicals may be all over the place

Depression can feel like 'nothing'

Bipolar disorder

Bipolar disorder (formerly called manic depression) is a kind of mental illness known as a mood disorder. It's made worse by drug and alcohol use.

A person with bipolar disorder has wild, seemingly random mood swings, with very down and listless periods and high, or "manic", madly busy ones. The swings can happen within a period of days, or one phase (high or low) can take over for weeks or even months.

High phases

During a manic period a person may:

✱ not sleep much

✱ have grand ideas and a sense of superiority

✱ rush into wild projects and actions that make no sense to anybody else

✱ behave recklessly, over-spending and acting out of character

✱ even experience psychosis so that they are not able to tell what's real and what's a delusion.

⑤ drugs or alcohol, usually with repeated use
⑤ a stressful or traumatic event such as trouble in the family, abuse, continual bullying or the death of somebody close
⑤ a recurring or chronic illness
⑤ a family history of mental illness.

Treatment for depression

Depending on your symptoms, these treatments can be combined or used separately:

⑤ counselling, with practical advice on strategies and coping
⑤ drugs to correct the brain chemical imbalance.

One of my closest friends now has depression and it's really, really painful for me to watch her go through this.   Samantha, 15

Depression is common. Some girls (me) are too scared to tell anyone and just paint on a happy face.

People in society have got to accept that some people aren't keeping up.   Anisha, 16

More info on depression

Childline: 0800 1111

sane.org.uk
Fact sheets on depression, and other help.
Helpline: 0845 767 8000.

youngminds.org.uk
Look here for loads of good info about
bipolar disorders and practical advice on
managing depression.

beyondblue.org
This Australian site has fact sheets on
various problems and info on help, as well
as a useful "Symptom checklist".

depressionalliance.org
Loads of help here covering all aspects and
forms of depression.

overcomedepression.co.uk
Learn more about depression and ways of
dealing with it. A good site for finding strategies
to help friends and family members who suffer
from depression.

I had depression – that affected me loads. I became paranoid and self-obsessed,
because in my head, everyone in the world was out to get me. It affected every part of
my life, and I was suicidal for a bit. My mum dragged me to counsellors and in the end
I went on drugs to help me get through it. I'm glad I did. Now I know how hard it is for
people in the same situation, and so I try my very best to be there for others and to
raise awareness among peers and adults that depression is an illness, not a sign
of a bad person.   Ellie, 18

I got heavily bullied in primary school because my dad is wealthy and the other
kids were jealous. I became very depressed and tried to hide my wealth by wearing
un-expensive clothes and not bringing flash toys to school.   Anonymous, 14

One of the perks (I like to look at it like that) of being diagnosed with depression is that
I have my own counsellor and I can sit in there and talk to her about me for an hour or
more straight, which is very therapeutic.   Bessie, 16

Severe anxiety

It's normal and sometimes even helpful to feel anxious about exams, a sports event or performing in a play. But severe anxiety gets in the way of enjoying life. It can be a feeling of possible imminent disaster or an overwhelming sense of worry, fear or embarrassment. It can include symptoms such as:

- ⑤ faster breathing and heartbeat
- ⑤ trembling and sweating
- ⑤ having to rush to the toilet all the time
- ⑤ feeling "frozen" – unable to move or talk.

Some anxiety disorders

Severe anxiety includes a number of disorders, which share some of the symptoms just listed but also have particular feelings and behaviours.

> I used to have panic attacks from getting worried so much. I don't get as worried but I do get worried mostly over tiny things like my maths teacher expects me to finish five pages in one night. People might say something like: "Don't do that, you'll get radiation poisoning and die!" At night I worry the most.
> Jessica, 13

Panic attacks   If anxious feelings get worse they can turn into panic attacks – sudden feelings of terror or complete weirdness. Sometimes a place or situation will cause one: for example, going over a bridge or being caught up in a crowd.

During a panic attack a person may feel:

- ⑤ their heart beating rapidly
- ⑤ dizzy
- ⑤ short of breath
- ⑤ sick in the stomach
- ⑤ disconnected from reality or "out of body", as though they've lost control of their body and mind.

Obsessive compulsive disorder (OCD)   With OCD the anxiety results in repeated thoughts or actions, which the person can't stop no matter how much they want to. Common repetitive behaviour can be many things, including:

- ⑤ washing hands
- ⑤ knocking a number of times before entering any room
- ⑤ counting things.

Post-traumatic stress disorder   A terrible or sad event can cause anxiety-related symptoms, including:

- "flashbacks" (sudden interrupting memories of the event)
- nightmares
- fear of the event happening again.

Trichotillomania   People with this form of anxiety pull their hair out by twisting, tugging or plucking: it can be the hair on their head, or their eyebrows or eyelashes.

> I think I might worry about food poisoning more than anything else. I worry not that something will happen to the people I love, but more that something already has and they haven't told anyone about it.
> Sarah, 18

Treatment for anxiety

If you feel anxious, see your GP. People who tend to become severely anxious usually need professional help to make changes in their life, and to become less shy, if that's what they want.

If you have an anxiety disorder

- Your GP should be able to refer you to a specialist or counsellor who can help.
- You may have cognitive behaviour therapy – talking about new strategies is usually very helpful.
- You may also find that medication is useful.

More info on severe anxiety

sane.org.uk
For fact sheets and other help.
Helpline: 0845 767 8000.

anxietyuk.org.uk
From the main page, choose "Young People and Anxiety": this site covers many forms of anxiety and fears (called phobias).

nomorepanic.co.uk
Lots of info on feeling worried or anxious, as well as suggestions for treatments and ways to cope.

dascot.org
The Scottish wing of the Depression Alliance has loads of online help and links to local contacts who can help.

> I always worry that I have something stuck to me!! I get so paranoid that people will stare at me because of it.   Suze, 13

Eating disorders

Eating disorders are not just about being concerned with food, being "vain" or going a bit too far with diets. They are complicated mental disorders that also affect the body.

Disordered eating behaviours are driven by emotions. They usually begin with thinking about weight, dieting, food control or exercise, and are accompanied by anxieties such as guilt, obsessive thoughts and a sense of being out of control. People who have an eating disorder are very unhappy, whatever their weight or size.

Disordered eating includes having very strict rules about foods and a wide range of unusual or otherwise odd behaviours – basically food weirdness. These can include:

- repeated dieting
- talking and obviously thinking about food a lot
- increased or obsessive monitoring of food (for example, checking fat content and kilojoules on all food labels)
- lying about not being hungry or having eaten already
- compulsive and strenuous exercising to lose weight
- trips to the toilet after or during eating, to try to purge food
- eating huge amounts or tiny amounts (sometimes restricting food to starvation levels)
- trying to ignore hunger or welcoming it
- drinking water before every meal, or instead of eating, to try to "fill up"
- taking "health" ideas to the extreme, such as aiming for no fat, instead of less fat; or only eating fruit and veg, instead of including proteins and carbohydrates
- only eating one sort of food
- only eating some meals
- using food as a reward
- inventing eating rituals, such as only eating in the same spot or with a certain spoon.

Other warning signs that someone has an eating disorder can be:

- weight changes
- fainting, tummy pain or headaches
- mood swings
- increased anxiety, depression, sadness or crankiness
- intense shame about their body image (often they wear baggy clothes to cover up), or guilt after eating
- involvement in elite athletics, ballet, gymnastics, modelling or another pursuit that focuses on body shape, weight or size

> I was diagnosed with anorexia at 13, but have since come the full cycle and now I binge eat and throw up everything.
> Emma, 16

⊙ they're a celebrity or a person who is constantly examined or commented on.

The two biggest risk factors for an eating disorder are low self-esteem and dieting. Disordered eating can start with a confidence problem, and be triggered by harsh self-criticism or unkind comments by somebody else – often a family member – about body shape or size. Girls don't usually choose to develop an eating disorder, but choosing to go on diets, restricting foods, making rules about eating or rigidly controlling food intake does make a disorder much more likely to develop.

The most common eating disorder   Known as "Eating Disorder Not Otherwise Specified", the most common eating disorder is a level of odd behaviour that includes some or many of the signs just listed, but is not full-on anorexia, bulimia or binge eating (explained below), although it might include a milder form of one of them, such as repeated dieting.

These dieting and food obsessions can be seen by some friendship groups and families as normal, but they are not normal and not healthy.

Anorexia nervosa

This is one of the most visible eating disorders because the person with anorexia eats as little as possible and often becomes very thin, haggard and bony. Eventually they look and are very, very sick. Anorexia often begins in the early to mid teens. People with the disorder usually have a very disturbed body image, seeing themselves as "fat", even when dangerously underweight.

At any weight anorexia causes severe sadness, self-loathing and an obsession with food and sometimes over-exercise. Signs of anorexia, apart from weight loss, are usually not obvious, but can include:

⊙ tiredness
⊙ dizziness when the person stands up
⊙ stomach pain and headaches
⊙ stopped periods.

Long-term effects can include:

⊙ stunted growth
⊙ an inability to become pregnant
⊙ easily broken bones
⊙ heart or other organ failure.

If you see someone you know losing weight really fast do something about it before it is too late. Don't tell them they look good. Tell them they are unhealthy and will get very sick and tell someone who you can trust. It is a mental disease, not something to tease them about or to join in on.
Lisa, 17

We're doing eating disorders in school and sometimes I wish I could just lose that much weight and look like a model. Eleanor, 14

Few people with anorexia actually die from it, and the majority can recover when they get help (see "Treatment for eating disorders" coming up). But most people with anorexia won't seek help themselves – it takes intervention from family and friends to move somebody towards treatment and recovery. Parents and friends will need to guard against online sites (and "friends") that encourage the illness.

Helping someone with an eating disorder

If some of these warning signs remind you of a friend or family member, ask the person whether they would like some help or information. Eating disorders support groups all have info and advice on how to approach a friend or relative you think may have a problem with eating (see "More info" coming up).

Bulimia nervosa

Bulimia nervosa is more common than anorexia nervosa, and also more hidden. Often it begins in the late teens or early twenties.

Bulimia is a cycle of binge eating (eating a lot more than the person needs), guilt and purging. Girls who develop it often have a history of dieting or restricting their food. Eventually they give in to cravings and eat what they think of as "bad" food – usually lots of it. They then feel ashamed of "losing control" and worried about gaining weight, so they try to get rid of the food by purging.

Purging efforts can include vomiting, over-exercising, fasting (not eating) and taking laxatives. None of these methods really works because the body has already taken in at least half of what it needs from the food before vomiting or pooing happens. Fasting as self-punishment just means the hunger will eventually tip into another binge.

As well as the feelings of shame and being trapped, bulimia can cause:

- ᏻ stomach and bowel problems
- ᏻ damaged teeth (because vomiting carries stomach acids into the mouth)
- ᏻ dangerous heart problems.

But the good news is that many, many girls recover from bulimia.

FACT

Not a "girls only" problem   There's so much publicity about eating disorders and young actresses that lots of people think only girls develop this problem, but guys and older women can too.

Binge-eating disorder

Binge-eating disorder is similar to bulimia. The difference is that people with binge-eating disorder don't try to purge the food and are often above a healthy weight. Bingeing becomes a way of dealing with their negative or difficult emotions. They often eat alone and feel ashamed of the amount they've had and of feeling out of control.

Treatment for eating disorders

People with an eating disorder need to be treated by a specialist doctor with experience in the area. The ones with the best chance of recovering are those who ask for help or are given help as early as possible – but part of the mental illness is that the sick person may not want treatment.

If you have an eating disorder   The most important thing to understand is that you can recover – but not by yourself.

Here are some steps to recovery.

- The first is to ask your local doctor for a referral to a specialist in eating disorders, if that's possible. You may have combined help from a psychiatrist or a psychologist, a dietician, and a specialist eating-behaviours counsellor. The help will usually be regular and ongoing, and may include attending special programs such as group therapy.
- Contact an eating disorders support group or foundation for help. It's a great place to start to talk with people who are going through the same thing (or have already been through it), so they can understand and support you while you decide what you're going to do, and afterwards. (To contact one see "More info" coming up.)
- Medicine may be prescribed to help change your feelings of depression or to correct chemical imbalances.
- You may need a stay in hospital for treatment if you are very sick.

Recovering from an eating disorder is often a long and hard road, but there's a much calmer place at the end of it, where people can declare a truce in the war against their body and find a way not to think about food all the time.

More info on eating disorders

b-eat.co.uk
Beat is the largest UK eating disorder charity.
The website has loads of info in the dedicated
FYP ("For Young People") section, and there's
loads of advice and links on finding help and
support.
Beat Youthline: 0845 634 7650.

nhsdirect.nhs.uk
NHS Direct has loads of info online as well as
on the phone.
NHS Direct health line: 0845 46 47

youthinformation.com
Buried in the "Health" section, this site has
some good info and links to more resources.

kidshealth.org/teen
Lots of general advice on diet and an in-depth
look at eating disorders.

childline.org.uk
The site's "Eating problems" section is very
useful, with lots of good info. There's also the
helpline for one-to-one advice:
Phone: 0800 1111

I first started myself out on a low-calorie diet. But things just declined from there.
I became extremely obsessed with losing weight and eating less/losing extra weight
by the day. I was admitted to hospital 6 times in the matter of a year and a half.
I'm still struggling today. Don't make the mistake I did.   Caroline, 18

I am recovering from an eating disorder which is a very difficult road. It has been tricky
because it did not spawn from any perception of myself as "fat" or "overweight". I think it
has been more about control and a fear of growing up, for me.   Mina, 18

I've had bulimia for about 3 years and even though I am aware of this and understand
that it's a sickness and everything, I do not want to change it. I am terrified of getting fat
and even though I'm at my healthy weight I'd still like to lose more.   Karen, 17

I learnt the hard way that the only person my weight matters to should be me.
I was anorexic.   Tanya, 16

Self-harm

Sometimes people deliberately hurt themselves, usually in secret, and try to hide any marks with their clothes. Examples of self-harm include cutting, burning, hitting, scratching or biting parts of the body, or using drugs or alcohol to put themselves in danger.

Self-harm is usually a way of trying to cope with painful or difficult feelings – often because the person finds it hard to put their feelings into words or to ask for help. It's most common in the mid to late teens and early twenties.

> Self-harm. I have been doing this for the last five years and it has only been in the last month that I have been able to talk to anyone about it, and this only was by chance. Encourage people to talk to someone about their problems.
> Lydia, 17

Treatment for self-harm

If you harm yourself:

- ⚷ it's very important that you see your GP for a referral to a psychiatrist or a psychologist who specializes in this problem
- ⚷ talking therapy can help you to change the way you think and to find strategies so that self-harm does not become a habit or the usual way you deal with something. Many girls have great success with talking therapy.

More info on self-harm

www.samaritans.org
Online info and someone to call.
Helpline: 0845 790 9090

www.harmless.org.uk
This voluntary organization has lots of info and personal stories from young people and their families about self-harm. A DVD is available featuring some real young people with a history of self-harm, and some professionals giving helpful advice.

www.sane.org.uk
Online info and other help.
Helpline: 0845 767 8000

www.selfharm.org.uk
Run by the National Children's Bureau, this site has tons of info and practical help.

> My brothers would pick on me and sometimes my parents would fight. I just thought I was worthless and nobody loved me. I'd run to my room and cry. Then I started cutting myself when nobody would come to my rescue.   Georgina, 17

Suicide

Lots of teenagers think about what it might be like if they were dead, but most of them won't try to kill themselves.

Most people who commit suicide believe, always wrongly, that they are doing the best thing. If teenagers succeed in dying they never find out how great the future could have been, or how devastated their family and friends are by their death – how haunted they are by guilt and sadness, sometimes for the rest of their lives. Lots of people think about committing suicide but don't carry it out, and are happy later that they didn't.

Suicide is never the right answer.

Worried about a friend or family member?

If you are worried that a friend or family member might try to commit suicide tell a calm, sensible adult you trust. Your friend or family member may insist you don't tell anybody, but it's more important to help save their life than keep a secret. You can also ring a helpline for advice (see "More info" opposite).

If you are having suicidal thoughts

You need to know that the thoughts:

- are a sign that your mind is not quite right at the moment, even though the thoughts seem logical to you
- can be caused by sleep deprivation
- are just thoughts – they don't mean you have to act them out
- won't go away with drugs and alcohol – these usually make them worse
- can be changed and won't always be there, even if you have them again, or a few times, or for a while. It may not seem that way, but you *can* be happy again.

Getting help

You have lots of options.

- Talk about your thoughts with someone. If they dismiss them, talk to somebody else. School counsellors, doctors, nurses and helpline staff are experienced in talking about this stuff.
- Promise yourself you'll never do anything at night to harm yourself, but instead will wait for the next day and talk it over with somebody: problems always seem harder at night.
- To get you through a bad night, call a friend, listen to music that's optimistic, or ring a 24-hour helpline (see "More info" below).

⚬ Talk to your GP or local health centre staff, who will know how to help you find ways to get to a happier place in your mind. Your doctor can refer you to a psychologist or a psychiatrist.

⚬ Try coping strategies, which can include making a list of things you can distract yourself with when you have suicidal thoughts; writing your thoughts and feelings down; setting small day-to-day goals that you can manage; and removing access to any dangerous items such as weapons or drugs.

More info on suicide

The Samaritans: 0845 790 9090
Ring 24 hours any day for help or a talk. You can ring anonymously.

childline.org.uk
The website has loads of info and help; they also provide someone to talk to, anytime about any problems or worries.
Childline: 0800 1111

papyrus-uk.org
This charity was set up to help prevent youth suicide. Its 24-hour helpline, called HOPEline UK, is on 0800 68 41 41. The website has lots of info and help. From the main page, under "Support When You Need It" choose "For You" to get immediate reassuring and useful info about your feelings and what you can do.

My friend is really depressed and he says that he wants to do things to hurt himself – this worries me a lot! Mandy, 13

A friend of mine told me she was going to kill herself then told me to keep it quiet. I told an adult at school and then my friend found out and said if she ever killed herself it would be my fault. I felt terrible but I would rather have a friend who hated me but was alive than a friend who still liked me and was dead. Holly, 17

Psychosis and schizophrenia

Psychosis (pronounced si-koh-sis) is a severe form of mental illness caused by a brain chemical imbalance, which mucks up a person's thoughts and causes them to be unable to tell reality from what's only happening in their mind. The most common time for the first "psychotic episode" to happen is in the late teens or early twenties, most often after a period of severe stress or using drugs, including cannabis (weed), speed, crystal meth (ice) or ecstasy. Schizophrenia (pronounced skitz-oh-freen-ee-a) is the most common psychotic illness.

Warning signs of psychosis

Psychotic symptoms can appear slowly and usually build up to a psychotic episode.

- ⑤ The person's ideas and conversations become stranger as time goes by.
- ⑤ During an episode a person with schizophrenia can see or hear things that aren't really there. They might try to make sense of it by thinking the voices are coming from a TV, or that another person is projecting or intercepting their thoughts. Other hallucinations can involve smell or visions. (Schizophrenia doesn't mean "split personality".)
- ⑤ Many people with schizophrenia also have delusions of being very important or having secret knowledge. Or they're afraid that someone or unseen forces are trying to hurt them. The delusions seem utterly real to the person having them.

Other signs can include:

- ⑤ a habit of pacing (walking back and forth)
- ⑤ complete withdrawal from family and friends
- ⑤ neglecting to wash or clean themselves
- ⑤ unusual sleeping patterns, such as sleeping in the day and being awake at night.

Treatment for psychosis

Somebody with symptoms of psychosis needs help quickly. Treatments are much better now than they used to be, and most people can recover well when they find the right treatment.

- ⑤ Many people with schizophrenia manage their condition by recognizing their need to take the right drugs, and take advantage of community services and rehabilitation programs. (Sadly sometimes a symptom of the illness can be rejecting the need for medication.)
- ⑤ Most people who have schizophrenia can learn to prevent psychotic episodes by avoiding their likely triggers (these include most illegal drugs, alcohol and stress). Many people with schizophrenia have "normal" family and work lives, like

anybody else. Statistically, someone with schizophrenia is far less likely to hurt someone else than themselves as part of their illness.

🌀 Sometimes a hospital stay is needed while the right drug combination is tested. There's no "magic" pill or pills for everyone.

More info on psychosis and schizophrenia

Ask your parents to take you to the doctor or speak to a school counsellor or chaplain if you think you have any symptoms described in this section.

The Samaritans: 0845 790 9090

www.childline.org.uk
Childline offer a 24-hour, 7-day a week helpline:
0800 1111

www.sane.org.uk
The national charity's one-stop shop for fact sheets and other help.
Helpline: 0845 767 8000.

Mental health

Mind health is like health in general – there are lots of things that you can do to maintain or improve it.

Self-help tips

These hints can help you enjoy life and get through any mind health problems.

- Talk about a problem and ask for help.
- Be around other people – keep communicating.
- Try to remember that bad thoughts are not necessarily true, but part of the problem or illness. Maybe you could make a poster or list to remind yourself of the good things about you and life.
- Have a routine so you don't have to think about some things such as what time to eat and go to bed.
- Eat a healthy diet (see the Food chapter). Your brain needs good food. A multi-vitamin supplement can be a useful idea.
- Exercise can help control mood swings and depression (see the Move chapter).
- Get more sleep – at the right times (see the "Sleep" section in the Brain chapter).
- Try some relaxation techniques such as meditation or yoga. Your local library, gym or community centre noticeboard should have details of classes, or you can find a website.
- Avoid smoking, drugs not prescribed for you, and alcohol.
- Keep a diary – it will help you see how your moods change.

Above all, always be kind to yourself. How would you treat a best friend going through a difficult time?

Five affirmations to say to yourself

1. "Like thousands of people who live with their mental illness successfully, I can control and manage my mental health."

2. "If one theory or possible solution doesn't help, it's not me that's failed, it's the theory or so-called solution that's failed me. I can try another one."

3. "New research, medication and other treatments are being developed all the time."

4. "For most people a mental health problem is only temporary."

5. "By acknowledging a problem I've already started work on fixing it."

PREGNANCY

? **22**

positive pregnancy test ←

what are your options?

There are lots of ways of saying somebody is pregnant: they've "fallen pregnant" (as if it was caused by tripping over a crack in the pavement), "got a bun in the oven" or "conceived" (the traditional word); or they're "up the duff", "in the family way" or even "in trouble" (the old-fashioned phrase).

Most teenage girls don't **want** to get pregnant, but thousands do each year, mostly because they didn't use contraception. This chapter explains the options open to pregnant girls so that if you need to you can make an **informed decision** about what to do. This is one of the most serious decisions anybody makes in their whole life. There may be a mix of strong emotions, including relief, guilt and regret, whatever you choose to do.

Being pregnant

You can get pregnant *only* if a guy ejaculates or a little pre-ejaculate semen leaks from the tip of his erect penis. But wait – pregnancy won't happen if he's on the other side of the room. Either his penis has to be in you at the time, or somehow his semen has to get near enough to your vagina for a sperm to wriggle up to a fallopian tube and fertilize an egg there. You'd have to be fairly unlucky for this to happen if he doesn't actually "come" inside you, but it is possible, and any sperm inside you do stay able to impregnate you for up to a week.

You can't get pregnant from any other form of sexual activity, such as thinking sexual thoughts, masturbation, kissing, sexual touching, oral sex, swallowing sperm, anal sex – or from toilet seats, wishing you were pregnant, having irregular or missed periods if you've never had sex, or anything else you can imagine.

Common signs of pregnancy

Some people have no idea they're pregnant; others have a feeling there's something different. There are some early signs but not everyone has these, and some people might get certain ones and not others. Getting a bigger tummy only happens much, *much* later in a pregnancy and you'll need to know a long time before that.

Pregnancy symptoms can include:

- ☺ a period doesn't arrive (it's very rare to have periods while you're pregnant)
- ☺ instead of your period you get a light spotting of blood, which could be a signal that an egg is implanting itself in your uterus
- ☺ you've missed a couple of periods (but don't wait this long to do a pregnancy test – missing one period is enough to suggest you're pregnant)
- ☺ your breasts are sore – they might be slightly swollen and tender, and the nipples or areola (area around the nipples) could get larger or darker in colour
- ☺ you start to feel sick in the stomach (nausea) or actually throw up ("morning sickness" can affect you at any time of the day)
- ☺ you have "stomach" cramps – many women say that the early days of pregnancy feel a lot like getting a period, which can make it hard to tell the difference
- ☺ you need to wee a lot – some women feel the need to wee much more when they are pregnant
- ☺ you're more tired than usual.

How to find out if you're pregnant

If you have one or more of the symptoms listed above or you suspect you may be pregnant, the best thing to do is to take a pregnancy test. Even if you have irregular periods and you're not usually worried about a missed one, do a test as soon as possible if you've had unprotected sex (without a condom or other contraception).

You can get tests from the chemist or some large supermarkets for around £5 to £10. These are very accurate and can sometimes show whether you are pregnant a couple of days before your period is even due. If you get a "negative" result after a missed period, do another test ten days later to be sure. Most people find it hard to trust just the one test so do another to confirm the result – it usually works out cheaper to buy two tests in the one packet than two separate tests.

> *I often fear that I may be pregnant, possibly because I am not fully aware and educated about the ways in which one can get pregnant.*
> Amber, 18

These tests usually involve weeing on a plastic stick. Follow the instructions and wee carefully. If there is a pregnancy hormone in your urine (wee) you'll get a "positive" result: usually a little window or line on the stick changes colour. You can also get a pregnancy test done for free at a local GP's surgery, contraception or young people's clinic, or a family planning clinic.

If the test shows you're pregnant

If the home test result is "positive", go to the doctor's, a family planning clinic or a contraception or young people's clinic in the next day or so. (Anything you tell them is in confidence.) Don't delay, no matter how confused or worried you feel. You may hope the problem will go away – it won't. Or you may believe that your parents will be angry when they find out – they may or may not be angry, but will definitely find out if you delay.

Going to a doctor, family planning clinic or young people's clinic means you can have important questions answered. And you must go straight away to be able to choose from the full range of options available. You can also anonymously call one of the counselling services listed under "Unbiased pregnancy counselling" further on.

Many girls who don't realize at first that they are pregnant, who are pregnant as a result of sexual assault, or who are too frightened to tell their family can end up far along in a pregnancy before they get help and won't have as many choices available to them.

Your options   If you are pregnant you have three options: to have the baby and be its mother; to have the baby and give it up for adoption; or to end the pregnancy by having a termination (also called an abortion) in a safe, professional medical way. You will have to make a deci-

You need to make a big decision pretty quickly

sion fairly quickly because after a short time a termination is no longer possible.

There isn't one option out of the three that you "must" choose. The important thing is to decide for yourself. None of the available decisions is likely to make you totally happy, and each option needs a lot of thought and talking through. To help you, the three are fully explained a bit later in this chapter.

Motherhood, which can be wonderful, isn't for everybody at every time of their life. Being a mum is too difficult, emotional, full-on and complicated a job to be compulsory, especially for a teenager. You have the right to choose when or if you have children. Nobody should ever be forced or pressured to continue a pregnancy they don't want – and nobody should ever be forced or pressured to terminate a pregnancy that they do want.

Pregnancy counselling services

Pregnancy counsellors will help you explore your options: you can get a referral to one from your doctor; speak to one at a family planning clinic or young people's clinic; or find them through one of the organizations in "More info" at the end of this section. But you need to be very careful because many pregnancy counselling agencies deliberately don't tell you about all your options.

Some things to consider

You may feel you want to be a mother now, and that you can manage whatever happens because you have full family support.

or

You may feel you're not ready to be a mum yet and may want to finish your education and grow up more, believing that you'll be a better mum later if you wait.

You may be aware pregnancy can be a health risk for teenage girls, and think it would be better not to continue.

or

You may feel you're full of energy so you'll be able to cope with a baby.

You may not like the idea of giving a baby up for adoption because you wouldn't be there to protect it through life.

or

You may like the idea of giving a baby to a family who wants one very much.

You may believe for religious or ethical reasons that anything after fertilization of the egg is a baby, no matter how undeveloped, and should not be terminated.

or

You may believe that something so undeveloped and incapable of surviving outside the uterus is not yet a human being.

Biased counselling services Some pregnancy counselling agencies are affiliated with anti-abortion and church organizations. Their main aim is to stop you having a pregnancy termination even if that's what you want to do.

These services can have posters in doctors' waiting rooms and other public places, and they may operate pregnancy helplines. They don't say that they have religious or other biases against termination of pregnancy when you visit or call them. So if you want pregnancy counselling that doesn't try to make you choose a certain way, but lets you make up your own mind, don't continue with an agency or counsellor that doesn't acknowledge all the options, and see "More info" coming up for unbiased helplines.

Some of the lies told by anti-abortion counsellors include claims that an abortion, whether you have surgery or take a pill, will create many physical and mental health problems for you. Let's just clear up some of those lies.

⑥ A safe, medical termination will not make it hard or impossible for you to have a baby in the future.

⑥ Statistically, carrying a baby to full term is a much bigger health risk to the pregnant person than having a safe, medical termination.

⑥ Termination does *not* increase your risk of getting breast cancer or any other major health problem.

⑥ You can't get a sexually transmitted infection from a termination.

⑥ You will not automatically develop a mental illness because you've had an abortion, although any stressful time or event can contribute to mental health problems. Statistically, having a baby is more likely to trigger a mental health problem – post-natal depression.

⑥ Although some girls who feel they were forced into an abortion, for example by their parents, can feel great regret (often linked to feeling powerless to make their own decision), most girls and women who have one don't suffer from terrible regret and grief afterwards. Most think it was the right decision at that time, even though they were saddened that they had to make it.

⑥ Doctors and counsellors who believe in a woman's right to have an abortion do not insist on or recommend it to anybody who doesn't want one. "Pro-choice" people want abortion to be one of the options a woman can choose for herself.

> The info I have been given about not getting pregnant is to keep your underwear on.
> Tara, 14

Biased pregnancy counselling services may try to get you to see gruesome pictures or films to frighten you into not considering a pregnancy termination.

Unbiased pregnancy counselling Go to an NHS family planning clinic, contraception clinic or young people's clinic in your area; or contact Brook Advisory Centres (for young people under 25) or the Family Planning Association (FPA) for information and advice (see "More info" coming up).

Your GP (local doctor) or a doctor or nurse at your community health centre can also talk to you about your options or refer you to a pregnancy counselling service. Some GPs, because of their religious convictions, will try to convince you not to include abortion in your list of options. But offical guidelines say that doctors should not let their personal opinions affect their advice, and that they should let you see another unbiased doctor instead.

Any clinic that offers terminations should ask you to undergo some form of counselling first to make sure you have considered all your options.

When you're pregnant you have a right to confidential, non-judgemental care and respect for whichever option you choose. You need to decide, not be forced into it by your parents, church, teachers, friends, boyfriend or anybody else. Talking to people who care for you often helps. You could be surprised by how supportive your parents are.

You may feel alone. But there are lots of people who can help you...

More info on being pregnant

www.brook.org.uk
The non-profit making Brook Advisory Centres offer free, confidential advice, info and counselling to young people, including under 16s. Choose "The facts", then "Pregnancy" for information, or "Find a centre" to get help in your area.
Helpline: 0800 018 5023

www.fpa.org.uk
The Family Planning Association offer confidential, non-biased info and advice. Choose "Find a clinic".
Helpline (UK): 0845 122 8690
Helpline (Northern Ireland):
0845 122 8687

I have had cousins who have had babies in their teens and have seen how much hard work a baby is. Sasha, 18

www.nhsdirect.nhs.uk

The "Emergency contraception zone" on the NHS Direct site has info on pregnancy tests and teen pregnancies, and tells you where you can get impartial help and advice. The "Pregnancy and childbirth zone" has info on being pregnant and having a baby. You can also chat with an NHS Direct advisor online. **NHS Direct health line: 0845 46 47**

www.ruthinking.co.uk

Government-funded sex and relationships site for under 18s. Click on "Need help in a hurry", then "Find help in your area" to find local contraception, pregnancy and abortion services and young people's clinics.

www.sexetc.org

This US site has stories from pregnant girls, showing each making a different decision, plus other stuff on being pregnant. Some of the legal facts and all the helplines on the site aren't relevant to the UK.

www.yoursexhealth.org

From the home page of this Australian site, choose "Reproduction", then "Pregnancy" for info on tests, options and what to expect.

Pregnancy termination (abortion)

An average pregnancy lasts about forty weeks (about three school terms). The fertilized egg is known as an embryo (pronounced em-bree-o) for about the first ten weeks, after which it's often called a foetus (pronounced fee-tus) and then a baby when it's "viable" (able to survive outside the mum's uterus). Some very premature babies have survived after being born at about twenty-four weeks, or even earlier.

A surgical pregnancy termination, also called an abortion, happens well before that, usually between seven and twelve weeks. (How many weeks pregnant you are dates from the first day of the last period you had, not the day you "got pregnant"). A pregnancy can also be terminated with a pill that causes the tiny embryo to come out (this looks like a period) within the first nine weeks (see "The abortion pill" further on).

Many pregnant teenagers choose termination. (But teenagers make up a small percentage of the total number of people who choose to abort.) Abortion is legal and free through the NHS in England, Scotland and Wales. In Northern Ireland the situation is a little different, with abortions being illegal, except under "exceptional circumstances".

Having a termination is not an easy option, even if you're sure that's the best choice for you. Many people believe a termination is a decision not to be a "bad mother", but instead to become a good mother at another time.

Surgical termination

Either your GP, a Brook Advisory Centre (see "More info", coming up), or your local family planning, contraception or young people's clinics will be able to talk you through the options and refer you for a termination. If you choose confidentiality, your parents don't have to know about the termination. Doctors will agree to refer a girl under 16 for a termination without telling her parents, as long as she can make it clear she understands what's involved.

Surgical termination is usually a safe, simple, low-risk procedure for the pregnant person, but the longer you have been pregnant the trickier and more confronting it can be, and most surgeons much prefer to do it in the first thirteen weeks. Pregnancy terminations later than fourteen weeks are sometimes done, but are more complicated, and terminations are only ever carried out beyond twenty-four weeks in exceptional situations (for example if the pregnancy is making you seriously ill).

The operation   A surgical abortion is done at a clinic or a hospital. You lie on an operating table for the procedure, with your knees apart, and are given either a light general anaesthetic, so that you are asleep, or some tablets to

The anti-abortion versus pro-choice debate

Polls done by independent organisations show that the majority of people in the UK are "pro-choice": say it's a woman's right to choose whether or not to have an abortion during the early part of pregnancy.

Anti-abortion groups continue to try to persuade politicians to make abortion illegal or much harder to get in England, Scotland and Wales. In Northern Ireland abortion remains illegal because of the political influence of the Catholic Church, which opposes it.

Anti-abortion groups, who call themselves "pro-life", can say hurtful things about abortion (including calling it murder) and can have some very nasty tactics, including harassing people outside clinics where terminations are performed.

make you more relaxed and then a local anaesthetic so you don't feel any pain.

The most common type of surgical pregnancy termination, called a suction abortion (or sometimes a "vacuum aspiration"), "vacuums" out the contents of your uterus through the vagina, using a special tube. It only takes about 15 minutes, and you should be able to go home the same day.

Support before and after the operation   It helps to have someone in the waiting room to support you on the day, and to help you get home afterwards (even if you have a licence, you're not allowed to drive after having anaesthetic).

Before the procedure a health worker will talk you through the process and the risks – make sure you ask any questions you have then. If you're worried that you'll for-

Not an option   Trying a do-it-yourself termination can cause terrible pain and damage to you, it doesn't stay secret and very often doesn't end the pregnancy. Before legal abortion was available women's hospitals had whole wards dedicated to trying to look after women who had tried to terminate their pregnancy. Many of them died. It's important for you to know that you can now end a pregnancy without harming yourself.

get the questions, write them down beforehand and bring them along, or take a trusted adult in with you. This could also be a good time to talk about what method of contraception to use when having sex in the future.

After the op you'll be asked to make another appointment for a couple of weeks time to make sure everything is okay. If you feel really poorly or get a fever after the op, however, you should go back to the clinic or see your GP straight away. It might mean you have an infection in the uterus and need to take some antibiotic pills to sort things out.

Although you'll probably feel a big sense of relief after the op, other emotions after an abortion can include guilt, anger, confusion, sadness wondering "what might have been", or a mixture of all these, even if you're still sure you made the right decision. Hormones can be very unsettled for a week or two after a termination, which doesn't help. You may want to keep your termination a secret, or within your family. It's probably not a good idea to tell anyone who might not keep your confidence – it's your own business. If you need help sorting out your feelings, go to a community health centre or a family planning clinic or get a referral from your doctor to a non-judgemental counsellor.

The cost of a surgical termination   If you are referred for a termination by your NHS GP or a local sexual health clinic, it will cost you nothing to have the op. In many areas the NHS has its own clinics, or instead you could be referred for a free operation at a private clinic, such as those run by the Marie Stopes organization or the British Pregnancy Advisory Service (see "More info" coming up). Or you can go directly to a private clinic without a GP's referral, but this may cost about £500.

The "abortion pill"

A non-surgical way to end a pregnancy is to take the pill called RU486 (mifepristone). Also known as a "medical abortion", it is available as an option on the NHS in most parts of the UK, but even though it is a pill, it is not available as a prescription or in a chemist. Instead, you need a clinic or hospital referral directly from your doctor or family planning clinic (see "More info on being pregnant" earlier in this chapter).

RU486 is successful 95 percent of the time, but needs to be taken in the first nine weeks of pregnancy. The pill works by stopping the action of the hormone progesterone, which is needed to continue a pregnancy. It's used with another tablet (prostaglandin), which is placed in the vagina a couple of days later and causes the uterus to contract and helps the foetal tissue come out (it's like having a crampy period). RU486 is not the morning-after pill for emergency contraception, which has to be taken within three days of unprotected sex (see the Sex chapter).

More info on pregnancy termination (abortion)

The Family Planning Association, Brook Advisory Centres, your GP and your local family planning, contraception or young people's clinics will help you if you decide to have a pregnancy termination (see "More info on being pregnant", a couple of pages earlier, for details).

www.bpas.org
Action Line (for confidential advice): 08457 30 40 30
The British Pregnancy Advisory Service was set up as a charity for people who choose to have an abortion. Choose "Young people" from the homepage of its site for info and help.

www.mariestopes.co.uk
24 Hour helpline for confidential advice: 0845 200 80 90
Mainly for private operations, the Marie Stopes clinics also take NHS referrals. The website has good info on terminations. From the home page choose "Services for young people", and then the link to "Pregnancy".

www.brook.org.uk
Brook Advisory Centres offer free, confidential abortion advice and counselling to young people, including under 16s.
Helpline: 0800 0185 023

www.likeitis.org
A joint UK and Australian site set up by Marie Stopes International, this site is especially for teens. Click on the Union Jack for the UK site, then on the Teenage Pregnancy main page choose the link to "Q and A section" to see details on all your options including abortion.

www.fpa.org.uk
The Family Planning Association also offers useful abortion and clinic information for all parts of the UK, with specific information for people living in Northern Ireland.

If you get pregnant there are ways that you can deal with it and still have a good life without ruining yours. Lisa, 17

Becoming a young mum

Between 5 and 10 percent of babies born in the UK have a teenage mum. Most girls who have a baby decide to stay its mum, especially after giving birth and spending time with the baby.

Making the decision

Having a baby is a responsibility that many older women feel daunted by, so it's a lot for a teenager to take on.

Good things about being a teenage mum

- ⑥ You tend not to get as tired as older mums (look for the zombies).
- ⑥ Teenage mums can be wonderful, loving mums. Older first-time mums are just as inexperienced with babies as you are.
- ⑥ You'll be closer in age to your kid – that means you may be able to understand them better, and are likely to be healthier and have more energy while they're growing up.
- ⑥ There are people whose job it is to help you, such as mother-and-baby health-centre nurses, who you can visit regularly in the early years of your baby's life. There are mothers' groups or special young mums' groups for support.
- ⑥ Being a good teenage mum is a truly great achievement and shows enormous strength of character.

Hard things about being a teenage mum

- ⑥ There's a higher risk of miscarriage and of a complicated birth in your teen years.
- ⑥ Very few schools help pregnant girls or young mums to stay on at school.
- ⑥ It can be lonely. Almost all the dads of the babies have broken up with the teenage mums by the time their baby turns one. Looking after a baby is so challenging, and takes away so much of the usual freedom of a young person, that it means most teenage mums end up being sole parents, caring for their baby themselves, perhaps with help from their family or perhaps not. Most friends don't understand the relentless commitment it requires 24 hours a day, seven days a week, 365 days a year.

◐ You will probably be poor, even very poor. On top of other UK benefits, you are entitled to a weekly "Child Benefit" payment and you will also get a "Child Tax Credit" if you work. But it isn't very much, and won't leave you with anything left over for extras such as clothes, make-up or haircuts for you, or entertainment or takeaway food that's good for you or your kid. It is almost impossible to save for something big such as a TV, sofa, fridge or car.

I got pregnant at 15 and had my son at 16 and now I'm 17 and he's a darling.
Angela, 17

◐ Unlike a pet, a baby (and older children) can't be left alone, ever. This can make you feel trapped, as it means you can't study, work or go out when you want to.

◐ Childcare (a place that minds kids) is very expensive, even with government "Childcare Vouchers". And if you live out in the country it might either not be available or might be difficult to reach.

◐ Being a teenage mum can mean you never get independence. Many teenage mums find that even if their family is not angry with them, the family still wants to tell them what to do and how to be a parent, especially if they are living with them or asking for their help and support.

When you've decided to become a mum

You'll need to think about telling your family and other people you're pregnant and have decided to keep the baby; prepare for the birth; and find out how much the baby's father wants to contribute. If he is not going to be around, you might want to think about claiming regular "maintenance" payments from him through the "Child Support Agency" (see "More info", coming up). It really helps if you have a good support network so, if that's not going to be the baby's father or your family, or somebody else, you'll need to start planning how to manage, and how to finish or extend your school and training years once you're a mum.

If you're frightened of how your parents may react to your decision, think about taking somebody with you when you tell them. It would be great if you could get the support teenage mums need during and after pregnancy from your family but, if not, your local doctor, community health centre or family planning clinic can help you find the right social workers to help you through.

Pregnancy and birth You and your unborn baby will need to have regular medical check-ups to make sure you're both healthy and progressing well. And you'll need

My friends all took off and moved on when I had my baby. I don't hear from them very often at all. Sharon, 18

advice about what you need to eat and what you can and can't do when you're pregnant (see "More info", coming up).

Pregnancy and birth specialists called midwives (usually women) and obstetricians (specialist doctors) will help you during your pregnancy and when you give birth. Your GP will help you choose them or they will be part of the staff at your local hospital.

After you've had the baby

- **Health and other costs**   If you have your baby through the NHS, the midwife and other costs are all paid for by the government.

- **Government support**   The government's Child Benefit payments start after the baby is born, but it's worth finding out what will be available to you before then. (See "More info", coming up.)

- **School**   The government provides what it calls the "Education and Maintenance Allowance" (EMA) payment to help teenage mothers stay at school. Some schools will even provide child-minding as well. If anyone pressures you to leave school, or your school is not co-operating, contact your local education authority, and ask for help. Don't take no for an answer.

- **Childcare**   If you know or think you might need childcare because of school or work, you need to organize it as soon as you have decided to keep the baby: call your local council and ask for the numbers of approved child-carers and nurseries near you. Call up as soon as you can and put your name down on the waiting list for a place. You can always say no if you don't need it when a place comes up. Some nurseries have several hundred people on the waiting list. You may be eligible for government help to pay for the childcare.

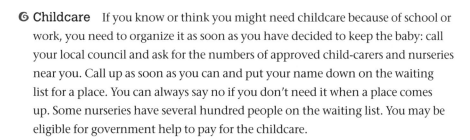

More info on becoming a young mum

www.oneparentfamilies.org.uk
Tons of factsheets and useful information on both practical day-to-day issues and legal benefit-related stuff.

csa.gov.uk
The UK Government's Child Support Agency will help you set up child maintenance payments. Telephone enquiries: 08457 133 133. The website has information you can download on what child maintenance is (payments from a child's other parent).

directgov.uk
You can apply for various government benefits online here. From the homepage choose "Do It Online" then "Money, tax and benefits online" then "Benefits and support for families with children".

www.surestart.gov.uk
www.childcarelink.gov.uk
SureStart is the government's agency for helping parents and their kids. It runs Surestart Children's Centres and provides info on childcare and gives parenting advice. The SureStart site will give you info about services. The Childcare link, accessed from the SureStart site, or through it's own website address (above), will tell you where to find the services in your area of England. You can also call them on: 0800 2 346346. Scotland has its own site: www.scottishchildcare.gov.uk.

www.ywca.org.uk/youngmums
The brilliant Respect Young Mums campaign site has stories by real girls who've had babies, a quiz on myths and facts, and lots more. From the main page, choose "Links and help" for a jump-off point to other great websites with support for young mums who need help, or about pregnancy, being a parent (including info for young dads) and contraception.

www.nctpregnancyandbabycare.com
The UK's leading childbirth organization, the NCT offers loads of good advice and run pre-birth classes across the nation. Or call:
Pregnancy and Birthline: 0870 444 8709
Breastfeeding line: 0300 33 00 771 or
Enquiries line: 0300 33 00 770

The Rough Guide to Pregnancy & Birth by Kaz Cooke, Penguin, UK
My book, which takes you through a pregnancy week by week. I check it all the time to make sure medical and other info is right up to date – so don't get an old copy from the library. Make somebody buy you a new copy or borrow a new one. Do the same for any other pregnancy or childcare book.

The Rough Guide to Babies & Toddlers by Kaz Cooke, Penguin, UK
Also by me, all about how to take care of your baby, how to get your baby to sleep, what to do about crying, breast and bottle feeding, and how to keep you and your baby healthy, right through to when they're a couple of years older and running around.

I'm a mum and the chores make me so depressed but no one else will do them, will they? I need braces to be fixed but I have no money.   Nicola, 18

Adoption

If you don't want to end a pregnancy, but know that you can't be a mother at this time, your best choice may be adoption. Many families are unable to have children themselves and are grateful for the chance to raise a baby as their own child. It can be heartbreaking to give up your baby, and very hard to stick to the decision, even if you don't feel able to be a mother yet. A very small percentage of pregnant girls choose adoption, with fewer choosing it each year.

Although you may have decided to have your baby adopted, you'll still find pregnancy and birth very big experiences physically and emotionally, and you'll need help and support throughout both (see "Becoming a young mum" above).

How adoption is organized

Somebody who is helping you, such as a social worker, your doctor or another adult, can contact your local authority social services departments and adoption agencies. A social worker will then work with you to arrange the adoption.

The social worker will discuss the decision with you, but you can't sign final adoption papers until the child is six weeks old. In most cases, once the adoption has been agreed you will have no further "rights" to make contact with the child, unless specific arrangements have been agreed.

You can talk to the counsellor about meeting the family if you'd like to, as well as whether you think you will want to contact your child in the future. Sometimes adoptions can be "open", which means you can see your baby as it's growing up. Some girls allow their baby to be adopted by relatives or family friends.

After the adoption

As mentioned above, you have at least six weeks to make a decision, so you can change your mind and keep the baby when it's born even if you had previously discussed adoption with your GP or a social worker. If, however, you've made the other decision and signed away the baby for adoption after the six week period, you could have no further legal rights or responsibilities.

A temporary option is "fostering": another family looks after your child for a time, but you keep your legal right to be the child's guardian, in the hope that you will soon be able to take your baby back and be the responsible parent.

MONEY

23

You mean I'm probably NOT going to marry the next Prince of Bratislava?

There goes my financial strategy

I know, you want more. Here's how to **save** it, how to hang onto it, how to **spend** it, and how not to get into **debt**. And see the Shopping chapter to find out how to avoid becoming a robot with a wallet.

How to hang onto it

You may get regular pocket money, but the older you get, and the more you want to choose and buy your own clothes or save for something big, the more you'll probably need an extra source of money (or you'll need to do some negotiating with a parent). The main way to get money is to work for it, and the Work chapter has lots of info on part-time and full-time jobs.

I guess it's kinda good that I work for the money to pay for clothes. It teaches me that I can't get everything I want.
Louise, 13

Saving

Saving is really the only way to get something major such as a car, a deposit for a rented flat, or a big holiday. If you're in your late teens see below for how to set up your own bank account. If you're too young to do this by yourself you can get your parents to help you.

rattle, rattle

FACT

The unavoidable truth about saving The only way to save is to spend less than you earn and put away what's left over. Even if you save only £1 a week from your pocket money that's £52 by the end of a year.

Opening a bank account

- Do some research online, in person or by phone. Compare the accounts on offer from different banks. Will some charge you whenever you take money out, or just deduct a monthly fee for keeping your money parked with them?

- Pick a bank or building society that has a branch office near your home or work. Although most banking these days is done automatically or online, which can be a lot quicker and more convenient, it can help to have a local outlet that you can go to with a query.

- Walk into the branch you've chosen and tell someone at the enquiries desk that you'd like to find out about opening an account. They'll

Pocket money

Pocket money is traditionally just for the odd little expenses, such as going to a movie with a friend, or lip gloss, or "just in case" money to keep in your – well, pocket (or bag).

Parents have different ideas about pocket money. Some believe their kids should do set chores in return for a fixed weekly amount so that they learn about earning money. Some feel their children should automatically have a small, regular share in the family's money, with no conditions attached. Some think pocket money is unnecessary because they look after all their children's needs and hand out money for anything special. And some believe teenagers should be given enough money each week to cover expenses such as fares, entertainment and casual clothes, so that they learn the value of handling money and budgeting.

Increasing your pocket money

✷ Explain to your parents why you want them to increase it. They may not know what you need, or how you're using it, or what other kids pay for. Try not to compare your pocket money with a friend's: maybe your family just can't afford more.

✷ Look at ways to earn more pocket money. Suggest to your parents that you do special one-off things around the house or extra chores.

At a certain point most parents will insist that you somehow earn your own extra money, usually in a part-time job (see the Work chapter).

give you a form to fill in, and about a zillion words explaining the bank's different accounts, fees and interest rates.

❻ Also ask a trusted, financially clever adult or a finance or business teacher which is the best deal before you make a final decision to go with a particular institution.

❻ If you have a full-time job, you can organize an automatic deduction from your pay so that each week some of it goes straight into your bank account (or a special savings account): that way you don't see it and immediately spend it.

I think you should save up your money for something special ... even if you don't know what you're saving up for at the time.
Amanda, 13

⊙ You'll probably be given a plastic debit card you can use to withdraw money from an automatic cash machine (ATM), or to pay for things in shops (see the later "Credit and debit cards" section). Find out what your ATM daily withdrawal limit is – you'll only be able to take this amount out in any one day. Although your card may work in any bank's ATM, your bank may charge you a fee for not using its branded ATMs.

⊙ Always check your bank account statements and ATM receipts, and keep them in case there's a mistake and you need to sort it out with your bank.

I think getting my first job made me a lot more appreciative of the money my parents gave me when I was younger. I think I've learnt to be more frugal with my money.
Bella, 16

Making a budget   A budget is a saving and spending plan based on the money (income) you receive. See "More info" later on for a head-start on working out what money you have "coming in" and which essential bills you have to pay regularly; how much to save; and what to do with any money left over.

Sometimes I feel guilty for having a lot but sometimes I feel that I never have enough!   Holly, 14

Don't waste it on superficial things. Save it up.   Lauren, 17

Why is it such a big issue how much money you have? I mean, who cares?
Mina, 14

FACT

Saving for a car   This is a big one. Factor into the price the high cost of road tax and insurance; a weekly fuel bill; maintenance (regular servicing isn't cheap but can prevent even more expensive repairs); any driving lessons; and a licence. Do as much research as you can on a car before you buy it, and don't let yourself get ripped off by smooth sales talk (see "More info" below).

More info on managing your money

financial-planning.uk.com
This useful site has some good info on saving and planning your finances, whatever age you are. From the homepage, click "Lifestages" and then choose the label that best suits you: "Students", "Children" or "Young adults".

www.teenissues.co.uk
Click "Family life" and then "Avoid pocket money problems" for some useful advice.

www.direct.gov.uk
This UK government site has pages and pages of helpful stuff Click "Young people" and then "Money" to find money-saving ideas, banking and other financial services info.

www.moneymadeclear.fsa.gov.uk
This is the UK's Financial Watchdog (FSA) site. There's lots here you really won't have to worry about just yet, but there's also lots that might apply to you. Click "Manage your money" and then take a look at the "Money saving tips". There's also stuff here to help you manage debt.

The Teenagers'Guide to Money by Jonathan Self, Quercus Publishing, UK
Jonathan Self explains how to get money, save money, spend it to your advantage and avoid owing any. Also has info on sticking to a budget when studying at university or college.

Cars:
www.dvla.gov.uk
The Driving and Vehicle Licensing Agency site: find out about fees and how to apply for a driving licence or register a car on this site.

www.which.co.uk
Which in the UK offers advice on buying, insuring and maintaining car safety. Choose "Cars and motoring" from the homepage.

How to spend it and not get into debt

Watch out for common money traps, which can get you into a spiral of owing money. These include mobile phones, dodgy contracts, loans, gambling and the very devil itself – credit cards.

Mobile phones

Mobile phones can cost you loads. Either research the best phone plan for you, or just get lots of £50 notes and start tearing them up right now.

Thousands of girls end up not being able to pay their phone bill, which can lead to legal problems; paying off a debt for years; and having their name put on a central registry or "credit black list", which may mean it's hard for them to get a loan or a credit card later or to get another phone service provider.

> I hate owing money. I owe people money now. Not much but enough to make me feel guilty.
> Fran, 14

Before buying a phone

- ⓖ Ask yourself why you're buying it. What do you need it for? Do you need it to take photos, watch DVDs and send messages into space? If you just need it to make and get calls, don't pay for extra whiz-bangery.
- ⓖ How much does the actual phone you want cost, and how much are the extras you'll also need? ("Free" or "cheap" phones might end up being expensive, depending on call costs, fees and downloads.)
- ⓖ Do you really need the latest, shiniest, tiniest (probably most expensive) phone?

Do some groundwork before you buy.

- ⓖ Look at websites or books on phone sales trickery (see "More info" coming up).
- ⓖ Consider using a prepaid "pay as you go" or "top up" account for your calls so you can't get into debt – essentially you're buying a certain amount of phone time in advance. And never top up your account with a credit card or using money from savings.
- ⓖ Shop around and look at different service providers or carriers (phone companies you'll have to sign a contract with) and their deals. Compare things such as flat call rates, special offers and discounts, and terms and conditions of contracts. Ask a trusted, money-savvy adult for help.

You can watch live wrestling on it!

SALES

'Special features' on a phone may just mean stuff you don't need

Mobile phone addiction

Does the thought of living without your phone for an afternoon make you anxious? How about a week? (Did you just scream?)

Some problems with phone overuse can include:

* feeling panicked or anxious because you can't use the phone

* spending money that could go on other things just to pay huge phone bills

* getting into phone debt

* sending messages to people you're not really interested in, about stuff that's not important or fun, just because they texted you

* not doing something, or making something, or playing something because you're too busy texting or saying "Where are you now?" 50,000 times

* having problems sleeping – some people leave their phone on all night and keep using it

* judging your worth or popularity by how many messages you get, regardless of who they're from or whether they're about anything

* stealing from parents or others, or lying ("I need money for . . .") to pay for the phone.

Some hints to keep sane

* Turn your phone off at least half an hour before bed and back on in the morning.

* Think about whether you spend more time interacting with a tiny screen than with people face to face. If you think you're losing social skills and the ability to relate to real people, cut down on phone time.

* When you're in the car all mobile phones get turned off. It's against the law to drive while using a mobile phone because it's so distracting: some drivers doing this have caused accidents which have killed people. (Hands-free phones in cars are distracting too.) Some people believe that the driving reactions of a person using a phone are worse than if they're drunk.

* Mobile phones emit low-level radiation so keep them away from your head and the middle of your body (near internal organs) as much as you can. Although no link to brain tumours has been proved, they're not proven to be harmless either. Experts worry about the effects on the teenage brain because it's still growing.

* Do an experiment – get a group of friends to turn off their phones for 24 hours. Oh, who am I kidding? Like that's going to happen.

◔ Consider using a second-hand phone, such as one somebody else has discarded (to get themselves the latest, shiniest one).

◔ Check out specials that are available if you use the same service provider as your friends do. Make sure you won't be paying extra for calling anybody (such as a parent) who is not with that service provider.

◔ Check out the difference between day and night rates to work out when to make cheaper calls.

◔ If you do sign a contract, remember it's legally binding (if you are over 18) and some can last for up to two or three years. This means that even if you want to change you still have to keep paying out until the contract expires. Read your contract thoroughly and make sure you understand it.

> Make sure you know exactly where your money is going and know exactly what is happening with it.
>
> Christina, 15

> I can't spend heaps of money because I live in the middle of nowhere and I hardly ever get into town.
>
> Karen, 13

◔ If you are "trapped" in the contract, and realize you're in trouble, see if a trusted adult or consumer legal service can help.

◔ Ask your service provider to put a "bar" on your phone, so that if you lose it or it's stolen nobody can make international, information, voting, timed or any other kind of call (like the thief who used my phone to vote for some idiot on *Big Brother* a gerzillion times, which cost more than £150). If your phone is stolen, report it to the service provider the second you find out, so that from that moment on you're not liable for any charges on the phone.

◔ Go through your bills: what service is chewing up the most money? Can you cut down or do without it? Voicemail and texts can be a typical money-eater.

◔ Texting is not always cheaper. Check your plan and your bills. Depending on your plan, if you send six text messages to organize to meet somebody, when one 10-second phone call could have done it, you lose.

◔ If your contract has a certain number of included texts and minutes, then stick to that limit. Your phone should be able to show you how many of each you have used by any point during the month.

◔ Find out exactly what a "standard call cost" is with your provider, and how the company defines it: local call of less than two minutes, local call of any length, or something else.

Credit and debit cards

Most people under 18 can't own a credit card, but some girls have a credit card that allows them access to a parent's account.

Credit cards are really debt cards. You use a credit card to "pay" for something, but actually you've just borrowed money from the credit card company (or department store) and they will charge you interest on the loan. (Some credit cards don't charge interest if you pay regularly every month, but they usually still charge a service or other fee.) This means that with every credit card purchase you pay more than the price on the tag: you are wasting money and possibly getting into a debt that you can't pay back.

Before you get a credit card, do some research. Many of the credit contracts are a rip-off when it comes to fees and conditions.

A better way of paying for things is to use a debit card, which just takes the money out of your bank account by the EFTPOS system (Electronic Funds Transfer, Point of Sale). You can only buy something with a debit card if the cost is covered by what you've got in your account, so you can't rack up any debts. Some debit cards can be used online, to buy concert tickets or to shop.

Shared finances

Whether you have a boyfriend, partner or husband, you always need to know what's happening with your finances.

✱ Have your own bank account and cards, and regularly check that you haven't overspent. You'll need a good financial reputation for your future transactions.

✱ If you pay off a business or housing loan together you can each pay money from your own accounts into the loan.

✱ Know your partner's debts, and don't sign on for a legal responsibility to pay these if something goes wrong.

✱ Don't share a credit card with a partner.

If I put it on credit, fairies will pay!

You May NeeD a MoRe GRowN·up appRoAcH to MoNeY...

Gambling

Gambling includes playing games for money at casinos, using gaming machines ("slot machines"), betting on races and other sporting events, and buying lottery tickets. Casino games and gaming machines are rigged so that the vast majority of money put into them goes to the profits of the people

Money rules

✳ Don't spend more than you have.

✳ Don't lend money.

✳ Don't borrow money from friends.

✳ Never guarantee somebody else's loan, even if they're your boyfriend, girlfriend or relative.

✳ Don't sign anything you don't understand: that won't be an excuse in court.

✳ If you're in debt, get help.

who own them: you can never win betting against "the house".

If you enjoy gambling and spend only what you can afford on it, such as the price of one lottery ticket every week or £10 at the races twice a year, then gambling isn't a problem. But many girls develop a gambling problem once they don't stick to a set limit and start to lose money. They keep trying to win back what they've lost, losing more and more, which has a disastrous effect on their finances and relationships.

If you think you – or a family member or friend – have a gambling problem you can get confidential advice by ringing one of the helplines given in "More info" coming up.

Email and phone scams

There are a million email and phone financial scams out there.

🗲 Don't open or reply to an attachment on an email from anybody you don't know.

🗲 Never, ever email (or give out) any bank account details, PIN numbers (personal identity numbers – codes for your bank account or other financial matters) or credit card numbers unless it's on a secure site.

🗲 Don't send money, a bank account number or a reply to someone who emails that they're going to send you money, lottery winnings or an inheritance (money left to you in a will), no matter how professional the email looks. And always hang up on somebody who calls you on the phone and talks about this sort of stuff. This is a dodgy way in which criminals steal money – they're successful because they send out thousands of spam emails and calls, and of every 100 people maybe one person will respond and be ripped off.

I've heard you can become a millionaire in a couple of months by doubling money – how?
[You really, really can't]
Bessie, 14

FACT

Scams   Schemes designed to take money from you include "pyramid" or "aeroplane" money-making schemes and games; financial offers or "cheap" handyman services from people who come to the door; any offer that you have to accept NOW or it will change; and some expensive seminars and training courses. Always be suspicious of a brilliant-sounding, low-risk "sure thing" or no-risk, high-return investment. There's no such thing. And never click a link in an email that asks you to log into your bank's website, even if it "appears" to be from your bank. This is often a scam called "phishing" and is just a way for criminals to get their paws on your secret password. Educate yourself: check out www.safefromscams.co.uk.

HINT

Your signature   Don't just copy your mum's signature, only substituting your initial. For business transactions you'll need to have your own professional-looking signature. Practise signing your name until it's easy for you. You'll be stuck with it for life, so don't make it little-girly or hard to do exactly the same way over and over again – no huge letters, hearts, smiley faces or elaborate swirly underlinings.

More info on debt, credit cards and scams, phones and gambling

www.debtadvisorycentre.co.uk
Info and advice on avoiding and getting out of debt. They also have a free, confidential helpline: 0800 970 7724

www.nationaldebtline.co.uk
Lots of info and separate sites for England, Wales, and Scotland. There's a phone number too.
Helpline: 0808 808 4000

www.adviceguide.org.uk
From the homepage of this Citizens Advice Bureau site, click "Debt" and then read the "Frequently asked questions".

www.connexions-direct.com
Connexions is a very useful site with info on all aspects of teenage life. From the home page search "debt" and then read through the articles that pop up.

Phones:

www.1affordablecall.co.uk
This no-frills independent UK site gives a
good overview of how to choose a mobile
phone package. From the homepage choose
"Introduction" under "Mobile users" to get
started.

www.which.co.uk/reviews/mobile-phones
Well-respected consumer organization Which
has loads of no-nonsense reviews of the latest
models and deals, so you know exactly what
you are getting.

Gambling:

Helplines:
GamCare   0845 6000 133
Gam-Anon   08700 50 88 80

www.gamanon.org.uk
Info and links for regional help.

www.gamblersanonymous.org.uk
For support and referral.

Every year, and sometimes twice a year (summer and winter) I get a set clothes
budget, and I can only spend that money. Mum won't give me any more for all the
clothes I need.   Kate, 14

I never have enough. I'm scared that I won't have enough when I grow up. I won't
be able to afford a car any time soon because I am going overseas.
Lisa, 17

Once you get in debt, it's so hard to get out of.
Daisy, 16

I want more! I don't get enough!
Samantha, 14

Save! Begin early!
Michelle, 17

Too many kids are spoilt and
just get what they want from
their parents straight away.
I have to save up for it, and it
makes me appreciate it more.
Anisha, 15

24

SHOPPING

Everybody wants you. **Every** clothes company, every shoe company, every fast-food company, drink company, TV network, major electronics company. The companies pay advisors, have "focus groups" and brainstorming sessions and then proceed to spend billions and billions of pounds on hype, **trying to get you to buy their stuff**. They want you to mix up the ideas of "want" and "need" so that you feel you must must must have something new **now now now**.

Marketing

Everybody wants you to spend money on their products – and they have some pretty clever ways of pretending that's not what they're trying to do. This section is about how to recognize marketing when the companies are trying to sneak it past you.

The big companies know that you're smarter and more cynical than your parents were in their teens – and harder to trick. So they spend loads finding new ways to fool you. These days they've changed tactics: they don't try to get parents to buy stuff for you ("My, these are sensible, long-lasting school shoes!"), they go after *you* ("These are the coolest!").

Advertising

Advertising tries to make you feel you want or need something. Look at the ads on a bus shelter, in a mag, on TV or on a website to see if you can spot these obvious strategies:

- "You deserve it, you're special, you've earned it. We get how special you are and how hard you work. We want to reward you."
- "Having this product will make you look more attractive. And your life will be transformed, somewhat like Cinderella's."
- "We have cool-seeming people in our ad so this product is cool, and because you like it you're cool too."
- "We have a nerdy person in our ad who isn't using our cool product, so let's all laugh at them. Ha ha! We're mean, but cool."
- "Check out this really cool song/amazing visual image/piece of animation. Now we have your attention, here's what we want you to buy."
- "Having this product will make you happy, oh so happy, ha ha, with laughing, very white teeth."
- "In the world where people use this product everything is sunny and fun."
- "You're one of a select group getting this text."
- "We care about you so buy our stuff."
- "We care about animals/the environment/poor people so buy our stuff."
- "This is such a funny ad you'll remember our brand name. (You don't? That's £15 million down the drain then.)"
- "This is such a weird ad it will intrigue you and get you talking about it."
- "If you buy our product you'll have an edge over competitors. In fact they will be CRUSHED."
- "Buy this because it's really exclusive and glamorous."
- "Buy this because it's really cheap."
- "If you have this takeaway your family will sit down together to eat and be happy."

- "Omigod, if you get this thing it will be so exciting. Lots of music and zoomy, colourful things will happen. And your life now is dull. And you bore the pants off everyone."
- "This celebrity says they use our stuff. If you want to be like them buy our stuff."
- "Everyone likes our stuff – don't be a left-out, sad, lonely loser."
- "We know you're too smart to fall for advertising and marketing. Smart people like you buy our stuff."
- "We have paid a lot of money for the rights to this really catchy song, so when you hear it you'll feel good and sing it, and that will remind you to buy our thing. And the ad is louder than the TV show, so don't try to ignore it."
- "Get a load of this scientific statistical stuff that makes it seem as if our product is proven to be the best. We paid someone to do the research and come up with those results." (And don't you love an ad where cartoon arrows bounce off the skin, because that proves . . . um . . . wait . . . yes, that proves that cartoon arrows bounce off cartoon skin.)
- "This ad is on high rotation. It's on TV, on radio, on public transport, on bus shelters and at the cinema, so you can't get away from our message. You can't hide from us."

Brand loyalty

Companies want your brand loyalty, which means that:

- instead of just saying, "I feel like a hamburger", you say "I feel like going to Burger King."
- instead of going into a shop and saying, "I want a sticking plaster" (Huh?), you say, "Can I have a Band-Aid, please," (Which is really a registered trademark.)
- instead of wanting any old pair of jeans, you only want the ones from the hot label. (Which might cost more than the other, identical pair without the label.)

Getting you early

Global corporations, local businesses and the advertising and marketing industry want to:

- grab your loyalty before you even turn 9 (in fact many companies aim to have kids telling their parents what to buy as soon as they can speak)
- get you now, as a teenage consumer, so they can keep you for life as a "L'Oréal lipstick girl" or a "Target undies buyer" – someone who always buys one brand rather than any other.

"Aspirational appeal"   This is a term used by marketers and advertisers for the feeling they wish to create in you – the feeling that you want the same kind of life/face/body/ boyfriend/hairstyle/acting career as the person in their ad – so that you'll buy the product. The theory is that you aspire to the image, so the product appeals to you. Basically it's creating envy.

Misleading advertising   Although there are laws that are supposed to protect us against fibbing ads, they're not always enforced. And ads can also be legal but misleading. Models in ads are not legally required to have used the stuff being advertised. That's right: Glossy Hair Model doesn't even use that shampoo. She just has nice hair.

The picture of a body used in an ad for cosmetic surgery usually belongs to a person who's never been in the same room as a surgeon. And here's a "shocking secret" (der): the person in the white coat isn't really a doctor/scientist/ researcher – they're an actor.

glossy hair model

When is an ad not an ad?

Ads are always ads, it's just that sometimes they come in the form of a "marketing campaign" that doesn't use the ad spaces you expect, such as in magazines and on websites, billboards, bus shelters, TV and radio. Here are some ads that don't always look like ads.

"Reports"   An article in a magazine can look as if it is written by a reporter, and be printed in the same style as the other articles, but can actually be a paid ad. Often an article – especially in free (giveaway) magazines, but also in some of the glossy expensive ones – will mention products from companies that regularly advertise in the

FACT

Thought association   Sometimes mere association is enough to create a reminder of a product. A big, curvy yellow M makes you think hamburgers – McDonald's hamburgers. The colour purple makes you think chocolate – Cadbury's chocolate. (Cadbury has even taken court action, saying that no other company should be allowed to use purple packaging on cakes, lollies or chocolates.)

magazine. It works on TV shows too. Did that travel reporter get a free trip? Then she's not likely to say the pool smelled like cheese, is she.

"Trend watchers"   Magazine pages called things like What's In, What's Cool or New Products are often really unpaid ads cobbled together by a reporter whose job it is to go through all the press releases of the magazine's advertisers to keep them happy.

"Direct marketing"   Companies make contact with you via mail, pamphlets, emails and phone calls you never asked for.

Videos, pics, messages and emails   You can sign up for stuff to be sent to your phone, which are obviously sponsored or which eventually turn out to be pushing a product.

"Viral marketing"   Companies try to spread their message like a virus. It looks like "word of mouth" – people telling each other about it – but it's really company employees using phone messages, websites, meeting sites, blogs, fake blogs ("flogs") and short films. The ads can look like an animation, a joke, inside info, a cute picture, a recommendation from a friend, a filmed romance story – anything but an ad.

Product placements   It's no accident that the cute guy in your favourite new movie is wearing that particular brand of watch or going into that particular restaurant chain in one scene – it's "product placement". This partly involves getting the brand name seen, and partly associating it with something cool such as a TV star or a hit film. Companies pay (sometimes several million pounds) for their drink to be the one poured at the table, or their cars to be the ones in the chase scene.

Some singers have even been paid to mention brand names in their songs. Luckily most singers, writers and other artists, and a few movie makers, reject being bribed to compromise their artistic vision. Just for fun, next time you watch a movie or TV show see how many product placements you can spot.

Freebies   Companies often give you a free sample of a product: you'll find it in your letterbox, stuck to the front of a magazine, in a "show bag" from a launch, or at a youth festival or careers night. It feels like a gift, but actually it's a small, cheap sample to persuade you to buy a (much bigger) packet or bottle.

Companies also send heaps of free products to people with "influence" – writers on newspapers and magazines, radio show hosts, celebrities – to get free mentions here and there.

Magazines
(and their websites)

✱ Magazines are expensive to produce – the price every reader pays for a copy isn't enough to pay for the printing and distribution – so their profits come from advertising (and other clever ideas such as phone-in competitions).

✱ Editors don't have total control over what goes in their magazine. The money to produce a mag comes from advertisers, so an editor who writes a story criticizing an advertiser's product, or any other aspect of the business, won't last long.

✱ Magazines have some fantastic stories and some great things to look at. But question why they want you to read what you're reading. Is the beauty editor influenced by all her freebies? Would the fashion editor recommend a look if an advertiser didn't stock it? Recently I saw a horoscope column that managed to squeeze in twelve ads: it recommended jewellery for each star sign, complete with prices and brand names.

Targeting   Companies often target a particular group for freebies: for instance, they go to schools, clubs and hangouts, identify the "cool kids" there and give them free new stuff to wear or use, and samples to give to friends. Suddenly everyone wants the product.

Endorsements   Endorsement ranges from celebrities paid to be in ads pretending they use the products, to radio hosts who are influenced by freebies faffing on about how yummy the doughnuts are from the bakery that just delivered them a boxful.

Celebrity handouts   Film and TV stars, models, singers, radio hosts, sporting "heroes" and all sorts of celebrities have stuff given to them by companies that want their products to be associated with glamour and fame. When the celebrities are photographed wearing an obvious label, holding a certain kind of drink or attending the opening of a certain club, assume they could have been paid to do it.

"Push marketing"   Girls with not a lot of clothes on, except high heels, hand out samples, or even pretend to be bar customers ordering a new drink, to get people talking about a product to create a buzz.

Merchandising   A company gets people to be walking ads by putting their name or logo on T-shirts, hats, matchbooks, lighters, stickers, pens, food or even cute toys.

Sponsorships   Companies can get their brand name everywhere by sponsoring an event such as a concert, sporting contest, festival or even a charity fundraiser. The idea is that the more you see a product associated with something you like, the more you'll like the product.

Competition prizes   A contest says, "To win a pack of Twang cosmetics worth £200, write down in twenty-five words or less why you need our stuff, and send it to . . .". So 10,000 girls write down how great the product is (and think about buying Twang), and the company has only had to pay £200 for stuff that they get out of the back room. And then they can even use the competition entries as unpaid "endorsements" of their products.

Donated prizes   Say a company donates a motorcycle as a prize for a competition in which you have to collect coupons from five packets of chips. The company gets ads for their motorcycle on millions of chips packets for the cost of only one motorcycle. The prizes you can win on radio, in magazines and on websites are all donated by companies to get their product mentioned and "out there".

Social conscience donations   Many companies say they are helping good causes and charities by donating a percentage of their profits. And they may be. It's just that the percentage of profit may be less than 1 percent, while the percentage they marked up on the price of their items was 5 percent. You'd be better off donating money directly to the charity and buying a cheaper product. Be careful when companies claim to be doing something out of the goodness of their hearts. Look closely and there's usually a profit.

More info on ads and magazines

www.adbusters.org
Choose the spoof ad gallery for some hilarious and clever send-ups of real ads.

www.asa.org.uk
The UK's Advertising Standards Authority has info on dodgy ads. From the homepage search for Ads.

Safe online shopping:

The Guardian Guide to Shopping on the Internet by Jim McClellan and
The Rough Guide to The Internet
by Peter Buckley, Rough Guides, UK
Both these books have ideas for shopping online, plus online financial security.

Some magazines are more independent than others. Try:

www.bbc.co.uk/switch/slink
The BBC's online magazine for teenage girls.

bust.com
From the homepage of this US site choose "Girl Wide Web" for links to other cool sites.

grrrlzines.net
Girl 'zines galore (independent magazines by older girls for older girls).

teenvoices.com
An online magazine for and by teenage girls with the slogan "Because you're more than just a pretty face".

Going shopping

Have you ever had that sinking feeling of arriving home with something in a shopping bag, knowing you shouldn't have bought it, you'll never use it, it's a waste of money, it doesn't look like it did in the shop, and now you can't even afford to buy a lolly snake? That's because shopping lures in the twenty-first century are very clever and hard to resist (or even see).

Sales techniques

Assistants who sell in shops and over the phone have often been trained in sales techniques. Somebody I know who used to sell gym memberships says, "I asked them what it was about their body they would change if they could, and then in different words I told them the gym could do that for them".

Here are some common sales techniques. The salesperson:

- 6 is friendly, asks how you are, chats about something other than the product (actually they're finding out things about you so they can work out the best way to persuade you to buy)
- 6 gets you to test or handle the product so you picture yourself having it and using it

- ☉ tells you stories about "real" people, including "other customers", who are so happy with their product ("I have one and it's great", "My friend has one of these and she's never had so many handsome, rich chappies wanting to take her to Hollywood")
- ☉ informs you the price or the great bonus is only available for another day or while the boss is out to lunch (they're trying to get you to hand over money or a signature in a hurry)
- ☉ makes you feel in charge, but pushes you by saying things such as, "It's up to you of course, but this is the last model available at this price".

Always remember that a salesperson wants to sell you something, no matter how nice they seem. So if you want an honest opinion don't ask Flossy behind the counter – take your mum or a friend shopping with you.

Shop atmosphere

Malls, department stores and smaller shops (sometimes called boutiques) spend thousands of pounds on consultants to create the right vibe to get customers in and keep them there (yes, that's why half the time you can't find your way out).

- ☉ Music is picked carefully, decor is artfully arranged, little things are temptingly left on counters, the assistants are wearing clothes that are on sale. Some shops even have perfumed candles. Others look like bargain basements, with stuff seemingly chucked into cardboard boxes with hand-lettered signs so that the items look more like a bargain than perhaps they really are.
- ☉ Lighting is kept low in changing rooms and near mirrors so you can't see any faults in the clothes.
- ☉ Mirrors may be angled to make you look thinner.
- ☉ A big, attractive display in a shop suggests the products shown are the best or the cheapest, but in reality it could mean the owner wants to get rid of the stuff quickly or a manufacturer paid for that spot in the store. (Drinks companies supply fridges to shops and don't let other companies put their drinks in them.)

SALE!
WE PUT UP THE PRICES AND THEN SLASHED THEM BY, OH 0.001%

BARGAIN

Spending

Your great-grandma would hardly recognize the way we go shopping now. She would always have gone out with a list of what she needed, and that's all she would have bought. She would have taken a purse full of cash to buy the things on that list,

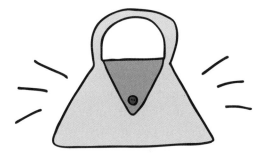

"You deserve it"

Don't ask, "Do I deserve this?", because of course you do. You deserve an emerald tiara and a holiday house in the Caribbean, but they're probably not going to happen. Instead ask yourself:

✱ "Can I afford it?"

✱ "Can I do without it?"

✱ "Is there a cheaper option?"

✱ "Would a laugh with a friend cheer me up just as much?"

✱ "Should I think about it for a couple of days?"

✱ "Do I want lots of small things now, or can I wait and save up for one really big, wonderful thing?"

or to pay off a short-term debt at the local store. She probably had an everyday handbag, and if she was very lucky another one for "best". Most people had one or two work outfits and a pair of work shoes, plus one "good" outfit including shoes. Back then most shops were almost all full of things you needed, not wanted. Only the super-rich could afford pretty but non-essential things, or extra clothes.

These days a handbag shop in a mall has more beautiful things in it than most major museums had a hundred years ago. We now have a huge choice of things to look at and buy – in one department store there is probably more pretty stuff than great-grandma saw in her whole lifetime.

Shopping centres today are places where we can choose from lots of shops, hang out with friends, eat, go to the loo, and stay dry, cool or warm. It's entertainment just to walk around and look at nice things, even if you can't afford them.

Shopping as therapy   Armed with a bunch of research about how girls and women use shopping as a social event and a kind of compensation for having a tough week at school, home or work, companies like the idea of "retail therapy": shopping as a feel-good activity. They've come up with advertising slogans and shop-assistant chat along the lines of "Because you're worth it", "Treat yourself", "You've earnt it" and "Reward yourself". The rise of salons, spas and home-grooming treatments is part of this self-pampering idea.

Staying in control of spending   Whether you "deserve it" or not, you may not be able to afford it. Be careful not to get giddy with wanting, and instead be happy with looking. Buying what you want can be a great way to celebrate having your own money from a part-time job, or your first real job. But it can be easy to blow all your money if you let yourself be manipulated by marketing.

don't get HYPNOTISED!
Remember your budget!

Don't get hypnotized by the shiny-shiny and forget the part about needing money for necessities. See the Money chapter for hints on how not to get yourself into trouble with cash and, even worse, credit cards.

"Shopaholics" Some psychologists think that being a "shopaholic" – always needing something new, and getting into debt – may be part of trying to fill up an emptiness people feel inside.

Shopping for some people has become a compulsion. If this sounds like you, have a think about your shopping habits.

- ⊙ Are you going shopping every week, or more, and spending more than you should?
- ⊙ Do you think it's become a habit or an addiction that you need to break?

Instead of shopping try:
- ⊙ visiting a gallery, an interesting place or a park
- ⊙ going on a nature walk
- ⊙ staying at home and creating something with a friend so you don't need to buy stuff
- ⊙ seeing how long you can go not buying anything except absolute necessities such as public transport fares.

And don't forget all the other ways of feeling good without spending.

25 CLOTHES & MAKE-UP

Is "What are you wearing?" a more common greeting in your group of friends than "Hi"? Are you a **"fashion tragic"**, with the attention span of a tadpole, who has to have something new every four days and wear the latest thing even if it makes you look like a colour-blind magician's assistant in a bubble skirt, gumboots and orange lipstick? Or do you wear the **same pair of jeans** until they are a bunch of threads held up by habit and hope?

In this chapter we'll look at aspects of clothes, style, fashion, accessories, make-up and why platform flip-flops are the **stupidest** things ever. (There are also those Skin and Hair chapters earlier.)

Clothes

Even without a T-shirt saying "Adidas" or "My Boss Sucks" you're saying something about yourself and the life you live with your clothes. If it was just about keeping warm, you'd just wear a sleeping bag suit in the winter and switch to your summer outfit of just a sunhat and some toe-nail polish. A school or work uniform sends a message. Wearing army pants and a black singlet says something different from a flouncy pink dress with ballet slippers.

Fashion

At any one time fashion can mean something quite different for different groups of people. For someone with £8000 to spare on a skirt, fashion may be what a starving, blank-eyed, flouncy model is wearing on the catwalk in Milan or Paris. To people who love reading about the lives of celebrities, fashion is what's worn by a Hollywood starlet on the red carpet on Oscars night. To some teenagers it's the zillion clothes they see in magazines and online. For you it's probably also what's popular at your school or in your group of friends – and what you can afford.

CLOTHES CAN MAKE A POLITICAL STATEMENT

The one thing that's true for every kind of fashion is that it changes all the time. Check out some of the "costume movies" in the list later in this chapter – it's a great way of seeing how fashions have changed and what was fashionable when, what still looks good and what an art form clothes can be. ("Vintage" is the fancy name given to old clothes kept long enough to have come back into fashion.)

Possible reasons for fashion always changing are:
- ⑥ fashion can be loads of fun
- ⑥ companies make more money if people think they need new clothes all the time, even when they've stopped growing out of them
- ⑥ fashion pages and TV shows are often put together by grown-ups who have their own money, and also get so much free stuff from the fashion and make-up companies as "samples" (or bribes) that it's easy for them to keep changing what they wear all the time

I like having something girly and fashionable to wear.
Mary, 15

I like comfort and quite baggy clothing.
Alex, 14

- ❻ fashion writers keep advertisers happy by featuring new clothes and looks and claiming that some things are "essential" when they're really optional extras
- ❻ people in the fashion world have very short attention spans.

> I am a model so that makes me feel very bad about my self esteem.
> Michelle, 17

What magazines tell you about fashion　Here's why the magazines tell you that this winter it's all chocolate brown and aubergine (fancy talk for purple) whereas last winter it was all lime and orange: they want you to buy NEW clothes. I'll say it again. Look carefully and you'll see that many of the "must-have" items are made by companies who advertise in the magazine.

When magazines have a shot of a famous actress in an outfit and tell you "How You Can Recreate the Look", then show you all the stuff you can buy that looks like hers – skirt, top, shoes, earrings, handbag, jacket, belt (complete with brand names, stockists and prices) – that's at least seven ways on one page to make you envious, suggest you need to look like someone else and spend your money.

Magazines tell you to buy what's "in fashion", not what suits you. It's hard to give individual tips so, apart from including the odd advice column and a few articles about "hiding your figure flaws" (as if everybody is some kind of biological error), what most magazines tend to do is tell you to buy what's in the shops – in other words, what the fashion companies have made and want you to buy, whether or not it looks good on you.

Labels

You probably know what the hot jeans label is at the moment, and the names of another couple of "must-have" labels. When you are paying for that sort of temporary cool, you're paying what's called a premium – a higher price for an item that's exactly the same as a cheaper one in another shop or with another label on it.

A "label queen" is a fashion tragic who has to wear the right label, even if the item is ugly, wrong or just plain stupidly expensive.

It's SO YOU!

Brand names make people feel poor.　Mina, 17

Models Models are not role models. You don't want to be one. Really you don't. Only one in hundreds of thousands makes good money, and most of them spend heaps of time being hungry and feeling that they're never right – never beautiful or thin or tall enough. Almost all of them have had experience with eating disorders and with obsessing about parts of their body.

It doesn't make sense to buy madly expensive clothes while you're still growing. And if you're just buying an item for the name on its label, not for its high quality or timeless style, then you're buying something that will look outdated in a flash.

Label traps

○ A lot of clothes, handbags and shoes are made cheaply in Asia, India or the Pacific islands, then chain stores pay to have their own label sewn into them.

○ Some "designers" create what's called a knock-off: they copy ideas from the genuine designer collections shown at fashion weeks. Sometimes a fake big-name label is just sewn onto stuff sold in a market for a fraction of the price (and usually the quality).

○ The items in a clothing range with a celebrity label, which ties in with an actress, a singer or a TV show, are usually the same ones you can buy in most chain stores – but you pay more for the name. And if you believe that the actress really designed all the clothes herself then . . . well, okaaay.

Style

Style is not the same as fashion, although "in style" is another way of saying "in fashion". Fashions come and go and are largely aimed at people who care about what other people think and want to fit in, not look different from everyone else. Style is something

"Most people wear 20 percent of their clothes 80 percent of the time."

Widely accepted fashion saying

Most
Models are not
Role Models

How to have style

Style isn't something you're born with. It takes some experiments and disasters along the way before you find your signature style. Here are a few hints.

✤ Don't buy clothes when you're hungry and light-headed, or exhausted but desperate to "get something".

✤ Don't buy clothes *just* because they're cheap.

✤ Don't buy this season's colour if it doesn't look good on you – blondes can look sickly in a yellow top, for example.

✤ Go for something you look great in – don't buy what's in fashion if it doesn't suit you.

✤ Dress for yourself. Don't worry too much about what you think others may or may not like – if you're confident, you'll look great.

✤ Make sure that even your "good" clothes are comfortable. If you wear a skirt so short you're always tugging it down and can't bend over, you're going to feel – and therefore look – uncomfortable and "wrong".

✤ Try a new kind of shop, check out a second-hand place, go shopping with an adult whose style you like.

more personal: a look that suits your personality, creativity and body shape. It's "you" – what *you* like, no matter what's in the shops.

During our teens and twenties most of us experiment with different styles until we find one or maybe a handful of looks that we like, that say what we want to say, and that are comfortable to wear. Many people eventually develop a "signature style" and stick with it – a way of dressing that's always around the same theme. It could be goth or sporty, Oxfam shoppy or girly.

Dressing to be noticed

These things say "look at me" (not that there's anything wrong with that):

   ⓖ big hairstyles
   ⓖ flashy jewellery (from swinging, sparkly bling to battery-operated earrings)
   ⓖ shiny fabrics
   ⓖ moving bits such as beads and tassels
   ⓖ bright colours
   ⓖ busy patterns.

Clothes that are very shiny, shimmery and glittery are best left to the over-eighteens at night, unless they're for a special school event.

Free advertising You know how some clothes manufacturers give themselves an advertising bonus by emblazoning their label's name or logo across bums, the front of T-shirts, the back of jackets and the side of shoes? Don't become a "walking billboard" advertising their stuff.

Dressing to "attract" guys

Some girls pile on the make-up, fake tan and clothes they think will make them look older or more "sexy". In fact it can just look "try hard" and a bit sad. If a guy really likes you he'll like you whether you're wearing tracky bottoms or a dress with heels.

> I love experimenting, finding things and dressing up a bit to get noticed. I have an eclectic style that's not really "in" but I love finding things and co-ordinating.
> Mandy, 15

Problem looks

- ⊙ Visible underwear, including G-strings, undies and bras: these always look like you didn't mean to show them, which is embarrassing, or like you did mean it, which is tacky.
- ⊙ Clothes that look like strippers' or sex workers' outfits, worn with heaps of dark make-up: these include anything that shows lots of skin, breast-revealing tops, really tiny skirts and way high heels. While some people promote this image as glamorous, most strippers and sex workers come from an abusive past and are working to feed a drug habit.
- ⊙ Clothes with sex images or slogans such as "Porn Star", or the Playboy bunny logo. (The logo is from *Playboy*, one of the exploitative "men's" magazines, with pictures of often topless or nude women in suggestive poses.)

Looking and acting as if they're sexually available to guys doesn't make girls strong and independent or popular. Instead of appearing grown up, girls can seem manipulated into presenting themselves as sexual objects whose brains, thoughts and feelings don't matter.

While a girl might be horrified that a 40-year-old guy is trying to pick her up, he might think her clothes are sending an unspoken invitation. A lot of guys don't know what's in fashion: they just think girls in revealing clothes are more likely to have sex with them. There is never an excuse for boorish, rude behaviour or sexual harassment or assault, no matter what you are wearing. No woman or girl is "asking for it".

All this doesn't mean you have to dress in a bag. You have a right to dress in whatever way you like. (After all, some people think bikinis on the beach are too raunchy.) Just be aware of why you present yourself in the way you do, and what various icons, outfits and messages can mean to other people.

> For the love of GOD people, keep your privates for private times. Some of us have eyes.
> Chloe, 17
>
> Seriously girls, be your own person.
> Matilda, 14

Dressing to suit a religion

Some girls wear certain items or a type of clothes because of their religion. Some Christian girls wear a cross; others always have long hair. Some Muslim girls cover their head with a hijab, or scarf. In the UK, many Muslim women who wear the hijab say it's their own choice, part of their personal dedication to Islam, but in some countries where Muslim religious leaders form the government women are forced to wear a veil. Many Muslim girls also wear sports uniforms or swimsuits that cover more of their body than the other players do. It's okay to ask a girl about her religion and her choice of clothes, but it's obviously not okay to take part in any bullying or rude commenting about it (see the Friends chapter).

Shopping for clothes

You'd think, given they want us to hand over money, that all sales assistants would be nice. But sometimes they're rude, snide, deceitful and more interested in talking on the phone than helping you.

Go back to shops where the sales assistants are helpful, don't try to pressure you, and say if something isn't right for you. Never let an assistant persuade you to buy something you're not sure of. First instincts are usually pretty good. You can always come back later and have another look. Just say, "I'm going to think about it, thanks." (See also "Going Shopping" in the Shopping chapter.)

HINT

If something doesn't fit Don't buy it. There's nothing wrong with you – there's something wrong with the clothes.

always try things on before you buy them

Sales   It's smart to wonder why something is on sale.

- ⑥ Badly cut?
- ⑥ Badly made?
- ⑥ A colour that hardly suits anybody?
- ⑥ Nobody wanted it so there are heaps left?
- ⑥ It's an "over-run" – meaning there's already a lot of it out there?

You can't always return clothes that are on sale (or second-hand), so always try things on: never assume it will look okay because it's "your" size. The cut may be bad, leaving it gaping at the waist, or it could be too tight across the shoulders or around your bot. Lots of clothes are fine in theory but look shocking on. And it's not your body's fault.

Accessories

You don't have to take any notice of them, but here are some accepted shoe and handbag "rules".

Shoes

- ⑥ Shoes should usually be slightly darker than your outfit. Most white and beige shoes are awful and don't go with anything, although white sandals will go with a summery white dress or a mainly white outfit.

Get a job if you want to buy expensive brand-name clothes.
Leanne, 18

Why can't mum pay for them?
Samantha, 16

Clothes disasters

You can wear any of the stuff on this list if you like. Just be aware that, whatever your intentions, others will consider them fashion mistakes.

✱ Clothes that are too tight, so they look and feel uncomfortable.

✱ Anything that shows bum crack, girly bits or undies when you bend over, stretch or get out of a car.

✱ Boob tubes: they look like some sort of bandage and create bulges over the top.

✱ Platform shoes: not unless you want to seem like you're walking on bricks.

✱ Socks or stockings with non-school sandals – especially dark socks.

Don't forget: it's fun to break the rules sometimes. Don't take fashion "laws" too seriously.

Basic handbag contents

✱ House keys

✱ Purse or wallet

✱ Phone

✱ Tissues

✱ Emergency period kit

✱ Lip gloss

✱ Sun cream

✱ Sunglasses

✱ Emergency public transport or taxi money

✱ Phone numbers written down in case your phone needs money or recharging

✱ Written-down contact numbers for you, but NOT your home address because you don't want someone getting that and your house keys if your bag is lost or stolen.

ⓖ If you're not comfortable and able to walk confidently in your shoes, don't wear them. I personally look like a drunken trainee drag queen in high heels.

ⓖ Don't wear really high heels or high heels every day: they damage your feet and toes, resulting in bunions and eventually even deformities, and cause foot and ankle injuries (from falling or "going over" on your ankle). At the very least don't wear them for more than a couple of hours. And don't wear them because you think all guys love them. They don't. And the ones who do love them can try them for themselves.

ⓖ The shorter the skirt, the flatter the heel should be (a fashion "rule" you don't have to listen to).

ⓖ Cheap shoes tend to fall apart quicker and not be as comfortable as more expensive ones. Plastic and non-breathing fabric will make your feet sweat more and slip, causing blisters. Get the best you can afford and ask a sales assistant's advice on caring for them.

ⓖ Until you've stopped growing, try to go to a shoe shop where the shop assistant can measure your feet and advise you on size – it's annoying to spend money on shoes only to discover you've grown out of them soon afterwards. Find out if you have a narrow or broad foot and ask which shoe styles are best for your type of foot.

ⓖ Don't drive in high heels – it's dangerous.

Handbags

ⓖ Handbags generally need to kind of match the feel of what you're wearing. That means a heavy, shiny black rucksack won't look quite right with a pale, flowery cotton dress. But when you're young you really can get away with anything – including lots of mixing and matching.

ⓖ Any handbag should be secured, with a zip or magnets, so that important things don't fall out. Big, open-topped bags are only good for the beach, but even those should have a zipper compartment for keys, period kit and money.

I have my own eccentric bohemian style, and I'm proud to be different.
Susan, 15

It's important these days to feel you fit in with the fashions otherwise you feel left out.
Charlotte, 15

Costume movies

Here's a list of films and DVDs that showcase fashion from different eras. The period given refers to the costumes – for example, *The Talented Mr Ripley* and *Funny Face* are both set in the 1950s, but *Funny Face* was made at that time and *Ripley* decades later. Check ratings to see if they're suitable for your age.

- ⑥ **Ancient Egypt**   *Cleopatra*
- ⑥ **Tang Dynasty**   (China, 859) *House of Flying Daggers*
- ⑥ **1500s**   *Elizabeth, Orlando, Shakespeare in Love*
- ⑥ **1600s**   *Lady Jane*
- ⑥ **1700s**   *Marie Antoinette, The Duchess*
- ⑥ **Qing Dynasty**   (China, 1770s) *Crouching Tiger, Hidden Dragon*
- ⑥ **1800s**   All the movies and TV series and films based on Jane Austen novels (*Pride and Prejudice, Sense and Sensibility, Emma, Persuasion*)
- ⑥ **Around 1900**   *My Fair Lady, Picnic at Hanging Rock, Doctor Zhivago*
- ⑥ **1920s**   *Chicago, Bullets Over Broadway, Thoroughly Modern Millie*
- ⑥ **1930s**   *Gosford Park, Cold Comfort Farm* (TV series), *The Cotton Club, Cabaret, The Aviator, Caddie, Tea with Mussolini, His Girl Friday, The Women* (the original)
- ⑥ **1940s**   *Land Girls, Charlotte Gray, All About Eve*

I only wear black and I love it.   Anisha, 16

I can't live without clothes, and my career is going to be a fashion designer.   Nicole, 14

- **1950s** *Funny Face, The Talented Mr Ripley, Children of the Revolution, Pleasantville, Designing Woman, Far from Heaven, Back to the Future, Gentlemen Prefer Blondes*
- **1960s** *What a Way to Go!, Walk the Line,* the Austin Powers movies, *Down with Love, The Avengers* (TV), *The Year My Voice Broke, Breakfast at Tiffany's*
- **1970s** *The Night We Called It a Day, Saturday Night Fever, Dick, Annie Hall*
- **1980s** *Working Girl, Desperately Seeking Susan, Heathers, Romy and Michelle's High School Reunion, Muriel's Wedding, The Breakfast Club, Ferris Bueller's Day Off*
- **1990s** *Clueless, Buffy the Vampire Slayer* (TV series), *Spiceworld*
- **2000s** *Josie and the Pussycats, Mean Girls, The Devil Wears Prada, Material Girls, Kath and Kim* (TV series)
- **Futuristic** *Barbarella, Star Trek, Blade Runner, The Fifth Element, Serenity*
- **Fantasy or crossover worlds** (a mix of historical and modern or imagined clothes) *Mad Max,* Baz Luhrmann and Catherine Martin's *Romeo and Juliet* and *Moulin Rouge, Amélie.*

More info on clothes

Remember that anything you read on a fashion site may be an ad.

fashion.net
Choose "Fashion", then "Green" for shops and labels with an environmental conscience or gimmick. Other options: "Designers", "Labels", "Art", "Jewellery".

www.green-uk.co.uk and cleanclothes.org and www.nosweat.org.uk
Campaigns to stop clothes workers being exploited by big companies. Find out which labels you shouldn't buy.

Many museums have specialist collections of fashion and costume, sometimes displayed online.

www.fashionmuseum.co.uk
The Fashion Museum.

www.ftmlondon.org
The London Fashion and Textile Museum.

ndm.si.edu
The US Smithsonian Institute's Cooper Hewitt Design museum.

www.vam.ac.uk
The Victoria and Albert Museum in London.

I wish we could wear costumes to school.   Karen, 13

I'm not the kind of person to be alternative. I go along with the trends.   Lucy, 18

Liking clothes does not necessarily mean you are materialistic. I love clothes but it's because I love the fabric, I love making them, I love putting them together, I love the look of things. I think the way you present yourself is important. Emma, 15

I love to look different from everyone else. Chlöe, 16

I feel confident about the way I dress, although it's different and a little "out there". It's who I am. If people don't like it, they can deal with it.

Bessie, 17

Yeah, I get really annoyed at the girls who insist on wearing a brand – that is not style! All their clothes are the same, they are really boring and really expensive.
Rhiana, 16

What's with all the popular girls dressing exactly the same? They're like an ARMY!!

Jess and Freya, 15

I like bargain hunting.

Isabelle, 13

The average size in the UK for women is 14, yet most of the clothes in shops are size 8–12. It's basically a slap in the face. Catherine, 16

Why are there no clothes for young, short people? Why is everything in traffic-cone bloody orange? Why are there no pants for anyone with an arse?

Anna, 17

Once someone buys it everyone gets it. Emma, 14

Unfortunately the majority of clothing promotes "thin is best". It's hard to find clothing made for real women with bums and hips and a waist. Amber, 18

I do judge people a lot by their clothes, like how high their jeans are and stuff.

Hannah, 13

Making your own clothes like a skirt or something isn't uncool or anything. If you get a good pattern and material, no one will be able to tell the difference and it'll be unique.

Rebecca, 14

I'm a ladies' size in a lot of shops and I'm only 13 and all the ladies' clothes are dull and boring.

Claire, 13

Why is stuff only made in a certain "common" size? Everyone likes groovy clothes.

Erin, 16

I get them for my birthday and Christmas generally and they last me the year.

Tracy, 17

I get bored clothes shopping.

Hannah, 18

My fave items are my toe socks, my bowler hat I bought from an Oxfam shop and my Dunlop shoes with skulls on.

Lucy, 13

Why can't we all just go around in the nude?   Ruby, 14

I like clothes but it really pisses me off that your status in groups is defined by what labels you wear.

Lily, 15

Clothes are my life. That is a bad thing.   Charlotte, 14

I hate it when girls analyse what you are wearing and decide what kind of person you are from that. It is so shallow.

Vanessa, 14

Face

We'll get to what to do with your eyebrows (ignore them or plait them?) later, but first here's the word on make-up. Make-up isn't supposed to hide your face. It's for accentuating and showing off the nice things about it such as your eyes, your lips, your teeth and your natural rosy cheeks. But make-up is basically used a lot by older women trying to look more like teenagers (minus the spotty moments).

tHe NatuRaL LooK
(USING HEAPS OF
MaKe-up)

tHe NatuRaL LooK
(No MAKe-up at ALL)

Make-up should be something you use as a bit of fun, or not at all. It's not compulsory. Lots of people never wear it. Some people only ever wear lipstick. Others only wear make-up on special occasions.

Make-up products

The following stuff has been described as "essential" by beauty magazines. If you really needed it all you'd have to have a suitcase on wheels and a fortune to fill it.

> I can't work out how to use eyeliner. Anyone I see wearing it has it smudged all around their eyes, it looks awful.
>
> Kate, 15

For skin

- **Primer**   This is a ridiculous "pre-foundation foundation" invented simply to sell more make-up. A waste of time and money.
- **Foundation**   It's used to make your face look exactly the same shade all over. It comes as a thick, skin-coloured fluid, applied with fingers or a sponge, or as a creamy stick that you use like a big crayon to draw the foundation on your face before blending it all over. Teenagers don't need it. If you have a tinted oil-free moisturiser it will do the job.
- **Powder**   Face-coloured powder is usually brushed or patted on over foundation to create a matt (non-shiny) look. It's available in a tub and brushed on with a make-up brush, or as pressed powder in an (easier to transport) compact and patted

on with the compact's pad. Powder doesn't
work without foundation because it doesn't
stick easily or smoothly, so it's a way of
making you buy two things. Teenagers
don't need it.

I only wear lip gloss to school and only wear eyeshadow and foundation when going out.
Bathany, 14

⊙ **Combined foundation and
powder**   This comes in a compact
or a stick, with a semi-matt finish.
Teenagers don't need it.

⊙ **Concealer**   This is mainly used to "cover" dark
circles under the eyes of older women so it's usually the wrong tint
to cover red pimples on girls. It comes in a tube, like a lipstick, or as a soft pencil.
To hide a spot it's better to carefully dab on some foundation that matches your
complexion.

⊙ **Blusher**   This is either brushed, in powder form, or rubbed,
in cream form, onto the roundest bit of your cheeks and up
your cheek bones. It's hard to avoid looking as if you have
patchy sunburn, severe embarrassment or a strange rash,
so use only a little, if any. Teenagers don't need it.

⊙ **Bronzer**   Too much of this glittery or shimmery powder or
lotion and you'll look like you've been rolling around in your
little sister's fairy costume.

CONCEALER
WARNING:
CAN MAKE
HEAD
DISAPPEAR
(OOPS)

For lips

⊙ **Lipliner**   Older women whose lip line is starting to get less distinct, because of
ageing skin, use a pencil to outline their lips. The inside area is then coloured in
with the pencil or with lipstick (sometimes using a lip-brush). Lipliner should be
the colour of the lipstick: lighter or darker looks odd. Teenagers don't need it.

⊙ **Lip gloss**   Cheaper than lipstick, this is a clear, shiny or tinted lip
ointment in a tube. Teenage girls have enough colour in their
lips already so a clear gloss is fine.

⊙ **Lipstick**   Sheer, pale and neutral colours look best on young faces. Don't wear
lipstick or lip gloss if, like most girls, you're doing something active or being a
normal teenager at school – you just end up with it everywhere else, such as on
your teeth, your sleeve and the basketball.

For eyes

⊙ **Eyeliner**   This is basically a pencil (or sometimes a liquid or paste
applied with a little brush) that is used to outline the eyes and
make them look bigger. Always put it outside, not inside, the line of

your lashes. Eyeliner (especially the liquid version) is best left to professionals or the very experienced. It's generally considered a dramatic, night-time make-up and not a good look for young teenagers.

beware
lippy on
teeth

◎ **Mascara**   Because it makes the eyelashes look darker, it can give the illusion of more length and thickness, and is a way of drawing attention to your eyes. If you have light-coloured eyelashes, black can look too heavy, so go for a brown instead. It comes as liquid in a tube, which you apply with a small "wand". When it smudges or runs it can make you look like a sad panda (and stain your clothes). Waterproof mascara must be removed with special eye-make-up remover every night, so that adds more trouble and expense.

◎ **False eyelashes**   Definitely best left to the professionals. Dangers include getting the glue in your eye, looking totally ludicrous, and having the eyelashes peel off and flap in the breeze.

◎ **Eyeshadow**   A temporary stain for your eyelids, it often looks unnatural and over-dramatic. It's generally considered to be for night-time, special-occasion or theatrical wear. Usually a neutral tone looks best. A shade close to your eye colour may make your eyes look dull in comparison, and most eyeshadow is best left to professionals to apply unless they've been drinking.

◎ **Eyebrow pencil**   Used to make eyebrows look thicker or darker, it's almost impossible to get right unless you're a professional. Sketched-on eyebrows tend to look like a 4-year-old's drawing. Give them a miss. (See also the "Eyebrows" section coming up.)

As well as all the above, professional make-up artists use lots of sponges and brushes, but you don't need to. Eyeshadow and blusher can be applied with clean fingertips or a cotton bud, then blended and rubbed in gently with the fingertips.

Heavy black eyeliner does not enhance your eyes, it makes them smaller. Waterproof mascara is overrated, it goes all clumpy and is impossible to get off.

Mia, 16

Safe make-up Cosmetics are full of chemicals (often preservatives) that can cause eye problems and skin rashes and reactions. Many people choose make-up that isn't tested on animals. Make sure make-up isn't tested on you. Choose a reputable brand.

The selling of make-up

If you buy make-up keep in mind that, like clothes and skin and hair-care products, it's big business, worth billions, and companies will use lots of tricks to convince you to buy loads of products.

Make-up is a fashion This means that, like clothes, it's subject to trends – new season's colours are brought out to try to encourage you to ditch last month's pale lipstick and go for the "dramatic colours" now all the rage. Or shiny. Or matt. Or autumn colours. Or bold shimmery stuff. Or purple and green (which together can make it look like you have two "black eyes").

So if what's hot one season is out a couple of months later, the only questions really are:

- ☉ "Do I like it? Why?"
- ☉ "Does it suit me?"
- ☉ "When would I use it?"
- ☉ "Can I afford it?"

false eyelashes are a drag

Make-up is expensive It's worth knowing that really expensive make-up isn't any better than less expensive make-up: you're just paying extra for packaging design, the label name and the companies' big advertising campaigns.

Even medium-quality make-up costs a lot: the total cost of buying most of the items for skin, lips and eyes listed earlier in "Make-up products" would be easily £200–400.

73.6 percent nonsense Don't ever believe the make-up ads. No matter what they say, make-up can't actually physically change any of your features. It's not possible for a lipstick to make your lips 40 percent plumper or for a mascara to make your lashes 20 percent longer or "three times thicker".

As with skin and hair products, watch out for silly claims and pretendy science-speak.

Brand loyalty   Cosmetics companies would like you to buy all your items from their brand range, but you don't have to. One brand may have the eyeshadow colour you like, while another has the SPF 15 you want in a tinted moisturiser that's oil-free.

> Make-up costs a lot of money if you use it daily.
> Sophie, 18
>
> It's too expensive.
> Grace, 16

Hard sell   Also watch out for make-up sales staff. They often get more money if they sell more stuff, so don't fall for being told that you're pale or washed-out and "need" certain things to "fix" yourself (and see the Shopping chapter).

Too much make-up

Heavy make-up in the movies, on stage and in photos looks good because there's a whole team of skilled and experienced make-up artists, lighting technicians and other professionals working on it. But in real life it looks waaaay overdone to any-one nearby.

28·7% more radiant than last Thursday...

Obvious make-up on anyone is a bad move because it:
- ↻ can look as if they've put on fancy dress or they've got into a crayon box and started drawing on their face
- ↻ can send a message that they want to look sexual when really they're just trying to look older
- ↻ would take less time and be easier to pop out for few hours and do a bit of coal mining every morning than put on all the products the magazine beauty pages say we should.

too MUCH make·up

a

Inside info   When an Oscar-winning American actress appeared on a television talk show, the producers agreed, as a condition of the ten-minute interview, to pay $4000 to her hair and make-up artist just to joosh her up.

If you want to use make-up

Here are some make-up hints you can adopt, or ignore.

✽ Any face make-up (foundation, powder or tinted moisturiser) should have a sunscreen of SPF 15, or higher (rare).

✽ If you have sensitive skin try hypo-allergenic make-up brands. Test any make-up on a bit of skin and wait 24 hours, to check that you don't get a reaction, before putting it on your face. Oil-free and "non-comedogenic" make-up is best for teenage skin prone to spots (see the Skin chapter).

✽ Use make-up that's close to your skin's natural colouring – pale and neutrals for pale skin, bolder colours for darker skin. Black eyebrows on a blonde look simply bizarre, like stuck-on fuzzy felt. Blondes look more natural with light brown or dark brown lashes and eyebrows. Girls with dark skin and very pale lipstick can look a bit like extras in a 1963 science fiction movie.

✽ Add colour gently, little by little. Experiment so you know what looks bad. Always use your face's natural shapes as a guide. In other words, don't draw outside the natural line of your lips; and only put eyeshadow on your eyelid, not up to your eyebrow. No, actually, do that so you can see how wrong it looks.

✽ Go outside and look at the make-up in a mirror. How does it look?

✽ Go to a department-store make-up counter and get the person to make you up with a natural look and then a party one. See how subtle changes can make you look a little different. Don't feel you have to buy the products.

✽ If you're really keen maybe you could ask for an hour's session with a make-up artist as a late-teens birthday present. Having a session at a department store may be free, but a make-up artist attached to a brand counter will only recommend what they're trying to sell at the moment rather than concentrating on what suits you, the person.

✽ You could have a make-up party for which a group of friends pitch in to hire a make-up artist.

✽ Always wash off all make-up before bed. You may need to buy a make-up remover.

So don't waste heaps of valuable sleeping, eating and activity time doing your make-up and hair. Many schools have rules against make-up anyway, and parents will probably want to have their say, too, about when it's okay to wear make-up. Dads can be more horrified than mums: it's one of those "Oh, my god, my little girl is growing up" things. Maybe a bit of sensible conversation is a good idea before you try to bounce out the door with bright red lipstick and spider-flappy false eyelashes.

Whether or not you care what guys think, it's worth knowing that most of them say they don't like it when a girl wears a lot of make-up. And it's also worth wondering why *guys* aren't expected to wear make-up to "look better".

Eyebrows

Eyebrows can frame and draw attention to the eyes, but most fiddling about ends up making them look worse than natural, never-touched ones. Disasters include eyebrows looking too thin, too straggly, too unnaturally shaped, too drawn on or too different from your natural skin and hair tones.

Most women who shape their eyebrows pluck them at home, or have someone at a beauty salon do it by plucking or waxing. (Yes, both ways hurt.) Unless you have the time and money to go to a professional every month (which, let's be honest, is a little obsessive for a teenager), it's best to leave your eyebrows alone in case you ruin them for life. Please don't just wade in – some eyebrow hair may not grow back because the follicles get damaged.

eyebrow monthly magazine

If you want to change your eyebrows

↳ Go to a popular beauty salon and talk to the beauty therapist about what you'd like and how to achieve it. Ask them to be conservative and take off less rather than more, so that you can assess the look and have a second go if it's needed. Don't stay if the eyebrow-shaper likes a thin eyebrow. Tell them you'll think about it, then run, run, run awaaaaay.

⊙ Once they've created the shape you want by waxing or plucking, you can try to follow the line when you're plucking your eyebrows at home.

⊙ Never pluck until your eyebrows look thin. The thinner the eyebrows, the more they look unnatural and strangely balding. The very worst are mean-looking, skinny eyebrows actually painted or drawn on.

⊙ Never shape your eyebrows into a sharp arch – it will make you look constantly astonished.

⊙ When you're plucking, use good tweezers that get a firm grip on individual hairs. Just remove a few hairs at a time or you'll go too far.

⊙ Never pluck hairs from the top of your brows, always just hairs underneath, outside the main shape.

⊙ Never shave or bleach your eyebrow hair. Sharp stubble quickly follows shaving, and bleaching can cause skin conditions or eye damage.

⊙ Only a professional should wax your eyebrows: hot goo can damage your eyes.

More info on make-up and eyebrows

Most make-up websites are full of ads disguised as advice. Some brands have site videos on how to apply make-up, or you can scan in a photo of yourself and play with pretend make-up on screen. You can find make-up artists at a local beautician, a theatrical agency or a department or cosmetics store. Your phone directory should list Make-up Artists, and bridal magazines have ads for them.

safecosmetics.org
About the chemicals and toxic substances that may be in your make-up.

bobbibrown.com
The site of US make-up "designer" Bobbi Brown has a teen page with make-up tips (and see also her book opposite).

paulaschoice.com
US make-up seller Paula Begoun's consumer advice. Choose "Make-up tips and tricks".

These (American) books assume you should use make-up a *lot*. Use them for ideas, fun and special occasions, but don't build your daily life around them.

Bobbi Brown: Teenage Beauty by Bobbi Brown, Collins, US
Hints for teenagers on how to look "pretty, natural, sexy and awesome" (but perhaps not all at the same time or you'll cause car accidents). A chapter each on girls of Asian and Latina heritage, and those with darker skin (called "African American" here). You don't have to buy her products.

Beautiful Brows by Nancy Parker and Nancy Kalish, Crown, US
Diagrams and step-by-step plans for not butchering your eyebrows.

I think some girls wear too much make-up EVERY DAY. I think it's stupid coz on a special occasion when you do get dressed up you look the same as you do every day.

Holly, 13

Fake eyelashes are tools of the devil.   Megan, 17

I can't be bothered. I hate make-up. As soon as I put it on I want to scratch it off.

Katharine, 18

Have a day when you're alone to just experiment with different make-up because if you leave the experimentation to just before you leave home, it won't look good or you'll stab your eye.

Louise, 17

I love make-up. I would die without it.   Ellie, 15

I used to hide behind big gothic make-up, but now my boyfriend who tells me I'm beautiful without any makes it easier for me to go out a lot of the time without any make-up on.

Tracey, 16

I absolutely LOVE make-up, without it I would probably die. I wear make-up nearly every day because I would not be seen in public without it. I think make-up, for me, is like a mask that I put on so no one will have to see the real me which I hate and I think that others won't accept. I'm very self-conscious and make-up lets me be this other person who I want to be.

Mollie, 16

DON'T OVERPLUCK!!!

Laura, 17

Make-up is for fun and for looking and feeling spesh at times, but I think it should never be compulsory. That's just crappy!   Alice, 13

I think boys look very nice in make-up and it's a shame it's so socially unaccepted.

Jade, 16

I like to use it to cover up pimples and things, but find that using too much just causes more because all of it blocks the skin.

Tia, 13

I will never leave the house without wearing a face full of make-up.

Jessica, 16

I'm not allowed to wear it to school, so I get into the habit of not wearing it.

Lydia, 16

I have 2 words to say to you – liquid eyeliner. Not a good look if you don't know what you're doing. I didn't know what I was doing! Anna, 13

REMOVE IT BEFORE YOU SLEEP!!! MY SKIN IS ICKY FROM NEVER REMOVING IT!!

Karen, 16

I dye my hair black, and I wear black eye make-up, and if I can be bothered black lipstick. It's not all that hard to put it on, but it takes a while to get it off.

Polly, 15

I hate make-up. HATE HATE HATE. The concept of it disgusts me.

Maya, 16

I went through a stage where I used a make-up base on my face every day at school and on weekends. This lasted about 3 weeks. It completely ruined my skin, I was breaking out. It's better now but not completely. Em, 14

I got into mum's make-up when I was about 4. Our family cat and I looked stunning.

Sarah, 14

Once I bruised my eyelid because I pinched it really hard accidentally with my eye lash curler. Charlie, 13

THE F WORD

Feminism or women's rights, **freedom** or girlpower: there are lots of different ways to describe the idea that girls should have as many opportunities as guys.

A lot of girls don't want to call themselves a feminist because they think that arguing for women's rights isn't needed any more, or the word signals that they don't like guys. But before you say, "I'm not a feminist", check out this chapter.

Thanks, feminism

Feminists have struggled hard to get rights and benefits for us women and girls: less than a century ago some of the suffragettes (women fighting for the vote) were sent to jail. Our rights have largely been "awarded" to us only in the last 200 years: in most cases the last 100 years, and in some cases the last 50.

> I'd like girls to become more aware about gender issues. I'm doing sexual politics at university, but I am often dismissed or called strange for insisting girls stick up for themselves, or that they do not take labels such as slut/bitch/whore.
> Melissa, 18

FACT

Did you know That your great-great-grandmother wasn't allowed to vote, and that in her time having paid work was considered not respectable? And that your grandmother, who *could* work – usually for low pay in a "woman's job" – was probably automatically sacked when she got married?

What we've gained

It's because feminists fought hard, against strong opposition each time, that we can:

- ☾ study at a college or university
- ☾ vote, and be a politician
- ☾ be on a jury, or made a judge
- ☾ choose our own career, including being allowed to be a lawyer, doctor or engineer
- ☾ earn, keep and spend our own money
- ☾ be paid at least a minimum wage
- ☾ get as much money as a man for doing exactly the same job (until 1970 UK law did not recognize than men and women deserved the same pay for the same job).

> Boys aren't superior to you! The world doesn't revolve around them like I used to think!

> Girls are more than half the population. Hell, we even live longer!

> We can make things happen! Marcella, 18

Did you know Traditionally you take on your husband's name when you get married because you are being passed on – as a possession – from your father's control to your husband's control.

- ◔ be legally protected from sexual harassment at work or in another public place, and from discrimination because we are female
- ◔ own and sell property
- ◔ as adults, ignore what our father – or our partner or husband – tells us to do
- ◔ participate in the Olympics
- ◔ keep working while we're pregnant, and get our job back later, instead of being sacked immediately
- ◔ have legal access to safe contraception and termination of pregnancy
- ◔ be a single parent and keep our children if we're not married or helped by a man, and get some government financial assistance
- ◔ decide to have medical treatment without the permission of our partner or husband
- ◔ legally stop our partner or husband from raping us
- ◔ go to a women's refuge (a safe house) if we or our children are being physically or mentally abused by a boyfriend or a husband
- ◔ not be accused of past "sluttish" behaviour during a rape trial.

> Girls (especially younger girls) need to know how important it is to believe in yourself and be your own person ... it really does make life a lot easier.
> Anisha, 18

Isn't everything okay now?

Women are still discriminated against here. And in some countries women still don't have any of the rights just listed, and are brutally oppressed. If the number of years humans have been around was expressed as a kilometre, we've had women's rights for about a millimetre. Unless we keep fighting, even the rights we've won recently can be taken away.

So if somebody tells you that all the fights are over, and nobody needs to bother about being a feminist any more, think about these questions.

- ⊙ How come, on average, girls do much better than boys at school and uni, yet women are more likely to be in the lower paid part-time or casual jobs with fewer benefits and worse conditions?
- ⊙ Why are most managers, bosses and politicians men?
- ⊙ How come the average full-time wage for women is still less than the average weekly earnings for men? (In most cases, less than or around 80 percent of the man's wage.)
- ⊙ What is the "glass ceiling" – and why do women keep talking about it?
- ⊙ Why is it that in many countries women who have been raped are arrested and punished because they are no longer "virgins"?
- ⊙ Why is it that in some cultures girls' genitals are mutilated? And why are girls in some countries forced to cover themselves entirely with fabric or risk being insulted or assaulted in public or legally punished?
- ⊙ Why is it that in many cultures young girls are "promised" to older men and forced to marry against their wishes?
- ⊙ How come so many guys in our own society don't respect girls and women or their achievements?
- ⊙ Why do some people persist in behaving as if girls are just toys for guys?
- ⊙ Why do some girls feel they need to know "What guys want" and "Will guys like it if I . . ."? Wouldn't it be nice if girls more often thought, "What would a guy have to do to impress *me*"?
- ⊙ Why is it that radio stations and music channels play songs in which guys call girls "hos", bitches and other brutal, disrespectful things, as if it was nothing – as if it was okay to do that?
- ⊙ How come more girl singers can't sing their own songs dressed the way they want, instead of having to look as if they're practically in a porn video?
- ⊙ Why do some religious leaders say that women who have their period can't enter a place of worship?
- ⊙ Why is a teenage girl who gets pregnant sometimes asked or pressured to leave school, but the father of the baby isn't?
- ⊙ How come most of the sports reports (and sponsorships) are for men's sports?
- ⊙ Why do large corporations sponsor only (or mainly) men's sports, not women's?
- ⊙ Why do so many radio and TV shows have lots of men but only one woman, never the other way round?

Why the bloody hell can't there be coverage of WOMEN'S sports on prime time television?

Karen, 17

⑥ How come male newsreaders and actors are allowed to get old and look "distinguished", but the women have to try to "look younger" by using cosmetic surgery?

⑥ How come the mostly male politicians in the government haven't fixed the childcare problem?

⑥ How come the mostly male politicians in the government make the rules about abortion when they will never be pregnant? And when most male politicians leave the raising of their families to their wives and disappear for weeks at a time?

⑥ How come even the women who work full-time with children usually do a lot more of the housework than their partners?

⑥ Why do so many children's stories have male heroes, rather than female ones?

⑥ How come women writers often write dramas and comedies with equal roles for guys and women, while most male writers tend to write interesting roles for guys but not so many good roles or lines for women? (Of course girls and women aren't always portrayed as just the passive, decorative or sexual interest in a story: see the lists of "Feisty girls and heroines" coming up.)

Calling yourself a feminist

Being a feminist doesn't mean you can't wear girly clothes, or you hate guys. Being a feminist means you support girls and women having equal rights with guys.

More info on girls' and women's issues

www.ywca.org.uk
This organization is run entirely by and for young women. It has lots of campaigns for women's rights, community projects and volunteer work, and classes for girls in communication and other skills.

www.equalities.gov.uk
The site of the UK government's Equalities Office. Yes, there really is a Minister of Women and Equalities.

rockrgrl.com
A site for girls who want to be in the band, not bringing it beers. Has a great messageboard for discussing hot topics.

now.org
The US National Organization for Women has info on all current women's issues and provides ideas for action.

globalfundforwomen.org
Inspiring projects worldwide.

www.thefword.org.uk
Up-to-the-minute feminism from England.

feminist.com
US site with ideas, info and links.

wluml.org/english
About women oppressed by Muslim laws.

Desert Flower by Waris Dirie, Virago, UK
An African girl's escape from nomadic poverty and cultural cruelty.

There are always going to be things you want to change about yourself, that's just the way a girl's mind works. But I like to think that everything about you makes you special and unique. Jessica, 14

You have to be strong to love yourself for who you are, especially when today's media is so strongly focused on beauty and image. Ruby, 16

If a boy treats you badly you are too good for him and you should leave.
Marianne, 18

Spanish people have a saying "Para el gusto se hicieron los colores", meaning "The colours were made for everyone's taste", as in people got different tastes and if one person thinks you are ugly another person may think you're cute. Alandra, 15

They all ditched me last year but that was at primary school and now I have a whole new group of friends at high school. Sarah, 13

Not all girls spend all their time thinking about sex, drugs, alcohol and boyfriends. Phoebe, 16

I feel confident about my ability to assert myself, my ability to see reason, responsibility, rationality, positivity and both sides in any situation. I feel confident about what I want and what I am passionate about. I am confident that I know who I am and how I feel. Sascha, 18

I would like to read why it is okay for guys to sleep with as many girls as they want and get congratulated for it, while girls get called sluts. [*Actually it's not okay.*]
Jane, 17

Put girls in power!!! Man, we need to kick these old men out of parliament! Who says they have the right to decide on such things as abortion!?! Girls need to realize their potential! And not be afraid of things such as law or maths simply because "boys are naturally better" – that's crap and we know it! Amy, 17

Feisty girls and heroines

Feisty is another F word, meaning sassy and bold. Here are some lists of great heroines and interesting girls and women in movies (on DVD), TV series and books. Add your own favourites to the lists. (See also the "Costume movies" list in the Clothes and Make-up chapter and "Lists for every stage of love" given at the end of the Love chapter.)

Books for girls

Teen-book specialist Rebecca Hutcheson from my local bookshop made this list. Ask your librarian or local bookseller which ones are right for your age (and reading level).

The Bermudez Triangle by Maureen Johnson, Puffin, US. Friends prepare for "after high school".

Becoming Bindy Mackenzie by Jaclyn Moriarty, Young Picador, UK. Bindy is a perfect overachiever. Or is she? Written entirely in emails.

Chinese Cinderella by Adeline Yen Mah, Puffin, UK. The true story of an unwanted daughter.

Does My Head Look Big in This? by Randa Abdel-Fattah, Marion Lloyd Books, UK. Amal, a 16-year-old Australian-Palestinian Muslim, tries for a "normal" life.

Dream Merchant by Isabel Hoving, Walker Books, UK. A marketing company hires kids to sell products into the world's dream realm, but three of them get stuck there.

Drums, Girls, and Dangerous Pie by Jordan Sonnenblick, Point, UK. A guy tries to make sense of his feelings for the hottest girl in school, his sick brother, his parents and his best friend.

The Illustrated Mum by Jacqueline Wilson, Corgi, UK. Dolphin loves her mum being so colourful, but her sister, Star, finds it hard to.

Jane Eyre by Charlotte Bronte, Penguin Classics, UK. An abused English orphan searches for love, belonging and independence (historical). (Also film and TV series versions on DVD.)

Little Women by Louisa May Alcott, Penguin Classics, UK. Four different sisters in a very close family make the best of things while their dad is away at war in this historical American story. (Also films on DVD.)

Looking for Alibrandi by Melina Marchetta, Puffin, Australia. Josie searches for the freedom to be herself, without the label of Australian-Italian. (Also a movie on DVD.)

Margaux with an X by Ron Koertge, Walker Books, US. Margaux's dad is a professional gambler and her mum's addicted to the Home Shopping Network, but she finds an unexpected friendship.

My Brilliant Career by Miles Franklin, Virago Press, UK. A historical Australian story about a bold girl who follows her dream to be a writer. (Also a film on DVD.)

Noughts and Crosses Trilogy: **Noughts and Crosses**, **Knife's Edge** and **Checkmate** by Malorie Blackman, Corgi, UK. In a world where the Noughts (whites) are downtrodden former slaves, and the Crosses (blacks) are mostly running things, one Cross girl searches for peace with her daughter from a relationship with a Nought boy.

Perfect World by Brian James, Push, US. After Lacie's dad dies, her new friend Benji helps her.

Persepolis by Marjane Satrapi. Jonathan Cape, UK. The story of a girl growing up in Iran.

Ruby Holler by Sharon Creech, Bloomsbury, US. Twins Florida and Dallas start a new life with foster parents.

Skin by A.M. Vrettos, Egmont, US. Donnie watches his sister get sick from not eating enough.

The Uglies Trilogy: **Uglies**, **Pretties** and **Specials** by Scott Westerfeld, Simon Pulse, US. Three hundred years in the future, Tally discovers the ugly side of becoming a Pretty.

Walking Home with Marie-Claire by Kirsty Murray, Allen and Unwin, UK. The ups and downs of having a best friend.

The Whale Rider by Witi Ihimaera, Robson Books, UK. In this New Zealand-based story, Pai needs to prove she has what it takes to be a Maori chieftain, despite being "just" a girl. (Also a film on DVD.)

_____

_____

_____

_____

_____

_____

_____

_____

_____

_____

_____

Girl movies

All About Eve Sisterhood versus scheming. The first stalker movie.

Bend It Like Beckham A girl from a strict family wants to play soccer.

Boys on the Side A film about friends.

Charlie's Angels Ultra-groomed action nonsense.

Clueless Hollywood does Jane Austen's *Emma*, with shopping.

Emma, Pride and Prejudice, Sense and Sensibility and any other Jane Austen novels made into a movie or a TV series. Eighteenth-century heroines that modern girls can identify with.

Erin Brockovich A lowly law-office assistant takes on corporate bad guys.

Freaky Friday A mum and her teenage daughter swap bodies – and lives.

Ghost World About two girls who aren't like everybody else.

The Golden Compass Fantasy adventure about a girl and a kick-ass polar bear.

Hairspray A lesson in high-school acceptance with dancing and singing.

Juno Tale of a US teen's pregnancy.

A League of Their Own Girls play their own game.

Mean Girls Beating the bullies.

Mermaids Single mother Cher makes her own fun.

Miss Congeniality Puts clever above glamour.

Muriel's Wedding About deciding to be yourself.

Norma Rae A woman takes on the bosses.

North Country Women take on sexual harassment.

The Prime of Miss Jean Brodie Scottish school movie.

Riding in Cars with Boys A young mum grows up.

Run Lola Run An unusual girl gets fast and furious.

Serenity Interesting women on a spaceship (and the captain is hot).

Silkwood A woman takes on the nuclear industry.

Spirited Away In this Japanese animated movie a plucky young girl enters the spirit world in search of her parents.

10 Things I Hate about You A Shakespeare comedy redone in an American high school.

Thelma and Louise The ultimate girlpower road movie.

13 going on 30 A 13-year-old wakes up 30 years old and isn't the woman she'd planned to be.

The Women Gossip and gowns.

Girl-friendly TV

Angel A *Buffy* spin-off.

Buffy the Vampire Slayer Buffy takes on demons, vampires and worse at high school.

Daria Animated teen queen of irony.

Gilmore Girls Single mother and daughter talk quickly.

Skins Award-winning, cutting edge UK drama about modern teen life.

Tracy Beaker A must-see spin-off from the Jacqueline Wilson book.

Ugly Betty Betty isn't, but the attitudes at her fashion magazine workplace are.

Veronica Mars Teen private investigator mixes school and sleuth stuff.

Wonderwoman It's the seventies so superchicks get big hair, hotpants and an invisible plane.

Xena, Warrior Princess Who doesn't want a leather skirt and a sword to take on the villains?

Movie and TV action heroines

Geena Davis in *The Long Kiss Goodnight*.

Jennifer Garner in the TV series *Alias*.

Sarah Michelle Gellar in the TV series of *Buffy*.

Holly Hunter voices Elastigirl and **Sarah Vowell** voices Violet in *The Incredibles*.

Angelina Jolie in the *Tomb Raider* movies.

Keira Knightley in *Pirates Of The Caribbean*.

Carrie-Anne Moss in *The Matrix*.

Mulan in, you guessed it, *Mulan*.

Lori Petty and **Naomi Watts** in *Tank Girl*.

Gina Torres in the movie *Serenity* and the TV series *Firefly*.

Sigourney Weaver in *Alien* and *Aliens*.

Michelle Yeoh in *Crouching Tiger, Hidden Dragon*.

that's quite enough book...
Now it's over to you!

Have fun out there, in the great, big, wonderful, exciting, sometimes scary, but generally excellent WORLD!

Acknowledgements

Well, there's no point flouncing about pretending I did it all by myself.

While the first version of this book was Australian, it has been translated into English (hmm), brought bang up to date and adapted for Britain by Tracy Hopkins and Peter Buckley (hurrah), with special help from Marie Stopes International and with medical checks and revisions suggested by an NHS GP called Dr Jon Tilbury. Andrew Lockett made it all happen.

From the beginning, this book benefitted from having access to some of the best and most generous minds when it comes to teenage health and welfare, including the world-renowned Centre for Adolescent Health in Melbourne. But first, thanks to Brendan Barlow for kicking off the project by setting up the website for the Girl Stuff Survey, not to mention collating the responses from the 4000 people who filled one in and allowed me to use their wonderful quotes. I couldn't have done it without you, girls! All quotes used from the Survey in this book are from girls who were aged 13 to 18. I changed names on the quotes whenever I thought somebody might need, or want, privacy. Answers from other responses to the Survey provided ideas and info for the book.

Emma Moss did all the preliminary research. For expertise, I need to thank many consultants and fact checkers. I was cheered and sustained by their generosity and dedication. (Annoyingly, I cannot blame any of them for mistakes in the book, nor hold them responsible for my opinions, conclusions or emphases.) Thanks to Professor Susan Sawyer, head of the Centre for Adolescent Health, dermatologists Dr Tanya Gilmour, Dr Josephine Yeatman, Dr Belinda Welsh, and Dr Ruth Morley. For info on drugs and alcohol, I am grateful to Paul Dillon, of the National Drug and Alcohol Research Centre, University of New South Wales, Geoff Munro, Director of the Community Alcohol Action Network, and his staff at the Australian Drug Foundation. Others who helped at the research stage were Anita Lal, Research Officer at the VicHealth Centre for Tobacco Control; Jane Martin, Policy and Information Manager, Quit Victoria; and Dr David Caldicott, Emergency Research Fellow, Department of Emergency Medicine and Trauma, Royal Adelaide Hospital.

For help with feelings and mental health issues, I thank Dr Louise Newman, Director of the New South Wales Institute of Psychiatry, Barbara Hocking at SANE, and Monica Hadges, adolescent mental health specialist. For info on eating, I'm indebted to clinical specialist dietician Mauren Humphrey, eating behaviours authority Dr Rick Kausman and paediatric specialist Dr Zoe McCallum, Senior Lecturer and Co-ordinator of the Child and Adolescent Health Course, Department of Paediatrics, University of Melbourne. Dr Melissa Cameron, Adolescent Gynaecology Fellow at the Centre for Adolescent Health, was especially helpful.

I'm indebted to sexual health specialists Dr Susan Bagshaw, Fellow of the Australasian Chapter of Sexual Health Medicine, College of Sexual Health Physicians, Chief Resident at the 198 Youth Health Centre, Christchurch, and Senior Lecturer in Adolescent Health, Christchurch School of Medicine, New Zealand; and the splendid Annie Rose, sexual and reproductive health educator and consultant. Advisors on young mums included Angela Steele, Manager of the Young Women's Health Program at the Royal Women's Hospital, Melbourne, and Kylie Houltham, a peer support worker at that hospital's Young Mums Clinic.

Readers of the Family and Friends chapters included Lorraine Rose, consultant psychotherapist, and Antony Gleeson, psychotherapist and consultant psychologist. For several useful contributions to the Friends chapter I thank Dr Helen McGrath, counselling psychologist, and member of the National Coalition Against Bullying. Thanks to Professor Michael Halmagyi, Professor of Neurology, Prince Alfred Hospital, Sydney; Dr Kathryn Strasser, a GP who's worked in general practice and psychiatry; and Professor Andrew Kornberg, neurologist, Children's Neuroscience Unit, Royal Children's Hospital, Melbourne.

Finance journalist and all-round brainy person Alan Kohler had smart things to say about the Money chapter. Advice on study and work was taken from Associate Professor Marcia Devlin, psychologist, higher education consultant; Julie Farthing, career and life–work consultant; and Cath Bowtell, industrial lawyer.

Various information was kindly provided by Dr Andrew Kennedy, Dr Frederike Veit, Pam Garcia and Dr Bill Cockburn at the Australian Society of Plastic Surgeons; Dot Henning, Co-ordinator of the Young People's Health Service centres; Dr Kathy McNamee, Senior Medical Officer, Family Planning Victoria; Ruth Trickey, herbalist; Cait Calcutt, Co-ordinator of Children by Choice, Queensland and booklister Rebecca Hutcheson.

Special thanks to Lesley Dunt for the editing and Julie Gibbs for the idea and the means to write the book.

"More Info" sections (suggested websites and books)

Index

Kaz Cooke is an Australian author and cartoonist, mum and former teenage girl. She has a background in journalism and faffing about. She is often a columnist; sometimes a radio broadcaster; the best-selling author of The Rough Guide to Pregnancy and Birth, The Rough Guide to Babies and Toddlers, The Little Book of Stress and Real Gorgeous; and the winner of the 2002 UK Diagram Prize for the Oddest Title of the Year, Living with Crazy Buttocks. Her books have been translated into many languages: in Latvian she is Keza Kuka and in Czech she is Kaz Cookeova. She has too many handbags and never knows where her mobile phone is.